CW01020252

ENGLAND AND T
THE PRACTICE OF DIPLOMACY IN LATE MEDIEVAL EUROPE

LEGENDA

LEGENDA, founded in 1995 by the European Humanities Research Centre of the University of Oxford, is now a joint imprint of the Modern Humanities Research Association and Maney Publishing. Titles range from medieval texts to contemporary cinema and form a widely comparative view of the modern humanities, including works on Arabic, Catalan, English, French, German, Greek, Italian, Portuguese, Russian, Spanish, and Yiddish literature. An Editorial Board of distinguished academic specialists works in collaboration with leading scholarly bodies such as the Society for French Studies and the British Comparative Literature Association.

MHRA

The Modern Humanities Research Association (MHRA) encourages and promotes advanced study and research in the field of the modern humanities, especially modern European languages and literature, including English, and also cinema. It also aims to break down the barriers between scholars working in different disciplines and to maintain the unity of humanistic scholarship in the face of increasing specialization. The Association fulfils this purpose primarily through the publication of journals, bibliographies, monographs and other aids to research.

M A N E Y
publishing

Maney Publishing is one of the few remaining independent British academic publishers. Founded in 1900, the company has offices both in the UK, in Leeds and London, and in North America, in Boston. Since 1945 Maney Publishing has worked closely with learned societies, their editors, authors, and members, in publishing academic books and journals to the highest traditional standards of materials and production.

The pope in council, from a late-14th-c. manuscript of the Decretum Gratiani
(BL MS Add. 15274, fol. 3ʳ). By permission of the British Library

England and the Avignon Popes

The Practice of Diplomacy in Late Medieval Europe

KARSTEN PLÖGER

LEGENDA

Modern Humanities Research Association and Maney Publishing
2005

Published by the
Modern Humanities Research Association and Maney Publishing
1 Carlton House Terrace
London SW1Y 5DB
United Kingdom

LEGENDA is an imprint of the
Modern Humanities Research Association and Maney Publishing

Maney Publishing is the trading name of W. S. Maney & Son Ltd,
whose registered office is at Hudson Road, Leeds LS9 7DL, UK

ISBN 1 904713 04 1

First published 2005

LEGENDA series designed by Cox Design Partnership, Witney, Oxon

Printed in Great Britain

CONTENTS

ABBREVIATIONS

❖

a.	*ante*
AA	*Acta Aragonensia*, ed. Heinrich Finke
abp.	archbishop
AHP	*Archivum Historiae Pontificiae*
ASV	Archivio Segreto Vaticano
BA	Bachelor of Arts
BAV	Biblioteca Apostolica Vaticana
BCL	Bachelor of Civil Law
B.Cn.L.	Bachelor of Canon Law
BEC	*Bibliothèque de l'École des chartes*
BEFAR	Bibliothèque des Écoles françaises d'Athènes et de Rome
BIHR	*Bulletin of the Institute of Historical Research*
BJRL	*Bulletin of the John Rylands Library*
BL	British Library
bp.	bishop
BPH	*Bulletin philologique et historique du Comité des Travaux Historiques et Scientifiques*
BRUC	Alfred B. Emden, *A Biographical Register of the University of Cambridge to AD 1500*
BRUO	Alfred B. Emden, *A Biographical Register of the University of Oxford to AD 1500*
B.Th.	Bachelor of Theology
BUJ	Bachelor of Canon and Civil Law (*utriusque juris*)
card. bp.	cardinal bishop
card. dcn.	cardinal deacon
card. p.	cardinal priest
CC	Adam Murimuth, *Continuatio Chronicarum*, ed. Edward M. Thompson
CCR	*Calendar of the Close Rolls*
CIC	*Corpus Iuris Canonici*, ed. Emil Friedberg, 2nd edn.
cl.	cleric

CPL	*Calendar of Papal Letters, 1198–1419*, ed. William H. Bliss et al. [all references are to vol. iii (1342–62) unless otherwise stated]
CPP	*Calendar of Petitions to the Pope, 1342–1419*, i: *1342–62*, ed. William H. Bliss (London, 1896; no further vols. published)
CPR	*Calendar of the Patent Rolls Preserved in the Public Record Office, 1232–1509*
CYS	Canterbury and York Society
D	*Innocent VI (1352–1362): Lettres closes, patentes et curiales se rapportant à la France*, ed. Eugène Déprez (followed by doc. no.)
Dau	*Benoît XII (1334–1342): Lettres closes, patentes et curiales se rapportant à la France, publiées ou analysées d'après les registres du Vatican*, ed. Georges Daumet (followed by doc. no.)
DCL	Doctor of Civil Law
D.Cn.L.	Doctor of Canon Law
DDC	*Dictionnaire de droit canonique*, ed. Raoul Naz
DGM	*Clément VI (1342–1352): Lettres closes, patentes et curiales se rapportant à la France*, ed. Eugène Déprez, Jean Glénisson and Guillaume Mollat (followed by doc. no.)
DHGE	*Dictionnaire d'histoire et de géographie ecclésiastiques*, ed. Alfred Baudrillart et al.
dk.	duke
DM	*Clément VI (1342–1352): Lettres closes, patentes et curiales interéssant les pays autres que la France*, ed. Eugène Déprez and Guillaume Mollat (followed by doc. no.)
D.Th.	Doctor of Theology
DUJ	Doctor of Canon and Civil Law (*utriusque juris*)
EHR	*English Historical Review*
EMDP	*English Medieval Diplomatic Practice, Part I, Documents and Interpretation*, ed. Pierre Chaplais
GC	*Les Grandes Chroniques de France*, ed. Jules Viard
GEC	G[eorge] E[dward] C[okayne], *The Complete Peerage of England, Scotland, Ireland, Great Britain and the United Kingdom*, rev. and enl. edn., ed. Vicary Gibbs et al.
GLG	*Innocent VI (1352–1362): Lettres secrètes et curiales*, ed. Pierre Gasnault, Marie-Hyacinthe Laurent and Nicole Gotteri (followed by doc. no.)
HBC	*Handbook of British Chronology*, 3rd edn., ed. Edmund B. Fryde et al.

HJb	Historisches Jahrbuch
HMSO	Her Majesty's Stationery Office
kt.	knight
LexMA	Lexikon des Mittelalters
Lic.	licentiate
MA	Master of Arts
MAHEF	Mélanges d'archéologie et d'histoire de l'École française de Rome
MIÖG	Mitteilungen des Instituts für Österreichische Geschichtsforschung
MD	Léon Mirot and Eugène Déprez, 'Les ambassades anglaises pendant la Guerre de Cent Ans: Catalogue chronologique, 1327–1450'
OC	Order of Carmel (Carmelite or white friar)
OESA	Order of Eremites of St Augustine (Austin friar)
OFM	Order of Friars Minor (Franciscan or grey friar)
OP	Order of Friars Preachers (Dominican or black friar)
OSA	Augustinian canon
OSB	Order of St Benedict (black monk)
PE	The Papacy: An Encyclopedia, ed. Philippe Levillain, Engl. edn., ed. John W. O'Malley
PUM	Publications of the University of Manchester
PUM/HS	Publications of the Univ. of Manchester, Historical Series
QF	Quellen und Forschungen aus italienischen Archiven und Bibliotheken
R	Foedera, ed. Thomas Rymer, 5th edn. ['Record Commission edn.'] (London, 1816–69)
RHD	Revue d'histoire diplomatique
RHE	Revue d'histoire ecclésiastique
RP	Rotuli parliamentorum, ed. John Strachey
RQ	Römische Quartalschrift für christliche Altertumskunde und Kirchengeschichte
RS	Rolls Series
SHF	Société de l'histoire de France
TNA: PRO	The National Archives of the United Kingdom: Public Record Office
TRHS	Transactions of the Royal Historical Society
V	Benoît XII (1334–1342): Lettres communes, ed. Jean-Marie Vidal (followed by doc. no.)
VM	Benoît XII (1334–1342): Lettres closes, patentes et curiales intéressant les pays autres que la France, ed. Jean-Marie Vidal and Guillaume Mollat (followed by doc. no.)

VPA	*Vitae paparum Avenionensium*, ed. Étienne Baluze, new edn. by Guillaume Mollat
VQ	Vatikanische Quellen zur Geschichte der päpstlichen Hof- und Finanzverwaltung

Note: All references to manuscript sources, unless otherwise indicated, are to The National Archives of the United Kingdom: Public Record Office (TNA: PRO).

ACKNOWLEDGEMENTS

History, I have come to believe since embarking on this project, is less about finding the 'right' answers than about finding the right questions. It is my pleasure to acknowledge my obligations to those who have helped me in this search.

In particular I must thank Prof. Dr Gerhard Fouquet (Kiel), who originally suggested that I deal with English diplomatic missions to the Continent, for his kindness and encouragement, which outlasted my temporary switching of academic allegiances. For advice on specific points I am indebted to Prof. Rees Davies and Dr Maurice Keen (Oxford), Prof. Dr Werner Paravicini (Paris), Prof. Dr Franz Josef Felten (Mainz), Prof. Dr Bernhard Schimmelpfennig (Augsburg), Mr Pat Corby (British Embassy to the Holy See), Dr Jan Hirschbiegel, PD Dr Arnd Reitemeier, Dr Harm von Seggern (Kiel) and especially to PD Dr Stefan Weiß (Augsburg). Dr Jeremy Catto, as my supervisor, offered counsel at every stage of my research.

The publication of this study has been made possible by a Historical Award from the Scouloudi Foundation in association with the Institute of Historical Research. I would also like to express my appreciation to The British Academy, Arts and Humanities Research Board and to the Faculty of Modern History at Oxford for supporting my project with Graduate Studentships. A research scholarship from the German Historical Institute in Rome made possible the examination of the source material preserved in the Vatican. James K. Farge, the librarian of the Pontifical Institute of Mediaeval Studies, Toronto, kindly extended library access rights to me.

Several of my fellow postgraduates at Balliol College have also been of great assistance. Jacqueline Fernholz, Joanne Wilson, Avery Willis and Alfonso Moreno have read and helpfully commented on parts of the draft. Special thanks are due to Dominik Zaum—though I am still not sure whether this is more for his probing questions on the aims of my research or for his patience in explaining the basics of contemporary International Relations theory to me.

My greatest debt, however, is to my parents, for their unwavering support over the years.

London, September 2004   K.P.

PREFACE

By the beginning of the twentieth century many of the basic tenets of those who concerned themselves with the study of diplomatic history had begun to be challenged.[1] History as an academic discipline, when it emerged during the professionalization process of the nineteenth century, was explicitly the political history of the nation state and its relations with other nation states. In other words, it was coterminous with the exploration of high politics and international diplomacy. Those who called themselves historians duly focused on the study of the intentions and deeds of the 'great men' who 'made history', taking a narrative and descriptive, rather than analytical, approach.[2] It was this latter feature of their works that caused George M. Young, as late as 1936, to remark that the greater part of what was passing for diplomatic history in his day was 'little more than the record of what one clerk said to another clerk'.[3]

Around 1900 historians, predominantly in France and Belgium, began to question the traditional paradigms of historical research and to advocate a history that accounted for social and economic factors rather than one that concentrated on leading personalities and isolated events. If this new, social-science-oriented history sought to replace the study of politics with that of society, historians from the 1960s onwards increasingly turned to the study of culture, understood as the conditions of everyday life and experience.[4] While conventional forms of political and diplomatic history dominated the profession until well after the Second World War, and although the view that history is essentially *political* history remains widespread even today, political history in its pure form is now written only by a minority.

The late nineteenth century, then, was the heyday of conventional diplomatic history. Although it retains an important place on university curricula today, it looks unlikely to regain its former prominence in the immediate future. Why, then, devote years of research to a subject that appears to be so out of date, and whose exponents have so often been accused of analytical short-sightedness? The present study takes as its starting point the assumption that it is possible to look at diplomatic history from two different perspectives. On the one hand, one can examine, as generations of medievalists have done, its contents and 'end products': alliances, truces, treaties and so forth. On the other hand, one can confine oneself to exploring the means and techniques of communication employed by two or more participants in a diplomatic dialogue in a given period of time. The present study is concerned with the latter: I shall attempt to move beyond the traditional, contents-oriented perspective and revisit the world of medieval diplomacy with an eye towards its functional aspects. In short, this book is concerned with the forms and structures, rather than the contents, of diplomatic communication in the late Middle Ages.

Although I am concerned here with diplomacy in its narrower sense—diplomatic practice—and not with 'diplomacy' as a synonym for 'foreign policy', it will not be possible to dispense wholly with digressions into 'eventist' history. A variety of factors—some pre-determined by the very nature of the relationship between the two protagonists, others historically contingent—set the parameters within which royal diplomacy had to operate. These will be discussed in two preparatory chapters. A prosopographical study of the official and unofficial diplomatic agents of the Crown then follows. In the final three chapters I will, as it were, look over the shoulder of Edward III's envoys as they set out on their missions and 'get down to work' after arriving at their destination. Chapters 5 and 6 are devoted to the interplay between written and oral discourse, to modes of bilateral and trilateral negotiation and to aspects of 'diplomatic culture'.

It is hoped that a new approach to diplomatic history that no longer privileges the concepts and tools of analysis of political and administrative history to the detriment of other analytical tools, such as those of the social and cultural sciences and of International Relations (IR), will allow us to gain a fuller understanding of the essence of medieval diplomatic communication.

Notes to Preface

1. For a concise survey of the main trends in modern historiography, see Georg G. Iggers, *Historiography in the Twentieth Century: From Scientific Objectivity to the Postmodern Challenge* (Hanover, NH, and London, 1997), 1–16. On medieval

history in particular, see Hans-Werner Goetz, *Moderne Mediävistik: Stand und Perspektiven der Mittelalterforschung* (Darmstadt, 1999), 72–6, 84–94, 106–25.

2. Jacques Le Goff, 'Is politics still the backbone of history?', in Felix Gilbert and Stephen R. Graubard (eds), *Historical Studies Today* (New York, 1972), 337–55 (337–40); Gordon A. Craig, 'Political and diplomatic history', ibid. 356–71 (356–8); Paul G. Lauren, 'Diplomacy: History, theory, and policy', in id. (ed.), *Diplomacy: New Approaches in History, Theory, and Policy* (New York and London, 1979), 3–18 (5–6).

3. George M. Young, *Victorian England: Portrait of an Age* (London, 1936), 103.

4. Iggers, 8.

CHAPTER 1

Methodological and Theoretical Considerations

1.1. Sources

Medieval diplomatic practice first became the subject of systematic studies in the last quarter of the nineteenth century when the general interest in diplomatic history was at its zenith. By the same time diplomacy itself had emerged as 'a distinguished vocation with specialized professional skills and a particular appeal to social and intellectual elites'.[1] However, the fact that, by and large, the political units of the Middle Ages lacked specialized institutions for the planning and conduct of foreign affairs meant that this particular aspect of governance had little chance of attracting the attention of mainstream constitutional and administrative historiography. Only few scholars of that early period, such as Viktor Menzel[2] and especially Marie Alphonse René de Maulde La Clavière,[3] made sustained efforts to understand the unique character of medieval diplomacy. Instead, the focus of attention of their contemporaries soon shifted towards the history of one of the hallmarks of modern statehood: the evolution of the practice of representation through permanent embassies and resident ambassadors, which, as the leading scholars came to agree, had Renaissance Italy as its birthplace and gradually diffused from there to northern and western Europe.[4] As late as 1939 the doyen of traditionalist diplomatic theory, Harold Nicolson, emphasized that in the Middle Ages 'there was little opportunity for any orderly or established system of international contact'.[5]

During the second half of the twentieth century only a few historians examined the available diplomatic documents, financial and administrative records and narrative sources systematically in order to gain a deeper understanding of the forms and methods of medieval diplomacy. Beside François Louis Ganshof, two Americans must be mentioned here as the authors of fundamental works: Garrett Mattingly and Donald E. Queller.[6] Since the early 1990s, foreign policy and diplomacy have found renewed interest mainly among French and German medievalists. A younger generation of scholars has made use of Ganshof's, Mattingly's and Queller's general findings in the context of individual case studies,[7] and major conferences were held in Berlin in 1997 and near Constance in 2001.[8]

In the course of the last few years monographs investigating the technique of communication employed by the rulers of Savoy and the Teutonic Order in their contacts with the late medieval papacy have been published.[9] Similar studies concerning Anglo-curial communication have so far been lacking. The first two parts of J. Robert Wright's *The Church and the English Crown, 1305–1334* consider some key aspects of Anglo-papal relations in the formative period of the Avignon papacy: the theory and practice of provisions, proctorial representation, the Crown's relations with the college of cardinals and English litigation in the Roman court.[10] However, Wright's focus is more on the Church, in its relations with the English State, than vice versa, and he devotes a mere five pages to Crown envoys. Roger Highfield has studied Anglo-papal and Church–State relations during the last thirty years of the Avignon period in his seminal 1951 thesis, but he, too, discusses the organizational aspects of these contacts but cursorily.[11]

From the late 1920s onwards a number of articles dealing with individual elements of English diplomatic practice in the Middle Ages were published in rapid succession: after Mary C. Salt and Betty Behrens had worked on some organizational problems of Anglo-French diplomacy under Edward I and on the first English resident ambassadors, respectively, Alfred Larson contributed an article on the payment of diplomatic personnel.[12] If we know a good deal more about the royal messenger service than about any other cog in the wheel of English medieval diplomacy, this is largely thanks to the meticulous research begun in those pre-war years by Mary C. Hill.[13] The first to explore the workings of the 'machinery of diplomatic intercourse' in late medieval England as a whole was her contemporary Henry S. Lucas, who placed his pioneering study in the wider administrative context of the early years of Edward III's reign.[14] In the same year, 1940, George P. Cuttino's *English Diplomatic Administration* appeared, with a large section devoted to the 'agents and mechanics of diplomacy'.[15]

However, the one scholar whose work has had the greatest impact on the present study is undoubtedly Pierre Chaplais, who, after a lifetime devoted to the study of Anglo-French relations, and of the 'diplomatic of diplomacy' in particular, published the two parts of his *English Medieval Diplomatic Practice* in 1975 and 1982.[16] This extensive and richly annotated selection of documents was intended to form the basis of a comprehensive manual on medieval English diplomatic practice, the first part of which, after many delays, was published in 2003.[17]

Englishmen travelled to Avignon for a variety of purposes. Bishops-elect went there to confirm their elections and receive their consecrations. The abbots-elect of monastic houses exempt from episcopal control and dependent directly upon the Apostolic See usually had to obtain confirmation of their elections from there, and often received their blessing there as well. A number of English scholars and theologians were drawn to the papal city as an intellectual centre.[18] Not least, there was a steady stream of Englishmen to the curia to seek absolution in reserved cases and to defend their rights in other matters of litigation. Each of these visitors presumably brought with him some pieces of information concerning the political situation in England. But it is the official diplomatic agents of the Crown with which I am here primarily concerned. It would certainly be rewarding to subject the whole of the Avignon period to such an examination; it would then become possible to ascertain what, if any, long-term trends and changes occurred in the development of Anglo-curial communication between the early years of Edward II's reign and the last years of Edward III's. However, I have found it necessary to focus on a comparatively short period of only two decades; if one aims to understand the intricacies of the communication process between these two protagonists, there is no choice but to opt for a decidedly 'microscopic' view and clearly define one's 'exploratory trench' (to use Michael Clanchy's expression[19]). This entails investigating the whole range of the material coming out of that 'trench' rather than a selection of a few well-known sources from the whole of the Avignon period—that is, from the years between 1309 and 1376 (I am aware that referring to Clement V (1305–14) as 'the first Avignon pope' is somewhat inaccurate and merely 'a historiographical trend that has reached the status of tradition'[20]). Only in this way does it become possible, for instance, to establish a precise chronology of diplomatic contacts.

The period that I have selected to investigate is more than just an arbitrary cross section of Edward III's reign and the Avignon period. The beginning of the pontificate of Clement VI coincided with a marked increase in the need for communication between Westminster and Avignon: the escalation of the conflict over papal provisions in England and especially the outbreak of the war in France provided powerful new stimuli for diplomacy. This thickening in the web of communication manifested itself in an increase in the amount of sources—our 'trench' promises to yield more material than any other that I could have chosen to dig elsewhere.

The England of Edward III and the curia of the Avignon popes stood out among the political units of their time because of their highly bureaucratized and efficient central administrations. On both sides an extensive use of literacy led to a proliferation of written records. A largely uninterrupted continuity of centralized record keeping in England and at the Holy See from the high Middle Ages to the twenty-first century has ensured the survival of most of the material relevant to our study.

Series C 70 (Chancery, Roman Rolls) in The National Archives/ Public Record Office consists mainly of enrolled copies of correspondence sent by Edward I, Edward II and Edward III to the pope and cardinals between 1306 and 1357. The twenty-five rolls include items concerning high royal policy as well as letters in favour of individual clerics and laymen. With only three exceptions, the fifty-seven extant papal letters to the English king from the two pontificates under examination[21] are today preserved in the series SC 7 (Special Collections, Papal Bulls). Fortunately, these documents did not share the fate of so many other papal letters to English addressees. While the Reformation led to a large-scale premeditated destruction of *papalia* and to the dispersal of most major monastic archives, the bulls in royal custody remained unharmed and later found their way into the national archives.[22] Thus—although, at a cautious estimate, less than a third of the total number of letters addressed to Edward III in 1342–62 survive[23]—SC 7 today contains the single most important collection of papal documents in England. Transcripts of most of the enrolments in C 70 and of most of the original bulls in SC 7 are printed in the various editions of the monumental compilation of Thomas Rymer, *Foedera*.[24]

The drafts of letters inserted in the *Registra Avenionensia* (RA) and, partly, copied into the *Registra Vaticana* (RV) at a later date supplement the original papal letters in England. In most cases their opening paragraphs contain precise information concerning the dates, personnel and tasks of English royal missions. As far as the British Isles are concerned, a valuable work of reference has existed for a long time in the *Calendar of Entries in the Papal Registers Relating to Great Britain and Ireland: Calendar of Papal Letters*, which gives short summaries of papal letters of English, Scottish, Irish and Welsh interest from the period from 1198 to 1492 (Innocent III–Innocent VIII). For several reasons, however, it appears insufficient to rely solely on this work. The *Calendar* uses as its only original source the copies of letter drafts from the *Registra Vaticana* without taking into account that by no means all these texts were copied into this series from the *Registra Avenionensia*.[25] For the years 1360–2 the *Registra Vaticana* volumes are missing,[26] which results in a gap in the *Calendar*. What is more, the process of copying was fraught with inconsistencies.[27]

In most cases these problems can be solved by consulting the editions of papal letters published by the French School at Rome.[28] Unlike the British *Calendar of Entries*, the French publication gives the full text of each letter, using the *Registra Avenionensia* as a primary source. However, the editing process is far from complete.[29] For this and the other reasons outlined above it has been necessary to supplement the information derived from the printed editions by examining the original documents preserved in the Vatican Archives.

Expense accounts of envoys and messengers form the backbone of this study. Besides providing exact chronological data and information concerning travel costs and routes, they sometimes offer insight into the emissaries' activities at their destination.[30] These original accounts (*particule compoti* or *compoti*) are today preserved in The National Archives: Public Record Office, series E 101. The core of this series is formed by various kinds of accounts and particulars of accounts deposited in the office of the King's Remembrancer after their enrolment on the Chancellor's Rolls (E 352, in the period 1323–40), Pipe Rolls (E 372, also called 'Great Rolls of the Exchequer') or, from 1367 onwards, Foreign Account Rolls (E 364). A parallel examination of E 101 and E 372/E 364 is essential for two reasons. First, it allows us to discover gaps in the Accounts Various. In many cases an envoy's original expense account has been lost and survives only in summarized form, drawn up by the staff of the Exchequer of Receipt (*Recepta Scaccarii*, Lower Exchequer) and subsequently inscribed on the Pipe Rolls or Foreign Account Rolls. (For the period 1342–62 there are twenty-eight copies of accounts of envoys to Avignon in E 372 but only eighteen extant original accounts in E 101). Secondly, the Pipe Rolls mention all advances and final payments received by an envoy at the Lower Exchequer, along with the date and contents of the privy seal letters authorizing these. This helps to illuminate the wider administrative context of diplomatic missions.

All payments out of the royal treasure made at the Exchequer of Receipt had to be authorized by the king's writ or by order of the barons of the Exchequer. In the course of the thirteenth century two new Exchequer offices emerged: that of the King's Remembrancer and that of the Lord Treasurer's Remembrancer. Both offices had their Memoranda Rolls. The Cowick Ordinance of 1323, which first defined the duties of the two Remembrancers, provided that the king's privy seal orders concerning the execution of payments were to be entered on the roll of the King's Remembrancer (E 159).[31] Hence this series contains some administrative material pertaining to the drawing-up of diplomats' final accounts, primarily enrolments of the privy seal writs that ordered the Treasurer and barons of the Exchequer to account with envoys or granted a discharge of a specific sum. The original writs and warrants ordering such payments survive in the files of E 404 (Exchequer of Receipt, Warrants for Issues). Both the originals and the enrolments contain details of diplomatic expenditure not always to be found elsewhere.

Like E 101, 372 and 159, the Issue Rolls (E 403) belong to the group of Exchequer sources comprising documents that initiated or recorded payments to English medieval diplomats. They give details of all money paid out of the Lower Exchequer, stating the name of the payee, the amount, the date and the reason for each individual payment. This makes them one of the most valuable sources of information about government expenditure in the mid-thirteenth to late-fifteenth centuries. In the context of a study of diplomacy the Issue Rolls gain special importance:[32] they state payments to simple messengers of whom neither original *compoti* nor their enrolments exist. As a direct result of the predominance of the Exchequer in the financial organization of diplomacy from the early 1340s onwards,[33] Wardrobe accounts are of minor importance for this study.

The rather complicated system of account at the Exchequer renders it impossible to gain a precise picture of English medieval Crown revenues and expenditure from a combined examination of the Receipt and Issue Rolls. The student of the *Introitus et Exitus* (IE)

series in the Vatican Archives is in a somewhat more fortunate
position. The Apostolic Camera dealt with all the financial transactions of the Holy See and soon became one of the most important
and highly organized curial departments. The cameral ledgers in IE
contain the cumulative monthly income and expenditure reports by
the papal treasurer.[34] Besides being a virtually inexhaustible source of
information on the economic, financial, military, social and art history
of the papal court itself, the IE volumes are immensely useful for the
exact dating of visits of envoys, proctors and clergy of all ranks.[35]
Although a great number of extracts from them have been published
by the German Görresgesellschaft in the eight volumes of the series
'Vatikanische Quellen zur Geschichte der päpstlichen Hof- und
Finanzverwaltung, 1316–1378', further research has proved to be far
from superfluous. Some additional material concerning English
members of the curial staff and the English delegation at the peace
conference of 1355 can be found both in the IE volumes used by the
German scholars, and in those not examined by them.[36]

   If the cameral ledgers are an important source for the understanding
of papal finances and the economy and social structure of the curia,
so are the 504 volumes of the *Collectoriae* (Coll.) series. They contain
mainly the reports and accounts submitted by the collectors appointed
throughout Christendom for the collection of those monies due to
the *Camera Apostolica* that were not directly paid to it. But apart from
that one also finds several stray items relating to other aspects of curial
and town life that were bound and stored with the collectors' reports
and became part of this series.

   The Registers of Supplications (RS), in which the papal scribes from
1342 registered petitions for all kinds of benefices and graces, include
a large number of supplications by English envoys for themselves or
on behalf of the king or other principals. Such references contribute
to our understanding both of the actual business transacted by them
and of their extra-diplomatic activities. Here, again, the present study
is indebted to the thorough scholarship of the late nineteenth century:
'British' and Irish material published from this series is included in
William H. Bliss's *Calendar of Petitions to the Pope*.[37]

   As has been seen, papal chancery documents can be said to
contribute more to a study of Anglo-papal diplomacy than the
material produced by the *Camera Apostolica*. Inversely, the sources
emanating from Edward III's Chancery, the chief secretarial
department of royal government, cannot match the importance of the

Exchequer material when it comes to obtaining information about the chronology and costs of communication between our two protagonists. The single most important series for our purpose (besides, obviously, the Roman Rolls) is the Treaty Rolls (C 76). These are Chancery enrolments of treaties and other diplomatic documents, mainly relating to France and the Holy Roman Empire. The enrolments for the period under consideration (C 76/17–45) all belong to the so-called French Rolls (C 76/17–215A) and include documents concerning the administration of the English possessions in France (excluding Gascony and the Channel Islands). Not all the credentials, appointments of attorneys and letters of procuration, protection and safe conduct for English diplomats sent to the papal court enrolled here have found their way into Rymer's compilation.

The king's commands were expressed, if not verbally, mainly through the privy seal or smaller seals. The various instruments (writs, bills, letters) that authorized the chancellor or the temporary keeper of the great seal to affix that seal to acts signifying the royal will are today preserved in the files of C 81 (Chancery, Warrants for the Great Seal, Series I).

Two more series of Chancery enrolments remain to be considered: the Close Rolls (C 54) and the Patent Rolls (C 66). They are of special interest for the student of diplomatic history since the former, which contain primarily royal orders to individual officials and subjects, also have a number of credentials, and in the latter many letters of procuration, protection and safe conduct were enrolled. Both series have proved to be exceptionally rich sources for the study of the English diplomatic personnel in that they provide a wide range of information on the careers of Edward III's leading diplomats and on the nature of their relationship with the king. Both the Patent and the Close Rolls are conveniently accessible thanks to detailed *Calendars.*[38]

Intermediate reports and other letters from envoys and proctors at the papal court are obviously a most valuable source for any study of this kind; from them most of our knowledge regarding the reception of envoys, the diplomatic protocol and the structure of negotiations derives. Perhaps the finest are those of the representatives of the Crown of Aragon in the late thirteenth and early fourteenth centuries, which have been edited by Heinrich Finke.[39] Of similarly great interest are the account books, legal papers and correspondence of the envoys representing the civic authorities of Hamburg in their

lengthy lawsuit against the local cathedral chapter between 1337 and
1356, especially since they contain some information on Englishmen
serving in the curial administration in those years.[40] Unfortunately we
have hardly any such letters or reports from mid-fourteenth-century
English diplomats; as regards contacts with Avignon, certainly many
embassies did not stay there long enough to make the dispatch of
reports and newsletters to Westminster necessary, and to justify the
risks and costs of doing so. But most of the blame, it seems, is to be
ascribed to contemporary practices of record preservation: in general,
once such reports and letters had served their immediate purpose they
were not regarded as worthy of transfer to the royal archives. Their
survival in England is thus intermittent and haphazard.[41] For the
period under examination there are, however, two remarkable
exceptions. John Offord, Hugh Neville and William Bateman, the
leading members of the English delegation to the Anglo-French peace
conference at Clement VI's court in 1344–5, reported on their
progress in fourteen letters close sent to Edward III and members of
his council between mid-September and early December 1344.
Additionally, Offord and Neville kept a detailed journal about their
discussions with the French (22 October to 29 November 1344). Late-
fourteenth-century copies of these documents were bound into one
of the volumes of Sir Robert Bruce Cotton's collection of manuscripts in the late sixteenth century and later printed in the appendix
to Kervyn de Lettenhove's edition of Jean Froissart's *Œuvres*.[42]

To what extent can chronicles be considered reliable sources of
information on day-to-day diplomacy? Historical writing on both
sides of the Channel was preoccupied with the grand themes of royal
governance, war and chivalry.[43] Works of this kind invariably served a
didactic purpose, their aim being to instil in their readers and
audience an appreciation of the chivalric code.[44] Indeed, 'despite the
fact that an undoubted administrative expertise was possessed by
several of the chroniclers of the time, an interest in administrative
procedures is one notable omission in contemporary writing'.[45] It is
not surprising that these writers were interested in diplomacy only in
so far as it appeared to fit into the general context of aristocratic
lifestyle and proto-nationalistic propaganda. A case in point is the
'coverage' of the Second Avignon Conference (January–February
1355), at which members of the elite of French and English knight-
hood were present. A number of fourteenth- and fifteenth-century
English chroniclers comment on the negotiations and their

breakdown. The conference was an event at which elements of chivalry and high politics fused with one another, and was still considered an interesting enough topic more than 100 years later for William Caxton to print a passage about it.[46] On the French side, there are short references in Froissart and in the *Chroniques des règnes de Jean II et de Charles V*.[47]

If any of the contemporary chroniclers can be called our principal witness for an examination of the technique of diplomacy, it is Adam Murimuth (*c*.1274–1347), who at the time he was writing could already look back on a distinguished diplomatic career of his own. A doctor of civil law, an able ecclesiastical lawyer and administrator and an experienced curial proctor, he served as a royal envoy to Avignon under Edward II.[48] Murimuth began his *Continuatio Chronicarum* after 1325, but probably wrote most of it around 1345. Throughout these later stages of his career he retained a sharp sense of observation of the diplomatic proceedings in which he had been so closely involved. He was in an excellent position to gather information: a canon of St Paul's from 1325, he was based more or less continuously near Westminster, the emerging power centre of the kingdom. Among the holdings of the archives of that church were newsletters, some of which he built into his narrative.[49] What is more, we know that Murimuth was acquainted with some of the most important English envoys to the curia during the 1340s, and we may assume that he received some pieces of first-hand information from them.[50] He has justly been called 'a terse, factual writer, meticulous about names and dates, with no gift for literary narrative'.[51] However, his strong anti-papal bias and pessimistic and at times even cynical tone do not detract from the value of his *Continuatio Chronicarum* for our study. Most of the information about the chronology and personnel of Anglo-papal diplomacy given in his chronicle is borne out by the corresponding administrative documents. Murimuth's work gives an example of how much information about routine diplomacy was available to a writer who took an active interest in it. Unfortunately, it covers only the period up to 1347, and no comparable work exists for the rest of Clement VI's and Innocent VI's pontificates.

In some regards, the quantity and quality of our source material are limited. Many English and Vatican documents have been lost or damaged.[52] Sources of a narrative nature exist for only very few missions. This means that we lack reliable information about the reception of envoys further down the social scale. Chronicles add some information not to be found in administrative records but were produced in a specific cultural and political context that has left its mark. Bearing all this in mind, one can still argue that the conditions for a study of contacts between Westminster and Avignon are better than for a similar analysis dealing with any other two protagonists.

1.2. Neither 'Foreign' nor 'Politics': Crown and Tiara

As part of the 'international society' of Latin Christendom, the *res publica* or *universitas Christiana*, the kingdom of England necessarily had to maintain close links with the Apostolic See, which before the Reformation and its formal rejection of papal authority was anything but an external power (Peter Moraw suggests as much in a recent publication with regard to the Empire when he refers to the curia as a stage for German 'quasi-foreign policy'[53]). This was not primarily because technically England had been a fief of the Holy See since 1213, when King John had been forced to surrender it to Innocent III (1198–1216) and receive it back as such. It is more to do with the well-known complexity of the relationship between Church and State in the Middle Ages. Even in the mid-fourteenth century, at a time when theories of national sovereignty had begun to develop, there were still a number of ways for the pope to curtail—at least temporarily—the king's authority within his own realm. Two examples may suffice: the privilege of 'benefit of clergy' and the existence of a distinct ecclesiastical legal jurisdiction in England,[54] and, secondly, the law of sanctuary, by which a number of ecclesiastical institutions were 'islands within the mesh of royal justice'.[55] In short, the universal, spiritual power of the Vicar of Christ penetrated the very sphere within which the kings of England strove to assert their secular dominion.

Furthermore, it is essential, when discussing contacts between any given secular power and the papacy, to beware of any confusion between content and form. Many, possibly most, decisions made by the popes on their own initiative or after negotiations with diplomatic agents had a decidedly 'political' dimension to them in that they had the potential to preserve or change the distribution of power within the geographic region in question. Perhaps the best example is John XXII's non-approbation of the election of Louis IV, followed in 1324 by his excommunication, both of which severely limited the emperor's capacity to pursue independent domestic and foreign policies. It was for a good reason that in the summer of 1336 Louis began spreading the rumour that his full reconciliation with the Holy See was imminent and a mere formality: according to the report of a French observer, this helped him regain the loyalty of clergy, aristocrats and townspeople all over Germany.[56] Nevertheless, even the most politically charged decisions were, from a strictly technical point of view, matters either of *iustitia* or of *gratia*: they invariably assumed the form of papal judgements, made with recourse to canon law, or of ecclesiastico-administrative measures. In this regard, they differed fundamentally from agreements reached by secular procedures of conflict resolution. Edward III's diplomats might attempt to convince the pope of the merits of the king's case, to persuade him to make a favourable decision, to influence him by altering his behaviour, beliefs and attitudes, maybe even—to some extent—to bargain with him, and in this respect their discussions at the curia displayed most of the characteristics of genuinely political forms of diplomatic discourse. But the phrasing of the official documents drawn up at the end of their missions makes it quite clear that it was the pope as the supreme judge in spiritual and temporal matters who had the final word.

Some stylistic features of the protocol (*superscriptio*) of English royal letters close reflect this inequality of status. While the emperor, kings and cardinals were usually addressed as *frater carissime*, *excellentissime princeps* and *amice carissime*, respectively, the family metaphor applied to the pope, *sanctissime in Christo pater* or *pater carissime*, was the only one to express a vertical power relation between sender and addressee.[57] This difference in position was also accentuated in the greeting (*salutatio*): from the late Middle Ages onwards it was customary to include in it the formula *devota pedum oscula beatorum*, a topos based on the gesture of reverence and obedience owed to the Supreme Pontiff by all visitors to his court.[58]

From what has been said so far we may deduce that most of the principal instruments of medieval foreign policy[59] could not be of much use to Edward III in his dealings with such a partner: he could not buy the pope's loyalty, extract oaths of fealty or homage from him, formally defy and wage war[60] against him, and—for even more obvious reasons—marry his daughters off to him. It will be one of our principal tasks to investigate how exactly diplomacy functioned in these conditions.

1.3. Some Definitions

From a twenty-first-century perspective such terms as 'diplomacy', 'diplomatic' or 'diplomat' may appear somewhat out of place in an analysis of medieval 'international' relations, since it was not until the late eighteenth century that they acquired their modern meaning.[61] Moreover, they have, as parts of the terminology of modern politics, unambiguously secular and political connotations, which seem to render them unsuitable for the examination of a relationship between a spiritual and a temporal power in which, as has been suggested above, legal and political issues were inextricably intertwined.

The political language of the Middle Ages had no specialized vocabulary for the particular form of interaction with which we are here concerned, nor did contemporary intellectuals attempt to create a theoretical framework for it. If, then, words such as 'diplomacy' and 'diplomat' appear throughout this study, it is simply for lack of alternatives. 'Diplomacy' will be taken to mean the peaceful conduct of external relations amongst rulers or ruling bodies (both spiritual and secular) and their representatives.[62] The difficulty here, of course, is that what qualified as 'external' was frequently unclear and the very source of many 'international' conflicts; there was no room in the socio-political structure of medieval feudalism for a sharp distinction between private, public and public international affairs. This is not, however, to deny in principle the awareness of a difference between domestic and foreign affairs on the part of the political protagonists of medieval Europe in general and England in particular—that is, an awareness that certain actions transcended a ruler's immediate sphere of power, thus assuming a 'foreign political' character. As Dieter Berg has convincingly argued, this awareness existed as early as the eleventh and twelfth centuries.[63]

What is more, I agree with those among today's International Relations scholars who, rather than restricting the concept of 'diplomacy' to specific (modern) practices and specific (State) actors, understand diplomacy in terms of generic concepts such as 'mediation', 'representation' and 'communication'.[64] Diplomacy, in this perspective, 'expresses a human condition that precedes and transcends the experience of living in the sovereign, territorial state of the past few hundred years';[65] it may, indeed, exist wherever there are boundaries for identity and those boundaries are crossed.[66]

In what follows the word 'diplomat' will be used to refer to anyone charged with conveying an oral message and/or participating in bilateral or multilateral negotiations—that is, anyone except simple letter-bearing messengers. When referring indiscriminately to anyone performing a diplomatic function, be it officially or unofficially, from the lowest-ranking *cursor* to the highest-ranking *nuncius solemnis*, I will employ the generic term 'diplomatic agent'. The use of the word 'ambassador' has been avoided, since it appears to be too closely associated with the post-medieval practice of representation through resident diplomats.

Notes to Chapter 1

1. Abba S. Eban, *Diplomacy for the Next Century* (New Haven and London, 1998), 34.
2. Viktor Menzel, *Deutsches Gesandtschaftswesen im Mittelalter* (Hanover, 1892).
3. Marie Alphone René de Maulde La Clavière, *La Diplomatie au temps de Machiavel* (Paris, 1892–3).
4. For a survey of the research done in this field in the late 19th and early 20th c., see F. Ernst, 'Über Gesandtschaftswesen und Diplomatie an der Wende vom Mittelalter zur Neuzeit', *Archiv für Kulturgeschichte* 33 (1950), 64–95 (68–70). See also Garret Mattingly, 'The first resident embassies: Medieval Italian origins of modern diplomacy', *Speculum* 12 (1937), 423–39, and the second part of his *Renaissance Diplomacy* (New York, 1970). The first chapter of Matthew S. Anderson, *The Rise of Modern Diplomacy, 1450–1919* (London, 1993), gives an overview of the innovations in diplomatic practice during the 15th and 16th centuries.
5. Harold George Nicolson, *Diplomacy*, 3rd edn. (London, 1963), 12.
6. François Louis Ganshof, *Le Moyen Âge* (Paris, 1953), is still useful as a general introduction (see esp. ch. xii on the late Middle Ages). Mattingly: *Renaissance Diplomacy*. Donald E. Queller: 'Thirteenth-century diplomatic envoys: *Nuncii* and *procuratores*', *Speculum* 35 (1960), 196–213, and esp. *The Office of Ambassador in the Middle Ages* (Princeton, 1967). Queller, 'Western European diplomacy', in *Dictionary of the Middle Ages*, ed. Joseph R. Strayer (New York, 1982–9), iv. 201–14, is the best short introduction to the subject.
7. See e.g. Christian de Borchgrave, *Diplomaten en diplomatie onder Hertog Jan Zonder Vrees: Impact op de vlaamse politieke situatie* (Courtrai, 1992), Arnd Reitemeier, *Außenpolitik im Spätmittelalter: Die diplomatischen Beziehungen zwischen dem Reich und England, 1377–1422* (Paderborn, Munich, Vienna and Zurich, 1999), and Petra Ehm, *Burgund und das Reich: Spätmittelalterliche Außenpolitik am Beispiel der Regierung Karls des Kühnen (1465–1477)* (Munich, 2002).
8. In both cases the conference papers have been published: Dieter Berg, Martin Kintzinger and Pierre Monnet (eds.), *Auswärtige Politik und internationale Beziehungen im Mittelalter (13. bis 16. Jahrhundert)* (Bochum, 2002) and Rainer Christoph Schwinges and Klaus Wriedt (eds.), *Gesandtschafts- und Botenwesen im spätmittelalterlichen Europa* (Sigmaringen, 2003).

9. Bruno Galland, *Les Papes d'Avignon et la maison de Savoie (1309–1409)* (Rome, 1998); Jan-Erik Beuttel, *Der Generalprokurator des Deutschen Ordens an der Römischen Kurie: Amt, personelles Umfeld und Finanzierung* (Marburg, 1999).

10. J. Robert Wright, *The Church and the English Crown, 1305–1334: A Study Based on the Register of Archbishop Walter Reynolds* (Toronto, 1980).

11. J. Roger L. Highfield, 'The relations between the church and the English crown 1349–1378—from the death of Archbishop Stratford to the outbreak of the Great Schism', D.Phil. thesis (Oxford, 1951). On English envoys and messengers to the curia see ibid. 29–32.

12. Mary C. L. Salt, 'English embassies to France in the reign of Edward I; Their personnel, powers, equipment and objects', *BIHR* 6 (1929), 29–31; 'List of English embassies to France', *EHR* 44 (1929), 263–78; Betty Behrens, 'The office of English resident ambassador', *TRHS*, 4th ser., 16 (1933), 161–92; 'Origins of the office of English resident ambassador in Rome', *EHR* 49 (1934), 640–56; Alfred Larson, 'The payment of fourteenth-century English envoys', *EHR* 54 (1939), 403–14.

13. Mary C. Hill, 'A study, mainly from royal wardrobe accounts, of the nature and organisation of the king's messenger service from the reign of John to that of Edward III inclusive', *BIHR* 18 (1940), 33–5; 'Jack Faukes, king's messenger, and his journey to Avignon in 1343', *EHR* 57 (1942), 19–30; 'King's messengers and administrative developments in the 13th and 14th centuries', *EHR* 61 (1946), 315–28; *The King's Messengers, 1199–1377: A Contribution to the History, of the Royal Household* (London, 1961); *The King's Messengers, 1199–1377: A List of All Known Messengers, Mounted and Unmounted, Who Served John, Henry III, and the First Three Edwards* (Stroud, 1994); 'The King's messengers in England, 1199–1337', *Medieval Prosopography* 17/2 (1996), 63–96.

14. Henry Stephen Lucas, 'The machinery of diplomatic intercourse', in James F. Willard and William A. Morris (eds.), *The English Government at Work, 1327–1336*, i: *Central and Prerogative Administration* (Cambridge, MA, 1940), 300–31.

15. George P. Cuttino, *English Diplomatic Administration, 1259–1339*. All references in this study are to the second, revised and enlarged edn. (Oxford, 1971).

16. *English Medieval Diplomatic Practice, Part II, Plates*, ed. Pierre Chaplais (London, 1975), *Part I, Documents and Interpretation* (London, 1982). For a list of Chaplais's publications, see Michael Jones and Malcolm G. A. Vale (eds.), *England and her Neighbours, 1066–1453: Essays in Honour of Pierre Chaplais* (London, 1989), pp. xxi–xxiv.

17. Pierre Chaplais, *English Diplomatic Practice in the Middle Ages* (London and New York, 2003).

18. See esp. Katherine Walsh, *A Fourteenth-Century Scholar and Primate: Richard FitzRalph in Oxford, Avignon and Armagh* (Oxford, 1981), 85–221, 406–51.

19. Michael T. Clanchy, *From Memory to Written Record: England 1066–1307*, 2nd edn. (Oxford, 1993), 20.

20. Sophia Menache, *Clement V* (Cambridge, 1998), 3; see also 23–6.

21. Thirty bulls by Clement VI, 27 by Innocent VI (*Original Papal Letters in England (1305–1415)*, ed. Patrick N. R. Zutshi (Vatican City, 1990), 89–142). Three letters are preserved in BL MS Cotton Cleo. E II, fos. 60–1, 66–7 and 100–1.

22. Walther Holtzmann, *Papsturkunden in England* (Göttingen, 1930–52), i. 10–13; Patrick N. R. Zutshi, 'The letters of the Avignon popes (1305–1378): A source

for the study of Anglo-papal relations and of English ecclesiastical history', in Jones and Vale (eds.), *England and her Neighbours*, 259–75 (260); *Original Papal Letters*, pp. xi–xiv. On the custody of papal letters in late medieval and early modern England, see ibid., pp. xxxiii–xxxvii.

23. This estimate has been made on the basis of a comparison between the number of *litterae apostolicae* to Edward III in ASV RV 137–213 (Clement VI) and RV 219–44N (Innocent VI) (173 letters) and the number of the surviving letters listed by Zutshi (*Original Papal Letters*, 89–142) (57 letters). I have not counted the letters to Edward III in the Avignon series. However, their number must be greater; usually all such outgoing letters were registered there. The fact that there is not a corresponding entry in the RV series for each letter in SC 7 (see *Original Papal Letters*, p. xxxiii and nos. 177, 179–80, 182, 187, 220, 237, 245, 248, 250–1, 253–4, 260, 262, 266, 269–70, 272–8) suggests that not all drafts were later copied into the RV volumes.

24. *Foedera, Conventiones, Litterae et cuiuscunque generis Acta Publica inter Reges Angliae et alios quosvis Imperatores, Reges, Pontifices, Principes, vel Communitates*, ed. Thomas Rymer, 5th edn. ['Record Commission edn.'], ed. Adam Clarke, Frederick Holbrooke and John Caley (London, 1816–69).

25. See, in detail, Leonard E. Boyle, *A Survey of the Vatican Archives and of its Medieval Holdings* (Toronto, 1972), 114–24.

26. There exists, however, a register of Innocent VI's *litterae secretae* from his ninth pontifical year (1361) in the Archivio di Stato, Rome. It was edited in the early 18th c. by Edmond Martène: *Thesaurus novus anecdotorum*, ii: *Urbani Papae IV epistolae* [...] *aliaque plura de schismate pontificum Avenionensium monumenta* (Paris, 1717), 843–1072.

27. Friedrich Bock, 'Einführung in das Registerwesen des Avignonesischen Papsttums (I. Textteil, II. Tafelbeilagen)', *QF* 31 (1941), 1–107 (23).

28. BEFAR, 3rd series: Registres et lettres des papes du XIVᵉ siècle.

29. The last volume of the series appeared in 1976 and covers only the first four years of Innocent VI's pontificate (i.e. c.1353–6). The work on the registers is being continued at the Centre de recherche sur la papauté d'Avignon. See Bruno Galland, 'La publication des registres de lettres pontificales par l'École française de Rome', *BEC* 154 (1996), 625–34.

30. For a detailed discussion of such accounts, see Karsten Plöger, 'Englische Gesandtschaftsrechnungen des Spätmittelalters', in Harm von Seggern and Gerhard Fouquet (eds.), *Adel und Zahl: Studien zum adligen Rechnen und Haushalten in Spätmittelalter und früher Neuzeit* (Ubstadt-Weiher, 2000), 247–54.

31. *The Red Book of the Exchequer*, ed. Hubert Hall (London, 1896), iii. 862–5. On the Memoranda Rolls (King's Remembrancer), see James F. Willard, 'The Memoranda Rolls and the remembrancers, 1282–1350', in Andrew G. Little and F. Maurice Powicke (eds.), *Essays in Medieval History Presented to T. F. Tout* (Manchester, 1925), 215–29.

32. Cf. Fritz Trautz, *Die Könige von England und das Reich, 1277–1377: Mit einem Rückblick auf ihr Verhältnis zu den Staufern* (Heidelberg, 1961), 52, and Reitemeier, 33.

33. In 1342 the Wardrobe transferred to the Exchequer what was left of the diplomatic functions that it had possessed since Henry III's reign (Thomas F. Tout, *Chapters in the Administrative History of Medieval England: The Wardrobe, the*

Chamber, and the Small Seals (Manchester, 1920–33), iii. 70–3, 149, 178; Cuttino,
English Diplomatic Administration, 166–7, 172, 177–83; Hill, 'King's messengers
and administrative developments', 323–8). It is important to note, however, that
this development was not irreversible: during Edward III's last French campaign
(28 Oct. 1359–18 May 1360) envoys' expenses were once more handled by the
Wardrobe, the king's mobile war treasury (see E 101/393/11).

34. On the account books of the Apostolic Camera see the superb recent study
by Stefan Weiß: *Rechnungswesen und Buchhaltung des Avignoneser Papsttums
(1316–1378): Eine Quellenkunde* (Hanover, 2003).

35. Leslie J. MacFarlane, 'The Vatican Archives: With special reference to sources for
British medieval history', *Archives* 4 (1959), 29–44, 84–101 (40).

36. The VQ series does not cover *Introitus et Exitus* in its entirety; the editorial
principles applied by Göller, Schäfer, Mohler and Hoberg have rightly been
criticized by Renouard, Boyle and Weiß (Yves Renouard, 'Interêt et importance
des Archives Vaticanes pour l'histoire économique du moyen âge spécialement
du XIVe siècle', in *Miscellanea archivistica A. Mercati* (Vatican City, 1952), 21–41;
Boyle, 169–72; Weiß, *Rechnungswesen*, 4–7).

37. The series was discontinued after the publication of this first volume: *Calendar of
Entries in the Papal Registers Relating to Great Britain and Ireland: Calendar of
Petitions to the Pope, 1342–1419*, i: *1342–62*, ed. William H. Bliss (London, 1896).

38. *Calendar of the Patent Rolls preserved in the Public Record Office, 1232–1509* (London,
1891–1916) and *Calendar of the Close Rolls preserved in the Public Record Office,
1272–1509* (London, 1900–63).

39. *Acta Aragonensia: Quellen zur deutschen, italienischen, französischen, spanischen,
zur Kirchen- und Kulturgeschichte aus der diplomatischen Korrespondenz Jaymes II.
(1291–1327)*, ed. Heinrich Finke (Berlin and Leipzig, 1908–22).

40. Accounts: *Die Rechnungsbücher der hamburgischen Gesandten in Avignon 1338 bis
1355*, ed. Th. Schrader (Hamburg and Leipzig, 1907). Their correspondence and
other papers have been published in the series *Rat und Domkapitel von Hamburg
um die Mitte des 14. Jahrhunderts: Die Korrespondenz zwischen dem Hamburger Rat
und seinen Vertretern an der päpstlichen Kurie in Avignon 1337 bis 1359*, ed. Richard
Salomon (Hamburg, 1968), *Das Prozeß-Schriftgut aus den Streitigkeiten des
Hamburger Rates und einzelner Bürger mit dem Domkapitel 1336 bis 1356*, ed. Jürgen
Reetz (Hamburg, 1975), *Ergänzungen sowie Namen- und Sachweiser zu dem in Teil
1 und 2 edierten Schriftgut der seit 1336 ausgetragenen Streitigkeiten*, ed. Jürgen Reetz
(Hamburg, 1980).

41. See Giles Constable, *Letters and Letter-Collections* (Turnhout, 1976), 21–2, and
Kenneth A. Fowler, 'News from the front: Letters and despatches of the fourteenth century', in Philippe Contamine, Charles Giry-Deloison and Maurice H.
Keen (eds.), *Guerre et société en France, en Angleterre et en Bourgogne, XIVe–XVe
siècle* (Lille, 1991), 63–92 (69). A number of newsletters from the Roman court
from the early Avignonese period survive in SC 1 (1/34/176, 50/29, 50/30,
50/37, 55/47, 56/14, 58/16).

42. Letters: BL MS Cotton Cleo. E II, fos. 47^r–57^r (Jean Froissart, *Œuvres complètes:
Chroniques*, ed. Joseph Marie Bruno Constantin Baron Kervyn de Lettenhove
(Brussels, 1867–77), xviii, doc. LVII). John Offord's first letter (14 Sept. 1344) has
also been edited by Chaplais (*EMDP* doc. 155). It seems that not all the reports
from this delegation have survived—there are no letters from the period 9 Sept.

to *c* 8 Oct. 1344. Journal: MS Cotton Cleo. E II, fos. 36^r–40^v (Froissart, *Œuvres*, xviii, doc. LVIII).

43. Antonia Gransden, *Historical Writing in England*, ii: *c.1300–c.1415* (London, 1982), 58–117, gives an excellent survey of the reign of Edward III. See also John Taylor, *English Historical Literature in the Fourteenth Century* (Oxford, 1987).

44. Malcolm G. A. Vale, *War and Chivalry* (London, 1981), 14–32.

45. Taylor, *English Historical Literature*, 41.

46. The fullest account is that by le Baker: *Chronicon*, ed. Edward M. Thompson (Oxford, 1889), 123–5. His chronicle was finished no later than four to six years after the conference (Herbert Bruce, *Notes on the Chronicle Ascribed to Geoffrey le Baker of Swinbrook* (Cardiff, 1918), 7). See also Ranulph Higden, *Polychronicon*, ed. Churchill Babington and J. R. Lumby (London, 1865–86), viii. 407; Robert of Avesbury, *De gestis mirabilibus regis Edwardi Tertii*, ed. Edward M. Thompson (London, 1889), 421; John of Reading, *Chronica*, in *Chronica Johannis de Reading et Anonymi Cantuarensis, 1346–67*, ed. James Tait (Manchester, 1914), 99–186 (118); *Chronicon Anonymi Cantuariensis*, ibid. 187–227 (195); *Anonimalle Chronicle, 1333–1381*, ed. Vivian H. Galbraith (Manchester, London and New York, 1927), 31–2 (with a confused chronology); Henry Knighton, *Chronicle, 1337–1396*, ed. and trans. Geoffrey H. Martin (Oxford, 1995), 126–9; Thomas Walsingham, *Historia Anglicana*, ed. Henry T. Riley (London, 1863–4), i. 278; *Chronicon Angliae, ab anno Domini 1328 usque ad annum 1388, auctore monacho quodam Sancti Albani*, ed. Edward M. Thompson (London, 1874), 31; John Capgrave, *The Chronicle of England*, ed. Francis C. Hingeston-Randolph (London, 1858), 215–16. For Caxton's account, see Higden, viii. 347–8.

47. Jean Froissart, *Chroniques*, ed. Siméon Luce et al. (Paris, 1869–1975), iv. 131–2; *Chronique des règnes de Jean II et Charles V*, ed. Roland Delachenal (Paris, 1910–20), i. 47–9.

48. See the biographical notes in *BRUO* 1329–30.

49. Gransden, ii. 65, 69. On the association of St Paul's with chronicle writing, see Taylor, *English Historical Literature*, 26, 28. On 14th-c. English newsletters, see ibid. 229–30.

50. On 20 Nov. 1337 Murimuth, John Offord and others were given a mandate to examine the nature of the Anglo-French dispute and to state their opinion on how best to defend Edward III's rights. Andrew Offord was among those ordered to inform them of the problems arising from the processes against Edward III in the *Parlement* and elsewhere in France (SC 1/11, printed in Richard Lescot, *Chronique (1328–1344), suivie de la continuation de cette chronique (1344–1364)*, ed. Jean Lemoine (Paris, 1896), app., doc. v.

51. Gransden, 64.

52. England: Alfred L. Brown, *The Early History of the Clerkship of the Council* (Glasgow, 1969), 1, 3, 52, and id., *The Governance of Late Medieval England, 1272–1461* (London, 1989), 47. Vatican: Heinrich Otto, 'Das Avignoneser Inventar des päpstlichen Archivs vom Jahre 1366 und die Privilegiensammlungen des Fieschi und des Platina: Ein Beitrag zur Geschichte des Vatikanischen Archivs im 14. und 15. Jahrhundert', *QF* 12 (1909), 132–88 (133–4); R. Ritzler, 'Die Verschleppung der päpstlichen Archive nach Paris unter Napoleon I. und deren Rückführung nach Rom in den Jahren 1815–1817', *Römische Historische Mitteilungen* 6–7 (1962–3, 1963–4), 144–90; Boyle, 8–11.

53. Peter Moraw, 'Über Rahmenbedingungen und Wandlungen auswärtiger Politik vorwiegend im deutschen Spätmittelalter', in Berg, Kintzinger and Monnet, 31–45 (39).

54. See in detail W. R. Jones, 'Relations of the two jurisdictions: Conflict and cooperation in England during the thirteenth and fourteenth centuries', in *Studies in Medieval and Renaissance History* 7 (1970), 77–210, and Robert N. Swanson, *Church and Society in Late Medieval England* (Oxford, 1989), 140–2, 149–53, 158–82.

55. Swanson, 149, 153–8.

56. *Nova Alamanniae: Urkunden, Briefe und andere Quellen besonders zur deutschen Geschichte des 14. Jahrhunderts*, ed. Edmund E. Stengel (Berlin and Hanover, 1921–76), doc. 408.

57. Cf. Lucas, 'Machinery', 305–6; Pierre Chaplais, 'English diplomatic documents to the end of Edward III's reign', in Donald A. Bullough and Robin L. Storey (eds.), *The Study of Medieval Records: Essays in Honour of Kathleen Major* (Oxford, 1971), 23–56 (46–7) and id., *English Diplomatic Practice*, 102–5.

58. Klaus Schreiner, 'Fußkuß', in *LexMA* iv. 1063–6 (1065). See also Section 6.3 below.

59. See the overview in Dieter Berg, *England und der Kontinent: Studien zur auswärtigen Politik der anglonormannischen Könige im 11. und 12. Jahrhundert* (Bochum, 1987), section 3.5.

60. It is worth remembering, however, that Louis IV may have considered a military operation against Avignon. See Jürgen Miethke, 'Der Kampf Ludwigs des Bayern mit Papst und avignonesischer Kurie in seiner Bedeutung für die deutsche Geschichte', in Hermann Nehlsen and Hans-Georg Hermann (eds.), *Kaiser Ludwig der Bayer: Konflikte, Weichenstellungen und Wahrnehmung seiner Herrschaft* (Paderborn, Munich, Vienna and Zurich, 2002), 39–74 (59 and n. 56).

61. See Stanislaw Edward Nahlik, 'Völkerrechtliche Aspekte der frühen Diplomatie', in Gerhard Pferschy (ed.), *Siegmund von Herberstein—Kaiserlicher Gesandter und Begründer der Rußlandkunde und die europäische Diplomatie* (Graz, 1989), 43–62 (43 and n. 1); James Der Derian, 'Diplomacy', in *Oxford Companion to Politics of the World*, 2nd edn., ed. Joel Krieger et al. (New York, 2001), 217, 223–3 (222).

62. See Keith A. Hamilton and Richard Langhorne, *The Practice of Diplomacy: Its Evolution, Theory and Administration* (London and New York, 1995), 1.

63. Berg. *England und der Kontinent*, 1–5; id., *Deutschland und seine Nachbarn, 1200–1500* (Oldenbourg, 1997), 1–4, 47–8.

64. See e.g. James Der Derian, *On Diplomacy: A Genealogy of Western Estrangement* (Oxford, 1987), and P. Sharp, 'For diplomacy: Representation and the study of international relations', *International Studies Review* 1 (1999), 33–57.

65. Sharp, 51.

66. Costas M. Constantinou, *On the Way to Diplomacy* (Minneapolis, 1996), 113.

CHAPTER 2

❖

Determining Factors and Points of Contact, *c*.1342–1362

Between the first Avignon pope and Edward I a state of almost perfect understanding had existed. Clement V (Bertrand de Got) had come from a well-known Gascon family with excellent connections with the English court. As archbishop of Bordeaux (1299–1305) he had been the king's vassal and the senior prelate in his continental domain. Earlier in his career, he had even served as a royal envoy to France. This friendly and close relationship had remained intact for some more years after Edward II's succession to the throne.[1] Relations with John XXII had lacked this personal aspect, and, at the same time, some political misunderstandings had arisen. But, if relations with Avignon had not been as cordial as before, they had remained, on the whole, friendly. This had also applied to the early stages of the reign of Edward III: before 1342, neither Edward's preparations for the war against France, nor his alliance with Louis of Bavaria, nor his assumption of the title of king of France had caused a rupture between Westminster and Avignon. What little conflict had arisen had been settled quickly and quietly by compromise.[2]

During the formative period of the Avignon papacy non-heretical (that is, non-theologically motivated) antipapalism had never assumed any major proportions in England. Those who participated in the political discourse during those years apparently did not take offence at the fact that the papacy was residing at Avignon, a stone's throw away from French territory. Only twice, in the Parliaments of 1307 and 1309, had the barons and commons launched attacks on the system of provisions. During the reign of Edward II there had been just a few, isolated instances of popular criticism. The same had been true of the early years of the reign of Edward III: antipapalism had never really been a sustained phenomenon.[3]

2.1. The Election of Clement VI (1342)

The news of the death of Benedict XII on 25 April 1342 reached Westminster within a week. In a letter dated 3 May Edward urged the Sacred College not to lose any time over the election of a successor.[4] While the king's letter was still on its way, Annibaldo Caetani da Ceccano, cardinal bishop of Tusculum, and Raymond des Farges, cardinal deacon of S Maria Nova, dispatched two messengers to England to inform Edward that the election had taken place on the day of their writing, and that the new pope was due to be crowned on the following Whit Sunday.[5]

Both Clement VI (Pierre Roger) and Innocent VI (Étienne Aubert) were natives of Limousin.[6] They received their academic education in France.[7] Charles IV and Philip VI of France lent crucial support to both of them in the earlier stages of their careers. Pierre Roger, abbot of Fécamp in the archdiocese of Rouen since June 1326, rose quickly in the French ecclesiastical hierarchy after the accession of the first Valois, becoming bishop of Arras in 1328, archbishop of Sens in 1329 and finally archbishop of Rouen (the richest see in the kingdom) in 1330.[8] Around the same time he was a member of the *Chambre des Enquêtes* and president of the *Chambre des Comptes*.[9] He soon became 'a leading figure in every major ecclesiastical and royal affair concerning France'[10] and one of the closest and most valued councillors of Philip VI.[11] Similar bonds of friendship joined Roger to John, duke of Normandy, Philip's eldest son and successor. In 1342 John was present at the coronation ceremonies in Avignon, and in 1350, during the first months of his reign, he visited the curia, where he stood godfather to Clement's niece.[12]

Roger had been closely involved in Anglo-French diplomacy from the outset. Shortly after Philip VI's coronation he was sent to England to demand Edward's homage for Guienne, and later in 1328 he travelled onwards to the duchy to supervise the confiscation of its revenues, which Philip had seized. In 1330 he was one of the eight French councillors who negotiated the Convention of Vincennes with Edward III's plenipotentiaries, and four years later he served on another committee deputed to talk with an English delegation at Senlis. When envoys of the two powers met at Arras in the summer of 1338, Pierre Roger represented the French king once more.[13] His diplomatic activities entailed the spreading of Valois propaganda. On 31 July 1335, in an official sermon preached in the royal palace in

Paris, he announced the decision made by Philip VI and his councillors to send a seaborne force to Scotland to support the cause of David II.[14]

Another focus of Roger's activity as diplomat and propagandist was Avignon, where his task was twofold. First, he was expected to promote the Valois cause in the war against England; at the outset of the hostilities he made the protest of France.[15] In January 1337, when Philip planned to divert the crusading tenths collected in his realm into his own war coffers, he charged him with pleading his case at the papal court.[16] At this time Roger had already formed his opinion about the Anglo-French conflict: Edward was a rebellious vassal, and Philip had every right to confiscate what was left of Aquitaine and lead a defensive war. In a sermon preached at Avignon on Ash Wednesday 1338 he assumed the role of Philip's military propagandist, basing his sermon on the Augustinian concept of the just war.[17] His second task was to promote the projected crusade to the Holy Land; he made three visits to Avignon in this connection, during the last of which he persuaded John XXII to confer the leadership of the expedition on the French king.[18] In the later years of the pontificate of Benedict XII Roger, permanently resident in Avignon from 5 May 1339, was one of the chief lobbyists of the French Crown.[19]

Étienne Aubert's activities in the service of Philip VI were even more exclusively centred on the papal court and on ecclesiastical matters than Roger's. As clerk of the great chamber of the *Parlement* (from 1336) he was at the papal court twice in 1337, three times in 1338 and once more in 1341.[20] Bishop of Noyon after 13 January 1338, Aubert was a peer of France and an important member of the king's council.[21] It is likely that Pierre Roger and Étienne Aubert knew each other well from the time when they both belonged to the circle of the king's advisers. Soon after his coronation Roger created his compatriot cardinal priest and Great Penitentiary. Aubert several times served as legate to the French court.[22]

Pierre Roger's election on 7 May 1342 has traditionally been attributed to the cardinals' weariness of the rigid, austere and autocratic government of his predecessor, and their hope that, with him as pope, they would enjoy a more tolerant regime.[23] But this somewhat superficial interpretation does not seem to take into account the fact that, in the situation of 1342, Roger was the French king's favourite candidate. In an attempt to influence the election Philip sent a high-ranking embassy headed by John, duke of Normandy, to Avignon to lobby the cardinals. John arrived too late, but would not have had much lobbying to do had he arrived in time: after a mere five days, the conclave had already elected a new pontiff.[24]

Although nothing is known about the actual negotiations among the cardinals, the circumstances do suggest that their decision was influenced by a double consideration. For a French-dominated college of cardinals at a curia whose financial foundation rested almost exclusively upon French resources, there was no reason to obstruct the accession to the papal throne of Philip's long-standing councillor and diplomat. In a moment of crisis for France it was an opportunity to establish closer ties with Philip's court than had existed under Benedict XII. In this regard, the electors of 1342 were making a conscious pro-Valois decision. Secondly, Roger's election must be seen in the light of a genuine desire for peace on the part of the cardinals at a moment when military escalation seemed imminent.[25] The Anglo-French conflict, halted by the truce of Esplechin on 25 September 1340, seemed likely to break out again soon. Of all the possible candidates, Pierre Roger, the eloquent preacher and skilled diplomat, appeared to be the only one qualified to bring about reconciliation.

On 21 May 1342 Clement sent coronation letters to the kings of Latin Christendom. The text is the same in all eleven letters, except for a long additional passage in the one addressed to Philip VI: Clement assured him that he intended not only to continue the special relations between them that dated back to the earlier years of his career, but indeed to intensify them.[26]

2.2. The College of Cardinals

In the early fourteenth century changes were made in the internal structure of the college of cardinals that had far-reaching implications for the balance of power in the curia. Clement V's promotions of 1310 and 1312 created a marked predominance of Frenchmen in the college, and this was to remain its distinctive feature to the time of Gregory XI (1370–8).[27]

Frenchmen (France in this context denoting all regions of the Valois kingdom) held a clear majority in the Sacred College through-out the pontificates of Clement V, John XXII and Benedict XII. They comprised 79 per cent at the end of both 1340 and 1341. Under Clement VI this strategy of recruitment was continued: of the twenty-five cardinals promoted between 1342 and 1352, twenty-one were French. His first promotion caused their percentage to grow to 81.5, and by the end of 1343 it had risen further to 88 per cent. The second promotion (27 February 1344) brought it back to 81,5 per cent, and it did not exceed 84 per cent in the pre-plague years. During the last two years of Clement VI and the first year of his successor the percentage of Frenchmen fluctuated between 88 and 92.5. It remained stable at between 80 and 83 per cent for most of Innocent's pontificate after his first promotion (15 February 1353).

The deaths of three non-French cardinals (Pedro Gomez da Barroso, Gozo Battaglia di Rimini and Giovanni Colonna) in 1348 drastically reduced what little counter-balance there was.[28] Between the death of the Castilian Pedro Gomez on 14 July 1348 and Clement's fourth promotion twenty-nine months later, only one member of consistory, Annibaldo Caetani da Ceccano from central Italy, formerly archbishop of Naples, was not a subject of the French king.

Among the Frenchmen, natives of the Langue d'oc held an overwhelming majority long before Pierre Roger succeeded to the papal see.[29] Clement VI promoted only two Frenchmen from the Langue d'oïl, and only towards the end of his pontificate (Guy de Boulogne and Gil Rigaud in 1350). Nineteen out of a total of twenty-five cardinals created by him came from Occitan France. Innocent VI, too, promoted only two northerners (Pierre de la Forêt in 1356 and Androin de la Roche in 1361) as opposed to eleven men from the *Midi*.

Before 1342 there had only been a few, isolated representatives of Limousin, compatriots of Roger's and Aubert's, in the college of cardinals.[30] The following twenty years witnessed what might most aptly be described as the development of a 'Limousin oligarchy'. Eleven of the nineteen southerners promoted by Clement VI came from the wider Limoges region; under his successor the number was five out of eleven. As a result, *Limousins* held ten out of twenty-five and ten out of twenty votes in the conclaves of 1352 and 1362, respectively.

For both popes the elevation to the purple of men of the same geographical origin was not the only means of ensuring the loyalty of the college. While Benedict XII had had the reputation of being a staunch opponent of nepotism, and had refused to promote any of his relatives,[31] Clement VI resumed the policy of John XXII and Clement V, supporting family members on an unprecedented scale by making use of his papal prerogative of choosing new cardinals.

Between 1327 and 1342, not a single Frenchman from the Langue d'oïl had received the red hat. Again, this was to change under Clement VI—further evidence of the political watershed marked by the year 1342. Royal support began to open the way for northerners into the Sacred College.[32] Guy de Boulogne, promoted in 1350, had been born to a noble northern family; his father was Count of Boulogne and Auvergne. His niece Jeanne had married John, heir to the French throne, in February 1349, and de Boulogne had thus become the king's uncle, taking an active part in government.[33] Gil Rigaud, an influential royal councillor from northern France, was elevated to the rank of cardinal at the behest of John II. He received the red hat at the royal court in Paris.[34] An exceptional case that illustrates the pro-Valois politicization of the Sacred College after 1342 was that of Andrea Ghini Malpighi, a Florentine, cardinal priest of S Susanna for eight months until his death on 2 June 1343. Ghini was a civil lawyer who had made his career in the financial service of the last Capetians. In the mid-1320s he had been Charles IV's private secretary, and between 1323 and 1334 he was involved in every significant diplomatic exchange between England and France. In the early years of Philip VI's reign he had been the king's main adviser on relations with England beside Pierre Roger, who in 1342 selected him as one of the first candidates for promotion.[35] Innocent VI admitted two men to the college of cardinals who were serving the Valois king as chancellors at the time of their promotion: Pierre de la Forêt in 1356 and Gilles Aycelin de Montaigu in 1361.[36]

By contrast, all Edward II's and Edward III's attempts to install an English cardinal in Avignon were thwarted. Seven months after the death of Thomas Jorz, cardinal priest of S Sabina (d. 13 December 1310) the Chancery received a

Mandate, as the king thinks that great damage may happen to him and his realm and great setback to his business if there is not an English cardinal made by the pope before this next general council,[37] to make letters to the pope praying his holiness to create some[38] cardinal before the council, also letters praying the cardinal of Pelagrue[39] and other friendly cardinals of the court to aid this business; and to send these letters by some messenger to master Adam de Hereford, the king's proctor in the court of Rome, to deliver them and sue the business with all diligence[40]

However, between Jorz's death in 1310 and the admission of Simon Langham to the Sacred College in 1368, the creation of an English cardinal appeared to be out of the question.[41]

2.3. The Diplomatic Agenda

In what follows I shall be concentrating on the two 'grand themes' of Anglo-papal diplomacy in the mid-fourteenth century, leaving aside such issues as royal petitions for matrimonial dispensations and episcopal appointments. These matters certainly could be of some political consequence, and often required the sending of envoys to appeal to the pope's *gratia* and *iustitia*, but arguably they constituted much less of a leitmotif than did the perennial twin problems of peace and provisions.

2.3.1. Iudex–arbiter–mediator? Papal peace efforts, 1342–1362

The idea that the Supreme Pontiff, as Vicar of Christ, 'the Prince of Peace',[42] had a special responsibility for the preservation of peace among the rulers of the Christian world was an integral part of contemporary conceptions of the nature of his authority.[43] For the post-Augustinian theorists, order and unity in the political world were an expression of the divine plan. Functioning as a link between the celestial and terrestrial spheres, it was the pope's duty to emulate in the latter—the earthly society of Christians—the same state of perfect harmony that existed in the former.

Since the high Middle Ages the popes, as holders of spiritual jurisdiction over all Christian rulers *ratione peccati*, saw themselves as having the authority to adjudicate the political disputes between temporal powers. In the early thirteenth century Innocent III was still eager to maintain the semblance of this competence as being purely spiritual, but his successors later renounced this pretext and aspired to the position of *iudex mundi*, empowered to enforce their decisions in all public and private feuds between temporal authorities.[44] From a more practical point of view, it had become clear by 1342 that a minimal amount of stability within the *res publica Christiana* was a prerequisite for a resumption of the crusading activities in the East. Benedict XII had largely followed a policy of retrenchment, but from 1342 onwards, and especially between 1343 and 1346, plans for a new crusade featured prominently on the pope's agenda. The demographic catastrophe of the Black Death and the continuation of the Anglo-French hostilities later caused these projects to be shelved, but Innocent VI again took the initiative towards the end of his pontificate.[45]

While hierocratic theory seemed to provide a master key for conflict resolution, the possibilities were considerably more limited in the reality of mid-fourteenth-century Europe. Nascent concepts of sovereignty were assuming an increasingly important role, and English and French claims to an unlimited right to govern without interference from pope or emperor virtually precluded acceptance of the former as a judge *in temporalibus*.[46]

Clement VI expressed his desire for a durable peace between England and France in his earliest letters to the French court.[47] Within a fortnight of his coronation he empowered two senior cardinals to negotiate a truce, referring to himself in a letter addressed to them as 'constituted by God as a vicar of peace on Earth'.[48] The first two articles of the four-year truce that the cardinal-legates helped to conclude at Malestroit in Brittany (19 January 1343) stipulated that English and French envoys were to come into the presence of the pope for further negotiations before the Feast of St John the Baptist (24 June 1343), and to conclude a final peace by Christmas.[49]

After deliberations in the Easter Parliament of 1343 (28 April–20 May), plenary powers for the English delegation were issued. Hugh Despenser, Ralph Stafford, William Bateman, William Trussell and Andrew Offord were authorized to talk about Edward's claim to the French throne, his continental possessions, the damages caused by the hostilities, and a final and perpetual peace.[50] However, around the same time it was decided to send only the envoys of lesser rank (Bateman, Trussell, Offord), on account of alleged breaches of the truce.[51] Bateman was back in Avignon by mid-June 1343, at the time when Andrew Offord paid the Roman court a hasty visit (1–20 June 1343), travelling via Paris.[52] Within four weeks of his return to England Offord travelled to Avignon again, this time in the company of Richard Chamberlain. It was a much longer mission, starting in mid-July and extending into early November.[53] It is to be assumed that the two diplomats reached their destination by 1 August, since on that day Clement VI granted a safe conduct for a most distinguished embassy, including five earls (Derby, Arundel, Warwick, Suffolk, Huntingdon), five barons (Hugh Despenser, Ralph Neville, Bartholomew Burghersh the elder, Reginald Cobham, Thomas Bradeston) and five archdeacons (William Bateman, John Offord, Henry Chaddesden, Robert Hereward).[54]

This was the pope's reaction to Edward's letter of 6 July, received through Andrew Offord, in which a safe conduct was requested for a grand embassy.[55] On 7 August Clement added that he had decided, in view of an increasing time pressure, to move the date for the start of the Anglo-French peace talks from 8 to 22 September.[56]

Offord and Chamberlain, having left Avignon on 17 October or shortly after, reached London on 5 November. During September the high-ranking mission announced in Edward's letter of 6 July had failed to appear in Avignon; on 29 August Edward had sent only John Grey, Robert Hereward and John Siglesthorn.[57] Among the documents they had taken to the papal court there had been a fresh appointment of plenipotentiaries. The line-up of 6 July had changed: there were now to be only twelve instead of fourteen envoys. The earls of Arundel and Huntingdon and Henry Chaddesden had been excluded, Hugh Despenser substituted with John Grey, and Andrew Offord, at that point in time still at the papal court, appointed as a new member.[58]

Although some preparations for this diminished but still imposing embassy were made, it soon became evident that it was not going to materialize.[59] When Andrew Offord and Richard Chamberlain left Avignon in mid-October, they took with them papal letters to the king and Henry, earl of Derby. Edward was asked to consent to a prolongation of the truce for a year, since the envoys that he had sent so far had declined to enter into full negotiations unless more precise instructions or higher-ranking emissaries (*majores nuncii*) arrived from England. Clement now expected an English delegation to appear in Avignon by Christmas 1344, and asked the king to signify his decision about further proceedings between 6 December 1343 and 3 July 1344.[60]

Four weeks after Offord's and Chamberlain's return to London, and on the day following the end of a council meeting at Westminster at which Offord had given an account of the proceedings at the curia,[61] Edward consented to the pope's proposal of a prolongation of the negotiations until Christmas 1344. In his letter of 29 November 1343 he announced a larger embassy for the eve of Palm Sunday (that is, for 26 March) 1344, with the earls of Derby, Warwick, Suffolk and Huntingdon, Bartholomew Burghersh, Thomas Bradeston, William Bateman and John Offord, as its principal members.[62] Andrew Offord set out for the French and Roman courts once more on 17 December 1343, his task being to procure safe conducts for the new delegation.[63] By 4 January he had achieved what he had come for: Clement had issued his safe conduct in the desired form and sent a letter to Paris asking Philip VI for his guarantees.[64] In the meantime, John Grey, who had been in Avignon since September, had met the French negotiators in the presence of the pope and a committee of cardinals for a formal prolongation of the truce until the following year (21 December 1343).[65]

Like Edward's grand embassy announced for September 1343, the one due to arrive in Avignon before 26 March 1344 was never sent; neither Hugh Neville nor William de Cusance, who both left London on 12 February, had been mentioned in Edward's letter of 29 November.[66] It was their task to inform the pope that the royal council deemed the current situation in France too dangerous for such an embassy to be dispatched, and the safe conducts issued by Philip's chancery were not considered sufficient protection. This was, as the pope insinuated, but another English attempt to play for time. The letter in which he referred to Neville's and de Cusance's arrival, and to the message brought by them, was written on 24 March 1344, by which date it was obvious that Edward's delegation would not come. What remained for Clement to do was to ask the king not to postpone any further the sending of envoys empowered to negotiate about an end to the breaches of the truce and about a final peace.[67]

When Henry, earl of Derby, finally travelled to Avignon—in late April or May 1344—it was for an unofficial visit.[68] In fact, Edward III probably did not learn of this until the end of June, when he sent a messenger to the papal city with letters for him—hence the complete silence of government sources regarding his journey.[69] On 31 May the leader of the French delegation, John, duke of Normandy, arrived, accompanied by Eudes IV, duke of Burgundy, and Guillaume Flote, Philip VI's chancellor. Other French delegates in June 1344 were the dauphin of Vienne and the counts of Boulogne, Auxerre and Eu. Little is known about the subsequent talks apart from the fact that, as well as meeting the pope for confidential discussions, Henry established contact with the French.[70]

The earl returned to London around 7 July 1344, and four days later a great council was convened. It seems that the decision finally to accept, after more than seventeen months, papal mediation and the briefing of the prospective envoys was made on the basis of his report. According to Adam Murimuth, it was decided to send John Offord, Niccolò Fieschi and Hugh Neville on the next mission.[71] On 3 August Edward requested the pope's safe conducts for these three and informed him that Offord and his colleagues would be ready to cross the Channel by 9 August at the latest and proceed to Avignon post haste.[72]

The complete line-up (William Bateman, John Offord, Thomas Fastolf, Hugh Neville, Niccolò Fieschi and Andrew Offord) was announced in their letter of appointment, which included their plenary powers, issued on the following day.[73] The first to set out were Offord and Neville, who left London on 6 and 8 August, respectively. They arrived in Avignon on 3 September 1344, a full six weeks before the French.[74] This allowed them to discuss the two main problems to be tackled—the infringements on the truce and the final peace—in a number of informal meetings with Clement and a select group of cardinals. Later in the month the arrival of Niccolò Fieschi completed the English delegation.[75] At the beginning of October John Reppes OC, Henry of Grosmont's confessor, brought letters from the earl and the archbishop of Canterbury. His diplomatic bag also contained other, more confidential letters from the earl and the king to Offord alone.[76] From these letters it is clear that, during his visit earlier in the year, Henry had proposed a secret meeting with the pope to discuss the English terms for a settlement.

The French delegation (the bishop of Clermont, Louis of Spain, Louis of Poitiers, count of Valentinois, Simon Boucy and Pierre de Cugnières[77]) did not come to Avignon until 18 October 1344, which led to an unexpected prolongation of Offord's and Neville's stay.[78] The conference began on 22 October, sixteen months behind schedule, and lasted until 29 November 1344.

Historians have become used to describing the role played by Clement VI in these negotiations as that of an arbitrator.[79] However, a close reading of the sources shows that Clement was never supposed to function as anything more than a 'mutual friend' (amicus communis) and mediator (amiable compositour) who, suspending, as it were, his pontifical status for the duration of the negotiations, temporarily became a 'private individual' (privata persona). Adam Murimuth notes that the two delegations were to meet 'non ad finem decisionis et ferendae sententiae sed melioris tractatus et pacis finiendae' (not to come to a final decision and judgment, but for the sake of a better discussion and peace agreement), and a number of governmental sources point out that Clement was to function 'non ut judice, sed ut privata persona et amico communi' (not as judge but as a private citizen and mutual friend), and that an agreement was to be reached 'non in forma nec figura judicii' (neither in the shape nor the form of a verdict).[80] A contemporary Chancery document may refer to the pope as acting 'come [...] persone prive et amiable compositour et arbitratour' (as a private individual, mediator and arbitrator),[81] but the latter two terms were frequently used as synonyms, and in many cases the *arbitrator* or *arbitrour* was actually nothing other than a mediator.[82] John Offord's and Hugh Neville's journal specifies Clement's role very clearly: he was to act as 'privata persona et amicabilis mediator de consensu ipsarum partium electus' (a private person and friendly mediator, elected by virtue of the parties' consent).[83]

The term *arbiter*, by contrast, is absent not only from the text of the agreement as given by Murimuth and Walsingham, but also from all papal letters written between May 1343 and October 1344 and from the reports of the royal delegation. Moreover, if arbitration in the diplomatic sense—a form of conflict settlement in which the parties involved agree to submit their differences to a third party to make a decision—had been intended, there would have to be evidence of the essential supplementary arrangements, such as an arbitral agreement (*compromissum*) that obliged the parties involved to abide by the arbitrator's judgement and sanctions against infringements.[84] It would seem, then, that Clement VI's role in 1344 was not supposed to go beyond that of a mediator or *amicabilis compositor*.[85] This would not have precluded a consideration of the problem from a legal standpoint, and the eventual rendering of a sentence, but before doing so, he and the two parties would have sought conciliation and amicable settlement.

At an early stage the Avignon talks reached a deadlock. From the French perspective, the war was a feudal conflict between lord and vassal, the origins of which lay in Guienne. Any settlement would have to be based on a solution of the problem of the duchy's status. The duke of Normandy and his co-ambassadors were empowered to make some limited territorial concessions on its margins, but only on the understanding that it was to be held as a fief of the French Crown. Any discussion of Edward III's claim to the French throne was out of the question. This, however, was the only point that Offord and his colleagues were empowered to discuss, apart from the breaches of the truce. No concessions were to be made; above all, an acknowledgement of Philip VI as Edward's sovereign in Guienne was out of the question. If the status of Guienne was at all to be talked about, it would have to be considered an allod, free of any feudal subordination to and interference of the French Crown, and in effect severed from the kingdom.[86]

Edward III had in the meantime received his envoys' request for further instructions and decided to send fresh agents, John Thoresby and Ralph Spigournel, in their support.[87] When they set out on 29 October 1344, they took with them plenary powers for themselves and the English delegation already at the curia. A comparison of this letter with those written for the first embassy (Despenser, Stafford, Bateman, Trussell and Andrew Offord) on 20 May 1343 and for the delegation that Thoresby and Spigournel were now supposed to join shows that Edward's position had remained entirely unchanged throughout the previous sixteen months: it contained verbatim repetitions of the earlier powers.[88]

By 12 November John Offord knew that Thoresby and Spigournel were on their way, and twelve days later they arrived.[89] Judging from the statements that Thoresby made during a first meeting with the pope, their diplomatic bag included plenary powers authorizing Offord and his associates to prolong the Anglo-French talks until early March 1345.[90] Nevertheless, at about the same time, the English delegation began to dissolve. On 21 November the pope commissioned Hugh Neville to travel back to England in order to present Edward with a first draft of a peace treaty and receive further instructions. However, he was not allowed to leave the curia until eight days later, since Clement feared that his departure—an implicit admission of the ultimate failure of papal mediation—might have a detrimental effect on the public image of the Holy See.[91] Neville left Avignon shortly after 29 November and joined Edward and his council on 1 January 1345, ten days before Thoresby and Spigournel, who had begun their return journey after 6 December.[92] William Bateman and John Offord stayed behind until late March, when they beat a hasty retreat, arriving in England on 5 April 1345.[93]

Edward's plan to send Henry of Grosmont and Bartholomew Burghersh the elder to Avignon had been known to the pope by 12 November 1344.[94] Preparations for their mission had been made in the first half of December.[95] But soon there appeared the first signs that the two would never set out. On 10 January 1345 Henry was still in England with the royal council, receiving Neville's report of the conference.[96] At the end of the month he was directly addressed by Clement, who expressed his growing concern about the delay of his mission.[97] Another week passed before the pope was informed by the residual members of the English delegation in Avignon, Bateman and Offord, that, after the plan to send Grosmont and Burghersh had been heavily criticized, their departure had been ordered on the seventeenth of that month.[98]

The original purpose of their mission may have been to prevent or at least to delay the final breakdown in the peace negotiations. However, Edward III and his advisers revised their policy in the early months of the new year. In February 1345, soon after the failure of the First Avignon Conference, it was decided to resume military activities on the Continent.[99] It is to be assumed that Neville's return to England and the subsequent deliberations in the king's council on the basis of his report played a crucial part in this.

Michael Northburgh and Nigel Loring, who set out in mid-February 1345 to join Offord and Bateman, were supposed to act as substitutes for Lancaster and Burghersh.[100] It must have been clear to all parties involved that no breakthrough towards a peaceful settlement was to be expected from this mission, and, already at the time of Northburgh's and Loring's first talks with the pope, Bateman, Offord and a number of other Englishmen were preparing to leave Avignon.[101] In mid-June John Reppes, who had been sent to Clement's court two months earlier to obtain a dispensation for the marriage between the prince of Wales and the eldest daughter of the duke of Brabant, received great seal letters that he was expected to present to the pope and four cardinals. In these Edward accused the French king and his officials of violating the truce in Brittany and Gascony, and declared war on Philip.[102]

After the escalation of hostilities in Brittany and Gascony in the summer of 1345 Clement VI reverted to his earlier method of mediation. Two nuncios, Annibaldo Caetani da Ceccano and Étienne Aubert, travelled to northern France in late November.[103] While several attempts to approach Edward III personally about the observance of the Malestroit truce failed, the cardinals succeeded in initiating the Anglo-French talks beneath the walls of Calais that resulted in the ten-month truce of 28 September 1347.[104] During the last five years of Clement VI's and the first three years of Innocent VI's pontificates, all papal efforts to convert this truce into a permanent settlement failed, although it was successively prolonged until June 1355.

Like its predecessor of 1343, the Calais truce was designed to pave the way for bilateral negotiations under papal auspices. Embassies were to be sent to Avignon before 2 February 1348 to talk about a final peace. Around 10 December 1347 Edward sent his first major delegation since the breakdown of the First Avignon Conference to make the necessary arrangements.[105] A report was expected to arrive from them in time for the January Parliament of 1348, but communication with England seems to have been interrupted by the outbreak of the Black Death in southern France: Carlton, Reppes and Neville arrived safely in Avignon, but Edward had still not heard of them by mid-February, which induced him to suspend the dispatch of the larger embassy.[106]

During their first audience Carlton and his colleagues requested that Clement grant permission for one of them to travel back to England to prepare the departure of the earls of Lancaster and Huntingdon, whom he would then accompany on their journey to the curia.[107] After obtaining the pope's consent, Hugh Neville left around 17 February; he arrived in London four weeks later.[108] At the end of March John Carlton, the head of the embassy, who had been vainly anticipating the results of Neville's efforts, left for England himself to speed up the dispatch of Edward's delegation.[109]

By mid-April 1348 Clement had realized that the projected conference would not materialize in the immediate future. Nevertheless, he was determined to secure at least an extension of the truce and wrote to Edward requesting him to send Carlton or another *procurator* with sufficient powers to renew it. At the same time, the king was reminded that his embassy was still expected at the curia.[110] After receiving a letter of procuration for an extension of the truce mentioning himself, John Reppes (who had stayed behind in Avignon after the departure of his two co-envoys) and Thomas Fastolf as the king's plenipotentiaries, John Carlton set out on his return journey to the papal court around 15 May.[111] At an uncertain date in June or July a meeting with French diplomats was held before the pope, and the Calais truce was prolonged for one year.[112]

Besides asking Philip to send his plenipotentiaries to negotiate with Carlton and his colleagues,[113] Clement also informed him that English senior envoys were expected in the papal city before Michaelmas for a confirmation of the arrangement. Clement's safe conducts were in fact requested for William Bateman, Henry of Grosmont, Richard Fitzalan and Bartholomew Burghersh on 28 July 1348, but in the event this embassy was never sent, because of the outbreak of revolts in Flanders, which necessitated an English intervention.[114]

When the truce was prolonged for the fourth time on 13 November 1348, it was agreed that envoys for either king were to meet between Calais and Guines on 22 March 1349.[115] In early March Clement VI sent two nuncios to join the English and French delegations.[116] The negotiations were completed by 2 May 1349: the truce was once more extended, and both sides agreed that their envoys would be sent to Avignon for 1 November to negotiate before Clement VI.[117]

The French decision, taken at the beginning of August 1349, to resume the war in the south-west, and the invasions of Saintonge and Bas-Poitou by Philip VI's armies in the following month, rendered the agreement a dead letter.[118] As in 1343–4, Edward III's envoys to the curia cited French violations of the truce as a reason for rejecting all requests for a larger and higher-ranking embassy to be sent to the Holy See.[119] In late March 1350 the archbishops of Braga and Brindisi prepared for yet another peace mission. They were given the pope's letter of procuration to negotiate with Edward's and Philip's envoys on the frontier between Calais and Guines.[120] After some delay in the sending of the English delegation, the truce was renewed for one year from 1 August 1350. As in the previous year, it was agreed that *granz et sollemnez messaiges* (great and high-ranking emissaries) should meet in the presence of the pope to continue the negotiations before 1 November.[121] On 18 June Edward informed Clement that he would send the bishop of Norwich, the earls of Lancaster and Arundel, and Bartholomew Burghersh.[122] In late July they were given a letter of procuration, although they were not scheduled to leave England until around Michaelmas.[123]

By late November 1350 Clement VI had realized that the proposed English embassy to his court would never come. Raymond Pelegrini, the papal collector in England, and Androin de la Roche, abbot of St Seine and Cluny, had been sent to Westminster and Paris, respectively, in early September to urge the kings not to delay the sending of their envoys any further, but, as Clement had learned from their letters, Edward III would at most consent to a meeting in a place between Boulogne and Calais, so that the truce could be prorogued.[124]

During the last two years of his pontificate Clement VI could do little more than continue to improvise. None of the three parties made any efforts to achieve anything more than a preservation of the status quo. The truce, which was due to expire on 1 August 1351, was twice renewed for short periods.[125]

The peace initiatives of Innocent VI between 1353 and 1355 were crowned with equally little success; again only prolongations of the truce could be negotiated. Cardinal Guy de Boulogne, who had discussed the possibility of a new peace conference with the earl of Lancaster in Paris in November and December 1352, was sent back there in the following January.[126] He succeeded in persuading Edward III and John II to reopen negotiations at Calais, but these led only to an extension of the truce until 1 August 1353. The diplomats undertook to continue their talks at Guines on 20 May,[127] but the meeting never took place. Instead, the French diplomats unilaterally extended the truce on 26 July.[128]

Instead of continuing negotiations in northern France, as agreed, Edward III decided to re-establish direct contacts with the curia in early summer 1353, four years after the last major mission of an English envoy. He sent John Woderove to Avignon to explain his conditions for a permanent peace, especially the full extent of his territorial demands.[129] Having received no news from his confessor by early July, the king charged William Whittlesey, archdeacon of Huntingdon, to travel to the curia to ask Innocent for an answer to these proposals, and to express his unwillingness to continue negotiations before Cardinal de Boulogne, whom he accused of partiality. According to Innocent's version of events, this prompted him to make plans for a new Anglo-French peace conference at his court. As a first step, the truce was to be prolonged for one or two years.[130]

By the terms of the preliminary peace concluded at Guines on 6 April 1354, Edward was granted Aquitaine, Ponthieu, Calais and Guines, Anjou, Touraine and Maine in full sovereignty.[131] The terms of the treaty were to be published by the pope in the autumn in the presence of the envoys of the two realms, who were thereupon to make the solemn and public renunciations of rights and territories for which it provided. Any dispute that might arise over the exact extent of the territories to be ceded to the English was, if necessary, to be settled by the pope. Edward III appears to have been eager to advance the beginning of the talks by several weeks. Almost immediately after the return of his embassy from Guines, preparations were set afoot. Richard de la Bere and John Woderove, who set out for Avignon on 20 and 25 May, respectively, procured safe conducts for the English envoys and their retinues.[132]

As regards the role of Innocent VI in the negotiations, apparently no lessons were drawn from the failure of the First Avignon Conference. According to the plenary powers issued to the leading members of the English delegation (the bishops of Norwich and London, the duke of Lancaster, the earl of Arundel, Bartholomew Burghersh and Guy de Brian), the embassies were to meet before the pope 'tanquam coram persona privata, non tanquam coram judice' (as

before a private individual, not as before a judge).[133] In keeping with
the stipulations of the treaty of Guines, papal arbitration was considered, but only with regard to narrowly defined territorial issues (the
exact boundaries of Aquitaine–Guienne), and only if the negotiators
should be unable to reach an agreement.[134]

The English envoys and their retinues set out at different times
between late August and early November 1354.[135] When Henry of
Grosmont and Richard Fitzalan arrived in the papal city, the French
envoys had still not come, and one of the leading members of their
own embassy, William Bateman, was terminally ill.[136] The actual
negotiations did not begin before mid-January, and it soon turned out
that positions would be just as uncompromising as ten years before:
the French refused to ratify the treaty of Guines (which effectively
would have sanctioned the dismemberment of John II's kingdom) and
to allow Edward III and his heirs to hold Aquitaine in full sovereignty.
By late February 1355 it was clear that the conference had been a
failure: it ended with the English reasserting Edward's claim to the
French Crown and rejecting any arrangement that would leave him
with the obligations of a vassal for his continental territories. The
most that Innocent could induce the parties to accept was an
extension of the truce for three months (1 April–24 June 1355).[137]

By the time the talks reached a stalemate, Edward III's envoys were
already engaged in diplomatic preparations for a recommencement of
hostilities by way of alliances with Charles of Évreux, the young king
of Navarre, and Emperor Charles IV.[138] Immediately after meeting
diplomatic defeat at his own court, in February 1355, Innocent VI
sent two nuncios to England and France to avert the outbreak of war.
They achieved little.[139]

Between the battle of Poitiers (19 September 1356) and the ratification
of the treaty of Brétigny at Calais (24 October 1360) the scene of
diplomacy shifted north to Guienne, England and northern France.[140]
In the aftermath of what had been a series of military disasters for the
Valois monarchy, five Anglo-French treaties were projected or
arranged in all of which the principle of territorial concessions in full
sovereignty in return for Edward III's renunciation of his claim to the
throne was stated or implied.[141] Innocent VI's nuncios were involved
in the negotiations preceding each of these agreements.

Nothing is known of the provisional treaty of Bordeaux, sealed by
the Black Prince and John II on 23 March 1357, but Talleyrand de
Périgord, cardinal bishop of Albano, and Niccolò Capocci, cardinal

priest of S Vitalis, are known to have been involved in the arrangement of the truce called later in the month.[142] At the time of John II's captivity in England, Talleyrand, Capocci and Pierre de la Forêt, cardinal priest of SS XII Apostoli, played a key role in the lengthy discussions of a permanent peace that took place in London and Westminster. Although the three parties reached an agreement before Christmas 1357 (First Treaty of London, finalized 8 May 1358), this was never fully implemented, and the peace process broke down in the May of the following year.[143] The truce of Bordeaux was prolonged for three months on 18 March 1359, and soon afterwards the parties concluded a second treaty, even more favourable to English interests (Second Treaty of London, 24 March 1359).[144]

When negotiations were resumed at Brétigny towards the end of Edward's inconclusive campaign of 1359–60, Innocent VI was represented by two nuncios, Androin de la Roche and Hugh of Geneva.[145] The provisional agreement signed on 8 May was ratified in a modified form at Calais on 24 October 1360.[146] The treaty was to be confirmed by Innocent VI, who was also to function as its supreme guarantor.[147] William Burton, who had taken part in the negotiations, left Calais on 26 November for the Roman court.[148]

If Innocent entertained any hopes of bringing English and French delegates together for a second round of talks at his court, these were thwarted during the last year of his pontificate. By March 1362 it had become clear that Edward III would make none of the renunciations stipulated in the agreement of Brétigny–Calais until all John II's obligations had been fulfilled. He also refused John's offer to submit their differences to a joint Anglo-French commission, the emperor or the pope, and instead made a treaty with his royal hostage (Treaty of Fleur-de-Lys, 21 November 1362).[149]

Between 1342 and 1362 none of the parties involved was able to enforce its interpretation of the precise nature of the war. Whereas Philip VI, John II and their advisers insisted that the conflict was an exclusively feudal one between an overlord and his recalcitrant vassal, in Edward III's view it was a legitimate defence of legitimate dynastic claims. If the combatants lacked the political and military power to achieve a peace that would best suit their interests, Clement VI and Innocent VI lacked the influence to end the feud once and for all and obtained only rather limited recognition of their peace-making powers. On two occasions their court became the focus of peace efforts that within weeks came to grief over the problems of sovereignty ('the problem of the whole war in microcosm'[150]) and of the indivisibility of kingdoms.[151] It was from this politico-legal inflexibility that war and diplomacy derived their dynamism.

2.3.2. Papal provisions

While the political power of the papacy can be said to have declined from the pontificate of Innocent III onwards, subsequent popes tightened their control over the machinery of ecclesiastical administration. The right claimed by the pope, as the universal ordinary, to collate to all vacant ecclesiastical benefices directly and without consultation of the ordinary collator was the most immediate expression of the process of centralization and fiscalization that transformed the relations between the provinces of the Western Church and its centre from c.1200 onwards.

Direct provisions by the pope or by another on apostolic authority had been an established practice for over a century when Clement IV (1265–8) published his decretal *Licet ecclesiarum* in 1265: it explicated, for the first time, the theoretical grounds of direct provisions in full and claimed the pope's exclusive authority to reserve benefices whose holders had died at the papal court to his disposition.[152] Every pope of the Avignonese succession made his own contribution to the development of the theory of provisions and reservations by modifying canon law regulations on that subject, thus continuing the extension of the class of benefices reserved to the Supreme Pontiff.[153] Clement VI's view on these matters did not differ from that of his predecessors: the right to full disposal (*plenaria dispositio*) of all churches, ecclesiastical dignities, benefices and offices by direct provision or reservation was grounded in the nature of his authority as defined by the concept of *plenitudo potestatis*; it was the manifestation of the sovereign power that he, as Vicar of Christ and successor of Peter, derived from God.[154]

Clement VI was not the first Avignon pope to provide to English benefices on a large scale. John XXII had been especially generous in granting provisions to foreigners, but, since most of these had been Italians rather than Frenchmen, and since in general the bilateral relations between England and the papacy had been relatively friendly during his pontificate, little cause for conflict had arisen.[155] Benedict XII's sparing use of provisions had diminished their importance as a matter of English legislation and diplomacy even further. Before 1342 the major bones of contention between king and popes had been of a different kind: it had mainly been the king's refusal to abandon the Crown's rights to appropriate the revenues of vacant bishoprics that had created some tensions.[156]

Again, the summer of 1342 marked a turning point. Anglo-papal relations in the field of ecclesiastical policy were strained from the succession of Pierre Roger onwards. It is possible to distinguish five major phases of this conflict during Clement VI's pontificate, the first lasting from his election in the summer of 1342 until the winter of 1344–5, the second until early 1346, the third through the summer of that year, the fourth from September 1346 until 1350 and the fifth until Clement's death in December 1352.

Immediately after Roger's succession to the Apostolic See, conflict with England broke out over the unprecedented extension of provisions and expectancies. The contrast with his predecessor's policy could hardly have been more striking: whereas Benedict XII had made twenty-three provisions and granted seventy-one expectancies to English benefices during the whole of his pontificate (1334–42), Clement, after his coronation on 19 May 1342, granted thirty-six provisions and no less than 122 expectancies during the remainder of that year.[157]

A mere nine weeks after the election at Avignon, Edward deemed it necessary to urge the auditors of the Rota to respect English customs regarding ecclesiastical jurisdiction and appointments to benefices.[158] His rather mild complaint was soon followed by the strong protest expressed in the celebrated Easter Parliament of 1343, in which the commons, outraged about the increase in the number of papal provisions (especially those to Frenchmen), painted a gloomy picture of the effect of provisions, reservations, annates, tenths and other charges on the realm and the Church of England. Edward asked the lords and commons to ordain a remedy, which came to be known as the Ordinance of Provisors of 1343.[159] The principal aim of the ordinance was to impose a limit on the papal say in English advowson matters. The twin problems it was designed to tackle were the provisions to aliens and papal grants that interfered with regalian rights.[160]

A number of orders were published with a view to enforcing the 1343 Ordinance. On 15 June 1343 the king ordered the arrest of all proctors of Englishmen or foreigners coming to England to claim possession of English benefices on the grounds of papal provisions. On the same day the proctors of the cardinal priest of S Anastasia and of the cardinal priest of S Sabina were arrested.[161] On 8 July the bishops of the realm were directed to certify the names of alien benefice-holders within their dioceses, and to state whether they resided in their benefices.[162] Later in the month Edward wrote to the sheriffs of England, informing them that he had forbidden all delegates, sub-delegates, executors, sub-executors and commissaries upon pain of forfeiture to allow alien provisors to take possession of English bene-fices.[163] Another royal writ followed on 30 July 1343: anyone arriving in England was to be searched for papal bulls or other letters the content of which might be prejudicial to the Crown.[164] Within half a year the king had put the petition of the Easter Parliament into effect.

As far as the treatment of the plenipotentiaries of the two cardinals was concerned, Clement VI had already complained to Edward in a letter dated 12 July. This was followed in early August by a second admonition: Edward should ignore the advice of those who were urging him to introduce new measures violating the liberty of the Church. The sharpness of the tone increased when, later in the month, again complaining about the expulsion of the cardinals' proctors, Clement indirectly accused Edward of rebellion against the Holy See and threatened him with excommunication.[165]

By the time these papal protests were entered, the curia had still not been officially informed about the discussions in the Easter Parliament and about the new ordinances published in the subsequent months. The man finally charged with taking the letters both of 'the princes, dukes, earls, barons, knights, citizens, burgesses and the whole com-munity of the realm' and of Edward himself[166] to Avignon was John Shoreditch.[167] On 16 October Clement wrote to Edward informing him that Andrew Offord, who had been at his court since early August to prepare peace negotiations with the French, would explain to him his views on the latest measures against provisors in England.[168]

Contrary to what such diplomatic clashes might suggest, Clement VI refrained from harsh measures against Edward in late 1343 and early 1344 in order not to put at risk what little willingness there was on the English part to cooperate in the peace process. On 2 January 1344 he thanked Thomas Bradeston, one of the king's advisers, for presenting his letters to Edward and striving to increase his devotion to the Roman Church. To this was added a request to send news from the royal court. At the same time he aimed to exert a restraining influence on the king by turning to his wife and son, the lay and ecclesiastical magnates and his advisers.[169]

The sending of these conciliatory signals, however, does not seem to have met with immediate success. On 20 January 1344 Edward, referring to an alleged series of incidents violating the rights of the *communitas regni*, reminded the English clergy of the ordinances of the previous year and admonished them not to attempt anything in contravention of the royal prerogative.[170] At the end of the month all sheriffs were once more ordered to make proclamations against provisors.[171] In the next Parliament, which met at Westminster in early June 1344, the commons' demands were further extended. They included draconian measures for anyone ignoring the prohibition of provisions: the penalty of perpetual imprisonment or outlawry, it was demanded, was to be imposed on those who had accepted provisions or occupied benefices by means of them since the 1343 Parliament. The same punishments were to be administered to those who sued in the Roman court to annul sentences passed by the king's judges. Moreover, the ordinance of the preceding Parliament was to be made a statute, and sterner measures were to be taken against curial provisions to bishoprics and against benefices in the hands of Frenchmen and other 'enemies of the realm'.[172]

This time, however, the reaction of king and lords was markedly more reserved. In contrast to what had happened in 1343, the Holy See was promptly informed of the latest developments in Parliament in the summer of 1344. Andrew Offord, who had set out for the curia on 13 March in the company of William Bateman, presented Edward's letter brought to Avignon by a messenger in early July.[173] A few days later Clement replied in a long letter, which Offord took back to England on his return journey: it had come to his notice that Parliament had made reservations and provisions dependent on the king's will, and that clerics bearing papal letters had been seized and imprisoned. Clement ended by entreating the king to end the attack on the liberty of the Church.[174] A year earlier, Edward and his councillors might have sent a sharp reply to the curia. But nothing of this kind happened after Offord's return to London; no direct reply to Clement's letter of 11 July is known to exist. In fact, tensions were beginning to lessen noticeably and remained at a comparative low from early 1345 until early 1346.

The mission of William Bateman, John Offord, Thomas Fastolf, Hugh Neville and Niccolò Fieschi from August 1344 to April 1345 deserves closer inspection in this context. Although the issue of provisions was clearly secondary to the two main points on the diplomatic agenda—the violations of the Malestroit truce and the establishment of a final peace—Edward's envoys were also authorized to discuss ecclesiastical business.[175] It was inevitable that the problem of provisions should come to the fore several times during their stay in the curia, especially since six weeks passed before the French delegation arrived. Having reached Avignon on 3 September 1344, the delegation first received Clement's protest against the antipapal measures in England three days later. The pope declared that no other Christian king dared to display such a blatant disregard for Church rights, and that his sort of conduct could not be tolerated any further. As far as Anglo-papal relations were concerned, these were considered the severest trespasses since the time of Thomas Beckett.[176] On the following day, a more constructive discussion in a closer circle took place. After a short meeting between Offord and the pope, Fastolf, Neville and Bateman joined in the late-night talks, which centred on the six essential points in dispute.[177]

As for Clement's replies of 7 September, two points are of special interest. Firstly, by referring to 'l'Eglise de Rome, laquele fuist et est fundee et establie cheveteyne et soverreyne sur toutes autres eglises par Dieu meismes et non pas par autre' (the Church of Rome, which was founded as, and still is, the head of all other churches through the power of God and none other), Clement restated the doctrine of papal sovereignty.[178] On the other hand, he also demonstrated his desire to reach a compromise: while defending the concept of sovereignty, he signalled his willingness to use his rights moderately, to refrain from promoting cardinals and other aliens to benefices with cure of souls, and to consider royal nominees in cases where alien benefices had fallen vacant *in curia* and the king's candidates appeared qualified.[179] The next meeting that Offord reported home about took place two days later. It seems that Clement was prepared for a compromise: he would limit the exercise of papal rights in England if Edward was prepared to end royal encroachments on them.

On 28 October 1344 the last major discussion of the subject took place. Since the previous meetings, the pope's stance had become more extreme and his tone markedly more aggressive. Edward's envoys suggested a compromise: provided that Clement demonstrated good will by refraining from providing cardinals and other aliens to curated benefices, and proceeded with moderation in all other matters, the king would revoke all antipapal measures since Easter 1343. Clement's answer was an outright rejection, consisting of two parts: first, a crude but concise reference to his supremacy and, secondly, a reminder of the feudal bonds that had technically existed between the kings of England and the Holy See since 1213.[180] His vision of a reconciliation was based on an inversion of the two stages of Offord's programme: first Edward would have all novelties revoked, and only then might he himself be prepared to restrict the exercise of his rights as he should see fit, without abandoning them.[181]

John Offord's personal views about the matter became more pronounced as the negotiations dragged on. Writing to the archbishop of Canterbury on 14 September 1344, he gave an account of how, days before their arrival, the English diplomats had been advised to come to Avignon as soon as possible, since rumours were circulating that a process against Edward III and other kings violating Church rights was under way, and that its publication was imminent. Allegedly, this had been the only discussion topic in consistory during the previous three weeks. By 18 October Offord had obtained confirmation of these rumours from the pope himself.[182]

During the following weeks Offord repeatedly warned the king and his advisers to ponder the potentially disastrous consequences of an open confrontation with the papacy. As the specialist on the scene, he clearly understood better than anyone else that a stalemate had been reached: Clement and his cardinals were adamant that the process against Edward would be made public unless all recent antipapal legislation were revoked. On the other hand, the diplomat knew the strategy of his sovereign well enough to know that he would never agree to such a concession without Clement first fulfilling his conditions.[183]

Neither his letter of 11 July nor his heated discussions with the English diplomats achieved the solution that Clement VI was doubtless seeking in the autumn of 1344. On 28 October Offord informed the king that two nuncios were about to travel to England; he and his colleagues had in vain asked for a postponement of their mission.[184] Within a fortnight Offord had received a reply from England: new Crown envoys were already on their way south. For a while Clement seemed willing to reconsider, but on 12 November 1344 antipapal letters reached the curia and were read out in consistory, much to the offence of pope and cardinals. According to Offord, this was what caused Clement to order the departure of his nuncios, notwithstanding that no royal safe conduct for them had been received and that Edward's own envoys, John Thoresby and Ralph Spigournel, were about to reach their destination.[185]

On 21 November 1344, three days before their arrival, Clement officially notified Edward of the appointment of his nuncios.[186] The two then began their journey northwards with a commission to mediate between the two courts and bring about the formal abolition of all recent antipapal legislation in the realm.[187] Rumours were circulating that they were bringing a bull of excommunication against the king with them, and Edward twice, on 3 and 21 November 1344, refused to grant his safe conduct. In early January, after the return from the papal court of Hugh Neville and a fortnight spent with deliberations,[188] it was decided that the nuncios were to meet the king at the beginning of Lent. Shortly afterwards the plan was changed: permission to enter the realm was given on 8 February 1345 and they were received at the archbishop of Canterbury's manor at Teynham. In their oration they demanded a continuation of all papal privileges regarding provisions to English benefices, and a revocation of all royal orders to the contrary.[189]

The king's evasive reply contained the same signals of appeasement as his letter of 23 February 1345, which the nuncios took back with them to the curia: Edward emphasized that it had never been his intention to attempt anything against the liberty of the Church, and, should there have been any such activities on the part of his officials, he would have them revoked without delay. He declared his willingness to work out a compromise acceptable to both sides. Additionally, the king distanced himself from the antipapalism of the commons by pointing out that there was as yet no law in his realm that, if by canon law an English benefice came to the collation of the pope, the king would fill it, nor was there one that the king would collate to benefices in the possession of Frenchmen or other enemies of England. No statutory form had been given to the commons' demands of 1343, and he was prepared to cooperate on the point of provisions. A council would be summoned to discuss these matters, and the pope would receive word through his envoys in due course. Apparently at that time a compromise had been reached, not least due to the repeated appeals by John Offord and the other members of Edward's delegation to the First Avignon Conference. After the end of that year, the ordinance of 1343 ceased to be enforced rigorously, although it remained a potential weapon for the Crown for years to come.[190]

During this brief lull in the conflict Edward III also showed signs of good will towards the Sacred College when he forbade the exaction of the triennal tenth on the possessions of eight cardinals who had property in England.[191] The détente of 1344–5, made possible by Edward's return to his earlier strategy of cooperation, which had been prompted in part by his envoys' advice, proved transient. Already in autumn 1345 Clement had issued two cardinals sent to England and France to negotiate for peace with letters authorizing them, if necessary, to use ecclesiastical censures against Edward III's subjects.[192] By February 1346 the financial situation of the Crown had deteriorated enough for the king to confiscate the fruits of all benefices held by non-resident aliens in his realm to help his administration cope with the burdens of the war.[193] Three months later the proctors of the benefice-holders concerned were ordered to hand over the due sums at the Exchequer. In an attempt to ensure the effectiveness of his ordinances Edward repeated the orders given out in July 1343: all bishops were directed to draw up lists of foreigners beneficed in their dioceses, including the titles, numbers and value of the respective benefices and an explicit statement whether these men were resident or not.[194]

The gentry, citizens and lower clergy of England had never in the meantime revised their position; their hostility to any papal interference with English affairs constituted an element of continuity throughout the Avignon period. In the Parliament that began on 11 September 1346, the commons demanded not only that all alien provisors leave the kingdom and that their benefices be transferred to English clerics, but also that those aliens be put outside the law. Although nothing came of this initiative, they gained the council's assent to a second petition: Edward would write to the pope informing him that the grants made to two cardinals of benefices worth 2,000 marks were null and void, and he would forbid English prelates to receive such provisions in future.[195]

After the victory at Crécy (26 August 1346) there was a short-lived change in English relations with both Paris and Avignon, although the issue of the cardinals' benefices remained unresolved. As the collective sense of threat among the public subsided, so did politically motivated antipapalism.[196] For the king there was no immediate parliamentary pressure to yield to, and no cause to follow a course of confrontation. The commons renewed their criticism of Clement VI's English policy only once, in January 1348, but without any short- or long-term impact. Reviewing what had been done against papal provisions on the part of the king since the Parliaments of 1343 and 1344, they criticized that, since then, cardinals and other aliens had been tolerated accepting benefices in this fashion and suing in the Roman court.[197] When it was demanded that the petitions of 1343 and 1344 be made a statute in perpetuity, Edward's response was hesitant: he asked the commons to put forward their suggestions in writing. In response nothing but a vague request was made to write a letter to Avignon explaining the evils of papal provisions. On 13 August 1349 Clement took the initiative and, sending one of his chaplains to England, exhorted the king in a conciliatory tone to allow the cardinals and other non-resident clerics to enjoy the fruits of their benefices.[198] After reaching a low in 1346–7, the number of papal provisions and expectative graces to English benefices rose again notably in 1348 and the two following years.[199]

It was in the context of this new surge in the number of provisions that a Parliament met on 9 February 1351, initiating a new phase in the 'cold war', which was to last until the death of Clement VI and beyond. The answer to the commons' complaints about the financial consequences of provisions was the Statute of Provisors. It is to be seen as supplementary to the ordinance of 1343 and as a belated royal answer to the commons' petition of June 1344. It provided that any appointments to elective Church offices in England that were made in violation of the law governing such appointments would be void. The right to fill the benefice in question would then revert to the authorities that had possessed the right prior to the papal encroachment, or, in default of that, to the king. The Statute of Provisors was chiefly concerned with the clerical patrons: the benefices at their disposal should be filled by free elections or presentation by the ordinary collator only.[200] In 1352 the English government again took action with regard to papal provisions. In the Parliament of that year the commons had petitioned that a person who obtained at the Roman court a provision to an abbey or a priory should be outlawed, together with his attorneys. The resulting statute said that none could be sued for any offence against the body or the goods of such a person.[201]

By the summer of his last pontifical year Clement VI seemed prepared for a full retaliation against Edward III unless the confiscation of the cardinals' benefices, ordered in 1346, was revoked. On 22 June 1352 he ordered the king to restore their possessions within four months or face excommunication. On 15 October, however, a few days before these censures were to go into effect, he postponed the date of the sentence by another four months.[202] He died long before this time elapsed.

Less than a month after the coronation of Clement's successor Edward III carried out his first strike against papal authority in England. On 20 January 1353 the collector of revenues, Hugh Pelegrini, was prohibited to levy first fruits where a provisor had not taken provision of the benefice in question.[203] The next piece of legislation concerning provisors followed in the September of Innocent VI's first pontifical year. The initiative for the Statute of *Praemunire* of 1353 lay with the royal administration. It was largely procedural in character: it threatened anyone who, by suing at, or appealing to, a foreign court (the Rota was not mentioned explicitly), withdrew from England cases cognizable in the king's courts with the penalties of imprisonment and final confiscation of property.[204] The statute in itself (like that of 1351) did not have any further foreign political implications; it was a legal tool designed to prevent papal encroachments in the legal sphere.[205] The right to try suits concerning advowsons had been the main issue between the Crown itself and the papacy for some time.[206]

No sustained parliamentary criticism is known to have been voiced between *c.*1351 and 1365, and Edward III refrained from antipapal measures during the rest of the period under investigation.[207] A noticeable lull in diplomatic activity occurred after the failure of the Second Avignon Conference: between January 1355 and the embassy of Richard Stafford and William Burton in mid-March 1359[208] there was no major mission to Avignon. For four years contacts with the papacy did not have political priority for Edward III. In 1359–60 he campaigned in France, and, like the victory at Crécy fourteen years earlier, the English success, marked by the conclusion of the treaty of Brétigny (8 May 1360), ultimately led to a more conciliatory policy towards the Holy See. In late October 1360 both Edward III and John II promised to order the restoration of the cardinals' benefices confiscated in their kingdoms. As of mid-February 1361 French priors could re-enter their possessions in England.[209] Although the problems that had come to dominate Anglo-papal relations under Clement VI were never resolved under his successor, neither side assigned them a role as crucial as during the preceding pontificate.

The antipapal acts of the period 1343–53 depended on the king for implementation, which has for long been known to have been imperfect: neither the Statute of 1351 nor those of 1352 and 1353 were ever published.[210] At the same time, by keeping the ordinance of 1343 in reserve as a potential weapon, Edward III retained ultimate control over how far specific papal provisions could take effect within his realm.[211] The commons' manifestations of discontent may have had enough momentum to influence his short-term policy towards the Holy See but never affected his long-term strategy.

If I have digressed into event-oriented history and at some length discussed the contents of diplomacy, it has been in the expectation that this may help us understand the basic conditions and identify the primary aims of English diplomatic communication with the curia between 1342 and 1362.

Much of the complexity of international affairs arises from the fact that policies operate in an interconnected environment in which the actors have diverse and potentially conflicting goals;[212] this applied to the late medieval *res publica Christiana* as much as it does to the world order of the twenty-first century. It was the discrepancy between papal claims to supremacy (as manifested in Clement VI's and Innocent VI's claims to peace-giving power and to the right to provide to benefices) and a political reality characterized by growing particularism that led to an increase in the need for Anglo-curial communication in the 1340s and 1350s.

The changing course of military events to a large extent determined the rhythm of day-to-day diplomacy, but the general temper of relations between Westminster and Avignon seems to have been more affected by the second issue on the diplomatic agenda: papal provisions to English benefices. The expressions of popular resentment against these became markedly more nationalistic and aggressive in tone after 1342: as far as such criticism had been voiced at all before that year, it had mainly been directed against papal fiscalism, but after the election of a clearly francophile pope and with war under way there were, in addition, growing suspicions that Church revenues from England were being diverted into the Valois war chest and that the pope's power of appointing to vacant benefices in England was used to provide an income for anglophobe functionaries and cardinals in distant Avignon. As a whole, antipapalism became more sustained and began to gain influence on high politics, reaching boiling point in 1343–4.

For the diplomatic agents of the Crown, the 'working conditions' at the papal court were worse than ever after 1342: Clement VI and Innocent VI had been protégés of the Capetian and Valois kings in the earlier stages of their careers, and as popes retained their pro-French bias. There was an inherent contradiction in the strategy, followed by the electors in 1342, of establishing closer ties with the Valois monarchy while, at the same time, reviving curial peace efforts. Moreover, almost all the cardinals were members of powerful south-western French families and maintained social and economic connections with their homeland. Their vested interest in the preservation of the status quo in that region made them natural opponents of any plans for a recovery of the lands ruled over by Edward III's predecessors.

Lastly, the English Crown at this time had a very definite defensive policy in papal relations: its central aim consisted in the safeguarding of the king's *ius* and *honor* regarding both provisions in England and the problem of the lost possessions on the Continent. In pursuing this policy, Edward III had to tread a delicate balance between, on the one hand, the extreme demands of his subjects concerning the first and his own ambitions concerning the second of these points, and, on the other, the necessity of maintaining good or at least stable relations with the Holy See.

Notes to Chapter 2

1. See in detail Menache, 7–13, 247–56, 258–78.
2. Guillaume Mollat, *Les Papes d'Avignon (1305–1378)*, 10th edn. (Paris, 1965), 424–31; Thomas Eckert, 'Nichthäretische Papstkritik in England vom Beginn des 14. bis zur zweiten Hälfte des 15. Jahrhunderts', *Annuarium Historiae Conciliorum* 23 (1991), 116–359 (157–71).
3. Eckert, 131–203.
4. R II. ii. 1193.
5. Ibid. 1194.
6. There exist two modern biographies by Antoine Pélissier: *Clement VI le Magnifique, premier pape limousin (1342–1352)* (Brive, 1951) and *Innocent VI. le Réformateur, deuxième pape limousin (1352–1362)* (Tulle, 1961). However, the author's nationalistic and pro-clerical bias much detracts from their value. On Clement, see instead Diana Wood, *Clement VI: The Pontificate and Ideas of an Avignon Pope* (Cambridge, 1989).
7. Roger studied arts, philosophy and theology in Paris, where the degree of a Doctor of Theology was conferred on him in 1323. For a detailed study of his early career, see John E. Wrigley, 'Clement VI before his pontificate: The early life of Pierre Roger (1290/91–1342)', *Catholic Historical Review* 56 (1970), 433–73. Having studied civil and canon law at the university of Toulouse, Aubert received his diploma as *licentiatus* in 1321, and his doctorate *utriusque juris* in 1329 or 1330. He was first judge in the court of civil appeals (June 1321) and then ordinary judge (July 1321) of Toulouse; from 1328 to 1329 he was lieutenant for the seneschal of Toulouse and Albi, and (probably) from 1330 to 1334 judge magistrate of Toulouse

(Raymond Cazelles, *La Société politique et la crise de la royauté sous Philippe de Valois* (Paris, 1958), 344; Pierre Jugie, 'Innocent VI.', in *PE* ii. 794–7 (795)).

8. Wrigley, 'Clement VI before his pontificate', 443–8; Wood, 10.

9. Cazelles, 70, 90–1.

10. Wrigley, 'Clement VI before his pontificate', 451.

11. *VPA* i. 263, 274. For Pierre Roger as councillor, see Cazelles, 91, 137, and Wrigley, 'Clement VI before his pontificate', 448–51.

12. Froissart, *Chroniques*, iv. 102 and doc. xli; Wood, 124.

13. Wrigley, 'Clement VI before his pontificate', 456–7, 461–2, 465–6.

14. Jonathan Sumption, *The Hundred Years War*, i: *Trial by Battle* (London and Boston, 1990), 145.

15. Ibid. 120.

16. Wrigley, 'Clement VI before his pontificate', 463–4.

17. Ibid. 464.

18. Last visit: July 1333. See Guillaume Mollat, 'L'œuvre oratoire de Clément VI', *Archives d'histoire doctrinale et littéraire du moyen âge* 3 (1928), 239–74 (no. 75); Philibert Schmitz, 'Les Sermons et discours de Clément VI, OSB', *Revue bénédictine* 41 (1929), 15–34, no. 67; Wrigley, 'Clement VI before his pontificate', 461.

19. Josef Lenzenweger, 'Clemens VI.', in *LexMA* ii. 2143–4 (2143); Bernard Guillemain, *La Cour pontificale d'Avignon (1309–1376)* (Paris, 1962), 123 and n. 139; Wrigley, 'Clement VI before his pontificate', 471–2.

20. Clerk of the great chamber: Jugie, 'Innocent VI.', 795. Missions to Avignon in 1337: Dau 284 (23 Apr.), 343 (18 July). Missions in 1338: Dau 399 (16 Jan.), 433 (21 Apr.), 544 (23 Dec.). Mission in 1341: Dau 852 (20 June). See Eugène Déprez, *Les Préliminaires de la guerre de cent ans: La papauté, la France et l'Angleterre* (Paris, 1902), 147 and n. 2, 184, 377, and Guillemain, *Cour pontificale*, 124.

21. Pélissier, *Innocent VI*, 36.

22. Ibid. 36–7.

23. Mollat, *Papes d'Avignon*, 90.

24. *GC* ix. 225.

25. See John E. Wrigley, 'The conclave and the electors of 1342', *AHP* 20 (1982), 51–82 (63–4, 81).

26. DGM 4, cf. 9–18.

27. Guillaume Mollat, 'Contribution à l'histoire du Sacre Collège de Clément V à Eugène IV', *Revue d'histoire ecclésiastique* 46 (1951), 22–112, 566–94 (23). On the composition of the Sacred College between 1350 and 1367, see Bernard Guillemain, 'Le Sacre Collège au temps du cardinal Albornoz (1350–1367)', in Evelio Verdera y Tuells (ed.), *El Cardenal Albornoz y el Colegio de España* (Bologna, 1972–3), i. 355–68. All figures mentioned in this chapter have been computed on the basis of Konrad Eubel, *Hierarchia catholica medii aevi* [...] (Münster, 1898–1910), i. 34–51. For the seven promotions under Clement and Innocent, see ibid. 17–19.

28. On the Italian cardinals of the Avignon period, see Bernard Guillemain, 'Les Italiens à Avignon au XIVe siècle', in *Rapporti culturali ed economici fra Italia e Francia nei secoli dal XIV al XVI* (Rome, 1979), 57–72 (61–3).

29. See Guillemain, *Cour pontificale*, 187 n. 33. Here, as in later chapters, I follow the definition of the Langue d'oc or *Midi* as opposed to the Langue d'oïl (northern

France) given by Guillemain, ibid. 185 n. 12 and 189 (see also map 5), and in 'Les Français du Midi à la cour pontificale d'Avignon', *Annales du Midi* 74 (1962), 29–31.

30. Guillemain, *Cour pontificale*, 188 n. 38.
31. Mollat, *Papes d'Avignon*, 76–7.
32. On those among the Avignonese cardinals who had made their careers in the service of the Capetian and Valois kings, see Pierre Jugie, 'Les cardinaux issus de l'administration royale française: Typologie des carrières antérieures à l'accession au cardinalat (1305–1378)', in *Crises et réformes dans l'église de la Réforme Grégorienne à la Préréforme* (Paris, 1991), 157–80.
33. Guillaume Mollat, 'Innocent VI et les tentatives de paix entre la France et l'Angleterre (1353–55)', *RHE* 10 (1909), 729–43 (736 n. 1). On de Boulogne's career, see Guillemain, *Cour pontificale*, 249–51.
34. Wood, 105–6; Cazelles, 179–80.
35. J. Pycke, 'Ghini Malpigli (André)', in *DHGE* xxii. 1174–7; Sumption, *Trial by Battle*, 119.
36. De la Forêt: *VPA* ii. 447 n.1; Guillaume Mollat, 'Forêt (Pierre de la)', in *DHGE* xvii. 1043–6 (1043–4). Aycelin de Montaigu: Jugie, 'Cardinaux', 174–5.
37. i.e. the Council of Vienne (16 Oct. 1311–6 May 1312).
38. i.e. English.
39. Arnaud de Pellegrue, card. dcn. of S Maria in Porticu (1305–32).
40. *Calendar of Chancery Warrants Preserved in the Public Record Office*, i: *1244–1326*, ed. H. C. Maxwell Lyte et al. (London, 1927), 377.
41. Mollat, 'Contribution', 35–6; Wright, 125–8.
42. See Isa. 9: 6.
43. Cf. Françoise Autrand, 'The peacemakers and the state: Pontifical diplomacy and the Anglo-French conflict in the fourteenth century', in Philippe Contamine (ed.), *War and Competition between States* (Oxford, 2000), 249–77 (260–1).
44. Michael J. Wilks, *The Problem of Sovereignty in the Later Middle Ages: The Papal Monarchy with Augustinus Triumphus and the Publicists* (Cambridge, 1963), 45–7, 354–6, 445–6; Walter Ullmann, *Principles of Government and Politics in the Middle Ages*, 4th edn. (London, 1978), 83–5; Wilhelm Georg Grewe, *The Epochs of International Law*, trans. and rev. Michael Byers (Berlin and New York, 2000), 93–4.
45. On Clement's and Innocent's crusading plans, see Norman Housley, *The Avignon Papacy and the Crusades, 1305–1378* (Oxford, 1986), passim, 'France, England, and the "national crusade", 1302–1386', in Gillian Jondorf and D. N. Dumville (eds.), *France and the British Isles in the Middle Ages and Renaissance* (Woodbridge, 1991), 183–98 (190–2), and *The Later Crusades, 1274–1580: From Lyons to Alcazar* (Oxford, 1992), esp. 55–62 and 423–5.
46. Pierre Chaplais, 'Règlement des conflits internationaux franco-anglais au xive siècle (1293–1337)', *Le Moyen âge* 57 (1951), 269–302 (269); Wilks, 426–7. For a concise analysis of the changing conditions for papal peace-making efforts in the period 1198–1377, see Jean Gaudemet, 'Le Rôle de la papauté dans le règlement des conflits entre états aux xiiie et xive siècles', *Recueils de la Société Jean Bodin pour l'histoire comparative des institutions* 15 (1961), 79–106 (esp. 95–106).
47. Eugène Déprez, 'La guerre de cent ans à la mort de Benoît XII: L'intervention des cardinaux avant le conclave et du Pape Clément VI avant son couronnement

(25 avril–19 mai 1342)', *Revue historique* 83 (1903), 58–76, docs. VIII and X; Wood, 30, 127.

48. DGM 94. On their mission (1 July 1342–*a*.24 Mar. 1343), see William E. Lunt, *Studies in Anglo-Papal Relations during the Middle Ages*, ii: *Financial Relations of the Papacy with England, 1327–1534* (Cambridge, MA, 1962), 636–8, and Marc Dykmans, 'Le cardinal Annibal de Ceccano (vers 1282–1350): Étude biographique et testament du 17 juin 1348', *Bulletin de l'Institut historique belge de Rome* 43 (1973), 145–315 (75–6).

49. The text of the agreement is given in *CC* 129–35, *Chronicon de Lanercost, MCCI–MCCCXLVI*, ed. Joseph Stevenson (Edinburgh, 1839), 335–40, Walsingham, i. 250–3, and Walter Hemingburgh, *Chronicon*, ed. Hans C. Hamilton (London, 1848–9), ii. 397–400. Cf. *GC* ix. 231–4.

50. R II. ii. 1224 (20 May 1343).

51. Ibid.

52. App. I, nos. IV and V.

53. Ibid., no. VI. Adam Murimuth lumps this mission together with that of John Grey and Robert Hereward, and also with that of John Shoreditch, all of whom set out later, in early Sept. and early Oct., respectively (ibid., nos. VIII/1–2 and IX).

54. DGM 315, cf. 327–8.

55. R II. ii. 1228.

56. DGM 326–8.

57. App. I, nos. VIII/1–2. It is to be presumed that John Grey is the *Johannes de Guliaco* or *Greliaco* mentioned in DGM 1844 and *CC* 180.

58. R II. ii. 1231–2. A different version, with more restricted powers: C 76/18, m. 12. See also DGM 581, with the pope's view of events.

59. Preparations: Already on 20 July a royal grant had been made to Robert Ufford, 'who is going as the king's envoy to the Roman court' (*CPR* 1343–5, 108). John Offord received money for a payment to be made to his brother Andrew, still in Avignon, on 22 Aug. (E 403/328, m. 32). On the same day an advance payment of wages for a 90-day journey was made to Henry of Grosmont. However, the earl later received two conflicting commissions: on 29 Aug. for a mission to the Roman court, and on the following day for a mission to Castile. There is no doubt that he was in Spain until Oct. 1343 (Kenneth A. Fowler, *The King's Lieutenant: Henry of Grosmont, First Duke of Lancaster, 1310–1361* (London, 1969), 45–6, 260). Thomas Beauchamp, earl of Warwick, was in Westminster on 29 Sept. to witness the sealing of patent letters in the king's presence (*CPR* 1343–5, 118). Robert Ufford, earl of Suffolk, appointed two attorneys on 13 Sept., and received a letter of protection on the same day, but the Issue Rolls record no payment for a mission to the Roman court or elsewhere (*CPR* 1343–5, 114; C 76/18, m. 2).

60. DGM 449, cf. SC 7/45/3.

61. *CC* 147–8.

62. R II. ii. 1239.

63. App. I, no. X. *CC* 152–3, gives 3 Dec. as the date of departure. For the exact dates, see the transcript of Offford's account in E 372/189, m. 44^{v} rather than the original (E 101/312/7, m. 1). Mirot and Déprez (no. C) give a wrong date (1344–5); the account is based on the Exchequer chronology.

64. DGM 581, 593.
65. ASV, Archivum Arcis, Arm. I–XVIII. 5014 (notebook of Guillaume de Bos, *clericus camere pape*), fo. 110; cf. Helmut Schröder, 'Die Protokollbücher der päpstlichen Kammerkleriker 1329–1347', *Archiv für Kulturgeschichte* 27 (1937), 121–286, no. 84.
66. App. I, no. XI.
67. DGM 743.
68. App. I, no. XIII. See Fowler, *King's Lieutenant*, 48–9.
69. The royal court believed him to still be in Spain in May 1344. On 15 May a messenger was sent there with a letter for him, but on his arrival in Bordeaux he learnt that the earl was in Avignon (Fowler, *King's Lieutenant*, 261 n. 37). *Ralph le Messager* was sent to the curia on or around 28 June 1344 (App. I, no. XV).
70. We owe most of the information concerning the informal contacts between Henry of Grosmont and the French representatives in the summer of 1344 to the account book of Guillaume de Sauvoigney, chamberlain of the duke of Burgundy, for the period 26 Nov. 1343 to 10 Nov. 1344. (See Ernest Petit, *Histoire des Ducs de Bourgogne de la race capétienne* (Dijon, 1885–1905), vii. 313–34, 370–3, 396–402, and Henri Dubois, 'Un voyage princier au XIVe siècle (1344)', in *Voyages et voyageurs au moyen âge* (Paris, 1996), 71–92.)
71. *CC* 159. See App. I, nos. XVI/1–3.
72. R III. i. 18.
73. Ibid. 19.
74. App. I, nos. XVI/1–2; Froissart, *Œuvres*, xviii. 202; *EMDP* 294–6.
75. App. I, no. XVI/3.
76. DGM 1155, 1158; cf. Froissart, *Œuvres*, xviii. 215–19, esp. 215–16. The date given by Kervyn de Lettenhove for this letter by John Offord to the abp. of Canterbury (28 Oct. 1344) is almost certainly wrong: John Offord explicitly refers to his meeting with the pope and John Reppes (*a.* or on 8 Oct.) as having taken place on the day of writing. Furthermore, the pope is said to be complaining about the absence of the French, who finally arrived in Avignon on 18 Oct. This suggests that the actual date of John Offord's letter (ibid. 215–19) is *c.*8 Oct. 1344. Hugh Neville praised Reppes's diplomatic skills, and asked for full credence to be given to his report, in his letter to the king of 17 Oct. (ibid. 212). Reppes probably left Avignon on that or on the following day, arriving back in London in early Nov. 1344 (*CC* 160). See App. I, no. XVI/4, on his mission.
77. Froissart, *Œuvres*, xviii. 212, 226.
78. On 29 Oct. 1344 60 li. were paid to Offord's attorney at the Exchequer, John Bedford. If the usual rate of payment of 20s. per day was maintained, this sum covered the wages for another sixty days. On the following day Neville's attorney received a similar payment (40s.), which also covered an additional sixty days (E 403/335, mm. 8, 9).
79. See esp. Eugène Déprez, 'La conférence d'Avignon (1344)', in Andrew G. Little and F. Maurice Powicke (eds.), *Essays in Medieval History Presented to T. F. Tout*, (Manchester, 1925), 301–20 (303–5); Chaplais, 'Règlement des conflits', 288; Bernard Guillemain, 'Les tentatives pontificales de médiation dans le litige franco-anglais de Guyenne au XIVe siècle', *BPH* 1957 (1958), 423–32 (425).

80. *CC* 130; R III. i. 19; C 76/19, m. 2.
81. C 76/19, m. 2 (20 Oct. 1344).
82. 'Arbitrator vero est amicabilis compositor, nec sumitur super relitigiosa ut cognoscat sed ut pacificet et, quod certum est, dividat; nec tenetur iuris ordinem servare' (Guillaume Durand, *Speculum juris*, ed. Alessandro Nievo (Frankfurt, 1594), I. 1. *De arbitrio*, 1). See also Ganshof, *Moyen Âge*, 294.
83. Froissart, *Œuvres*, xviii. 235.
84. See Adolf Berger, *Encyclopedic Dictionary of Roman Law* (Philadelphia, 1953), 366, and William W. Buckland, *A Textbook of Roman Law from Augustus to Justinian*, 3rd, rev. edn., ed. Peter Stein (Cambridge, 1963), 531–2. The differences between mediation and arbitration are stressed by Ganshof, who gives succinct descriptions of each (*Moyen Âge*, 291–3).
85. The phrase cited as evidence for papal arbitration by Wood ('non auctoritate nostra, sed ex potestate attributa nobis a partibus' (Wood, 131–2)) refers to Clement's ideas about his role in the preservation of the truce, and not to that in the projected peace conference (cf. DGM 812).
86. Froissart, *Œuvres*, xviii. 252–3; Craig Taylor, 'Edward III and the Plantagenet claim to the French throne', in James S. Bothwell (ed.), *The Age of Edward III* (Woodbridge, 2001), 155–69 (163).
87. *CC* 159–60; cf. Froissart, *Œuvres*, xviii. 229, 230. Their mission: App. I, no. XVI/5.
88. Cf. R II. ii. 1224, R III. i. 19 and C 76/19, m. 2.
89. Froissart, *Œuvres*, xviii. 229, 254. Arrival: ibid. 232, 254.
90. Ibid. 255.
91. Ibid. 231–2, 253, 256; cf. DGM 1305.
92. DGM 1305, also printed in R III. i. 25; Froissart, *Œuvres*, xviii. 234. For Neville's arrival at Wymondham, see also *CC* 160–1.
93. DGM 1574; R. III. i. 27, 32. Return to England: E 372/189, m. 44[r], cf. *CC* 163.
94. Froissart, *Œuvres*, xviii. 229.
95. The treasurer was instructed on 10 Dec. to pay wages to Lancaster and Burghersh for a mission to Avignon, but the mandate (E 404/5/31) bears the following note on its dorse: 'Nichil fiat per hoc breve quia infrascripti Henricus et Bartholomus hunc viagium infrascriptum non assumpserunt'. On 13 Dec. the papal chancery issued a safe conduct for Lancaster, Burghersh, Bateman, the Offord brothers, Neville and Fieschi. The wording is the same as in the letter of 19 Aug. 1344 (DGM 1305, cf. 1039).
96. *CC* 161.
97. DGM 1446.
98. Ibid. 1475–6.
99. Sumption, *Trial by Battle*, 453.
100. App. I, no. XVII; R III. i. 32; DGM 1574.
101. DGM 1574.
102. Reppes: App. I, no. XVIII. For the original purpose of their journey, see R III. i. 35.
103. See R III. i. 64; DGM 1850–2, 2074, 2076–2135, 2194–6, 2201–2, 2173–4, 2198–9, 2440. On their mission, see Dykmans, 77–82.
104. *CC* 192; cf. Clement's version of events in the memorandum summarizing the papal peace efforts since 1340, addressed to da Ceccano and Aubert

(DGM 2726, cols. 220–1); Sumption, *Trial by Battle*, 473, 513. Truce: Avesbury, 390, 392. The text of the truce (ibid. 396–402) is also printed in Rymer (R III. i. 136–8).

105. App. I, nos. XXVII/1–2. Michael Northburgh received an advance of 20 li. for a journey to the Roman court around 31 Dec. 1347, but later returned the money (E 403/340, m. 23; cf. E 401/393, m. 7).

106. DGM 3703; cf. R III. i. 151–2.

107. DGM 3703.

108. Ibid. 3742; E 372/192, m. 46^r.

109. DGM 3797.

110. Ibid. 3812. The pope's letter was taken to England by Guy de Brian, who had been at the curia to discuss the grant of a tenth (DGM 3811; see App. I, no. XXVIII).

111. Powers to renew the truce: R III. i. 161. Clement VI was informed that Carlton intended to return to his court by the Feast of Corpus Christi (15 June 1348) (DGM 3890). See App. I, no. XXIX. It is unlikely that his journey to Avignon began on 6 May 1348, as stated in his account at the Exchequer (E 372/194, m. 45^v). This would not only lead to a contradiction with E 372/192, m. 46^r, which mentions 14 May as the day of Carlton's return from the previous journey (App. I, no. XXVII/2), but also imply that he set out nine days before receiving his plenary powers. Carlton returned to London on 15 Sept. 1348.

112. R III. i. 166.

113. DGM 3890.

114. R III. i. 165; Fowler, *King's Lieutenant*, 76–7; Jonathan Sumption, *The Hundred Years War*, ii: *Trial by Fire* (London: Faber and Faber, 1999), 13–18.

115. R III. i. 177; Fowler, *King's Lieutenant*, 84–5. The French and English envoys were appointed on 8 and 10 Mar., respectively (R III. i. 182).

116. See DGM 4092–4101 and 4104, esp. 4092 and 4098–4101.

117. R III. i. 184–5.

118. Sumption, *Trial by Fire*, 51–8.

119. See Clement's complaints in his letter to Philip VI of 27 Oct. 1349 (DGM 4289). The English envoys in the summer of 1349 were Michael Northburgh, John Carlton and Robert Askeby (see App. I, nos. XXXV–XXXVII). A papal safe conduct for Bartholomew Burghersh the elder was issued on 20 May 1349, but he never travelled to Avignon (DGM 4169).

120. DGM 4442–6.

121. R III. i. 197–8; GC ix. 325.

122. The original of the king's letter is lost, but is mentioned in the pope's response of 31 Aug. 1350 (DGM 4684).

123. R III. i. 201.

124. DGM 4813. When one of Edward's sergeants, Robert Tanny, who was on his way to Gascony to announce the truce, was murdered at Tours in the summer of 1350, this was used as a demonstration of how the French safe conducts could not be trusted, and as a reason for not sending the proposed delegation to Avignon (DGM 4639–40, 4813, 4819). Raymond Pelegrini had been in Avignon since at least Jan. 1350 (see VQ v. 571). For his mission to Edward, see DGM 4699 and 4701–4. Androin de la Roche was instructed to try and obtain a safe conduct for the English envoys from John II and have it sent to Pelegrini

(DGM 4710). At the beginning of Nov. Robert Herle and Andrew Offord were empowered to confirm the truce (R III. i. 207).

125. On 27 June William Bateman, William Clinton, Bartholomew Burghersh and Robert Herle were empowered to negotiate for its renewal and a final peace. They returned to London *a*.21 July, having concluded only a short truce for a few weeks' duration. Six days later Robert Herle was empowered to extend this arrangement by up to twelve days (R III. i. 225, 227). Edward's envoys left London on 4 Aug. and were back on 1 Sept. (E 101/313/8, m. 2). The truce, which was to last for one year, was published on 11 Sept. 1351 (R III. i. 232). See also Fowler, *King's Lieutenant*, 101–2.

126. GLG 61, 83–4.

127. Text of the agreement (10 Mar. 1353): R III. i. 254–5. See Sumption, *Trial by Fire*, 115–16.

128. Extension of the truce (until 11 Nov. 1353): R III. i. 261–2. See Fowler, *King's Lieutenant*, 112–13.

129. App. I, no. XLV. A summary of Edward's territorial claims as stated in the *cedula* sent to Avignon through Woderove in June 1353 is contained in Grosmont's and Fitzalan's secret *charge* of 31 Oct. 1354 (Friedrich Bock, 'Some new documents illustrating the early years of the Hundred Years War (1353–1356)', *BJRL* 15 (1931), 60–99 (75, 95), and *EMDP* 190, ll. 5–15).

130. GLG 466. On Whittlesey's mission, see App. I, no. XLVI.

131. Bock, 'Some new documents', 71–3, 91–3. See also George P. Cuttino, *English Medieval Diplomacy* (Bloomington, IN, 1985), 89–90, and Sumption, *Trial by Fire*, 132–3. R III. i. 276–7 contains only the text of the one-year truce that formed the first part of the Guines agreement.

132. A safe conduct for Woderove and de la Bere, accompanied by up to thirty riders, was requested earlier in the month from Cardinal de Boulogne, then in Paris (Édouard Perroy, 'Quattre lettres du cardinal Guy de Boulogne (1352–54)', *Revue du Nord* 36 (1954), 159–64 (163)). The king's confessor and the knight obtained the desired safe conduct from Innocent VI on 10 July 1354 (GLG 1019, see also 1026). On Woderove's and de la Bere's journeys, see App. I, nos. XLVIII/1–2, and Mollat, 'Innocent VI et les tentatives de paix', 739.

133. R III. i. 283 (28 Aug. 1354). Again, this phrase has been mistaken to mean that the pope was expected to function as arbitrator between England and France (Mollat, 'Innocent VI et les tentatives de paix', 739; Guillemain, 'Tentatives pontificales', 432 n.1). In his letter to Innocent of 15 Aug. 1356 Edward referred to the peace talks of 1355 as having taken place 'in vestra presencia, ad vestram mediacionem solicitam' (C 70/25, m. 1).

134. R III. i. 284. Cf. the treaty of Guines (Bock, 'Some new documents', 72, 92). See also the sixth article of Lancaster's and Arundel's secret *charge* (ibid. 95–6, and *EMDP* 190, l. 35–191, l. 1).

135. App. I, nos. XLIX/1–6.

136. Our key sources for this mission are in disagreement as to the exact date of Grosmont's and Fitzalan's arrival. While Knighton (126–9) describes their ceremonious entry into the city on Christmas Eve, and the records of the Apostolic Chamber contain a reference to Grosmont dining with the pope on the following day (VQ iii. 558), an intermediate report of two English diplomats, dated 26 Dec., begins as follows: 'Tresredoute seignour. Voliez savoir que voz

messages de Lanc' et Darondell' ne sont pas unqore venuz' (BL Cotton MS Cleopatra E II, fo. 86^r; *EMDP*, doc. 156). It seems that the authors (almost certainly Guy de Brian and Michael Northburgh, and not, as Chaplais believes, Gérard du Puy—the initial 'M' (for 'Michaelis' [Northburgh]) is missing from his edition), who expressed their hope that the duke and the earl would arrive before Christmas ('Nus quidoms qils serront a Avign' devant ceste feste'), accidentally put down a wrong date.

137. Discussions: Le Baker, 123–5. Extension of the truce: *Chronique des règnes*, i. 49. See Sumption, *Trial by Fire*, 142, and, in more detail, Fowler, *King's Lieutenant*, 133–8.

138. Fowler, *King's Lieutenant*, 138–46.

139. GLG 1389–91, 1394, 1397. According to Avesbury (423–4), the nuncios were given short shrift by Edward III himself, who was not prepared to consent to any further prolongations of the Calais truce.

140. On the military and diplomatic course of events during this period, see esp. Roland Delachenal, *Histoire de Charles V* (Paris, 1909–31), ii. chs. II–VI, and John Le Patourel, 'The Treaty of Brétigny, 1360', *TRHS*, 5th ser., 10 (1960), 19–39.

141. Michael Jones, 'Relations with France, 1337–1399', in Jones and Vale (eds.), *England and her Neighbours*, 239–58 (249–50).

142. On Talleyrand's and Capocci's mission (21 June 1356–Apr. 1359), see GLG 2022–85 and in detail Norman P. Zacour, *Talleyrand: The Cardinal of Périgord* (Philadelphia, 1960), 45–6, 51–64. Text of the truce (to last until 9 Apr. 1359): R III. i. 348–51. See Delachenal, ii. 48–9, 52–3.

143. On London I, see Delachenal, ii. 55–6, 59–67, and Le Patourel, 22–7. BL Cotton MS Cal. D. III, fos. 64–8, contains what is probably an early draft of the agreement; it is printed in Delachenal, ii, doc. XXIII. No formal document is known to have survived.

144. London II demanded unprecedented territorial concessions from France: the whole of the old Angevin Empire, together with the counties of Ponthieu, Boulogne and Guines, and the town of Calais, all in full sovereignty and completely detached from the kingdom of France. Text: Froissart, *Œuvres*, xviii, doc. CI. See Delachenal, ii. 80–8, and Le Patourel, 28–30. Article 29 of London II stipulated that envoys were to be sent to the curia for final negotiations (the Estates-General and the Dauphin rejected the agreement outright: *Chronique des règnes*, i. 232–6).

145. On the Brétigny conference and treaty, see esp. Delachenal, ii. 193–231, Le Patourel, 20–1, 31–9, and Cuttino, *English Medieval Diplomacy*, 93–4. The texts of both the truce (7 May) and the treaty (8 May 1360) are printed in Rymer (R III. i. 486 and 487–94). On de la Roche's mission, see *CPL* 629–30.

146. R III. i. 514–18.

147. Ibid. 492–3 (articles 34 and 36).

148. App. I, no. LXXII.

149. R III. ii. 682; Cuttino, *English Medieval Diplomacy*, 94.

150. John J. N. Palmer, 'The war aims of the protagonists and the negotiations for peace', in Kenneth A. Fowler (ed.), *The Hundred Years War* (London, 1971), 51–74 (53).

151. Autrand, 268–74.

152. *CIC* i. 1021, trans. in William E. Lunt, *Papal Revenues in the Middle Ages* (New York, 1965), ii. 220; Geoffrey Barraclough, *Papal Provisions: Aspects of Church History, Constitutional, Legal and Administrative, in the Late Middle Ages* (Oxford, 1935), 8–11.

153. Bernard Guillemain, *La Politique bénéficiale du pape Benoît XII (1334–1342)* (Paris, 1952), 21–33; Wright, 5–14.

154. See Clement VI's letter to Edward III of 11 July 1344 (DGM 957), in which he refers to the pope as *pastor universalis* of all churches and to his *primatum super omnibus mundi ecclesias.*

155. Andrew D. M. Barrell, 'The Ordinance of Provisors of 1343', *Historical Research* 64 (1991), 264–77 (271); Eckert, 160–73.

156. Guillemain, *Politique bénéficiale*, 79–86; Mollat, *Papes d'Avignon*, 424–30.

157. Lunt, *Studies*, ii. 326–7.

158. R II. ii. 1208 (28 July 1342).

159. *RP* ii. 141, 143.

160. Barrell, 265, 277.

161. R II. ii. 1226; *CC* 142–3; cf. the pope's reaction in DGM 275, 375, 393–4.

162. *CCR* 1343–5, 224.

163. R II. ii. 1230.

164. Ibid. 1230, 1237.

165. DGM 275, 326, 375.

166. *CC* 139–40 and 143–6. The date given by Murimuth is 26 Sept. 1343. Johannes Haller (*Papsttum und Kirchenreform: Vier Kapitel zur Geschichte des ausgehenden Mittelalters*, i (Berlin, 1903), 414 n. 4) points out that different sources give different dates for Edward's letter, ranging between 3 and 26 Sept. 1343 (e.g. R II. ii. 1233–4: 10 Sept.). See also Lunt, *Studies*, ii. 330. However, it seems that Edward's letter to the pope 'pur arester la malveiste des provisours' was written much earlier: on 6 July 1343 the king ordered the earls and barons, and the commons of the cities and towns, to put their seals to it (R II. ii. 1228). If this is correct, the king delayed its dispatch for about three months.

167. See App. I, no. IX.

168. DGM 449; SC 7/45/3. On Offord's mission, see App. I, no. VI.

169. Request: DGM 587. Letters to relatives, magnates and advisers: ibid. 318, 393, 450, 519–20.

170. *CC* 153–4.

171. R III. i. 2–3.

172. *RP* ii. 153–4; *CC* 160–2; Haller, i. 416; Guillaume Mollat, 'La collation des bénéfices ecclésiastiques à l'époque des papes d'Avignon (1305–1378)', in id. (ed.), *Jean XXII (1316–1334): Lettres communes* (Paris, 1904–46), i. 9–152 (106); cf. R III. i. 31.

173. App. I, nos. XII/1–2, XIV.

174. DGM 957.

175. Froissart, *Œuvres*, xviii. 203–4 (John Offord's letter to Edward III, 14 (not 13) Sept. 1344). In the same letter, Offord requested 'un powair especial de tretier sur mesmes les attemptats de un les et d'autre' (205).

176. Ibid. 206–7.

177. 'Videlicet de liberis electionibus, de non promovendo alienigenas infra regnum, de beneficiis vacantibus in curia et alibi per mortem capellanorum suorum, de

reservationibus beneficiorum virorum ecclesiasticorum notabiliter in Anglia promotorum, de gratia domini Ademari Roberti cardinalis et de moderatione facienda quoad gratias jam factas indigenis linguae nostrae' (ibid. 208). These six points for discussion were taken from a great seal letter given to Offord before the departure from London (ibid. 215). For the subsequent discussion, see ibid. 209–10.

178. Ibid. 204.

179. Ibid. 210.

180. 'Et ipse [Clement VI] dicit: "Nos sumus superior suus, non ipse noster. Angeli, Archangeli, Troni, Dominationes et Potestates habent caput in coelis, et nos a Deo sumus in terris [...] Nonne advertit rex quod ipse est vassallus et homo ligius Ecclesiae Romanae, et tenetur homagium nobis facere pro regnis Angliae et Hiberniae' (ibid. 217).

181. Ibid.

182. Ibid. 206, 213.

183. Ibid. 218.

184. Ibid. 219–20, 225.

185. Ibid. 227–9. Adam Murimuth gives an account of the council meeting at which the dispatch of the two *nuncii mediocres* was agreed on (*CC* 159–60). On Thoresby's and Spigournel's mission, see App. I, no. XVI/5. They arrived in Avignon on 24 Nov. 1344 and met the pope on the following day (Froissart, *Œuvres*, xviii. 232, 254). Spigournel and Thoresby were not authorized to discuss ecclesiastical business. Their letter of recommendation states that their task was to negotiate 'super reformacione attemptatorum contra treugas et super pace inter nos et Philippum de Valesio' (C 70/20, m. 2). Cf. their own statement concerning their limited competence in Froissart, *Œuvres*, xviii. 255.

186. DGM 1268; Barrell, 275.

187. *CPL* 12–14; Mollat, 'Collation des bénéfices', 107; Lunt, *Studies*, ii. 335.

188. Here again, the chronological details given by Murimuth (*CC* 160) are confirmed by the archival sources. Neville met the king on 1 Jan. and stayed with him and the council until 15 Jan. (E 372/189 m. 44ᵛ). The next mission leaving for Avignon was that of Michael Northburgh and Nigel Loring, who set out on 16 Feb. 1345 (App. I, no. XVII).

189. R III. i. 29; *CC* 161.

190. R III. i. 31; Barrell, 276. Eckert (185) unconvincingly argues that it was the failure of the peace talks that caused Edward III to give up the policy of confrontation pursued in 1343–4.

191. R III. i. 29–30 (20 Feb. 1345), 33 (12 Mar. 1345). It is to be noted that even a staunch anglophobe like Talleyrand, branded by the commons as 'le plus fere Enemye qe soit en la Courte, et plus contrair a les busoignes nostre Seign' le Roi' less than two years before (*RP* ii. 144), enjoyed royal protection in 1345.

192. DGM 2076–8. The entry of the two nuncios into England was prevented by Edward's refusal to grant them safe conducts on the grounds that he himself was about to come to France (*CPL* 195–8; Lunt, *Studies*, ii. 336).

193. R III. i. 68.

194. Ibid. 81–2, 90.

195. *RP* ii. 162.

196. Eckert, 190.

197. *RP* ii. 172–3.

198. DM 2044.

199. Lunt, *Studies*, ii. 338. Between 1 Jan. 1348 and 31 Dec. 1350 at least 449 provisions to English benefices were issued (J. Roger L. Highfield, 'Correspondence', *History*, NS 39 (1954), 331–2 (332)).

200. *The Statutes of the Realm (from Magna Charta to the End of the Reign of Queen Anne), and a Chronological Index* (London, 1810–28), i. 316–18. See Édouard Perroy, *L'Angleterre et le grand schisme de l'occident: Étude sur la politique religieuse de l'Angleterre sous Richard II (1378–1399)* (Paris, 1933), 24–5, and esp. C. Davies, 'The Statute of Provisors of 1351', *History*, NS 38 (1953), 116–33. A summary of the conflicting views concerning the origins of the statute is given by Eckert, 193–5.

201. *Statutes of the Realm*, i. 323–4.

202. DGM 5431 (full text in ASV RA 120, fos. 525^v–526^r and RV 146, fos. 70^r–71^r); Mollat, 'Collation des bénéfices', 109. On 1 May 1353 Innocent VI suspended the censures once more until 15 Aug. of that year (GLG 260).

203. R III. i. 250.

204. *Statutes of the Realm*, i. 329.

205. See W. T. Waugh, 'The Great Statute of Praemunire, 1353', *EHR* 37 (1922), 173–205, and Edgar B. Graves, 'The legal significance of the Statute of Praemunire of 1353', in Charles H. Taylor and John L. La Monte (eds.), *Anniversary Essays in Medieval History Presented to Charles Homer Haskins* (Boston and New York, 1929), 68–80.

206. Anne Deeley, 'Papal provisions and royal rights of patronage in the early fourteenth century', *EHR* 43 (1928), 497–527 (505, 508).

207. Eckert, 195, 202–3.

208. App. I, no. LXVII.

209. R III. i. 545, 620.

210. Mollat, 'Collation des bénéfices', 109; Perroy, *L'Angleterre et le Grand Schisme*, 24–7. The commons' petition in early 1352 to have the Statute of Provisors published and put into execution was in vain (*RP* ii. 241).

211. Lunt, *Studies*, ii. 346; Barrell, 276.

212. Robert Jervis, 'Systems theory and diplomatic history', in Lauren (ed.), *Diplomacy: New Approaches*, 212–44 (239).

CHAPTER 3

Diplomatic Personnel

3.1. Official Diplomatic Agents

The list of crowned heads who travelled to the papal city is long,[1] and among the many illustrious guests at John XXII's table were two close relatives of English monarchs: Edmund of Woodstock, half-brother of Edward II, and John of Eltham, brother of Edward III.[2] But neither of these two kings ever met any of the seven Avignon popes in person; the last meeting of this kind had been that between Edward I and Gregory X at Orvieto in February 1273, and there were no further meetings until April 1903, when Edward VII visited the Vatican.[3] Summit diplomacy, as it would be called today, played no role in Anglo-papal diplomacy in the period with which we are here concerned. A 'multiple career line analysis'[4] of the group of men who went in the king's stead therefore forms an essential part of our investigation.

3.1.1. Aristocrats

The Crown depended on the cooperation of the aristocracy in the conduct of foreign affairs as much as it did in administration, finance and warfare. From an aristocratic viewpoint, engagement in public life was a form of 'giving counsel', a prime expression of the power and responsibility of that estate since the early Middle Ages. In the absence of any rigid separation between domestic and foreign politics, the men who considered themselves the king's natural companions and counsellors saw diplomatic missions to the Continent as a continuation of their participation in administrative business within the realm.

The middle years of Edward III's reign have often been described as a period of harmonious relations between the king and the nobility. A decade of instability during which Edward had failed both to enforce aristocratic discipline at home and to secure the magnates' support for his military ambitions abroad had culminated in the political crisis of 1340–1. The following twenty years, marked by military success abroad, saw a process of reconciliation and the revival of the tradition of aristocratic service destroyed in the conflicts of Edward II's reign.[5] This had a beneficial effect on English diplomacy: the pool from which the Crown could recruit its lay envoys was larger in those years than it had ever been under Edward's predecessor.

Edward III's two highest-ranking lay envoys to the papal court between 1342 and 1362, Henry of Grosmont and Richard Fitzalan, had for some years been among the main recipients of royal favour, and their social standing had improved correspondingly. Fitzalan, restored to his father's earldom of Arundel in 1330, was of about the same age as his king, and remained firm friends with him until his death in 1376. Grosmont was one of the six new earls created in the Parliament of March 1337.[6] He had been summoned to royal councils since 1335 and had become a banneret by 1337.[7]

A full survey of the involvement of these two earls in military and diplomatic activities would be beyond the scope of this study (Henry of Grosmont, for example, served on fifteen separate military expeditions, headed six major diplomatic missions abroad, participated in twelve peace conferences and took part in crusades in Spain, North Africa and Prussia). Here I need give only an outline of the earlier stages of their careers. At the time of their first selection for missions to Avignon,[8] their military experience was significant. Arundel and Lancaster had both commanded English forces in Scotland between 1333 and 1338. When the king had set out on his expedition to Flanders in 1338, Henry had been in his company as an adviser and military commander, while Fitzalan had remained in England as a member of the regency council.[9] He is also to be found among the magnates appointed in August 1338 to oversee the array of troops and the keeping of the peace in the various regions of the kingdom.[10] He had accompanied Edward on his expedition from June to November 1340 and taken part in the naval battle off Sluis.[11] When a new Parliament had been summoned on 11 July of that year, the king had sent him and others to present an eye-witness report on the recent military operations.[12] In 1346–7 Arundel fought at Crécy, and in the following year he and Lancaster were with Edward's troops at the siege of Calais. Henry of Grosmont had been in the royal entourage as early as 1329 as one of the king's attendants at the homage ceremony of Amiens. Negotiations with French representatives took him abroad in

1348 and 1353. During his missions to Guines in February and November 1353 he was accompanied by Fitzalan, his co-envoy to the curia towards the end of the following year.[13]

Grosmont and Fitzalan belonged to the politically most active section of the English nobility. In his doctoral thesis William Mark Ormrod analysed witness lists to royal charters from the period 1346–56 to support his argument that only a small circle of lords temporal took an active part in domestic affairs, whereas for most magnates 'to be a royal councillor was [...] to act in an advisory, rather than in an executive capacity'.[14] The names of the earls of Oxford, Salisbury, Devon, Hereford and Essex rarely appear on such lists, while Henry of Grosmont and Richard Fitzalan were among those who frequently witnessed important transactions. The parliamentary records of the same period confirm Ormrod's findings. The same names of magnates appear with a great degree of regularity when the auditors of petitions for each parliament are listed.[15] Richard Fitzalan was an auditor in 1341, 1348, 1352, 1354 and 1362. When Henry of Grosmont was not campaigning on the Continent, he was equally involved in this important business. He audited petitions in both 1348 Parliaments, in 1354 and in 1362.

An examination of the careers of the English barons, bannerets and knights who travelled to Avignon between 1342 and 1362[16] confirms the impression that distinction through loyal service to the Crown and proximity to the king were the most important criteria for the selection of envoys from the ranks of the nobility. Richard de la Bere, Thomas Bradeston, Guy de Brian, William de Cusance, Nigel Loring and Hugh Neville had all been recruited to the service of the Crown as squires or knights of the king's household within the first ten years of Edward's reign.[17] The *scutiferi* or *milites hospitii regis* were a group of fighting men attached to the household, although they did not normally reside at court. Their primary duty to the king was military; they formed the nucleus of his household troops and served as commanders, recruiting agents and captains of castles. Occasionally, however, household squires and knights were also used as commissioners, councillors or diplomats.[18]

Bartholomew Burghersh the elder and Guy de Brian were prominently engaged in the administration of the royal household. The offices connected with the Chamber involved a particularly close personal contact with the sovereign and thus opened a prime channel in bringing matters to his personal attention and conveying his decisions.

The reign of Edward III saw the revival of the Chamber as an organization of administrative importance. As the monarch's privy purse, it supplemented the efforts of the Wardrobe and the Exchequer in financing military operations. It was important also as providing an organized staff close to the king, at his disposal for confidential business of every kind.[19] Above all, by virtue of its keepership of the secret seal, the Chamber served as a secretariat prepared to give expression to the king's personal will in times when the keeper and office of Privy Seal were no longer readily available.[20] Guy de Brian became sub-chamberlain in 1348.[21] As steward of the household (29 August 1359–30 May 1361) he was later the chief lay officer of the *domus regis*, responsible for order, discipline and overall efficiency within it, and, jointly with the Keeper of the Wardrobe, for the general supervision of the king's domestic expenses.[22] Beside serving as seneschal of Ponthieu and warden of the Tower, Bartholomew Burghersh the elder was Edward's chamberlain at the time of his journeys to Avignon in 1348, 1349 and 1354–5.[23] Like the post of steward, this office involved confidential relations with the king and was held by men of high status.[24] The fact that Burghersh was selected for these missions to the curia is indicative of their special importance— owing to his onerous duties within the king's household, the chamberlain could not normally spared for diplomatic tasks.[25]

Richard de la Bere and Richard Stafford, envoys to the papal court in 1354 and 1359, respectively, made their careers outside the king's household. As has been mentioned above, de la Bere was originally a household squire, but between 1347 and 1351 he served Edward, prince of Wales, as chamberlain.[26] Stafford was closely attached to the prince from an early age, and by 1347 he was a member of his council. In that year he also became steward and surveyor of Edward's lands, an office that he probably held until 1360. In 1358 he served as auditor of the accounts of Edward's Wardrobe.[27] Nigel Loring was another squire of the king's household who was later in his career employed by the Black Prince: as his chamberlain he was sent to England in October 1356 to inform the community of London about the victory at Poitiers.[28]

Most—perhaps all—the lay envoys to the courts of Clement VI and Innocent VI had at some point in time been appointed members of the body that assisted the king in coordinating the administrative machinery of the realm: the royal council. William Burton became a councillor with an annuity of 40 li. at the Exchequer on 16 March

1360.[29] No such exact dates are available for the admission of Thomas Bradeston, Hugh Neville, Guy de Brian and Bartholomew Burghersh the elder to this advisory body, but we know that Bradeston was a councillor by 1339, Neville by 1344, de Brian by 1347 and Burghersh by 1337.[30]

Distinction during one or more of Edward's earlier military campaigns is perhaps the most striking common factor among the aristocrats who later served the Crown as diplomats. Some of them— Thomas Bradeston, Guy de Brian, William de Cusance and Nigel Loring—had been in the king's retinue during his expeditions to the Low Countries and the Rhineland in 1338–40.[31] Guy de Brian, Bartholomew Burghersh, William Burton and Richard Stafford had fought at Crécy in 1346 and taken part in the siege of Calais in the following year.[32] In 1356 Nigel Loring and Richard Stafford served in the Poitiers campaign.[33]

By the time they set out on their missions to the curia in the 1340s and 1350s most of the aristocratic envoys had already had the opportunity to gain some diplomatic experience. Bartholomew Burghersh the elder had been sent to Hainault in 1328 and to Paris in 1332. He had also participated in the Anglo-French talks at Antoing in August 1341.[34] After its capture in 1347 Calais became an important venue for negotiations between English diplomats and their French counterparts; William Burton and Guy de Brian each travelled there at least once before or between missions to Avignon.[35] Burghersh, Stafford, Loring and Burton were members of the English delegation that negotiated the truce of Bordeaux in 1357, and Burghersh, Loring and de Brian were among Edward III's plenipotentiaries at Brétigny three years later.[36] Throughout the early stages of the war Flanders remained of vital importance to the English because of its geo-strategic position and economic strength. William Burton, Edward's most important agent at the curia in 1359–60, was sent to the county twice in 1351.[37] Burghersh and Burton had also travelled the Empire, especially its north-western principalities. The former had served on embassies to Hainault in 1328 and to Frankfurt in 1339, and the latter on three embassies to the Low Countries in 1351–2.[38]

Missions to the Roman court, on the other hand, had only rarely been an aristocrat's first diplomatic assignment. Bartholomew Burghersh's first embassy had been the one that had taken him to John XXII's court in 1327 in the retinue of the bishop of Hereford. He had returned there in 1330.[39]

Finally, a rather unusual career remains to be considered: that of Niccolò Fieschi DCL, a Genoese nobleman who joined Edward III's 'diplomatic service' in 1336 and soon came to hold such a prominent position in Anglo-papal diplomacy that in 1341 it was declared in an Exchequer document that 'Celui Nicholin' soit demorez en nostre service a la Court de Rome par nostre comandement ou sa presence nous est taunt necessare que nous ne la puissons desporter qant a ore sanz grant damage de nous, et empeschement des grosses busoignes qe nous avons afaire illoqes' (Niccolò has stayed in our service and by our order at the Roman court where his presence is so essential for us that it would be much to our detriment, and to the hindrance of our important business there, if we had to do without it).[40]

Niccolò was probably the eldest son of Luchino Fieschi (d. between 1331 and 1335) and a member of one of the leading Guelph families of Genoa.[41] In many regards he was the perfect envoy to the papal court; his services could help the English king compensate for the fact that there were no dynastic ties whatsoever between himself and the popes or the cardinals. During the thirteenth century the Fieschi had been the best-represented non-Roman family in the curia.[42] Among Niccolò's paternal ancestors there had been two pontiffs— Innocent IV (Sinibaldo Fieschi, 1243–54) and Adrian V (Ottobuono Fieschi, 1276, Niccolò's great-great-uncle)—and two eminent cardinals, Guglielmo and Luca Fieschi. Furthermore, his mother Constanza was a member of the mighty Orsini clan, which had produced one pope and several cardinals and had played a pivotal role during the earliest phase of the Avignon papacy, when Napoleon Orsini, leader of the French faction of cardinals, had become 'pope-maker' in the conclave of 1305.[43]

Little is known about Niccolò's early years. He spent some years at university, probably in northern Italy, and earned a doctorate in civil law. From the very start of his career he was a full-time diplomat in the service of his home town Genoa, and the geographical range of his activities spanned the whole of the Mediterranean basin. His first mission in 1320 took him to Cyprus and Armenia, and in the mid-1320s he travelled to Avignon for the first time. Between 1328 and 1331 he visited the courts of Aragon, Cyprus and Naples.

The Ghibelline coup of 27 February 1336 drove the Fieschi into exile. Giovanni Fieschi, Niccolò's uncle, became supreme commander of the troops of his brother-in-law, Luchino Visconti of Milan. Niccolò and his son Giovanni turned their backs on Italy and moved to England. While Giovanni started studying theology in Oxford, his father became one of the key figures in English continental diplomacy in the early years of the Hundred Years War.[44]

3.1.2. Clerics: The King's Council, Chancery, Privy Seal

The great majority of the English *clerici regis* known to have been commissioned to negotiate with Clement VI and Innocent VI, or to participate in their peace conferences, had spent several years studying Roman civil law in Oxford or Cambridge before entering the service of the Crown. A conspicuous number among them had earned a doctorate.[45]

Theirs was not an exceptional case. By the end of Edward I's reign the English judiciary had been transformed by a process of laicization. For most of the thirteenth century there had been some clerks, trained in Roman civil law, among the king's judges, but the legal system that they represented had little in common with the common law practised by the large majority of courts in the land, and gradually those who dispensed justice ceased to borrow from it.[46] This did not, however, lead to the study of civil law falling into neglect: an ever-increasing number of young men studied the subject at the two English universities with a very real intention of applying it. Three main avenues of advancement remained open to those who could afford the time and money to take a degree in civil law: aristocratic, ecclesiastical or royal administration.[47]

For some of Edward's leading clerical emissaries to Avignon in the mid-fourteenth century it is possible to ascertain more or less exactly the date of their admission to the king's council. John Piers became a *consiliarius regis* on 17 June 1333.[48] William Bateman seems to have been appointed during his first visit to England as a papal nuncio in the late summer of 1340.[49] Andrew Offord, John Carlton and Michael Northburgh all became councillors on 10 May 1346.[50] For John Thoresby and John Offord, two of Edward III's most important diplomats, we do not have such exact dates, but we know that they had already joined the ranks of the royal councillors when they went to the Continent with the king in mid-July 1337.[51]

Many clerical councillor-diplomats distinguished themselves when in the king's company during his continental campaigns. John Offord, John Thoresby and Robert Askeby accompanied Edward III on his 1338–40 expedition to the Low Countries, Germany and France.[52]

Offord stayed with the king until January 1339, when he was appointed his proctor at the papal court.[53] Askeby performed the function of a messenger keeping up the communication between Edward and the regency council in England.[54] John Thoresby again accompanied the king on his short expedition to Flanders in July 1345, combining the keepership of the privy seal with the custody of the great seal.[55] A year later, on the eve of Edward's passage to France, Thoresby again received from Chancellor Offord the great seal of the realm, exchanging it for the great seal of absence.[56] Staying with the king throughout the Crécy–Calais expedition of 1346–7, Thoresby kept both the great and the privy seal during the siege of Calais and was occasionally sent to England on confidential business.[57] Other participants in this campaign were Andrew Offord and Michael Northburgh.[58]

Through the process of handling—that is, copying and enrolling—documents relating to foreign relations, the Chancery clerks, 'the most important and the ablest of medieval civil servants',[59] acquired a degree of familiarity with that particular field of administration that recommended them for active participation in diplomacy. The case of John Piers, who was responsible for the keeping of important diplomatic documents by 1333, illustrates this point. He was sent to the French court once and to the curia four times between 1334 and 1342.[60] After an early career as an Exchequer clerk, John Thoresby served as a notary in Chancery from at least 1336 onwards.[61] In a letter to Benedict XII four years later Edward referred to him as *clericus de cancellaria principalis* (principal clerk of the Chancery), which indicates his dominant role in the office at that time.[62] From 21 February 1341 onwards he was also keeper of the Chancery rolls (a senior clerk, almost the chancellor's deputy).[63] In this capacity Thoresby was responsible for the custody of the rolls once they had been compiled and supervised the work of enrolment and the drafting and writing of the Chancery engrossments.[64] He was still holder of this office when visiting the papal court in the autumn and winter of 1344–5.[65] A distinguished clerk, Thoresby was the obvious choice when, after the death of Chancellor Parving on 26 August 1343, three temporary keepers of the great seal were appointed. On 16 June 1349 his career culminated in his appointment as chancellor, an office he was to hold for more than seven years.[66] Andrew Offord, 'one of the leading Chancery clerks of the younger generation', served with the department from 1345 until at least 1353[67]. His elder brother John was made chancellor on 26 October 1345, when the great seal was delivered to him at a council meeting in Westminster.[68] When Thomas Brayton set out for Avignon in the company of the duke of Lancaster and the earl of Arundel in late 1354,[69] he had been employed in the office of the great seal for more than thirty-five years, and had become one of the leading senior clerks of his time. Whenever commissions in charge of the great seal had been appointed between 1340 and 1353, he had been one of the members. Brayton's outstanding importance as a Chancery clerk of the first grade (*de prima forma*) is further underlined by the fact that he served for some time as 'clerk of parliament' charged with the compilation of the Parliament rolls.[70]

As the opening of the Hundred Years War led to a marked increase in diplomatic activity, the Privy Seal office gradually became the ordinary channel through which the Crown directed its relations with foreign powers. It may still have been in the form of Chancery writs that letters close and patent addressed to foreign rulers were drawn up and enrolled, and the great seal continued to be used extensively for those letters to curia that demanded a greater degree of solemnity.[71] But by 1360 the privy seal had superseded it as the normal seal for diplomatic correspondence, and its head had become an important officer of state.[72] From 1345 to 1354, with only a short interruption, its keepership was in the hands of men who also served as envoys to the Roman court at some stage of their careers (John Offord, John Thoresby and Michael Northburgh), although only one of them, Offord, actually travelled there *as* keeper (in 1344). He had succeeded William Kildesby on 4 June 1342, and, since he was immediately sent on a three-week embassy to France, Thoresby temporarily acted as the seal's deputy keeper during his absence.[73] On 3 July 1345 Thoresby became keeper himself, vacating the office in September 1347.[74] Simon Islip, keeper between then and 1350, was not directly involved in Anglo-papal diplomacy, but his successor Michael Northburgh, keeper from 1350 to 1354, was one of Edward III's most active diplomats. John Welwick had become a Privy Seal clerk in 1353, during the short period when the office was the main centre of notarial and diplomatic activity.[75] Adam Hilton, envoy to Innocent VI in 1358–9 and 1360–1, was a member of its staff by August 1359.[76]

For the large majority of the English clerics entrusted with missions to the Roman court during the middle years of Edward III's reign, these journeys were not their first diplomatic assignments; like their aristocratic colleagues, they would usually have had the opportunity to gain experience in negotiations elsewhere. Some of the curial envoys of the early and mid-1340s—John Offord, John Piers, John Carlton and Laurence Fastolf—had been sent to northern France, Flanders, or the Low Countries both before 1336, at a time of mounting Anglo-French tensions, and later in the same decade, when war was beginning to appear inevitable.[77] The Offord brothers and Michael Northburgh soon came to be considered experts on the legal intricacies of the Anglo-French conflict. On 20 November 1337 Northburgh and John Offord were appointed members of a panel of advisers who were to enquire into the causes of the problem, and to make recommendations to Edward III as to how to go about the defence of his rights. Andrew Offord was to furnish additional information about the processes against the king in the French courts.[78]

Many clerics who later became royal emissaries will have had the opportunity to familiarize themselves with the route to Avignon, the city and the papal court during previous journeys made as proctors of English petitioners. John Thoresby travelled to the curia several times between 1323 and 1327, and again in 1330, while still serving as a clerk in the archbishop of York's household, in connection with the proposed canonization of Thomas of Lancaster.[79] Michael Northburgh was at the curia in 1336, but it is unclear in what function.[80] William Whittlesey was licensed to travel there in November 1350 with two companions on business for Archbishop Islip.[81]

Between their missions to Avignon, John Offord, John Carlton, Adam Hilton and Michael Northburgh continued the diplomatic dialogue with their French counterparts by conducting negotiations in northern France or Flanders.[82] Perhaps the most notable example, however, is that of William Bateman, bishop of Norwich, one of the dominating figures in English diplomacy at the time, who travelled to Calais eight times between September 1348 and March 1354 to meet representatives of Philip VI and John II.[83]

3.1.3. Clerics: Notaries

Robert Askeby, John de Branketre, Adam Hilton, William Ludeford, William Loughteburgh, John Thoresby and John Welwick all belonged to a growing group of specially trained administrative experts, the notaries public. While the institution of notary, which had been 'imported' from Italy around the middle of the thirteenth century, was alien to English common law, clerks who had acquired the skills of the *ars notarie* could expect to find employment in ecclesiastical law and administration and in royal government, especially in the Chancery and the Privy Seal.[84]

The spread of the institution of notary was a result of the spread of Roman civilian and canonical procedure. With Roman law coming to be recognized as an 'international' code of conflict resolution, there were obvious advantages in using the experts in diplomatic, whose transcripts and other documents would be widely accepted, as experts in diplomacy. The English notary came into his own in the negotiations with France and the Low Countries—'whenever truce or treaty is in question some of the most important documents in debate are drafted or transcribed and certified by permanent officials'.[85] John Thoresby, a notary public by 1336, played a key role in the English delegation at the First Avignon Conference of 1344. Ten years later, when again a peace agreement was to be negotiated, John de Branketre and John Welwick were acting in the curia on Edward III's behalf. Branketre, a senior Chancery clerk, had been appointed *notarius regis in cancellaria* on 28 January 1355, three weeks before leaving for Avignon with letters addressed to Henry of Grosmont and Richard Fitzalan.[86] As holder of this post, he was responsible not only for the preparation of notarial instruments but also for the writing and enrolling of diplomatic texts. Branketre was to direct and supervise the diplomatic work of the Chancery for the following twenty years, during which time he is believed to have introduced a number of innovations.[87] A large part of the curial business of John Welwick, the Privy Seal clerk, during his 1354–5 mission was to do with clerical matters: he obtained a number of special graces for Edward III and the royal family as well as privileges for St George's Chapel at Windsor.[88] But at the same time Welwick was also a member of the large English delegation to Innocent VI's peace conference. He was one of the proctors appointed to represent the bishops of England and a group of eighty-eight aristocrats and to consent on their behalf to any forthcoming agreement.[89] The diplomatic activities of the English notaries were not, however, limited to the great conferences of 1344 and 1355. During the period under examination Adam Hilton, William Ludeford and Robert Askeby all travelled to the curia on their own or as members of smaller embassies.[90]

3.1.4. Clerics: The king's confessor

The king's confessor was usually in constant attendance on his master, and as one of the most important members of the royal household he not only played a central role in its spiritual life but often also gained considerable influence in political and administrative matters.[91]

Friars Preachers were the sole English royal confessors from the reign of Henry III to the fall of Richard II, and later under Henry V and his son. From the very beginning they also served as judges, councillors and diplomats. They took on a particularly prominent part in governmental business under Edward III's grandfather, and continued to stand high in favour at court under his father.[92] The constitutions of the Dominicans of 1228 granted to superiors the power to dispense from the order's various observances, which enabled its members to participate in more secular activities.[93] When Innocent IV gave the English Dominicans permission to relax their rule so far as to ride on horseback (30 April 1250), this further enhanced their physical freedom of movement, and made them even more suitable for diplomatic missions to such remote destinations as Avignon.[94] The prior provincial, who often had to travel overseas to a general chapter or to the curia on his order's business, possessed special qualifications for the functions of a confidential envoy. An agent who was also a *persona grata* at the papal court was extremely useful, and consequently provincials or friars who had formerly held this office were frequently found on missions to Rome and Avignon from the mid-thirteenth century onwards.[95]

Richard Winkleigh OP DTh, who held this office from 1336 to 1339, first acquired diplomatic experience when he accompanied Henry Burghersh, bishop of Lincoln, on his two continental missions in the spring and autumn of 1337.[96] His first journey to Avignon (1 May–31 August 1340[97]) came shortly after his appointment as confessor to Edward III. Less is known about John Woderove OP DTh. He became *confessor regis* in the spring of 1349, and vacated his post only in 1376, shortly before or at his death.[98] The use of the personal confessor as an agent of diplomacy was not limited to the king. When John Reppes OC (to whom Hugh Neville and John Offord referred as *message Blank* in their reports, alluding to his white habit[99]) came to Avignon as a Crown envoy in early October 1344, it was not his first visit. As confessor to Henry of Grosmont he had been sent to the papal court almost exactly a year before.[100]

The fact that a large part of Winkleigh's, Reppes's and Woderove's tasks on their missions was to do with entirely secular issues is indicative of the degree to which royal and aristocratic confessors had become involved in all aspects of government by the middle years of the fourteenth century. In the spring of 1342 Winkleigh's primary task was of a private nature: the petitions that he put forward reflected the king's concern for his own spiritual well-being.[101] But two years earlier he had been instructed to expound his lord's views concerning a peaceful settlement of the Anglo-French conflict, and to announce his intention of sending *nuncii solemnes* (high-ranking emissaries) to the curia.[102] The secular element clearly dominated in John Woderove's mission of June 1353: after the truce of 10 March he was to explain to the pope the exact territorial demands made by Edward and his advisers as compensation for the French Crown.[103] He returned to the curia with Richard de la Bere in June 1354.[104] Besides using his insider knowledge of the machinery of papal administration to advise John Welwick on how to obtain graces and privileges, how to have them copied into the Register of Supplications, and how best to have the bulls sent to England, Woderove supported the work of the English delegation to the Second Avignon Conference until the spring of 1355; it was on the basis of his findings, probably written down in report form and taken back to England by de la Bere, that the first group of English envoys set out for the curia.[105] There is nothing improvised about Woderove's ten-month mission; the king's confessor had become a regular diplomatic agent in his own right. Although primarily a Crown envoy on his second mission to the curia, John Reppes was authorized to represent the earl of Derby and to explain his peace policy: he reported on Grosmont's attempts to win Edward over for a peace agreement that would be modelled on what had been discussed a few months earlier during the earl's own stay in Avignon.[106]

Interestingly, both Winkleigh and Woderove were Edward III's first envoys to the curia after the papal elections and coronations of 1342 and 1352. It is unlikely that this was coincidental; the sending of a person who 'by profession' was more privy to the king's intentions than anyone else could be read as a sign of trust and good will and thus help to establish good relations with a new pontiff from the outset. For the pope, on the other hand, it made sense to try and influence the king's policy indirectly by exerting pressure on a man who enjoyed such an exceptional degree of royal confidence. As recent research has shown, his unique position at court rendered the French *confesseur du roi* a key figure in Franco-curial relations between the early and the late fourteenth century.[107]

The king's confessor was the perfect tool for confidential communication with the Holy See. His journeys alone or with a small number of companions did not require lengthy preparations, and he could enter and leave the papal city without attracting too much attention. The crucial point, however, was that the status of the oral message that he conveyed was a unique one. It was, technically, a 'confession by proxy': the king would entrust a certain piece of information to his confessor as confessor, authorizing him, as diplomat, to reveal the contents of this 'confession' to the pope. Thus in October 1344 Clement VI told John Offord and his co-envoys that he wished to be informed 'com en confession' (as if in confession) about Edward III's and Henry of Grosmont's suggestions for a peace agreement, and assured Henry that he would treat this particular piece of information as if it were given to him 'sub secreto [...] confessionis sigillo' (under the secret seal of confession).[108] In the summer of 1353 Bartholomew Burghersh addressed the peers and commons in the White Chamber at Westminster. Reporting on the king's latest peace efforts, he told them how Edward had sent John Woderove to the curia in June to explain his ideas about a final peace to Innocent VI: 'Il envoya son Confessour a la Court de monstrer a nostre dit Seint Pier en confession, com pres il se vodra prendre, aufyn qe la Guerre [...] purroit cesser' (He sent his confessor to the curia to show the Holy Father as if in confession how great an effort he was prepared to make so that the war should end).[109] In August 1356 Edward himself referred to Woderove's mission; regarding his opinion about Innocent VI's peace plans, he had 'secretly opened his mind', as he put it, to the pope through his confessor.[110]

Sacralizing the diplomatic message in this fashion was an effective means of ensuring secrecy and secure communication: anyone interested in disrupting the flow of communication from England to Avignon would have to think twice about laying hands on men like Winkleigh or Woderove and forcing them to divulge what Edward III had 'confessed' to them. Every Christian knew that a priest was bound to inviolable secrecy regarding what was revealed to him in sacramental confession, and that the only possible release from this obligation was a formal permission given by the penitent himself.

Without it, any violation of the seal of confession constituted not only a grave sin but also a sacrilege.[111] This inflationary use of the sacrament of confession—its instrumentalization for diplomatic purposes—was facilitated by the fact that as late as the fourteenth century there was still some debate among theologians and canon lawyers as to whether it was only the actual sin itself that had to remain secret, or whether the canon law regulations applied to everything said by the confessant.[112]

3.1.5. Messengers

So far we have been looking at the backgrounds and careers of 'diplomatic part-timers'—that is, men for whom going on embassies was only one among several forms of service to their king. By contrast, in its messengers the Crown had had a group of regularly employed professional transmitters of information from the early thirteenth century onwards. In two respects the successful government of medieval England depended on the king employing an efficient body of messengers. Within the realm, *nuncii* and *cursores* formed a link between the central authority and its main local agents, their primary function being the conveyance of letters of great, privy and secret seal or of personal letters of the king or of his household officers to their addressees: bishops, magnates, sheriffs, port authorities, tax collectors and so forth.[113] Moreover, messengers were indispensable for the maintenance of contacts with the courts of continental Europe (no distinction was made at this period between home-service and foreign-service messengers). All this was achieved, during the reign of Edward III, by a permanent corps of between seven and twenty-one mounted messengers (*nuncii regis*) and a fluctuating number (anything between fourteen and fifty-two) of foot messengers (*cursores*).[114] The former were permanent members of the king's household, in which they formed a distinct unit, from the thirteenth century, whereas the latter achieved this status only later.[115]

The function of mounted and foot messengers in Anglo-papal diplomacy was twofold. Firstly, they conveyed letters to the papal court that would subsequently be presented to their addressees by higher-ranking official envoys or by whoever would agree to take on this task—simple messengers probably did not present letters to the pope themselves.[116] Secondly, they played a key role in what may be called 'secondary diplomacy': the longer the duration of a mission, and the greater the complexity of the business to be discussed, the more necessary it was for the king and his councillors and their representatives abroad to maintain the flow of communication in both directions. The latter had to send intermediate reports and requests for new instructions to Westminster, while the former had to see to it that the necessary communications reached them safely and in time. Extensive use of secondary envoys was made, for example, during the Second Avignon Conference. Between mid-November 1354 and late February 1355 six messengers were charged with taking royal privy and secret seal letters to the leading members of the English delegation.[117]

3.1.6. Qualifications

Having examined the available prosopographical data, we can now proceed to ask what precisely qualified a cleric or layman for diplomatic missions to the papal court. As has been said above, aristocrats considered themselves the king's natural counsellors by virtue of their noble birth. Moreover, peers were indispensable for embassies that had to be headed by a person of considerable social prestige; the sending of an emissary with insufficient status could be interpreted as disrespectful of the ruler to whom he was sent and as an inadequate approach to the business in hand (thus Clement V on one occasion complained to the king of France that he had sent him someone of humble status, who had travelled on foot, and warned him to send more suitable envoys ('nuntios ipsi negotio congruos') in future[118]). It is not surprising that the exceptional influence that noblemen were presumed to have in the curia should have attracted interest in them as lobbyists for third parties. Thus in early December 1354 Hinricus de Monte and Johannes Wunstorp, envoys of the council of the City of Hamburg, advised their masters to send letters to the duke of Lancaster, who was on his way to Avignon for the Anglo-French peace conference, requesting him to intercede with Innocent VI and the cardinals on the council's behalf.[119]

Provisional agreements between Edward III and the kings of France usually stipulated that their final form was to be negotiated and concluded by envoys 'of royal birth' or 'royal blood'. By the terms of the Malestroit truce (19 January 1343), 'aliqui de sanguine dictorum regum' (some of the blood of the said kings) were to be sent to the curia before 24 June. Article 7 of the treaty of Guines stipulated that its terms were to be published by Innocent VI 'in presencia solempnium nunciorum [...] quos dicti domini Reges mittent [...] tam prelatos quam dominos temporales; et inter alios aliquos de genere eorundem' (in the presence of envoys of high rank whom the said kings will send, both prelates and temporal lords, and among these some of their families).[120] This stress on consanguinity with the monarch as a qualification for diplomatic activity seems to be nothing other than a manifestation of the ancient (and, in fact, pre-feudal) notion that ties of kinship were channels for the transmission of power: '[in the Middle Ages] it was universally accepted that power was transmitted by consanguinity, or blood ties, for it was by blood that the virtues and charisma necessary for the exercise of power were also transmitted [...] All claims to power thus had a genealogical basis.'[121] Only through confirmation by blood relatives of the kings concerned did agreements become fully valid.

Lesser aristocrats possessed prestige sufficient for all but the most solemn missions. Furthermore, what rendered them (as well as the higher-ranking nobles) useful as agents of diplomacy was their organizational skills, their experience in on-the-spot decision making, and their leadership qualities, developed and proved both at home in England and on the battlefields of France.

This archaic element in the 'diplomatic service' of the Crown—the participation in diplomacy of men whose privileged position in the socio-political hierarchy was based on birth, blood and lineage—coexisted with a more progressive one: 'It could be said that no one in 1300 conceived of an important embassy without its great noble, no one in 1500 of one without lawyers.'[122] Among the three legal traditions that converged to form what may be called the international law of the Middle Ages—feudal customary law, canon and Roman civil law—the latter was the most important one: 'To Western sentiments of unity, civil law, backed by the traditions of imperial Rome, seemed even to the most zealous defenders of local customs the only possible and general code for governing the relations of the whole complex community which thought of itself as the Christian protraction of the Roman empire.'[123] Those who had systematically studied this law came closest in concept to the present-day international lawyer.[124] Their special skills enabled them to see two sides of a problem, apply highly abstract principles to practical situations, defend their actions articulately and draft diplomatic texts.

After 1259, when the Treaty of Paris failed to define the English rights in the south-west of France and the exact legal relation between the two Crowns, English continental diplomacy became increasingly legalistic, and the rise of the civil lawyer as an agent of diplomacy began. An impression of the legal complexities that Edward III's envoys to the curia had to be able to cope with can be gained from the document stating Edward III's claims to the throne of France drawn up by William Bateman, John Offord, John Thoresby, Niccolò Fieschi and John Piers in Avignon in December 1340. The king's case was thoroughly set out, the possible objections were stated, and the refutation of these objections was demonstrated. Thanks to Pierre Chaplais's meticulous research, we can fully appreciate the importance of civil-law principles to the argumentation (with all due caution necessary in such a purely quantitative approach): on less than twelve folio pages there are 115 references to passages from the Digests, Institutions, Codex or Novels, thirty-seven references to canon-law texts and only twelve to collections of feudal law.[125]

Civil-law graduates also seemed to be best qualified to defend what were considered the rights of the Crown with regard to the second major issue on the diplomatic agenda, the problem of provisions. Suffice it to say that, while the very nature of canon law required canonists to elevate the authority of the pope (and, later, general councils) and to favour more extensive powers for the Church, civil law was more friendly to the independence of the secular power. Originally imperial law, it could, by the second half of the fourteenth century, also be used by able jurists to defend the sovereignty of territorial princes.[126]

To sum up: the status of Edward III's aristocratic diplomats was to a large extent an *ascribed* one: their privileged position in the socio-political hierarchy was assigned to them on the basis of birth, blood and lineage. His clerical envoys, on the other hand, owed their position at the centre of the royal administration and/or in the ecclesiastical hierarchy to their individual accomplishments. These were more often than not men of humble origin who had 'worked their way up' over the years (although it must be conceded that the method of recruitment was highly nepotistic: in many cases doors had been opened by a recommendation by a magnate or bishop, or by a relative or neighbour already established in the king's admini-stration[127]). These men possessed invaluable skills—a thorough knowledge of civil law, training in the *ars notarie*, or the 'spiritual expertise' of the confessor—and had proved their exceptional competence in years of Crown service; theirs was an *achieved* status.[128] But, just as mere descent did not guarantee an aristocrat access to the inner circle of the king's advisers—the group from which his diplomatic representatives were selected—their academic degrees and administrative experience alone were not sufficient qualifications for clerics. Members of both groups had to gain the king's complete confidence through years of loyal service in administration at home and war abroad. Only then would they be referred to as his *secretarii*—his 'confidants'—in diplomatic correspondence.[129]

3.2. Englishmen at the Papal Court

Virtually any envoy from any region of the *universitas Christiana* could expect to find, on his arrival in Avignon, compatriots of his among the townspeople or the resident curialists.[130] Among the latter group Frenchmen predominated, though there was still a fair proportion of Italians. Englishmen formed only a minute proportion of the known curial officials, reaching their largest raw number, as well as their largest percentage, under John XXII—that is, well before the period with which I am here concerned.[131] Indeed, Bernard Guillemain, in his ground-breaking study of the society of papal Avignon, has concluded that the city was not a good place for Englishmen to find themselves in.[132]

In what follows I will be asking to what extent it was possible for Edward III and his advisers to integrate what few English resident *curiales* there were into the diplomatic process and to use such official and unofficial channels in their pursuit of the ultimate aim of English diplomacy: the safeguarding of the Crown's *ius* and *honor*.

3.2.1. *Proctors*

The rapid expansion of the curial bureaucracy and the increase in papal provisions during the Avignonese period forced petitioners more than ever to rely on the services of experts familiar with the workings of the curia's legal and administrative machinery (especially that of the chancery), but also with its less official mechanisms of decision making.[133]

Until the early thirteenth century legal representation through proctors remained a preserve of the ecclesiastical and secular elites:

only archbishops, bishops, abbots, deans, archdeacons, kings, the higher nobility and corporations enjoyed the right of charging curial proctors with defending their interests. Under Innocent III the foundations for an extension of the proctorial system were laid.[134] A new regulation introduced in 1215 by the Fourth Lateran Council conceded to all *petentes* the right to employ proctors if these could produce a specific mandate (*mandatum speciale*) on demand.[135] These representatives can be categorized according to their fields of activity: proctors *ad agendum* or *ad causas* transacted their clients' business in the law courts (Rota, *Audientia litterarum contradictarum*, Penitentiary), while *procuratores ad impetrandum* sought to obtain privileges, indulgences and other letters of grace in the Apostolic Chancery.[136] Once the regulations imposing a time limit of two years on an individual proctor's activity had been removed, a group of standing professional proctors evolved who took over more and more legal business from their more occasional, 'visiting' colleagues (although these continued to be sent by their principals).[137]

Individual rulers as well as secular and ecclesiastical corporations soon recognized the value of representation through at least semi-permanent proctors. English kings, queens and princes called upon their services from the early thirteenth century onwards. Under Edward I and his successor the *procuratores Regis Anglie* in the Roman court seem to have been exclusively Italian.[138] A Florentine, Andrea Sapiti, was Edward II's and Edward III's permanent proctor between *c.*1308 and 1338, providing an element of continuity in English curial contacts during that period.[139] His activities illustrate the indissolubility of the connection between legal, ecclesiastical and diplomatic business at the papal court: besides making payments on behalf of English bishops and promoting the election of royal candidates to episcopal sees, Sapiti was also expected to persuade John XXII to increase the pressure on Robert Bruce in 1321.[140] His proctorial endorsement can be found in the margin of a number of papal letters relating to petitions by Edward II and his successor, and on at least one occasion he 'lent' one of his scribes to a travelling diplomat for secretarial work.[141] The remnants of Sapiti's corres-pondence with the king are scanty, but what evidence there is shows that he played a key role in the transmission of information from Avignon to Westminster: in 1314, for example, he sent reports on the general state of affairs at the curia and on the preparations for the election of a new pope.[142] He travelled to England at least six times to receive outstanding payments and instructions, and cooperated with many of Edward III's diplomats.[143]

However, Sapiti did not hold office uninterruptedly. William Weston, a king's clerk who had arrived in Avignon on 12 May 1328, received a great seal letter on 1 April of the following year through which he was appointed Edward III's proctor, and was ordered to receive all letters and memoranda concerning the king's business at the papal court from the Florentine. Weston stayed in Avignon *in officio procuratoris* until 14 March 1330, when two royal emissaries, William Montague and Bartholomew Burghersh, revoked his mandate.[144]

Andrea Sapiti afterwards held office again and finally resigned in November 1338. Two trends can be observed regarding the period from *c*.1340 onwards: the disappearance of the permanent royal proctor and the 'anglicization' of English proctorial representation.

Sapiti was soon replaced by John Offord, who had accompanied Edward III to the Netherlands as a clerk of the royal council in the summer of 1338. He was appointed on 12 January 1339[145] and left for the papal city eleven days later. He seems to have stayed there continuously or at least for extended periods of time until 31 January 1341. Two privy seal letters, one issued on 18 January 1339 and the other on 19 July 1340, ordered the Exchequer staff to pay Offord the same wages as Sapiti and Weston before him, plus an additional annuity of 100 marks.[146]

As regards the rest of Benedict XII's pontificate, and those of his two successors, the sources do not allow us to identify a permanent *procurator Regis* with certainty, although Richard Thormerton may be an exception. He had taken up residence in Avignon after becoming notary public under John XXII and was recommended to Benedict XII on 28 October 1340 as *noster in sanctitatis vestre curia procurator*, commissioned to support the travelling envoy Reginald Cobham in his negotiations.[147] What little evidence there is of his activities in the 1340s and 1350s suggests that his employment by the Crown was not as continuous as that of Sapiti or Offord. While in Avignon Thormerton was appointed a member of the delegation coming to the curia to lodge the king's protest against William la Zouche (18 January 1341).[148] Although the Registers of Supplications mention him as Edward's proctor in December 1342 and August 1343, there is no corresponding information to be found in the English sources.[149] His participation in the mission of 1341, and the support he lent to a royal petition on behalf of Thomas Brembre in March

1353, seem to have been isolated cases.[150] If Thormerton actually served Edward in this function with any regularity after 1344, he would have had to coordinate his activities with those as curial advocate, a title he bore from *c.*1344 on.[151]

While there is some lack of clarity about Richard Thormerton's exact status, other independent English proctors at Avignon were charged with transacting royal business only when the needs of Edward's diplomacy demanded it. Alan Setrington was another *magister* who had moved to Avignon during the pontificate of John XXII.[152] Like Offord and Thormerton, he was appointed a member of William Bateman's mission of 1340–1.[153] Setrington acted as the bishop of Norwich's proctor until his death in Avignon in 1347, but no evidence exists for a later involvement in royal policy.[154]

The Issue Rolls of the 1340s and 1350s show the designation 'royal proctor' being used occasionally, but not as a term exclusively applied to resident curial representatives. Michael Northburgh, archdeacon of Suffolk, travelled south in the summer of the following year and was probably back in England by late September. Nevertheless the Exchequer scribe compiling the list of departmental expenses used the title *procurator Regis* to describe his status.[155] This confusion may be due to the fact that by the mid-fourteenth century *proctor* and *nuncius* could be treated as synonyms.[156]

Proctorial endorsements usually appear in the central upper margin of letters issued by the papal chancery in response to petitions.[157] Regarding the period under investigation, these notes hint towards only one such person transacting royal business: Richard Middelton OFM, who acted as a chancery proctor (*procurator ad impetrandum*) for Edward III's petitions on behalf of St George's Chapel, Windsor, between 1349 and 1352.[158]

The rise of the non-resident English proctor as a representative of English interests may partly be explained by the improved accessibility of the Avignonese curia to English travellers.[159] A reason for the disappearance of the permanent *procurator regis Anglie* and for the diversification and anglicization that can be observed in royal representation through proctors from the early 1340s onwards is probably to be seen in the noticeable surge in Anglo-papal diplomatic contacts through itinerant envoys following the truce of Malestroit and the Easter Parliament of 1343. In Clement VI's view, representation through resident proctors and representation through envoys were two fundamentally different, perhaps even mutually exclusive, techniques of diplomacy. In a letter sent to the chancellor of France on 19 August 1349 he complained about the absence of a French royal proctor to deal with on a continuous basis. Instead, he was finding his court swarming with ever new delegations of envoys:

Vix est aliquis catholicorum principum orbis terre qui non habeat apud Sedem Apostolicam negociorum suorum aliquem promotorem preter [...] Philippum, regem Francie illustrem, qui crebris missionibus plurium nunciorum, qui importunis petitionibus et alias multipliciter nos fatigant, non levibus subicitur oneribus expensarum. Igitur, quieti nostre ac utilitati etiam regie consulere cupientes, fraternitatem tuam attente rogamus quatinus procures quod prefatus rex Francie apud eandem sedem hujusmodi habeat, si expedire crediderit, promotorem.[160]

[There is hardly one among the Catholic princes of the world who does not have some kind of promoter of his affairs at the Apostolic See other than Philip, the illustrious king of France, who, owing to frequent missions of a multitude of emissaries harassing us with their impudent petitions and in other ways, is burdened with considerable expenses. Therefore we, eager to take our own peace and quiet as well as the king's benefit into account, request you, Brother, to see to it that the aforementioned king of France appoint such a promoter, if he should deem it expedient to do so.]

As Bernard Barbiche has shown in his study of French royal proctors, the Valois kings did not have a permanent representative of this kind before the second half of the fourteenth century, but instead relied on the short-time services of a diversity of non-professional proctors (notaries, chancery scribes, *familiares* of French cardinals) and travelling envoys.[161] By comparison with the resident *procurator Regis*, the itinerant *nuncius* (or *nuncius et procurator specialis*) may have been deemed a more flexible instrument of diplomacy by the French king before 1350 and the English king after 1340.

There has been considerable discussion as to how far, if at all, resident proctors at the papal court performed the functions of permanent diplomatic representatives. Ultimately, this raises the important question whether they are to be looked upon as the first resident ambassadors. Most of the confusion regarding this point seems to have been caused by a basic conceptual imprecision. Even such authorities as Mattingly, Queller and Cuttino fail to give a clear definition of 'diplomacy', although they do operate with certain a priori assumptions about its nature. Mattingly and Queller, for instance, implicitly claim to know where to draw the line between legal proceedings and other forms of diplomatic communication, and accordingly, while admitting that resident proctors occasionally *did* perform diplomatic functions, they discard these out of hand as non-diplomats.[162]

It seems difficult to uphold this view, which seems to be based on 'a confusion between the form and the content of the activities of these men',[163] if what has been said so far about the essence of the diplomatic relations between the English Crown (or any secular ruler, for that matter) and the curia is taken into consideration. Legal and diplomatic issues were inseparable from each other—in fact, very often to the point where they became indistinguishable. The task of men like Andrea Sapiti or John Offord was to defend what were perceived to be the rights of the Crown before the pope as the supreme judge in spiritual and secular matters; nothing stands in the way of referring to these *procuratores regis* as permanently resident legal *and* diplomatic representatives.

On the other hand, it must be emphasized that there is no discernible connection between the resident curial proctors of the early and mid-fourteenth century, those legal experts and insiders to the administrative structures of the papal court, and the resident ambassadors who made their first appearance at the lay courts of Renaissance Italy a century later. Both may have been diplomatic agents, but the modern practice of representation through permanent embassies developed in an entirely different political context. William Urban thus seems to be going a step too far when he concludes that the Teutonic Knights, who undoubtedly had continuous representation through a general proctor at the papal court from the early thirteenth century onwards, 'should be allowed to boast that they were indeed the first to practise Renaissance diplomacy'.[164]

3.2.2. Penitentiaries and chaplains

The *Poenitentiaria Apostolica*, one of the tribunals of the Roman Church, was arguably the most 'cosmopolitan' department of the Avignonese curia. To enable it to perform its function—namely, to handle jurisdictional matters affecting the spiritual good of individual Christians—clerics from the principal linguistic areas of the Christian world (in most cases members of the regular orders) were aggregated to the college of minor penitentiaries.[165]

Three English Dominicans are known to have served as

poenitentiarii minores under Clement V, John XXII and Benedict XII: John Ecclescliff (*c.*1304–18), Nicholas Wisbech (1318–19) and John Wrotham (*c.*1319–35). The Crown made repeated efforts to position its candidate in this tribunal: Wisbech and Wrotham were both named as penitentiaries by John XXII at the explicit request of Edward II, and both also served at times as envoys to the curia.[166] Under Clement VI and Innocent VI, and in the first pontifical year of Urban V, the office of 'minor penitentiary for the English language' (*primarius Anglie*) was held by Thomas de Lisle OP D.Th. (*Thomas de Insula*, between *c.*1341 and 1345), John Reppes OC (*c.*1345), William Charnels OP D.Th. (from 21 October 1348), Thomas Ringstead OP D.Th. (from 7 September 1349), Robert Wyghen OSB (*c.*1357), John de Tatenhall OP D.Th. (from 22 June 1361), Thomas Appleby OSA B.Cn.L. (*c.*1362–3) and Thomas Brinton OSB D.Cn.L. (from 26 June 1363).[167]

It was not at all uncommon for minor penitentiaries to function as emissaries of the Holy See.[168] De Lisle had originally, in the spring of 1341, been Edward III's envoy charged with securing the promotion of William Kildesby to the see of York but had stayed on in Avignon.[169] In 1343 Clement VI sent him back to England with a letter asking Edward III to nominate envoys who would represent him in the negotiations that were intended to convert the truce of Malestroit into a final agreement.[170] He was certainly back in the curia by January 1345, when royal letters requesting support for the bishop of Worcester's proctors were directed to him, William Bateman and John Offord.[171] Thomas Ringstead had been a penitentiary for seven years when he was sent to England in July 1356 to explain the pope's peace policy to Edward III and inform him and his counsellors about the forthcoming mission of Cardinals Talleyrand and Capocci.[172]

John Reppes, whose activities as a royal envoy in 1344, 1345 and 1347–8 have been discussed above, became a papal chaplain at the request of the earl of Derby and Queen Isabella during a mission to Avignon in the earl's service in October 1343, and a penitentiary some two years later.[173] In September 1346 he was Clement VI's envoy to Gascony, and in the following spring he received another commission for a journey to England and France.[174]

Information on the careers and activities of Englishmen who served as chaplains in cardinals' households,[175] or bore the titles of *capellanus commensalis* or, from the reign of Clement VI onwards, honorary chaplain, is much harder to come by, but it may be assumed that they played a certain role in maintaining contacts and transmission of information between England and Avignon (although honorary chaplains visited the curia only rarely, if at all).[176]

3.2.3. Advocates and auditors

In order to succeed before the curial tribunals it was essential for a plaintiff or petitioner that his cause be defended by a person versed in canon and civil law who would also give professional advice. Advocates differed from proctors in that they dealt directly with the legal aspects of a given case. The advocate assumed the facts delivered to him by the proctor to be true, and built his legal argument on them.[177]

'Advocates in consistory', who had the right to speak before the pope and cardinals, were considered the elite of these experts, and were nominated by the pope himself.[178] Richard Wimundewold DCL (d. *a.* November 1362) belonged to this group by 10 February 1343.[179] He actively promoted the king's curial business in the late 1340s and early 1350s. When Geoffrey de la Mare arrived in Avignon at the end of May 1349 to claim the deanery of York for the king's candidate, Philip Weston, he could count on Wimundewold's support during his audience with the pope. Four months later Wimundewold, as a member of a delegation including Michael Northburgh, Andrew Offord and Robert Askeby, was empowered to negotiate with the French about a prolongation of the Calais truce. In May 1351 he travelled to Spain to negotiate with the king of Aragon about an alliance.[180] It was one of the tasks of William Whittlesey during his mission in July 1353 to pay the advocate 33li. 6s. 8d. 'for good services rendered to the king in the curia'.[181] As an advocate in consistory, Wimundewold was ideally suited to carry out legal work complementary to that of the English delegation to the 1355 peace conference. He was one of the five proctors empowered by a group of 104 English prelates and aristocrats to give their consent to any forthcoming Anglo-French agreement.[182] One of his colleagues on this team was Richard Drax DCL (d. 1361), a curial advocate since *c.*1352 and, like Wimundewold, classed as a *iuris civilis professor* in the letter of appointment.[183] E 101/313/39, one of those rare expense reports that contain evidence for cooperation between resident Englishmen and travelling envoys, shows that Drax and his staff supported the work of Richard Stafford and William Burton five years later.[184]

No direct evidence has as yet come to light as to how far English consistorial and curial advocates other than Fastolf, Wimundewold and Drax—Robert Thresk MA, William Sallowe MA, Thomas Michel DCL, John Appelby DCL[185]—were charged with diplomatic business by their king, or interacted with English embassies during the 1340s and 1350s.

By 1342 the Court of Audience (*Audientia sacri palatii*) was established as the supreme court of the Western Church. At a time of an extension of provisions at the expense of the ordinary collators, the auditors of the papal palace (*domini auditores sacri palacii apostolici*) concerned themselves primarily with the growing amount of routine litigation over benefices.[186]

Auditors had been appointed since early times. When towards the end of the twelfth century the centralization of Church administration increased the amount of judicial business to be transacted by the pope as supreme judge, the investigation of minor cases began to be entrusted to cardinals and, later, chaplains. These were appointed to hear the evidence of the litigants and to make a report to the pope, who would then take his decision. Innocent III was the first pontiff to give his auditors the power to hand down verdicts in less important cases while reserving confirmation to himself.[187] His successors extended this concession, and in the course of the thirteenth century the auditors' procedure became regularized. By the early fourteenth century the *Audientia* had developed into a collegiate body.[188]

The recruitment of William Bateman DCL for service in the Rota in 1329 indicates that, at a time of increased provisions to English benefices, it appeared expedient to have an expert on English affairs in a leading position at the curia. Shortly after becoming archdeacon of Norwich on 8 December 1328 Bateman transferred to Avignon, where, according to his contemporary biographer, he was in high favour with John XXII and soon established a reputation as a chaplain and auditor of outstanding legal expertise.[189] It seems possible, therefore, that he was prominent in reorganizing the Rota in 1331. During the pontificate of Benedict XII he attended two consistories in which relations with the Crown of Aragon were treated.[190]

Bateman, a Norfolk man, born in Norwich, was not the first Englishman to make a career as an auditor in Avignon—the Oxford canonists Adam Orleton (d. 1345) and John Ross (d. 1332) had served before him—but with him the English contribution shifted for several years to Cambridge civil lawyers, or at least to civil lawyers of East Anglian origin.[191] Thomas Fastolf DCL was most probably one of this circle, and closely connected with Bateman, although his university is not known positively.[192] He is not mentioned as an auditor before 1340, but it is very likely that he entered the papal service under John XXII.[193] Like Bateman, Fastolf soon became a canonist of some distinction, and, as author of the earliest known collection of *decisiones* of the Rota (dated 1336–7), he is today considered a pioneer of the law reporting tradition.[194] He is possibly also to be identified with the English canonist who wrote the *Memoriale presbiterorum* at Avignon in 1344.[195]

A nephew and protégé of Bateman's from Suffolk, Simon Sudbury (d. 1381), became papal chaplain and took the auditors' oath on 8 December 1348.[196] His university is not known for sure, but by 1344 he was a doctor of civil law, and in the following year acted as Bateman's *commissarius specialis* in his quarrel with the abbot of St Edmund.[197] Sudbury's association with his uncle was so close that in late 1346, at the height of the conflict between the latter and Edward III, he fled to Avignon to escape royal disfavour.[198]

East Anglian lawyers continued to be employed in the Rota under Innocent VI. William Lynn DUJ (of King's Lynn in Norfolk, d. 1373) was serving in this capacity by November 1359.[199] Thomas Paxton (or Paston) DCL (d. 1370), another Norfolk lawyer, one-time fellow of King's Hall, Cambridge, and long-standing member of Bateman's household, had joined the *Audientia* by December 1361, but there is some evidence that his career in Avignon began well before his promotion to this post.[200] Robert de Stratton DUJ (d. 1380), the first master of Trinity Hall, will have acquired some experience in curial business when in Avignon as a member of Bateman's staff during the second Anglo-French conference, and may indeed have stayed on after the bishop's death on 6 January 1355. By November 1362 he had become an auditor himself.[201]

Between 1331 and 1335 three pieces of legislation regularized the work of the college of auditors further, and, at the same time, made for closer relations between them and the pope. John XXII's constitution *Ratio iuris* (16 November 1331) drew up the definite regulations for the working of the Court of Audience.[202] His successor Benedict XII promulgated *Ad regimen* (10 January 1335) and *Cum, sicut accepimus* (1 October 1335). The former added the auditors to the officials of the Roman court, assigning them a place in the curial hierarchy, and by virtue of the latter they joined the pope's *familiares domestici commensales ac speciales ac veri officiarii*.[203] All auditors were elevated to the rank of papal chaplain upon joining the Rota and received distinctive clerical garb after taking the oath.[204] Benedict, Clement and Innocent would sometimes invite the college of auditors to lunch or dine with them on certain feasts.[205] This enhanced importance and confidentiality, but also the increased activity of the college (which was made up of between fifteen and twenty members between 1342 and 1362[206]), found its visible expression in architectural rearrangements. From a building to the south of the papal palace, where it held its sessions under John XXII, the *Audientia* moved to the bay at the east end of Clement VI's great hall in 1344.[207]

The account books and correspondence of the envoys representing the city council of Hamburg in its lawsuit against the local cathedral chapter give a good impression of how clearly the value of maintaining good relations with these men was realized by those who came to Avignon to seek papal grace or justice. Between 1341 and 1348 Thomas Fastolf was in charge of five suits involving Hamburg's council or individual citizens—in at least two cases at the envoys' request.[208] Although *Ratio iuris* forbade auditors to accept donations of any kind, Heinrich Bucglant made several payments to Fastolf himself, to the notaries assisting him and to his chamberlain.[209] His successors as envoys established contact with Simon Sudbury, who was to be involved in at least part of the litigation against the cathedral chapter during the 1350s, as early as April 1348, even before he had taken the auditors' oath. Sudbury, to whom the Germans would refer as *consiliarius noster*, and members of his household received considerable sums and gifts in kind in 1353–6.[210]

Between 1340 and 1344 William Bateman was valued as a transmitter of information by Edward III, Benedict XII and Clement VI alike. His activities during this period show to what extent expertise, authority and papal favour made auditors of causes the obvious choice for diplomatic tasks.[211] Bateman started on his first mission a nuncio on or around 29 August 1340, his task being to urge the king, then in the Netherlands, to abandon hostilities with France.[212] By the time he, accompanied by John Offord, John Thoresby and Niccolò Fieschi, set out on his return journey (on or after 10 November) he had become a royal councillor and a central figure in Edward's communication with the curia.[213] Only five weeks after his arrival in Avignon he was appointed one of the proctors supposed to make the king's protest against William la Zouche's election to the archbishopric of York.[214] While Offord and Thoresby were back in England by mid-March 1341, Bateman probably stayed on until the spring of the following year, managing his affairs in England by attorney.[215] His second appointment as nuncio was made by the college of cardinals shortly after Benedict XII's death.[216] Having left the curia in early May 1342, Bateman reached Westminster four weeks later. It seems that he stayed in England until his return to the curia in mid-June 1343 as the first English envoy to negotiate for peace after the deliberations in the Easter Parliament. During that summer he was nominated as a royal diplomat twice more while engaged in his normal business as auditor.[217] In early August 1344—he had made two more journeys to England in the meantime—Bateman was called upon to present royal letters to Clement VI.[218] When he was appointed a leading member of the English delegation to the First Avignon Conference (4 August 1344), this marked the completion of his integration into royal diplomacy.[219]

Thomas Fastolf was more 'stationary' than Bateman in that he remained at the papal court throughout the 1340s, but nevertheless he was assigned a similar role as an official representative of Edward III. Considering that the average duration of service in the Rota was less than five years,[220] the English were exceptionally fortunate in being able to rely on the experience of two men who had been auditors for fifteen (Bateman) and ten years (Fastolf), respectively. By virtue of a letter of procuration of 4 August 1344 Fastolf became a full member of the English delegation, alongside his senior colleague.[221] Like Bateman, he was present at the meeting between John Offord, Hugh Neville and the pope on 7 September.[222] According to a report of the two Hamburg proctors, Hermann Vrackel and Heinrich Bucglant, he neglected his normal duties as an auditor during that time.[223] In May 1348 Fastolf once more cooperated with an English embassy: he received plenary powers for an extension of the truce concluded at Calais together with John Carlton and John Reppes.[224]

Like William Bateman himself, his protégé Simon Sudbury seems to have been integrated into the English 'diplomatic service' after a journey to Westminster as a papal nuncio. He left for England in late February 1356 for the first time since going into exile almost ten years earlier and stayed in London for more than five weeks.[225] A year later

Sudbury was requested to provide advice and help to Nicholas d'Amory and Thomas Fulnetby, and to help them gain access to the pope.[226] The activities of William Lynn at about the same time (1354–7) were not restricted to the curia: he participated in the Second Avignon Conference as plenipotentiary of eighty-eight English aristocrats but was also Edward III's envoy to Cardinals Niccolò Capocci and Talleyrand de Périgord in the autumn of 1356. In March 1357 Lynn was involved in the negotiations leading up to the truce of Bordeaux.[227] It is unlikely that he severed all ties with the English court on becoming an auditor.

The nature of the sources imposes certain limits on our analysis. It is difficult to gauge the full extent of informal cooperation between the king's envoys and English curial officials when having to rely almost exclusively on financial and administrative records. Furthermore, sources of this kind do not usually reveal how much influence Englishmen who were not proctors, penitentiaries, chaplains, advocates or auditors wielded—how much truth, for instance, was there to the rumour in circulation in Avignon and England around 1351 that Nicholas Hethe, a cleric from the diocese of Coventry and Lichfield who had been living in the papal city for several years, was 'on more intimate terms with the Holy Father at Avignon than any other person of the English nation'?[228]

But even given the scarcity of direct evidence, some conclusions can be drawn. By the middle of the fourteenth century Edward III and his advisers had come to prefer the services of English curial advocates and auditors, and, to a lesser degree, individual proctors, to those of a permanent *procurator regis Anglie*. Men who moved as easily between England and Avignon as Reppes, de Lisle, Bateman, Fastolf, Sudbury, Lynn, Drax and Wimundewold were in an ideal position to gather information (*nova curie*) about the latest developments at the papal court and elsewhere in Europe and transmit it to England,[229] and to support and complement the work of itinerant envoys by helping to establish connections, providing advance information as to the moves that would be made in the curia, or otherwise employing their inside knowledge to smooth their way. At the same time, if formally appointed, curial penitentiaries, auditors and advocates could become official diplomatic agents in their own right. The fact that de Lisle, de Tatenhall, Ringstead, Bateman, Fastolf, Lynn and Sudbury were all eventually provided with episcopal sees in England, Wales or Ireland is indicative of the favour in which these men were with both sides alike.[230]

3.3. Non-English Lobbyists

3.3.1. Cardinals

From the mid-eleventh century onwards the cardinals assumed an ever-increasing importance as electors, assistants and permanent councillors of the Supreme Pontiff, and by the time the papacy moved to Avignon they had gradually taken over a large share of the general government of the Western Church.[231] The members of the Sacred College exercised their judicial and administrative functions in the curial law courts, the Apostolic Chamber and Chancery and, above all, in the consistory, the reunion of the cardinals and the pope. In it the so-called *causae majores* were regularly treated: questions of faith and important disciplinary matters, all matters regarding dioceses and bishops, the questions that arose concerning the properties of the Church, the papal fiefs, the crusades and political problems such as the settlement of disputed royal elections, the approbation of newly elected kings and the deposition of princes.[232]

An exact knowledge of who among the cardinals could be expected to promote one's interests was essential for the successful transaction of any business at the curia. At the beginning of the century Edward I had appreciated the value of his links with Thomas Jorz, cardinal priest of S Sabina, who had been promoted thanks to royal intervention. In September 1306 he wrote to the Englishman, requesting him to supply information frequently concerning developments at the papal court.[233] The envoys representing Hamburg's city council between 1337 and 1356 were no less aware of the cardinals' importance. One of the members of the first mission (1337–48) compiled a short list of cardinals, ranking them according to their approachability.[234] A similar memorandum was drawn up by the members of the 1354–5 embassy.[235]

During the pontificate of John XXII, when Anglo-papal relations were not yet as strained as they were to become later, individual cardinals had been appointed nominal councillors of the English king and granted annual pensions (usually fifty marks per year). Gaucelme de Jean Duèsne, cardinal priest of SS Marcellinus and Peter from 1316, later cardinal bishop of Albano, was a member of the king's council in Aquitaine from October 1313, and became a member of Edward II's council and household in January 1314 'in consideration of his good services in the court of Rome and elsewhere'.[236] Bertrand de Montfavès, cardinal deacon of S Maria in Aquiro, had been appointed a councillor in March 1320.[237] Annibaldo Caetani da Ceccano, cardinal bishop of Tusculum, had been retained by Edward III by 1333.[238]

The practice of paying pensions to individual cardinals thought to be unusually influential and/or favourable to English interests went back at least to the reign of King John. Calculated *largesse* of this kind was all the more necessary during periods when there was no Englishman among the members of the Sacred College. On 24 January 1311, only five weeks after the death of Thomas Jorz, Edward II asked the lieutenant and keeper of the realm, the chancellor and the treasurer for information concerning what cardinals were receiving pensions from the Crown, and what amount, and to state their opinion as to whether he should retain more of them 'to advance his business in the court of Rome', and, if so, how much they should draw.[239] In those earlier years of the Avignon papacy the news of grants of such pensions were often taken to the curia by the more important royal envoys, and these often made the payments as well.[240]

While five cardinals are known to have received annual pensions from Edward III up to late 1334,[241] I have found no evidence of such payments, or of new appointments to the king's council, being made at the time of Benedict XII or afterwards. The conclusion seems tenable that at a time of growing antipapalism in England a return to this practice was no longer politically feasible. However, before the violent reaction to provisions in the Easter Parliament of 1343 Edward III had no compelling reason to lay hands on the cardinals' benefices in England.[242] On 27 January 1343 he informed the earl of Leicester that, 'in view of the affection for the English Crown of the cardinals beneficed in England', he had cancelled the debts they owed to the Crown by reason of their benefices in his realm.[243] As late as mid-March of the same year Gaucelme de Jean and Pierre Després were exempted from the payment of the subsidy recently granted by the English clergy.[244]

The king's policy towards the cardinals after 1343 has been outlined above.[245] Throughout the 1340s and 1350s Edward succeeded in pursuing an independent policy—that is, a policy free from interference by the commons—vis-à-vis their officials and property in England, and exemptions from the seizure of revenues could be obtained by royal favour. Renewing an earlier privilege, Edward took the proctors and other officials in England of Raymond des Farges, cardinal deacon of S Maria Nova, into his special protection on 21

January 1345.[246] When the Italian officials of Annibaldo da Ceccano crossed over to England in February 1348, they were given the same protection as his lands. It was renewed twice in 1350 at the cardinal's request.[247] It is important to note that by then Annibaldo was the only non-French member of the Sacred College.

In addition to this, two non-French cardinals enjoyed economic privileges. Pedro Gomez da Barroso, cardinal priest of S Praxedes, a Castilian, had been permitted to export sixty sacks of wool yearly free of customs duty for the clothing of his household in November 1340 'in recognition of his furtherance of English affairs in the curia'. The grant was renewed after his promotion to the cardinal-bishopric of Sabina.[248] In early July 1343 Annibaldo da Ceccano was given a free hand to export 100 sacks of wool, while the Exchequer took over the payment of the 200 li. due to the London customs authorities.[249] In the autumn of 1343, when the commons' protests against provisions and payments to aliens had made it virtually impossible for da Ceccano and Pierre Després, the long-standing vice-chancellor of the papal court, to exercise an earlier privilege for the free export of 200 sacks of wool, Edward III granted each of them 200 li. in recompense.[250]

We have already seen that in February 1345 eight of the thirteen cardinals beneficed in England received the guarantee that their property would remain unaffected by the general levy of a triennial tenth.[251] Although the fruits of the benefices of all non-resident aliens were confiscated on 12 February 1346, most cardinals and other beneficiaries, while having to accept the loss of their revenues until further notice, were allowed to retain their titles. One way for the king and his councillors to 'get done what they wanted' at the Roman court was to assist certain cardinals in maintaining financial control over their benefices in the realm. On 6 October 1349 Annibaldo da Ceccano was exempted from the payment of the latest tenth granted by the English clergy for his two parish churches.[252] By 1352 Pierre Després had obtained a privilege that enabled him to receive an annual sum of 600 florins out of the revenues of his archdeaconry of York.[253] 'Out of reverence for the pope' Pierre Roger de Beaufort, Clement VI's 18-year-old nephew, cardinal deacon of S Maria Nova and archdeacon of Canterbury, was allowed to have the revenues from his English benefice collected without interference in September 1348.[254]

Because of the largely informal nature of the collaboration between

English envoys and individual cardinals, it is no surprise that evidence of it is scanty. However, where it can be found, the same names tend to occur. Annibaldo da Ceccano and Raymond des Farges were the cardinals who on 7 May 1342 dispatched messengers to England to inform Edward that a new pope had been elected, and that his coronation was due to take place soon.[255] One of them may well have been the unknown anglophile cardinal who in early September 1344 advised John Offord and Hugh Neville through his messenger to speed up their journey to the papal court in order to avert the impending publication of the processes against Edward III.[256] In the following year the king even made an attempt to use four cardinals as mouthpieces for his policy: da Ceccano, des Farges, Pierre Després and Talleyrand de Périgord were to see to it that the content of a royal letter to the pope branding Philip VI as a *violator treugarum* (violator of truces) and Edward's *inimicus et prosecutor capitalis* (principal enemy) became publicly known.[257]

One possible indication of the relative importance of various cardinals to Edward III can be seen in the frequency of letters to them as recorded on the Roman Rolls, which are probably the major surviving source of such correspondence.[258] When the king addressed a petition of some importance to the pope, he would send numerous duplicate requests *mutatis mutandis* to selected cardinals whom he considered well disposed to further his interests.[259] According to this series, less than a quarter of all cardinals who lived during the period 1342–1358 received letters from the English Chancery. The overwhelming majority of these (ten out of thirteen) were men who had been promoted to their first cardinalates under Benedict XII, John XXII or Clement V.[260] Among them were three members of the dwindling non-French minority in the Sacred College: one Spaniard (Pedro Gomez da Barroso) and two Italians (Giovanni Colonna and Annibaldo da Ceccano).

The lack of evidence poses a serious problem in considering the question of the king's relations with individual members of the college of cardinals, and therefore only a few tentative conclusions appear valid. For Edward III and his diplomats there were no obstacles to cooperation with Italian or Spanish cardinals, and the king clearly appreciated the value of this 'non-French connection'. Among the Frenchmen from the *Midi*, those who enjoyed special prestige and influence because of their seniority and administrative functions, such as Raymond des Farges, Gaucelme de Jean Duèsne, Élie Talleyrand de

Périgord, Gailhard de la Mothe, Pierre Després[261] and Jean de Comminges, 'veterans' from times when relations between Crown and Tiara had been less strained, were at least occasionally viewed by Edward III as men whom he could 'do business with'. The fact that this group also included a man like Talleyrand, a protégé of the French Crown but also one of the most influential figures at the papal court,[262] is testimony of a good deal of pragmatism on the part of Edward III. On the other hand, there are hardly any signs of cooperation between the Crown and the men newly promoted under Clement VI and Innocent VI.

3.3.2. Other curiales

On 27 February 1334 Edward III ordered the Exchequer to reimburse Richard de Bury, bishop of Durham, for his expenses at the Roman court in the previous year. He had not only settled the king's debts to John XXII and members of the Sacred College but had also paid the annual pensions of some curialists retained by the English Crown ('[gens] qi sont de nostre retenance en mesme la cour').[263]

To speak of a pro-English party at the curia at this time would almost certainly be an overstatement, but there were certainly some anglophile individuals among the members of the papal household and of the curial administration. Like the pensions awarded to members of the college of cardinals and the gifts given to certain curialists, which will be discussed below, the more or less regular payments made at the Exchequer to these men were intended to create an obligation to render counter-services to the Crown.

The coronation of Clement VI (19 May 1342) was announced to Edward III by Pierre de Saint-Martial, a squire of the papal household from the diocese of Tulle.[264] Pierre was appointed a member of the king's household with an annuity of 20 li. and the robes of a valet on 28 July 1342 and returned to Avignon four weeks later.[265] What seems to have rendered him a particularly useful contact in Avignon in the following years was the fact that for at least six years (1343–9) he was, as a *magister hostiarius prime porte* (master-doorkeeper of the first door), responsible for guarding the main entrance to the apostolic palace.[266] If encouraged to do so by financial means, he could thus grant English envoys access to the place where they strove to transact their business. In March 1343 Edward III wrote to him requesting him to speak to Clement VI in favour of William Northwood, a member of the queen's household.[267] The Issue Rolls record payments of his annuity in 1346 and 1349.[268] In October 1351 Clement VI requested the leading members of Edward III's council to persuade the king to allow Pierre and his three sons to collect the revenues of their benefices in England, pointing out his consistency in promoting the interests not only of the king but of all Englishmen in the curia.[269]

Pierre de Podensac, another squire of the papal household and between c.1335 and c.1348 a guard and, later, master-doorkeeper of one of the palace's interior doorways (*ostiarius* or *custos*, later *magister hostiarius secunde porte*),[270] probably came from a town by that name in the hinterland of Bordeaux. We do not know what, if any, services he rendered to the English, but during the First Avignon Conference John Offord deemed it necessary to remind a member of the king's council that the Exchequer was in arrears with the payment of both his and de Saint-Martial's pensions.[271]

It is quite possible that there were other men like Pierre de Podensac and Pierre de Saint-Martial among the curialists from south-western France; men who came from areas still under English control or were members of families that had entered into alliances with the English Crown and who were thus prepared to assist at least temporarily English Crown envoys in their work.

3.3.3. Merchants

Faced with expensive continental commitments and only a modest domestic income, the English kings from Edward I onwards came to rely heavily on loans from the nascent banking systems of Flanders, the Rhineland and, above all, Italy. Their great wealth, business capacity and advanced methods of international credit and exchange made the Italian merchant-banking companies practically indispensable for a successful conduct of domestic and foreign policy.

The Society of the Bardi was the largest of the Florentine companies of the first half of the fourteenth century. Active in England since 1267, the Bardi effectively became bankers to the Crown by 1329.[272] Additionally, they were prominently involved in the transfer of the papal collections from the British Isles to the Holy See from 1316.[273] Another one of their main functions was the provision of money for the maintenance of the royal household, as well as for the households of other members of the royal family, between c.1329 and 1341.[274] Although after 1345 Italians ceased to be the principal bankers of the English Crown, their presence in the British Isles continued. In 1342, early in the crisis of the Florentine companies that ended in the bankruptcy of the Peruzzi and Bardi in 1343 and 1346, respectively, Clement VI had given the Malabaila, Asti's leading merchant bankers, the monopoly on the transfer of the revenues collected throughout Christendom to the Apostolic Chamber.[275] Later that year he had ordered Bernard de Sistre, his collector in England, to deliver all funds to be transferred to the Holy See to the Malabaila's representative in London.[276]

Florentine merchant-bankers played a key role in the financing of royal diplomacy, especially in the preparation of missions, throughout the 1320s and 1330s. The Exchequer documents up to c.1339 contain many references to money being advanced by them to messengers and envoys of all ranks shortly before their setting out for the curia. Moreover, the Bardi's international banking network could be relied upon for the provision with cash of diplomats already in Avignon as well as of the *procurator regis*.[277]

While payments by the Bardi accounted for approximately one-third of the total sum paid to English envoys staying abroad in the first ten years of Edward III's reign,[278] there is no evidence of the merchants performing similar functions in the 1340s, and it seems certain that the company ceased to give financial support to royal diplomacy some six or seven years before its collapse in April 1346. This would underpin what has been noted elsewhere about the general trend in the company's English activities: the Bardi's lending to the Crown escalated between 1336 and 1338, but dropped from Michaelmas 1338 to February 1340. Around that time they also discontinued the transfer of money collected in the British Isles to the Apostolic Chamber. Lending after 1340 was relatively modest, and ceased to be of any vital importance after 1343.[279]

Later in that decade, and throughout the 1350s, the representatives of the Malabaila company in London, Pietro and Daniele Provana of Carmignano (Tuscany), rendered services to the Crown as money-changers. In this capacity they were sometimes involved in the preparation of missions to Avignon.[280] At the same time other members of the company gave financial support to English diplomats when they had arrived at the curia. It was to the Malabaila that Guy de Brian and Michael Northburgh turned in December 1354 when they found that even before the official beginning of the Anglo-French peace talks their stay in Avignon was already putting some

strain on their resources.[281] Without the 90 li. that Lodovico
Malabaila advanced to him, Philip Codeford in 1356–7 might have
found it impossible to carry out the task he had been assigned: the
renewal of the privileges of the king's free chapels at Westminster and
Windsor.[282] On behalf of the prince of Wales another member of the
company delivered 300 florins (47 li.) to Nigel Loring when he was
at the papal court in the winter of 1361–2; the money was to be used
'for certain business that the prince had in hand there'.[283]

What merchants and popes had in common was that they pursued
interests spanning the whole of Latin Christendom, requiring
elaborate networks of communication. Each of the Italian companies
had its own informants, correspondents and messengers at its disposal.
Associates as well as couriers of the Bardi, Peruzzi, Buonaccorsi,
Acciaiuoli and Malabaila could be found travelling between the
branches of their firms in Cyprus, Spain, England and southern Italy.
Secular and ecclesiastical rulers attempted to use these private
networks for their own ends to obtain information and to have oral
and written messages conveyed.[284]

Considering the range of their activities, it is not surprising that
members and couriers of the Italian companies should sometimes have
been suspected of collaboration with the enemy by either side in the
Anglo-French conflict. Accusations of this kind occurred early in the
war: in November 1338 Benedict XII was forced to intervene with the
authorities in Paris on behalf of the Bardi, Peruzzi and Acciaiuoli. Some
of their *socii* had been imprisoned in France, and their money and goods
confiscated, on a charge of collusion with Edward III (who at that time
was staying in the Netherlands, making financial preparations for the
invasion of France).[285] After the collapse of the Bardi, the Malabaila,
their successors in England, became a target for similar allegations,
which again triggered papal protests. On 12 April 1347 Clement VI
wrote to the French king, recommending to him Giacomo Malabaila,
whom Philip suspected of having had letters from England and Flanders
transported to the papal city by his couriers. By way of reprisal,
Giacomo's representative in Paris, Bertrand Coquerant, had been
arrested and his goods confiscated. Giacomo, the pope asserted, had
done no more than to present entirely non-political letters relating to
certain English benefices.[286] In the summer of 1355 Antonio, Giacomo's
successor as head of the company, was arrested by French officials at
Villeneuve-lès-Avignon, apparently on similar grounds. Again, the
Holy See lodged its complaint.[287]

French suspicions of Italian merchants giving logistic or other support to English diplomacy were not always unfounded. The letter that John Offord wrote to the archbishop of Canterbury on 12 November 1344 shows that the English delegation at the First Avignon Conference had established contacts with the Bardi office in the city. We can see from this letter that Edward III's chief envoy had at some stage attempted to persuade members of the company to reimburse English *cursores* arriving in the city for their expenses, perhaps even to have letters taken back to England by the company's own messengers. He had also obtained information about the forthcoming arrival of John Thoresby and Ralph Spigournel from one Giacomo Nicholai, *magister in curia, societatis Bardorum*.[288] The perhaps most obvious example of Italian merchants becoming involved in Anglo-curial diplomacy is that of Pietro and Daniele Provana, who accompanied the papal collector Hugh Pelegrini from England to Avignon and back as Edward III's official *nuncii* in the autumn of 1352. The aim of their mission was to reach a compromise concerning the benefices of clergy not resident in England.[289] One *Johannes Phessane, mercator de societate Luc'* (possibly Giovanni Spiafame, one of the *socii* of the Society of the Spiafame[290]) received 4 li. 16s. 8d. from Bartholomew Burghersh the younger, Edward III's envoy to the court of Urban V, in the summer of 1366: he had seen to it that a number of letters found their way from Avignon to England.[291]

Between 1345 and 1362, when it went bankrupt, the Society of the Malabaila operated from Avignon, where its directors (Giacomo, then Guido and Antonio) were in almost permanent residence.[292] This meant that they and other family members were ideally positioned to assist English petitioners, which is known to have happened on at least four occasions: in late 1351 or early 1352, when Antonio Malabaila advanced 40 li. to Nicholas Hethe; in September 1354, when one *Mynotus Maillebaille* submitted a supplication on behalf of John Welwick, then at the curia; in March 1358, when Guido Malabaila presented a petition in favour of a clerk of the bishop of Winchester; and in May 1360, when Antonio Malabaila gave the same kind of assistance to two other English clerics.[293]

Our examination of the official, semi-official and unofficial channels of communication has shown that the work of the Crown's itinerant diplomats was supported by compatriots and anglophile foreigners both at the curia and in the papal city at large. Short-, mid- and long-term ties had to be created and maintained with these men, usually at considerable material expense, to facilitate the flow of diplomatic information. In what follows we will look, first, at the central problems of organization and logistics and, secondly, at the means and practices of communication.

Notes to Chapter 3

1. See Guillemain, *Cour pontificale*, 517.
2. VQ ii. 60 (Woodstock, 23 May 1320) and 130 (Eltham, 1–8 Sept. 1329).
3. Meeting in 1273: Michael Prestwich, *Edward I* (New Haven and London, 1997), 83. Edward VII's visit: by kind information of Mr Pat Corby, Chancery Assistant, British Embassy to the Holy See. According to Matteo Villani, Edward III contemplated visiting Avignon during his continental expedition of 1359–60 and sent envoys to make preparations, but Inncocent VI and the cardinals managed to dissuade him (Matteo Villani, *Cronica, con la continuazione di Filippo Villani*, ed. Giuseppe Porta (Parma, 1995), ii. 386).
4. Laurence Stone, 'Prosopography', in Gilbert and Graubard, *Historical Studies Today*, 107–40 (107).
5. Anthony Tuck, *Crown and Nobility: England 1272–1461*, 2nd edn. (London, 1999), 129–34.
6. Chris Given-Wilson, *The English Nobility in the Later Middle Ages: The Fourteenth-Century Political Community* (London and New York, 1987), 34; Andrew Ayton, 'Edward III and the English aristocracy at the beginning of the Hundred Years War', in Matthew Strickland (ed.), *Armies, Chivalry and Warfare in Medieval Britain and France* (Stamford, 1998), 173–206 (188, 192–3).
7. GEC vii. 401; *CCR 1337–9*, 41.
8. Grosmont: 1344. Fitzalan: 1355. See App. I, nos. XIII and XLIX/6.
9. Grosmont: GEC vii. 403; R II. ii. 1050, 1055, 1063, 1068. Fitzalan: *CPR 1338–40*, 112; Tout, *Chapters*, iii. 84; v. 322.
10. *CPR 1338–40*, 141–2.
11. For Fitzalan's service at Sluis see *CCR 1339–41*, 493–4, and le Baker, *Chronicon*, 70. See also Ayton, 193.
12. *RP* ii. 118.
13. Amiens: GEC vii. 403; Froissart, *Œuvres*, ii. 232. Negotiations in 1348: E 372/193, m. 34^v. Mission to Guines in Feb. 1353: E 101/313/19 (Grosmont) and E 101/313/18 (Fitzalan). Mission in Nov. 1353: E 101/313/14 (Fitzalan) and E 372/198, m. 39^v (Grosmont).
14. William Mark Ormrod, 'Edward III's government of England, *c*.1346–1356', D.Phil. thesis (Oxford, 1984), 109–13.
15. This analysis is based on the proceedings printed in *RP* ii.
16. Baron: Thomas Bradeston. Bannerets: Bartholomew Burghersh the elder. Knights: Richard de la Bere, Guy de Brian, William Burton, Richard Chamberlain, William de Cusance, Nicholas d'Amory, Thomas Fulnetby, Niccolò Fieschi, John Grey of Ruthin, Nigel Loring, Hugh Neville, Richard Spigournel, John Shoreditch.

17. Squires of the king's household: Richard de la Bere (*CPR* 1334–38, 172), Thomas Bradeston (*CPR* 1328–30, 146; *CPR* 1340–3, 82), Guy de Brian (BL Cotton Nero C VIII, fos. 225^v, 229^v, 231^r), Nigel Loring (ibid.), Hugh Neville (*CPR* 1334–8, 167). Knight: William de Cusance (BL Cotton Nero C VIII, fo. 230^v).

18. Chris Given-Wilson, *The Royal Household and the King's Affinity: Service, Politics and Finance in England, 1360–1413* (New Haven and London, 1986), 21–2, 204–12.

19. Malcolm G. A. Vale, *The Princely Court* (Oxford, 2001), 56–68.

20. Stanley B. Chrimes, *An Introduction to the Administrative History of Medieval England* (Oxford, 1952), 197.

21. Tout, *Chapters*, iv. 255

22. *HBC* 76; Given-Wilson, *Royal Household*, 9.

23. Tout, *Chapters*, vi. 46.

24. Given-Wilson, *Royal Household*, 10.

25. Chaplais, *English Diplomatic Practice*, 166.

26. *CPR* 1345–8, 373; *CPP* 154; Tout, *Chapters*, v. 360.

27. Councillor: *Register of Edward the Black Prince* (London, 1930–3), i. 119. Steward and surveyor: ibid. 48; Tout, *Chapters*, iii. 328; v. 439. Auditor: Tout, *Chapters*, iii. 328.

28. Loring as Edward's chamberlain: *Reg. Black Prince*, ii. 64, 94. Poitiers: Delachenal, ii, doc. XI.

29. *CPR* 1358–60, 329.

30. Bradeston: R II. ii. 1099. Neville: R III. i. 25. De Brian: Tout, *Chapters*, iv. 255. Burghersh: *Das deutsch–englische Bündnis von 1335–1342: I. Quellen*, ed. Friedrich Bock (Munich, 1956), doc. 593. In his accounts of his wages for serving on the council in the period from 1351 to 1355 (E 101/96/4–7) Burghersh appears as constantly involved in government work and court business: 'In the many ordinary tasks of administration no name occurs more frequently than his' (James F. Baldwin, *The King's Council in England during the Middle Ages* (Oxford, 1913), 89).

31. Bradeston: E 36/203, fos. 103^r, 122^r. De Brian: ibid., fo. 123^r. De Cusance: ibid., fo. 103^r. Loring: ibid., fo. 123^r.

32. De Brian: *CPR* 1345–8, 474; *CPR* 1348–50, 444. Burghersh: *RP* ii. 157–8; *CPR* 1325–8, 474. Burton: E 159/128, m. 110^r. Stafford: Tout, *Chapters*, v. 390 n. 2.

33. Loring: *Reg. Black Prince*, 136, 171; le Baker, 155. Stafford: Tout, *Chapters*, v. 390 n. 2.

34. Hainault: E 403/236. Paris: E 101/310/31 (MD no. XXX). Antoing: E 101/389/8, m. 25; R II. ii. 1168, 1169. See Henry Stephen Lucas, *The Low Countries and the Hundred Years War, 1326–1347* (Ann Arbor, 1929), 468–9, and Sumption, *Trial by Battle*, 381, 383, 385–6.

35. Burton: 1349: E 101/312/36 (MD no. CXXXVII), 1360: E 101/314/11 (MD no. CCVI). De Brian: Feb. 1353: E 101/313/17 (MD no. CLIX), Nov. 1353: E 101/313/13 (MD no. CLX).

36. Bordeaux: R III. i. 348. Brétigny: Loring: E 101/314/7 (MD no. CCV). De Brian: E 101/314/11 (MD no. CCVI). See also R III. i. 493–4.

37. E 101/313/6 (MD no. CXLIV) and E 101/313/5.

38. Burghersh: Hainault: see *Deutsch–englisches Bündnis*, docs. 12, 18; Frankfurt: Trautz, 282–4 and n. 220–2, 225. Burton: E 101/313/5 and E 101/313/9 (MD no. CLI).

39. Mission in 1327: E 101/309/37 (MD no. IV). For his confidential journey in 1330, which aimed at securing papal backing for Edward's assumption of personal rule, see BAV Barb. lat. 2126, fo. 12ʳ; *CPL* ii. 494–3; *CPR* 1327–30, 513; *Deutsch–englisches Bündnis*, 160–3; Charles G. Crump, 'The arrest of Roger Mortimer and Queen Isabel', *EHR* 26 (1911), 331–2.

40. E 159/117, m. 91ʳ.

41. For what follows, see in detail Karsten Plöger, 'Die Entführung des Fieschi zu Avignon (1340). Zur Entwicklung der diplomatischen Immunität in der Frühphase des Hundertjährigen Krieges', *Francia* 30/1 (2003), 73–105 (74–85).

42. Agostino Paravicini Bagliani, 'Innocent IV.', in *PE* ii. 790–3 (793).

43. Bernhard Schimmelpfennig, *Das Papsttum: Von der Antike bis zur Renaissance*, 4th edn. (Darmstadt, 1996), 223. On the Orsini popes and cardinals, see George L. Williams, *Papal Genealogy: The Families and Descendants of the Popes* (Jefferson, NC, and London, 1998), table IIIa, and 36–7, 41.

44. Giovanni: *CPR* 1338–40, 190; *The Register of John de Grandisson, bishop of Exeter (AD 1327–1369)*, ed. Francis C. Hingeston-Randolph (London, 1894–9), i. 58. Niccolò: Plöger, 'Entführung des Fieschi', 79–85, 95–7.

45. See App. IV.

46. Christopher T. Allmand, 'The civil lawyers', in Cecil Holdsworth Clough (ed.), *Profession, Vocation, and Culture in Later Medieval England* (Liverpool, 1982), 155–80 (155); Jean Dunbabin, 'Careers and vocations', in *The History of the University of Oxford*, i: Jeremy I. Catto (ed.), *The Early Oxford Schools* (Oxford, 1984), 565–606 (582).

47. John L. Barton, *Roman Law in England* (Milan, 1971), 27–8; id., 'The study of civil law before 1380', in Catto, 520–30 (522); Dunbabin, 576–8, 581–92.

48. *CPR* 1330–34, 437.

49. VM 2981.

50. *CPR* 1345–48, 80, 91; Baldwin, 82.

51. Thoresby: E 36/203, fos. 122ʳ, 139ʳ. Offord: ibid., fo. 134ᵛ.

52. Thoresby: C 76/12, mm. 3, 4, 7; C 76/13, m. 5; *CPR* 1338–40, 459.

53. E 36/203, fo. 134ᵛ; Tout, *Chapters*, iii. 160, and v. 17. See in detail above, Section 3.2.1.

54. *The Wardrobe Book of William de Norwell, 12 July 1338 to 27 May 1340*, ed. Mary Lyon, Bryce Lyon and Henry Stephen Lucas (Brussels, 1983), p. lxxxiv; E 36/203, fos. 7ʳ, 7ᵛ, 8ᵛ, 94ᵛ, 120ᵛ; *Treaty Rolls Preserved in the Public Record Office*, ii: *1337–1339*, ed. John Ferguson (London, 1972), ii, nos. 450, 713, 739–40; Tout, *Chapters*, iii. 98.

55. R III. i. 53; *HBC* 94.

56. R III. i. 85.

57. *CPR* 1345–8, 80; *CCR* 1346–9, 238: Tout, *Chapters*, iii. 169–70.

58. Offord: Tout, *Chapters*, iii. 170, and v. 22. Northburgh: Avesbury, 357.

59. Thomas F. Tout, 'The English civil service in the fourteenth century', *BJRL* 3 (1916), 185–214 (196).

60. Documents: Cuttino, *English Diplomatic Administration*, 43–4. See e.g. *CCR* 1333–7, 72, and R II. ii. 881. France: E 372/178, m. 42ʳ. Curia: 1334: E 372/178, m. 42ᵛ. Two missions in 1335: E 101/311/15 (MD no. LVII). 1342: C 70/18, m. 2; C 81/1331/45; C 81/1332/9; E 36/204, fo. 77ʳ; E 403/325C, m. 1; E 404/5/29; E 404/5/31.

61. Exchequer: Tout, *Chapters*, iii. 85 n. 6. Chancery: *CPR* 1334–38, 329.
62. C 70/17, m. 2 (18 Oct. 1340).
63. R II. ii. 1151; *HBC* 94.
64. Bertie Wilkinson, *The Chancery under Edward III* (Manchester, 1929), 72–3.
65. App. I, no. XVI/5; *CCR* 1343–6, 474.
66. Keeper of the great seal: R II. ii. 1231. Chancellor: *HBC* 86; Tout, *Chapters*, vi. 14.
67. Tout, *Chapters*, iii. 159; Wilkinson, 167. See e.g. *CCR* 1346–9, 605, and *CCR* 1349–54, 84, 619.
68. *CC* 177; *CCR* 1343–6, 661; *HBC* 86; Tout, *Chapters*, iii. 206, 160.
69. After the failure of the Anglo-French talks at Avignon in Feb. 1355, Brayton was sent to Pisa, where he met Emperor Charles IV. His letter of credence and a memoir of the negotiations are printed in Froissart, *Œuvres* (xviii. 362–5). See also Fowler, *King's Lieutenant*, 144–6.
70. Wilkinson, 81 and n. 2.
71. See e.g. R II. i. 549–51, 553–7, 560, 563–4, 575–6, 581–2; R III. i. 259, 328–9, 338, 341–2.
72. J. H. Johnson, 'The king's wardrobe and household', in Willard and Morris, 206–49, (226–7); Cuttino, *English Diplomatic Administration*, 152–3, 186; Chaplais, *English Diplomatic Practice*, 99–100.
73. Tout, *Chapters*, iii. 162; ibid. v. 18, 21.
74. *HBC* 94.
75. *CPP* 258, 288; Tout, *Chapters*, v. 112; Cuttino, *English Diplomatic Administration*, 173–4.
76. E 403/397, m. 31; Tout, *Chapters*, iii. 226.
77. Offord: mission to the Low Countries with Henry Burghersh, bp. of Lincoln, in 1337: E 101/311/31, fol. 6ᵛ (see Trautz, 250–60). Piers: France, 1333: E 372/178, m. 42ʳ. Carlton: Brabant, 1334: E 372/179, m. 40ʳ. Fastolf: Hainault, 1337: E 403/235.
78. SC 1/11, printed in Lescot, *Chronique*, app., doc. V.
79. VQ i. 60–1; Tout, *Chapters*, iii. 85 n. 6. Mission in 1330: R II. ii. 782; *CPR* 1327–30, 493.
80. BAV Barb. lat. 2126, fo. 76ʳ.
81. *CPR* 1350–4, 11.
82. Offord: Antoing, 1341 and 1342: E 101/389/8, m. 25 (cf. E 101/311/40 (MD no. LXXXIV)); R II. ii. 1168–9, 1175, 1177, 1185; *CPR* 1340–3, 255; *CCR* 1341–3, 195; Sumption, *Trial by Battle*, 381, 383, 385–6. Meetings with French diplomats in Flanders and Brabant, 1342: E 404/5/29; R II. ii. 1191, 1196; Tout, *Chapters*, v. 17–18. Member of the English delegation at Malestroit, Jan. 1343: *Cartulaire des comtes de Hainaut*, i. 198 n. 2; *CC* 130, 134; Tout, *Chapters*, iv. 111. Carlton: Calais and Brabant, 1348: E 372/194, m. 45ᵛ. Calais, Brabant and Flanders, Jan. 1349: ibid. Flanders, Mar. 1349: E 101/319/40 (MD no. CXXXI). Adam Hilton: Brétigny and Calais, May and Oct. 1360: R III. i. 493–4; *GC* vi, 172–3; Delachenal, ii. 197; Tout, *Chapters*, iii. 226, 229. Northburgh: Calais, Feb. 1353: E 101/392/12, fo. 37ᵛ. Calais, Oct. 1353: ibid. Calais, Mar. 1354: E 101/313/24 (MD no. CLXV).
83. Sept. 1348: E 101/312/33 (MD no. CXXIX). Mar. 1349: E 101/312/33 (MD no. CXXXII). May 1350: E 101/313/1 (MD no. CXL). June 1351: E 372/196,

m. 41^r. Aug. 1351: ibid. Feb. 1353: E 101/313/12 (MD no. CLVI). Nov. 1353: E 101/313/15. Mar. 1354: E 101/313/24.

84. Christopher R. Cheney, *Notaries Public in England in the Thirteenth and Fourteenth Centuries* (Oxford, 1972), 40–71, 135–6, 140; Patrick N. R. Zutshi, 'Notaries public in England in the fourteenth and fifteenth centuries', *Historia, instituciones, documentos* 23 (1996), 412–33 (421, 426–7).

85. Cheney, 62.

86. *CPR* 1354–8, 168. See App. I, no. LV.

87. For a full treatment of Branketre's career, see Pierre Chaplais, *Essays in Medieval Diplomacy and Administration* (London, 1981), ch. xxii: 'Master John de Branketre and the Office of Notary in Chancery, 1355–1375'.

88. E 101/313/22 (MD no. CLXVII), cf. E 372/202, m. 37^r. A transcript of the privileges for St George's Chapel is in ASV RS 27, fo. 110 (*CPP* 265–7).

89. R III. i. 284–5, cf. *Registrum Johannis de Trillek, episcopi Herefordensis*, ed. J. H. Parry (London, 1912), 225–7.

90. App. I, nos. LXIV, LXX, LXXIII (Hilton), XVIII (Ludeford), XXXVII (Askeby).

91. William A. Hinnebusch, *The Early English Friars Preachers* (Rome, 1951), 461; Bernhard Schimmelpfennig, 'Beichtvater', in *LexMA* i. 1819. England: Bede Jarrett, *The English Dominicans* (London, 1921), ch. vi. France: Robert-Henri Bautier, 'Confesseur du roi', in *LexMA* iii. 125–8, Georges Minois, *Le Confesseur du roi: Les Directeurs de conscience sous la monarchie française* (Paris, 1988), esp. ch. vii, and Xavier de la Selle, *Le Service des âmes à la cour: Confesseurs et aumôniers des rois de France du XIIIᵉ au XVᵉ siècle* (Paris, 1995), esp. ch. vi.

92. On their excursions into diplomacy, see Jarrett, 111–13, and in some more detail R. D. Clarke's unpublished 'Some secular activities of the English Dominicans during the reigns of Edward I, Edward II, and Edward III (1272–1377)', MA diss. (London, 1930), *passim*. See also William A. Hinnebusch, 'Diplomatic activities of the English Dominicans in the thirteenth century', *Catholic Historical Review* 28 (1942), 309–39; id., *Early English Friars Preachers*, 458–91; David Knowles, *The Religious Orders in England* (Cambridge, 1948–59), i. 167–70; Wright, 233–4. For a list of Friars Preachers who acted as royal confessors, see C. F. R. Palmer, 'The king's confessors', *The Antiquary* 22 (1890), 114–20, 159–61, 262–6.

93. Heinrich Denifle, 'Die Constitutionen des Prediger-Ordens vom Jahre 1228', *Archiv für Literatur- und Kirchengeschichte des Mittelalters* 1 (1885), 165–227 (194).

94. *Bullarium Ordinis fratrum praedicatorum*, ed. Thomas Ripoll and Antonius Bremond (Rome, 1729–40), vii. 24, cf. C. F. R. Palmer, 'King's confessors', 114–15.

95. Jarrett, 111–12; Knowles, i. 168.

96. *Deutsch–englisches Bündnis*, doc. 186 (Apr. 1337); R II. ii. 998–9 (Oct. 1337). On his career, see *BRUO* 2060, and C. F. R. Palmer, '*Fasti Ordinis Fratrum Praedicatorum*: The Provincials of the Friar-Preachers, or Black Friars, of England', *Archaeological Journal* 35 (1878), 134–65 (150–3).

97. E 101/311/38 (*EMDP*, doc. 377; MD no. LXXXII; E 372/185, m. 42^r). See also R II. ii. 1121, 1130, and Dau 742.

98. C. F. R. Palmer, 'King's confessors', 263–4; Alfred B. Emden, *A Survey of Dominicans in England Based on the Ordination Lists in Episcopal Registers (1268 to 1538)* (Rome, 1967), 68, 468.

99. Froissart, *Œuvres*, xviii. 211–15.
100. Reppes became honorary papal chaplain on this occasion (*CPP* 25).
101. 'Confessorem itaque nostrum fratrem Ricardum de Wynkeleye [...] cum quibusdam supplicationibus curam et salutem anime nostre [...] concernentibus ad sanctitatem vestram presenciam [...] duximus transmittendum' (C 70/18, m. 2).
102. Dau 742 (R II. ii. 1130); Déprez, *Préliminaires*, 305, 312.
103. See Section 2.3.1. Woderove accompanied William Bateman, Henry of Grosmont, Richard Fitzalan, Bartholomew Burghersh, Guy de Brian and Michael Northburgh to Guines in Nov. 1353 (C. F. R. Palmer, 'King's confessors', 263; cf. E 101/313/13, E 101/313/14, E 101/313/15, E 101/313/16, E 101/313/20 (MD nos. CLX–CLXIV).
104. App. I, nos. XLVIII/1–2.
105. Welwick: see E 372/202, m. 37ʳ: 'Idem [John Welwick] computat de diversis solutionibus et expensis suis factis in supradicta curia in prosecution diversorum graciarum regi a domino papa concessarum [...] ut in scriptura bullarum illarum et nota earundem graciarum pergameno [...] ac conducione nuncii pro eisdem bullis una cum aliis bullis subscriptis in Angliam deferendis, iuxta ordinacionem et avisamentum fratris Johannis de Woderove confessoris Regis.'
106. See DGM 1155.
107. De la Selle, 250–4. For instances of Dominican friars being employed as envoys by other medieval rulers, see Jarrett, 111–12.
108. Froissart, *Œuvres*, xviii. 211, 214; DGM 1155.
109. *RP* ii. 251–2
110. 'Sub illa per confessorem nostrum sanctitati vestre mentem nostram [...] aperuimus sub secreto' (C 70/25, m. 1).
111. Canon 21 of the Fourth Lateran Council (1215) had laid down the obligation of secrecy (*Constitutiones Concilii quarti Lateranensis*, ed. Antonio García y García (Vatican City, 1981), 68).
112. Peter Browe, 'Das Beichtgeheimnis in Altertum und Mittelalter', *Scholastik* 9 (1934), 1–57 (26–8, 52–3).
113. Hill, *King's Messengers: Contribution*, 87–103.
114. Ibid., app. I.
115. Ead., 'King's messengers in England', 67.
116. Ead., *King's Messengers. Contribution*, 89–90.
117. See App. I, nos. L–LV.
118. *Registres et letters des papes du XIIIᵉ siècle: Les Registres d'Innocent IV, , publiées ou analysées d'après les manuscrits originaux des Archives du Vatican et de la Bibliothèque Nationale*, ed. Élie Berger (Paris, 1884–1911), i, pp. xl–xli.
119. Advice to council: *Korrespondenz*, 225. De Monte and Wunstorp were received by Grosmont several weeks later, and the duke agreed to do what he could to help them (ibid. 234). Contact with Henry had probably been established with the help of *dominus Richardus de Anglia* (Richard Wimundewold?), the advocate of the Hamburg envoys between 1353 and 1355 (see Section 3.2.3.), who was present at the meeting.
120. CC 130. Guines: Bock, 'Some new documents', 93.
121. Georges Duby, *France in the Middle Ages 987–1460: from Hugh Capet to Joan of Arc*, trans. Juliet Vale (Oxford and Cambridge, MA, 1991; repr. 1999), p. xi.

122. Bernard Guenée, *States and Rulers in Later Medieval Europe*, trans. Juliet Vale (Oxford, 1985), 146.

123. Mattingly, *Renaissance Diplomacy*, 21.

124. Allmand, 'Civil lawyers', 158.

125. See *EMDP* doc. 239(b), iii, esp. 439–49. In his edition of the diplomats' dossier (Froissart, *Œuvres*, xviii, doc. LVIII) Kervyn de Lettenhove suppressed most of the legal citations and some key passages from the original text (cf. C. Taylor, 158). The envoys' sealed *cedula* delivered to Benedict XII and copied into the RV series (VM 2982 and *CPL* ii. 586–8) omitted all the arguments based on canon, civil and feudal law (see *EMDP* 438 n. 74).

126. Antony Black, *Political Thought in Europe, 1250–1450* (Cambridge, 1992), 9, 11; Grewe, 46–7.

127. Tout, 'English civil service', 197–8.

128. On the distinction between 'ascribed' and 'achieved' status, see Bryan S. Turner, *Status* (Milton Keynes, 1988), 3–5.

129. L. B. Dibben, 'Secretaries in the thirteenth and fourteenth centuries', *EHR* 25 (1910), 430–44 (432–3).

130. See esp. Guillemain, *Cour pontificale*, chs. VI–VIII. On the English, see ibid. 612–15.

131. Ibid. 329, 336, 344, 352, 369, 441, 447, 451, 454.

132. Ibid. 614.

133. Rudolf von Heckel, 'Das Aufkommen der ständigen Prokuratoren an der päpstlichen Kurie im 13. Jahrhundert', in *Miscellanea Francesco Ehrle* (Rome, 1924), ii. 290–321 (295–9). These *procuratores* are to be distinguished from the travelling envoys to whom the same term was applied, but who could also be called *nuncii*. While both kinds of proctors were administrators of the affairs of the represented, it may be argued that the resident curial proctor resembled more the *procurator litis* from post-classical Roman law, whose primary task was legal representation, than the *procurator negotiorum* occupied with more general administrative business (Feliciano Serrao, *Il Procurator* (Milan, 1947), 17; Queller, 'Thirteenth-century diplomatic envoys', 205). In this chapter I deal only with professional *procuratores* who were more or less permanently resident at the papal court (cf. Guillemain, *Cour pontificale*, 568).

134. See von Heckel, 300–13, and the historical and bibliographical overview in Andreas Sohn, *Deutsche Prokuratoren an der römischen Kurie in der Frührenaissance (1431–1474)* (Cologne, Weimar and Vienna, 1997), 61–70, esp. 61–7 and 63 n. 12.

135. Canon 37 (*Constitutiones Concilii quarti Lateranensis*, 79–80). See von Heckel, 312–13.

136. von Heckel, 313–15. On proctors' activities in specific curial departments, see Peter Herde, *Beiträge zum päpstlichen Kanzlei- und Urkundenwesen im dreizehnten Jahrhundert*, 2nd edn. (Kallmünz, 1967), 126–7 (Chancery), and id., *Audentia litterarum contradictarum. Untersuchungen über die päpstlichen Justizbriefe und die päpstliche Delegationsgerichtsbarkeit vom 13. bis zum Beginn des 16. Jahrhunderts* (Tübingen, 1969–70), i. 26–30 (*Audientia*); Franz Egon Schneider, *Die römische Rota: Nach geltendem Recht auf geschichtlicher Grundlage* (Paderborn, 1914), §11 (Rota); Emil Göller, *Die päpstliche Pönitentiarie von ihrem Ursprung bis zu ihrer Umgestaltung unter Pius V.* (Rome, 1907–11), i. 183–4 (Penitentiary); Mollat, *Papes d'Avignon*, 473, and Jean Favier, *Les Finances pontificales à l'époque du Grand Schisme d'Occident* (Paris, 1966), esp. 378–83 (*Camera Apostolica*).

137. Time limit: see the *Institutio cancellarie super petitionibus dandis et recipiendis* (c.1192–1236), printed in *Die päpstlichen Kanzlei-Ordnungen von 1200–1500*, ed. Michael Tangl (Innsbruck, 1894), 55, §12; Herde, *Beiträge*, 128–9.

138. Jane E. Sayers, 'Proctors representing British interests at the papal court, 1198–1415', in Stephan Kuttner (ed.), *Proceedings of the Third International Congress of Medieval Canon Law, Strasbourg, 3–6 September 1968* (Vatican City, 1971), 143–63 (144–5, 152–3).

139. Start of his career: see SC 1/50/29 (printed in Ch.-V. Langlois, 'Notices et documents relatifs à l'histoire du xiiie et du xive siècle', *Revue historique* 87 (1905), 55–79 (76–7)). The date of this letter is most probably 13 May 1308; Adam Orleton had been sent to the curia in mid-Apr. to promote the canonization of Thomas Cantilupe, the business referred to in William Ros's letter (R II. i. 43). Sapiti had been a notary from 22 Jan. 1304 on, when he was granted the *officium tabellionatus* while at Benedict XI's court in Rome (see *Registres et letters des papes du XIIIe siècle: Le Registre de Benoît XI: Recueil des bulles de ce pape, publiées ou analysées d'après le manuscrit original des archives du Vatican*, ed. Charles Grandjean (Paris, 1905), 277). On Sapiti, see also Wright, 110–11, and Patrick N. R. Zutshi, 'Proctors acting for the English petitioners in the chancery of the Avignon popes (1305–1378)', *Journal of Ecclesiastical History* 35 (1984), 15–29 (24–5).

140. Payments: VQ i. 45, 58, 125, 138, 141, 143, 147, 165, 178, 184, 188, 199, 222; Bishops: R II. i. 295, 407; R II. ii. 949; *Registrum Palatinum Dunelmense: The Register of Richard de Kellawe, Lord Palatine and Bishop of Durham, 1311–1316*, ed. Thomas D. Hardy (London, 1873–8), iv. 391–3; *The Register of John Kirkby, Bishop of Carlisle (1332–1352), and the Register of John Ross, Bishop of Carlisle (1325–1332)*, ed. Robin L. Storey (Woodbridge, 1993–5), i, no. 393. Bruce: R II. i. 443 (where Sapiti is explicitly mentioned as having diplomatic papers in his possession).

141. Endorsement: SC 7/25/7, 25/13, 24/5, BL MS Cotton Charter VI, 6 (see *Original Papal Letters*, nos. 109, 128, 147, 148). Scribe: see John Stratford's gift of 6 flor. to Sapiti's clerk Walter around Christmas 1322 (App. VII.2).

142. SC 1/34/176 and 55/47 (printed in Ch.-V. Langlois, 'Le fonds de l'*Ancient Correspondence* au *Public Record Office* de Londres', *Journal des Savants* (Aug. 1904), 446–53 (450), and id., 'Notices et documents', 77 n. 2).

143. Journeys to England in 1313 (CPR 1313–17, 45), 1314 (E 43/528; CPR 1313–17, 118), 1317 (CPR 1317–21, 16), 1325 (CPR 1324–7, 121, 125), 1334 (BAV MS Barb. lat. 2126, fo. 106^v; Johann Peter Kirsch, 'Andreas Sapiti, englischer Prokurator an der Kurie im 14. Jahrhundert', *HJb* 14 (1893), 582–603 (593–4); CPR 1330–4, 558; CPR 1334–8, 7), 1336 (CPR 1334–8, 316). Cooperation with English embassies: R II. i. 161, 197; E 101/309/27, m. 3 (John Stratford, 1322–3), BAV MS Barb. lat. 2126, fos. 183^v–184^r (William Trussell, Richard Bentworth, 1334), fo. 192^r (Laurence Fastolf, 1336), E 101/311/25 (Paolo Montefiore, 1337). Sapiti received the arrears of his wages as proctor through royal emissaries: C 62/114, m. 7 and E 404/3/19 (5 May 1339).

144. E 101/309/32, cf. E 372/177, m. 40^r. During his term as proctor Weston received the same annual emoluments as Sapiti: 50 marks and two robes at the value of 4s. each. Cf. similar payments to Sapiti: C 62/113, m. 6 and E 403/288, m. 20 (1336), and C 62/114, m. 7 and E 404/3/19 (1337).

145. Offord stayed with the king from 22 July 1338 to 22 Jan. 1339 (E 36/203, fo. 134^v). Appointment: *CPR* 1338–40, 197. The office of *procurator Regis* did not become vacant because of Sapiti's death, as Kirsch (595–6) assumes. The Florentine was still alive in May 1339, when he received a payment of 58 li. from the Wardrobe through his son Otto (E 36/203, fo. 174^v).

146. E 36/203, fos. 28^r, 121^r, 134^v; E 101/389/8, m. 7. Orders of payment: *CPR* 1338–40, 197, and E 36/203, fo. 121^r. During that period a number of messengers were sent to Avignon with instructions for him while others carried back his reports: ibid., fos. 104^v, 116^r, 118^v.

147. C 70/17, m. 2. Thormerton as notary public: *CPL* ii. 207. Residence in Avignon: ASV Coll. 52, fo. 62^r. Thormerton acted as proctor of the hospital of Ledbury in 1323 (*Original Papal Letters*, doc. 125), of the abp. of York in 1326 (VQ i. 76), of the bp. of Worcester in 1328 (VQ i. 213), of the Benedictine priory of Luffield (*Original Papal Letters*, docs. 154–5), the prior of Winchester in 1332 (*Chartulary of Winchester Cathedral*, ed. Arthur W. Goodman (Winchester, 1927), doc. 177), and of the bp. of Worcester in 1340 (*Calendar of the Register of Wolstan de Bransford, Bishop of Winchester, 1339–49*, ed. Roy Martin Haines (London, 1966), 55).

148. *CPR* 1340–3, 109–10.

149. Thormerton was provided with firewood, hay, grain and wine by the Apostolic Chamber on 6 July 1342 and 12 Aug. 1343 (ASV IE 207, fos. 3^v, 26^r). Mentioned as royal proctor: *CPP* 4, 16–17.

150. C 70/25, m. 2 (royal letter to Innocent VI, 16 Mar. 1353), where Thormerton is merely referred to as *lator presencium*.

151. ASV IE 207, fo. 49^r (under the date 9 Sept. 1344), *CPP* 263–4.

152. In mid-Feb. 1329 Setrington was sharing a room with an English colleague (ASV Coll. 52, fo. 177^r).

153. *CPR* 1340–3, 109–10.

154. *CPP* 10, ASV IE 242, fo. 15^v (VQ v. 112). *Memorials of St Edmund's Abbey*, ed. Thomas Arnold (London, 1890–6), iii. 68–73, is an account of Setrington's proceedings in Bateman's suit against the abbot of Bury St Edmund before Cardinal Aimeric de Châtelus in Apr. 1346.

155. E 403/347, m. 25.

156. Queller, 'Western European diplomacy', 205.

157. Thomas Frenz, *Papsturkunden des Mittelalters und der Neuzeit* (Stuttgart, 1986), §141.

158. *Original Papal Letters*, nos. 227, 230, 232–3. On Middelton's activities in Avignon in 1349–50, see Zutshi, 'Proctors', 22. Around 1 Sept. 1351 he was 'prosecuting the king's business in the Roman court' (*CPP* 219). He was probably the man that John Faukes was supposed to contact when sent to Avignon in Apr. 1352 'cum quibusdam litteris directis procuratori Regis ibidem tangentibus appropriacionem ecclesiarum ad liberas capellas Regis Westm' et Wyndesore' (E 403/362, m. 7). Middelton died in Avignon *a*.8 Feb. 1355 (*CPP* 278).

159. Zutshi, 'Proctors', 22. Zutshi cites the erosion of linguistic barriers as another factor, pointing out that French rapidly replaced Italian as the predominant vernacular language at the papal court. However, it is worth remembering that 'French' in this context meant Occitan (or, to be more precise, its Gascon dialect), which shared some phonetic characteristics with the French spoken in

northern France and England but was closer to Catalan and Italian (Nathaniel B. Smith, 'Occitan Language', in *Medieval France: An Encyclopedia*, ed. William W. Kibler and Grover A. Zinn (New York and London, 1995), 677–80). It is to be doubted, therefore, that this linguistic change made the work of English proctors and envoys at Avignon much easier (cf. Section 5.3.).

160. DGM 4231.

161. Bernard Barbiche, 'Les procureurs des rois de France à la cour pontificale d'Avignon', in *Aux origines de l'état moderne: Le Fonctionnement administratif de la papauté d'Avignon* (Rome, 1990), 81–112.

162. Mattingly, for instance, declares forcefully that 'the diplomatic procurators were not residents, and the resident ones were not diplomats' (*Renaissance Diplomacy*, 67). See also Queller, 'Thirteenth-century diplomatic envoys', 198 n. 16, 205, and *Office of Ambassador*, 75–84.

163. Zutshi, 'Proctors', 26.

164. William Urban, 'The diplomacy of the Teutonic Knights at the curia', *Journal of Baltic Studies* 9 (1978), 116–28 (127).

165. Göller, esp. i. i. 132–53, i. ii. 48–95, 96–131, and 172–80; Johannes Vincke, 'Volkstum und Apostolische Pönitentiarie im 14. Jahrhundert', *Zeitschrift der Savigny-Stiftung für Rechtsgeschichte* 58, Kanonistische Abteilung 27 (1938), 414–44 (422–34); Timotheus Majic, 'Die Apostolische Pönitentiarie im 14. Jahrhundert', *RQ* 50 (1955), 129–77 (146–50, 160–70); Filippo Tamburini, 'La Penitenzieria apostolica durante il papato avignonese', in *Aux origines de l'état moderne*, 251–68 (265).

166. Eclescliff: Wright, app. 5, no. 23. Wisbech: 'engaged in the king's service' by June 1318 (*CPL* ii. 172); see also Clarke, 144–6, 158, 164–6. Wrotham: *EMDP*, doc. 367; R i. ii. 964; R ii. i. 127–8, 399, 424, 443; VQ iii. 24; CCR 1302–7, 212, 213; *CPR* 1301–7, 238; *BRUO* 2095–6. Cf. Wright, 102.

167. Reppes: DGM 2802; *CPL* 33; VQ iii. 391 (*Johannes de Anglia*). Charnels: ASV Coll. 456, fo. 22ᵛ; VQ iii. 391, 419 (*Guillelmus de Anglia*); *BRUO* 2161. Ringstead: Coll. 456, fo. 23ᵛ; ASV IE 199, fo. 32ᵛ; IE 267, fo. 180ᵛ; *CPP* 249, 285, 290; VQ iii. 614. See also Walter Gumbley, *The Cambridge Dominicans* (Oxford, 1938), 17–18. Wyghen: ASV RA 135, fo. 33ʳ; *CPP* 370. De Tatenhall: *CPP* 370; *BRUO* 2221. Appleby: *CPP* 396; *BRUO* 2144. Brinton: RA 198, fo. 422; IE 304, fo. 159; VQ vi. 19, 280; *BRUO* 268–9. On Brinton's career in Avignon and Rome, see Mary Aquinas Devlin, 'Bishop Thomas Brunton and his sermons', *Speculum* 14 (1939), 324–44 (328–9), and Knowles, ii. 58–60.

168. Guillaume Mollat, 'La diplomatie pontificale au XIVᵉ siècle', in *Mélanges d'histoire du moyen âge dédiés à la mémoire de Louis Halphen* (Paris, 1951), 507–12 (507); Majic, 175–7; Guillemain, *Cour pontificale*, 338.

169. R II. ii. 1118 (giving a wrong date); cf. C 70/17, m. 3, and E 101/389/8, m. 17. De Lisle received grain, wine, firewood and money for clothes in 1342 and 1344 (ASV IE 207, fos. 25ᵛ, 45ʳ; VQ iii. 235). See also CC 172. On the early years of de Lisle's turbulent career, see John Aberth, *Criminal Churchmen in the Age of Edward III: The Case of Bishop Thomas de Lisle* (University Park, PA, 1996), 7–10. De Lisle was consecrated bp. of Ely at Avignon on 24 July 1345 and lived there in exile following his banishment from England in 1356 until his death on 23 June 1361 (James Bentham, *The History and Antiquities of the Conventual and Cathedral Church of Ely*, 2nd edn. (Norwich, 1812), 162; Aberth, 161–80).

170. R I. ii. 981–2 (the letter is mistakenly dated 1306; cf. *Original Papal Letters*, 91–2).
171. R III. i. 27.
172. C 70/25, m. 1; *CPL* 620, cf. R III. i. 388.
173. Chaplain: *CPP* 25. Penitentiary: see above.
174. 1346: DGM 2802; *CPL* 29, 33. 1347: DGM 3212; *CPL* 33.
175. Henry Harowdon, John Bateman, Walter Segrave (Raymond des Farges, *c.*1342–4; ASV IE 207, fo. 15^v; *CPP* 31, 103, *CPL* 203–4; IE 207, fo. 48^r), Robert Thresk (Bertrand de Déaulx, *c.*1344–50; IE 207, fos. 48^v, 125^r; *CPL* 415), Thomas Bridekirk (Talleyrand de Périgord, *c.*1350–3; *CPP* 207–8, *CPL* 498), William Kellesey (Guillaume Court, *c.*1354–7; *CPP* 257, 301), Thomas Mount (Pierre de Monteruc, *c.*1361–2; *CPP* 382, 393), William Clinton (Rinaldo Orsini, *c.*1362; *CPP* 387).
176. The sources do not always distinguish clearly between a *capellanus commensalis* and a *capellanus honoris* (Guillemain, *Cour pontificale*, 367). The former actually fulfilled an office at the papal court and were maintained by the pope, whereas the latter were simply aggregated to his household *honoris causa*, enjoyed certain privileges and exemptions, but did not perform any specific function in the curia. English papal chaplains under Clement VI: Richard Havering (*CPP* 10), Robert Stratford (ibid. 14), John Reppes OC (ibid. 25), Thomas Multon (ibid. 40), John Stacy OESA (ibid. 110), William Beaufitz OFM (*CPL* 27, 230), Robert Nacton OSB (DM 1552; *CPL* 250), Thomas Bradpole OP (ASV Coll. 456, fo. 6^r), Robert Southeby OSA (ibid., fo. 6^v; *CPL* 282), Peter Driffield (Coll. 456, fo. 7^v), Roger of Chester OFM (ibid., fo. 8^v), Reginald Manning OSA (ibid., fo. 9^r; *CPP* 179), John Worthin OP (Coll. 456, fo. 9^r), Walter of Cambridge OESA (ibid., fo. 9^v), Benedict Boder OSA (ibid., fo. 12^r), William Stanwoulde OESA (ibid., fo. 13^r), William Kirketon OSA (ibid., fo. 44^r; *CPL* 461) and William Askeby (*CPL* 462). Under Innocent VI: William Edingdon (*CPP* 290), Hugh de Chyntriaco (ibid. 285), William Northores (*CPL* 595), John Heventre OSA (ASV RA 144, fo. 296r), John Clement (*CPP* 348), John Woderove (ibid. 356). On the office of papal honorary chaplain, see Karl Heinrich Schäfer, 'Päpstliche Ehrenkapläne aus deutschen Diözesen im 14. Jahrhundert', *RQ* 21 (1907), 97–113, Gerd Tellenbach, 'Beiträge zur kurialen Verwaltungsgeschichte im 14. Jahrhundert', *QF* 24 (1932–3), 150–87 (161–3), Bernard Guillemain, 'Les chapelains d'honneur des papes d'Avignon', *MAHEF* 64 (1952), 217–38, and Charles Burns, 'Vatican sources and the honorary papal chaplains in the fourteenth century', in Erwin Gatz (ed.), *Römische Kurie. Kirchliche Finanzen. Vatikanisches Archiv* (Rome, 1979), i. 65–95. On the *capellani commensales*, see Guillemain, *Cour pontificale*, 367–70, and Bernhard Schimmelpfennig, 'Die Organisation der päpstlichen Kapelle in Avignon', *QF* 50 (1971), 80–111. On English honorary chaplains under Urban V, see Anne-Marie Hayez, 'Anglais présents à Avignon dans le pontificat d'Urbain V', in *La 'France anglaise' au moyen âge* (Paris, 1988), 569–86 (581).
177. P. Gillet, 'Avocat', in *DDC* i. 1524–35 (1527).
178. Guillemain, *Cour pontificale*, 573.
179. *CPP* 13, see *BRUO* 2230–1.
180. De la Mare: DM 2009 (*CPL* 40). I have not found any other evidence for de la Mare's mission (App. I, no. XXIII), nor have I been able to identify this envoy. Truce: R III. i. 188. It seems that eventually only Robert Askeby

travelled to Avignon (E 403/347, m. 26; DGM 4313). Spain: R III. i. 219.

181. E 403/368, m. 16 (where he is incorrectly referred to as *auditor in curia Romana*).

182. R III. i. 284–5; cf. *Reg. Trillek*, 225.

183. On Richard Drax, see *BRUO* 2171. A *dominus Richardus de Anglia* (Richard Wimundewold?) was employed as advocate by the Hamburg envoys from Feb. 1343, receiving a regular salary and monetary gifts (*Rechnungsbücher*, intro. 55, text 34–5, 42–4, 48–9, 51–2, 54–7 *passim*; *Korrespondenz*, docs. 175, 177). Both this *dominus Richardus* (or *Richardus maior*) *de Anglia* and Richard Drax (*magister Richardus de Anglia*) worked for the council's second major embassy between 1353 and 1355 (*Rechnungsbücher*, intro. 56, 89, text 93, 105–7, 109, 111; *Korrespondenz*, docs. 252–3; *Prozeß-Schriftgut*, 326), the use of the comparative *maior* is probably to be explained by the fact that *dominus Richardus* had taken up residence in Avignon nine years before Drax. *Dominus Richardus* was ill in Sept. 1355 and probably died in the following year (*Korrespondenz*, doc. 259; *Rechnungsbücher*, intro. 56). ASV Coll. 53, fo. 114^r, mentions a *hospicium quondam Richardi Anglici in curia advocati* near St Geniès in the city centre (28 Mar. 1357). Richard Drax died on 16 Apr. 1361. A third *Richardus de Anglia* identified by Schrader never existed (for both see the letter in *Rechnungsbücher*, intro. 97–9, which has been misdated by Schrader, cf. *Korrespondenz*, doc. 249; for Drax's correct date of death, see also VQ vii. 357).

184. E 101/313/39 m. 2: 'Item cuidam servo Ricardi Drax pro quodam nuncio, xxiij s. iiij d.' (later crossed out).

185. Thresk: proctor by 1334 (*Literae Cantuarienses: The Letter Books of the Monastery of Christ Church, Canterbury*, ed. Joseph B. Sheppard (London, 1887–9), ii. no. 549; cf. *CPP* 105, VQ v. 140, 153), advocate by 28 Sept. 1348 (ASV IE 207, fo. 125^r), dead by 11 Oct. 1350 (VQ v. 441). Sallowe: advocate by 3 Sept. 1349 (*CPP* 174), dead by 31 Jan. 1352 (*CPP* 224; cf. *BRUO* 2212). Michel: advocate by 1 Mar. 1357 (*CPP* 298; E 30/1367), dead by 28 Sept. 1361 (*CPP* 377, 382; cf. *BRUC* 405). Appelby: proctor by 1350 (VQ v. 225, 258, 281, 303, 316, 324; VQ vii. 139), advocate by 1363, vacated 1365 (The Queen's College, Oxford, 2 P, fo. 111^r; *CPP* 396; *BRUO* 40). See also Anne-Marie Hayez, 582–3. On 7 Jan. 1346 an advocate from northern Italy, Francesco da Ravenna DCL, became a clerk of Edward III's household (*CPR* 1345–8, 22).

186. Guillemain, *Cour pontificale*, 345.

187. Charles Lefebvre, 'Rote Romaine (Tribunal de la Sainte)', in *DDC* vii. 742–71 (743); Pierre Jugie, 'Consistory', in *PE* i. 413–15 (415).

188. Lefebvre, 'Rote Romaine', 744; Bernard Guillemain, 'Les tribuneaux de la cour pontificale d'Avignon', in *L'Église et le droit dans le Midi (XIIIᵉ–XIVᵉ s.)* (Toulouse, 1994), 339–60 (343–4).

189. *Desiderata Curiosa*, new. corrected edn., ed. Francis Peck (London, 1779), i. 240. Bateman was a chaplain by 1330 and an auditor by 1332 (*CPL* ii. 323, 356, 380, 525). On his career before 1344, see John W. Clark, 'Bishop Bateman', *Proceedings of the Cambridge Antiquarian Society* 9, NS 3 (1894–8), 297–336 (306–7), Alexander H. Thompson, 'William Bateman, Bishop of Norwich, 1344–1355', *Norfolk and Norwich Archaeological Society* 25 (1933–5), 102–37 (103–7), and *BRUC* 44.

190. Schröder, nos. 40, 55.

191. John H. Baker, 'Dr Thomas Fastolf and the history of law reporting', *Cambridge Law Journal* 45 (1986), 84–96 (88–90).

192. *BRUO* 2174 mentions him as studying in Italy in mid-Dec. 1332.
193. Emmanuele Cerchiari, *Capellani papae et apostolice sedis auditores causarum palatii apostolici seu Sacra Rota, ab origine ad diem usque 20 Septembris 1870* (Rome, 1919–21), ii. 26; first mentioned as auditor: *CPL* ii. 547.
194. Baker, esp. 85–7.
195. *Decisiones*: Gero Dolezalek, 'Quaestiones motae in Rota: Richterliche Beratungsnotizen aus dem vierzehnten Jahrhundert', in Stephan Kuttner and Kenneth Pennington (ed.), *Proceedings of the 5th International Congress of Medieval Canon Law* (Vatican City, 1980), 100–37 (102 n. 23); André Fliniaux, 'Contribution à l'histoire des sources du droit canonique. Les anciennes collections de "Decisiones Rotae romanae" ', *Revue historique de droit français et étranger* 4e sér., 4ème année (1925), 61–93, 382–410 (390–1). *Memoriale*: William A. Pantin, *The English Church in the Fourteenth Century* (Cambridge, 1955), 21 n. 3 and 205–11.
196. ASV Coll. 456, fo. 7^r; Hermann Hoberg, 'Die Rotarichter in den Eidregistern der Apostolischen Kammer von 1347–1494', *QF* 34 (1954), 159–72 (163). According to Cerchiari (ii. 31), Simon's brother Thomas Sudbury DCL was an auditor under Innocent VI.
197. *CPP* 80; *Memorials of St Edmund's Abbey*, iii. 63–5. After Bateman's death Sudbury was one of the executors of his will (VQ vii. 88, 97).
198. *CPL* 304–5; Thompson, 119.
199. *CPP* 349. According to Cerchiari (ii. 30), William Lynn became an auditor under Clement VI, but there is no evidence for this. Emden assigns him to Oxford because he was one of the university's proctors in a dispute before Bishop Bateman in 1345 (*Munimenta Academica, or Documents Illustrative of Academical Life and Studies at Oxford*, ed. Henry Anstey (London, 1868), i. 149). This view is challenged by Baker (89 n. 36), who holds that the engagement resulted from a connection with Bateman rather than with Oxford.
200. Paxton and Cambridge: *BRUC* 445; Paxton and Bateman: *CPP* 9; curial career before *c*.1361: *CPL* ii. 366 (appointed notary public by John XXII, 11 Nov. 1331), VQ iv. 72 (proctor of the bp. of Worcester, 1339), *CPP* 2 ('proctor general of suits in the papal palace', 1342). Paxton held the post of auditor until his death (ASV Instr. Misc. 2239; *BRUC* 445). He died on 6 Nov. 1370 and was buried in the chapel of the Cistercian convent of Sainte-Catherine in north-eastern Avignon (today 8 rue Sainte-Catherine, where his gravestone can still be seen) (Anne-Marie Hayez, 585–6).
201. Stratton in Avignon, 1354–5: E 101/313/21, m. 2. He received wine from the papal Chamber on 17 Nov. 1358 and 11 Sept. 1360 (ASV IE 199, fos. 98^r, 126^v). Auditor: ASV RA 198, fo. 410^r; *CPP* 395, 421. See also *BRUC* 562, and Anne-Marie Hayez, 583–4.
202. Cerchiari, ii, doc. 50. See also *Die päpstlichen Kanzlei-Ordnungen*, 34.
203. *Die päpstlichen Kanzlei-Ordnungen*, docs. 52 and 53. Hence the designation *capellanus et familiaris domini nostri pape* for Thomas Fastolf and Simon Sudbury (ASV IE 207, fos. 134^v, 167^r).
204. Guillemain, *Cour pontificale*, 347–8; Hoberg, 161.
205. See ASV IE 162, fos. 54^v, 47^v; IE 165, fo. 54^v; IE 220, fo. 72^v; IE 216, fo. 83^v; IE 282, fo. 154^v; IE 286, fos. 154^r, 168^r (by kind information of Dr Stefan Weiß).
206. Guillemain, *Cour pontificale*, 352.

207. Id., 'Tribuneaux', 346.
208. *Korrespondenz*, doc. 97 (against Konrad von Hetfeld, from 4 or 5 May 1341); *Prozeß-Schriftgut*, pp. 123, 168 (against Hamburg cathedral chapter, from 14 Nov. 1341 and again 19 July 1342–21 Feb. 1345), doc. 28 (chapter against council and two former councillors, 11 Nov. 1342–5 Dec. 1347), p. 235 (Erich against Johann Holdenstede, 4 Feb. 1343–27 Mar. 1348), docs. 18–19 (council against chapter, about the costs of the main suit of 1338–45 (cf. docs. 12, 13, 15), 4 Apr.–2 May 1345).
209. Fastolf's *notarius* or *scriba* was Philip Bugwell, an Exeter clerk (*Rechnungsbücher*, 33, 42, 43, 45, 50, 55; cf. *Prozeß-Schriftgut*, docs. 14, 28c–e). Legal restrictions: Lefebvre, 'Rote Romaine', 745.
210. First contacts: *Rechnungsbücher*, intro. 98; Sudbury as auditor in these cases: *Korrespondenz*, docs. 215, 217; Payments and gifts: *Rechnungsbücher*, 89, 105–6 (Christmas 1355), 107 (Easter 1355), 111, 125–6, and *Korrespondenz*, doc. 191.
211. Cf. Guillemain, *Cour pontificale*, 351–4.
212. VM 2871, 2876, 2877, 2926; Dau 766, 768 (*CPL* ii. 582–3); Lucas, *Low Countries*, 419.
213. VM 2926; *EMDP*, doc. 239a (*CPL* ii. 583–4). Arrival in Avignon (12 Dec. 1340): Dau 801 (*CPL* ii. 589).
214. *CPR* 1340–3, 109–10; Thompson, 105.
215. Offord and Thoresby: C 70/17, m. 3; E 101/389/8, m. 7. Attorneys: *CPR* 1340–3, 158.
216. R II. ii. 1199; Déprez, 'Guerre de cent ans', docs. I–III. On 1 Oct. 1342 Edward III thanked the cardinals for their letters he received through Bateman (C 70/18, m. 1).
217. Stay in England: VQ iii. 196. In early June 1342 Bateman met an English delegation going to Flanders and Brabant somewhere at the Channel coast (Déprez, *Préliminaires*, 394–6).
218. First journey to England (late Jan.–7 Apr. 1344): DGM 607–8, 610, 657, 759, 794, 957 (*CPL* 5, 7, 8); CC 157 (arrival in London, c.2 Feb.); E 101/312/7, m. 1 (departure from London in the company of Andrew Offord, 13 Mar.); Thompson, 133. Second journey (c.23 May–11 July 1344): DGM 957 (*CPL* 9, 182); Thompson, 133
219. Froissart, *Œuvres*, xviii. 231–3, contains two reports by William Bateman to Edward III, written between 26 and 29 Nov. 1344. The draft agreement taken to England by Hugh Neville around 29 Nov. bore Bateman's seal (ibid. 234).
220. Guillemain, *Cour pontificale*, 348.
221. R III. i. 19.
222. Froissart, *Œuvres*, xviii. 204, 209.
223. 'Vos scire cupimus, quod ad instanciam nostram in omnibus et singulis causis vestris coram domino Thoma auditore pendentibus XIIII. die mensis Junii proxime preteriti fuit conclusum et expedicioni causarum predictarum dictus auditor intendere non potuit, primo propter vacaciones generales, item quia palacium dominorum auditorum fuit destructum et ipsi caruerunt sedibus per omnes vacaciones, item quia rex Anglie ipsum specialem una cum aliis in negociis suis contra regem Francie deputavit ambassiatorem, de quo negocio fuit apud papam et cardinales multum occupatus' (*Korrespondenz*, 119).
224. R III. i. 161.

225. GLG 1946–7; R III. i. 328; Avesbury, 458. See also *Reg. Grandisson*, ii. 1187–8.
226. R III. i. 356 (27 May 1357).
227. 1354: R III. i. 284–5. 1356: ibid. 341; E 403/385 mm. 9, 16. 1357: R III. i. 348.
228. *Calendar of Letters from the Mayor and Corporation of the City of London, c.AD 1350–1370* (London, 1885), 8–9. Cf. R III. i. 255. On Hethe, see *BRUC* 302.
229. On 28 Jan. 1355 William Tydirleye, proctor of the prior of Christ Church, Canterbury, added information on the political situation in the Empire to a report to his client: Charles IV had been crowned king of Italy in Milan three weeks earlier, and his imperial coronation in Rome was believed to be just a matter of time (*Literae Cantuarienses*, ii, no. 810).
230. De Lisle (Ely): 1345 (*HBC* 244). De Tatenhall (Ossory): 1361–2 (*HBC* 369). Ringstead (Bangor): 1357 (*HBC* 291). Bateman (Norwich): 1344 (*HBC* 262). Fastolf (St Davids) 1352–3 (*CPL* 462; *HBC* 297). Lynn (Chichester): 1362 (*HBC* 239). Sudbury (London): 1361–2, (Canterbury): 1375 (*HBC* 258, 233).
231. A. Molien, 'Cardinal', in *DDC* ii. 1310–39 (1317–18); Mollat, *Papes d'Avignon*, 497–503; Charles Lefebvre, 'Les origines et le rôle du cardinalat au moyen âge', *Apollinaris: Commentarius canonicus* 41 (1968), 59–70; Schimmelpfennig, *Papsttum*, 154–5, 216, 227.
232. On the judicial, administrative and advisory functions of the cardinals, see Johann Baptist Sägmüller, *Die Thätigkeit und Stellung der Cardinäle bis Papst Bonifaz viii, historisch-canonistisch untersucht und dargestellt* (Freiburg, 1896), 46–96, 101–13; Paul Maria Baumgarten,*Untersuchungen und Urkunden über* die Camera collegii cardinalium *für die Zeit von 1295–1437* (Leipzig, 1898), passim; Mollat, 'Contribution', 80–112, 566–86, 593; Guillemain, *Cour pontificale*, 225–51; Lefebvre, 'Origines et rôle', 68–9.
233. R i. ii. 998.
234. Bertrand de Poujet, card. bp. of Ostia, and Jean de Comminges, card. bp. of Porto, are referred to as *bonus*, Gaucelme de Jean Duèsne, card. bp. of Albano, even as *optimus*, while Annibaldo da Ceccano, card. bp. of Tusculum, is described as *malus* (*Rechnungsbücher*, intro. 89–90).
235. 'Dominis infrascriptis scribantur bene littere supplicatorie' (ibid., intro., 89 and n. 1; cf. *Korrespondenz*, doc. 200).
236. Aquitaine: *Gascon Rolls Preserved in the Public Record Office, 1307–1317*, ed. Yves Renouard (London, 1962), p. xxv and nos. 1120–1, 1123–4. King's clerk: *CPR 1313–17*, 79. Payment of Gaucelme's annual pension by Richard de Bury and John Shoreditch in Sept. 1333: E 101/386/11, m. 1.
237. R II. i. 421 ('Attendentes laudabilia merita quibus venerabilis pater Bertrandus [...] noscitur insigniri, necnon et locum praecipuum quem nobis in nostris agendis in curia Romana et alibi tenet et tenere potuit in futurum intime considerantes'). Payments of his pension through English envoys: E 372/177, m. 40ʳ (William Weston, 1326); E 101/309/37 (Bartholomew Burghersh, 1327), E 101/386/11, m. 1 (John Wawayn, 1333).
238. E 101/386/11, m. 1; cf. E 43/104.
239. *Calendar of Chancery Warrants*, 338.
240. Wright, 119. Wright found evidence of at least eighteen cardinals pensioned by the English Crown out of a total of some seventy cardinals who lived during the pontificates of Clement V and John XXII (ibid. and app. 3, nos. 2, 3, 5, 7, 11, 17–23, 28, 29, 34, 38, 39, 41).

241. Annibaldo da Ceccano, Gaucelme de Jean Duèsne, Bertrand de Montfavès, Pierre de Montemart, card. p. of S Stephanus in Coelio Monte, Napoleone Orsini, card. d. of S Adrianus. See ibid., app. 3, nos. 5, 17, 22, 23, 28.

242. There had been one exception, however: on 27 Dec. 1341 the king had confiscated a Lincolnshire prebend held by Élie Talleyrand de Périgord, card. p. of S Petrus ad Vincula, because Talleyrand was suspected of supporting the French crown (R II. ii. 1184). In the Easter Parliament of 1343 he was branded as 'le plus fere Enemye qe soit en la Courte, et plus contrair a les busoignes nostre Seigneur le Roi' (RP ii. 144).

243. R II. ii. 1218.

244. R II. ii. 1223, cf. E 159/119, m. 136^v (de Jean).

245. Section 2.3.2.

246. R II. ii.1192 (13 Apr. 1342); R III. i. 28 (21 Jan. 1345). An extension was granted on 6 Oct. 1345 (ibid. 61).

247. R III. i. 154. Renewal in 1350: CPR 1348–50, 448; R III. i. 200.

248. R II. ii. 1141, cf. CCR 1341–3, 218, 443. This was a conversion into a grant for life of a one-off concession made in the summer of that year (ibid. 1133, 1135). Renewal of the grant (2 June 1342): R II. ii. 1199. On 18 Apr. 1343 Edward forbade a group of Flemish and Italian merchants to demand such payments from the cardinal or his officials (ibid. 1222).

249. R II. ii. 1227.

250. Ibid. 1234 (20 Sept. 1343).

251. R III. i. 29–30.

252. E 159/126, m. 21^r.

253. CCR 1349–54, 431; cf. E 159/128.

254. CPR 1348–50, 191. Three years later Clement VI once more tried to persuade Edward III to permit Pierre Roger de Beaufort to enjoy the fruits of his benefices 'cum idem cardinalis prefati regis honorem zelatus fuerit et zeletur' (DGM 5079, 5 Oct. 1351).

255. Da Ceccano and des Farges pointed out that the pope-elect had chosen them for this task: 'Qui, sciens nos vestrae serenitati stricta amicitia fore conjunctos et speciales honoris regii zelatores, nos ad se vocavit [...] nobisque dixit quod vestrae serenitati scribere deberemus' (R II. ii. 1194). Their messengers received 5 li. each for bringing the news of Clement's election to England (ibid. 1199). They received their money on 6 June 1342 (E 403/326, m. 15). Poncio Dynant, a valettus of Cardinal des Farges, had taken Edward's congratulatory letter to Avignon a fortnight earlier (R II. ii. 1195; E 404/5/29).

256. Froissart, Œuvres, xviii. 206.

257. R III. i. 41 (26 May 1345).

258. App. V. Cf. Wright, 122 and app. 4.

259. The same is true of English envoys' letters of credence. It was customary for medieval diplomats to carry multiple credentials, addressed to influential members of the recipient's entourage (Queller, Office of Ambassador, 113). In Anglo-papal diplomacy the obvious addressees would be cardinals from whom the Crown could expect some measure of support to its interests. See e.g. C 70/17 (inserted pages), C 70/19, m. 4; C 70/21, m. 3; C 70/22, m. 2; R II. ii. 1118; R III. i. 145; EMDP, doc. 45.

260. Promoted by Benedict XII: Bertrand de Déaulx (1338). Promoted by John

XXII: Gaucelme de Jean Duèsne and Gailhard de la Mothe (1316), Pierre Després (1323), Giovanni Colonna and Pedro Gomez da Barroso (1327), Jean de Comminges (1329), Élie Talleyrand de Périgord (1331), Annibaldo da Ceccano (1333). Promoted by Clement V: Raymond Gulhem des Farges (1310).

261. Gaucelme de Jean: vice-chancellor under John XXII, 15 Sept. 1316–9 Jan. 1319 (Paul Maria Baumgarten, *Von der apostolischen Kanzlei: Untersuchungen über die päpstlichen Tabellionen und die Vicekanzler der Heiligen Römischen Kirche im XIII., XIV. und XV. Jahrhundert* (Cologne, 1908), 96–9). Grand penitentiary from *c.*1327 (*VPA* ii. 219). Gailhard de la Mothe: see *VPA* ii. 229–31. Pierre Després: vice-chancellor, 20 Apr. 1325–7 May 1361 (Baumgarten, *Von der apostolischen Kanzlei*, 104–7). See also *VPA* ii. 245–8.

262. On Talleyrand de Périgord, see *VPA* ii. 272–83, and Zacour, *passim*. He had owed his promotion to a strong recommendation on his behalf by Philip VI, and for most of his long curial career was known as a staunch anglophobe (Zacour, 5–6, 10, 20–1; Guillemain, *Cour pontificale*, 248; Wrigley, 'Conclave and electors', 69). However, his relations with Edward III improved markedly after a personal visit to England in 1357–8 (Zacour, 59–63).

263. E 404/3/17.

264. DGM 839, 911, 1078, 1496, 2823.

265. R II. ii. 1207, 1210.

266. VQ iii. 233, 289, 324, 360, 389, 418; DGM 839, 1496. On the doorkeepers of the papal palace, see Guillemain, *Cour pontificale*, 418–19, and Mollat, *Papes d'Avignon*, 467.

267. R II. ii. 1221.

268. E 403/338, m. 14, E 403/344, m. 28; C 62/126, m. 4.

269. DGM 5079, in which de Saint-Martial is referred to as 'negotium non solum regiorum, sed Anglicorum omnium apud nos director et promotor'.

270. VQ iii. 27, 43, 60, 93, 118, 158, 201, 233, 271, 289, 324, 360, 389, 918.

271. 'Sire, jeo entenks que vous aiderets que le conseil pense par temps [...] de la dette [...] de Piers de Seint-Marcel et de Piers de Poddinghake, com estoit acorde devaunt mon departir' (Froissart, *Œuvres*, xviii. 215).

272. Edmund B. Fryde, 'Italian merchants in medieval England, *c.*1270–*c.*1500', in *Aspetti della vita economica medievale* (Florence, 1985), 215–31 (221–4); Edwin S. Hunt, 'A new look at the dealings of the Bardi and Peruzzi with Edward III', *Journal of Economic History* 50 (1990), 149–62 (151).

273. Yves Renouard, *Les Relations des papes d'Avignon et les compagnies commerciales et bancaires de 1316 à 1378* (Paris, 1941), 125, 130–8, and *Recherches sur les compagnies commerciales et bancaires utilisées par les papes d'Avignon avant le grand schisme* (Paris, 1942), 12; Guillemain, *Cour pontificale*, 588–9.

274. E. Russell, 'The Societies of the Bardi and Peruzzi and their dealings with Edward III, 1327–45', in George Unwin (ed.), *Finance and Trade under Edward III* (London, 1962), 93–135 (104–7 and 118–19).

275. ASV RV 138, nos. 501–4 (cf. Renouard, *Relations*, 116, 200, 444–5). On the family's history, see Mario Chiaudano, 'Note sui mercanti astigniani: I Malabaila', *Bollettino storico-bibliografico subalpino* 41, NS 5 (1939), 213–28. Comparatively little is known about the Malabaila's business activities (Renouard, *Recherches*, 44–5).

276. Cf. Renouard, *Relations*, 205–8.

277. See *Registrum Ade de Orleton, episcopi Herefordensis, AD MCCCXVII–MCCCXXVII*, ed. Arthur T. Bannister (London, 1908), 131–2 (Adam Orleton, 1320), E 101/309/32 (William Weston, 1326, 1328); E 101/310/40 (Richard de Bury, 1333), E 101/311/15 (John Piers, 1338). Royal proctor: *CCR* 1337–9, 3, *CCR* 1333–7, 247 (Andrea Sapiti); E 361/2, m. 38^r, E 361/3, m. 15^r (John Offord).

278. 645 li. 5s. 6d. out of 2,041 li. 18s., according to Larson, 'Payment', 407–8.

279. Edmund B. Fryde, 'The financial resources of Edward III in the Netherlands, 1337–40 (2nd part)', *Revue belge de philologie et d'histoire* 45 (1967), 1142–1216 (1146, 1153, 1159). Transfer of funds: Renouard, *Relations*, 138. Activities after 1343: Russell, 98.

280. Daniele Provana: E 403/343, m. 12, E 403/344, mm. 19, 28, E 403/347, mm. 2, 22, 25, E 403/368, m. 23, E 403/371, mm. 18, 20, 24, 28. Missions to Avignon: 'Magistro Michaeli de Northburgh procuratori Regis in curia Romana in denariis solutis Danieli Pruan' pro escambio c li. in auro eidem magisto Michaeli liberatum super feodo suo, xvj s. viij d.' (E 403/347, m. 25; 18 Aug. 1349), 'Petro Prouan mercatori. In denariis sibi liberatis in persolucione lxxv s. xj d. quos ipse solvit cuidam nuncio nuper misso versus curiam Romanam cum litteris domini Regis de excusacione adventus Justic' domini Regis versus curiam predictam, lxxv s. xj d.' (E 403/385, m. 15; 24 Nov. 1356).

281. E 101/620/9 (de Brian's account): receipt of 220 li. 'per manus societatis de Maillebaille' (cf. E 403/375, m. 18).

282. C 62/135, m. 1.

283. *Reg. Black Prince*, iv. 305.

284. Yves Renouard, 'Comment les papes d'Avignon expédaient leur courier', *Revue historique* 180 (1937), 1–22 (17–19); id., *Relations*, 385–401; id., 'Information et transmission des nouvelles', in Charles Samaran (ed.), *L'Histoire et ses méthodes* (Paris, 1961), 95–142 (107–9, 121–3).

285. *CPL* 571–2.

286. Clement's letter: DGM 3224. The details of the case are described in some more detail in Philip's letter ordering Coquerant's release and the restoration of the goods (*Documents parisiens du règne de Philippe VI de Valois (1328–1350), extraits des registres de la Chancellerie de France*), ed. Jules Viard (Paris, 1899–1900), ii. 367). The bp.-elect of Lincoln (*esleu de Nicole*) mentioned in the letter is not, as Viard believes, Thomas Bek, but John Gynwell, provided on 23 Mar. and consecrated on 23 Sept. 1347 (*HBC* 255).

287. GLG 1635–6. Antonio Malabaila remained imprisoned for at least seventeen months (ibid. 2486).

288. Messengers: 'Socii Bardorum nolunt solvere cursoribus pro suis expensis aliquid nisi de eo ipsis voluero respondere. Propterea mitto meos nuntios meis sumptibus successive' (Froissart, *Œuvres*, xviii. 228). Thoresby and Spigournel: ibid. 229.

289. The group left England in early Sept. (*CPR* 1350–4, 325) and arrived in Avignon before 22 Oct. 1352 (*CPL* 469). Their return journey began around 11 Nov. 1352 (DGM 5446–8, 5450, 5457).

290. Yves Renouard, 'Compagnies mercantiles lucquoises au service des papes d'Avignon', *Bollettino storico lucchese* 11 (1939), 42–50 (44–5).

291. E 101/315/16.

292. Renouard, *Relations*, 105, 110.

293. 1351: *Calendar of Letters*, 8–9. 1354: E 101/313/22. 1358: *CPP* 328. 1360: ibid. 355.

CHAPTER 4

Organization

4.1. The Problem of Security

4.1.1. Diplomatic immunity

The immunity of the envoy and his entourage, residence, papers and
means of transport and communication from local jurisdiction,
together with the duty of the receiving government to accord special
protection to his dignity and security, constitute the most fundamental
feature of diplomacy.[1]

In theory, those who set out to the Roman court on diplomatic
business in the fourteenth century were among the best-protected
travellers of their time. Clerical envoys could invoke canon 15 of the
Second Lateran Council (1139) to claim physical inviolability; by
any aggression against secular or regular clerics was punished by
anathema *ipso facto*.[2] A number of later decretals commented on this
canon and clarified it further; generally, the higher the rank of the
victim, the more severe was the penalty imposed on the culprit.[3] Both
Roman civil law, as codified under Justinian, and medieval canon law
emphasized the inviolability of the diplomatic representative, his right
to safety from any hindrance or violence, and attributed to him a
quasi-sacral status (*sanctitas legatorum*); an attack on him was equivalent
to an attack on the *ius gentium*.[4] In addition, envoys to Rome or
Avignon were eligible for the same special protection that had been
granted to all travellers to the curia by Boniface VIII in 1302–3:

Declaramus [...] omnes [...] qui [...] incolis im-perii, regnorum seu terrrarum
suorum, vel transeuntibus per ea [...] ad Sedem venientibus [...] vel
redeuntibus ab eadem, equitaturas limitant, vel subtra-hunt que deferunt seu
reportant, pro suis opportunitatibus vel expensis, vel quevis alia res et bona,
aut aperiunt litteras vel auferunt, seu taxant numerum personarum vel
familiarum seu quantitatem expensarum aut evectionum, vel alias [...]
talibus venientibus vel redeuntibus impedimentum vel obstaculum praestare

praesumunt, impeditores fore ad dictam Sedem venientium et redentium ab eadem, et anathematis et excommunicationis sen-tentiam incurrere supra-dictam, ipsosque sic ligatos a sacramentorum perceptione nunciamus exclusos.[5]

[The following persons we declare hinderers of those coming to or returning from the Holy See, and impose upon them the sentence of anathema and excommunication: all those who limit the number of horses used by the inhabitants of the Empire, its realms and lands, or by those who pass through these territories on their way to or from the curia; furthermore, all those who, for the sake of their own profit, seize what these persons are taking to the curia or bringing back from there, or any other of their belongings, or who seize or open their letters, or restrict the number of persons or their retinues, or the amount of their expenses or means of transport, and all those who otherwise dare create direct or indirect obstacles for those travelling to and returning from the Holy See. Such persons we declare excluded from receiving the sacraments.]

For English envoys to the Roman court, the privilege of 1302–3 meant that, unlike their colleagues travelling to other destinations, they could, in theory, rely at all stages of their journey on the 'total protection' provided by a host whose sphere of influence was coextensive with Western Christendom.

The ultimately theological doctrine of the *sanctitas legatorum* laid more emphasis on the origins of diplomatic immunity, and on the sanctions against those who violated it, than on its practical purpose. But there were also more pragmatic grounds for the pope to insist that anyone, cleric or layman, envoy or private petitioner, should be able to travel to his court without fear of molestation. In 1339 the English knight Robert Littlebury and his companions were waylaid near Valence and subsequently imprisoned in Philip VI's castle at Beaucaire, south of Avignon. In his letter of protest to the French court, Benedict XII deplored that, in the light of recent events, many pilgrims and other *romipetentes* had decided not to make the dangerous journey to Avignon and the papal court. He declared that the maintenance of free access to the curia (referred to elsewhere as the *communis patria*[6]) had to be in the interest of any Christian concerned about his spiritual well-being. Moreover, he pointed out that any interruption of the stream of visitors threatened to create a potentially dangerous information deficit: without visitors, no news from the trouble spots of Europe; without news, no papal mediation; without mediation, no peace.[7] In the sixteenth century, in the context of the transition from a theological to a rational and pragmatic basis for diplomatic immunity, this argument, the 'theory of functional necessity', began to occur in the writings of theorists on international law. According to it, a diplomat's freedom of movement and communication and his immunity from local jurisdiction are essential prerequisites if he is to perform his functions fully, and if a constructive dialogue between states is to be maintained.[8]

A second pragmatic consideration that today ensures that it is exceptionally rare for international actors not to honour a diplomat's immunity is the principle of reciprocity. In a situation where both parties involved in a diplomatic dialogue have reason to fear the other's reprisals against their representatives, respect for diplomatic immunity is in their mutual interest.[9] That such considerations were not at all alien to medieval practitioners of diplomacy follows from a passage in John Offord's letter to the archbishop of Canterbury of 12 November 1344. It had come to Offord's attention that during a session of the consistory on the previous day an influential figure, probably a cardinal, had recommended harsh measures against the members of Edward III's delegation if Clement VI's two nuncios, Niccolò Canali and Pedro Alfonso, should be imprisoned on their arrival in England.[10] This rumour, and the realization that his own position in Avignon would become untenable if open conflict between the papacy and the English Crown (*guerra inter sacerdotium et regnum*) should break out, prompted Offord to ask the king for his immediate recall. It never came, nor was Clement VI prepared to release him, as Offord repeatedly requested. In mid-March 1345, when news had arrived about the cancellation of Henry of Grosmont's and Bartholomew Burghersh's projected mission to the curia, and when the war was about to be resumed, Offord and William Bateman, together with 'many other Englishmen staying at the papal court', made hasty preparations for their return.[11]

4.1.2. Safe conduct

If, in theory, the inviolability of Edward III's envoys to the curia was guaranteed not only by Roman and canon law precepts, but also by practical imperatives, this was not always deemed sufficient in everyday practice.

To messengers, some degree of security will have been afforded by the royal arms painted on the boxes or pouches in which they carried their letters, a visible expression of their status.[12] Presumably, higher-ranking envoys were not so readily identifiable as such, and needed other forms of protection. The term *conductus* (safe conduct) first appeared around the turn of the millennium in continental sources. All the various forms of safe conducts that developed during the Middle Ages had one thing in common: they offered, for a limited time, protection to people on the move who had reason to fear for their safety.[13] They were often granted to individual travellers of high rank and/or special status, whose protection was in the special interest of the ruler of the lands that they intended to cross. This type of *conductus* could take two different forms: its receiver could be given an armed escort (a 'physical' or 'human' safe conduct) or a document authorizing his free passage (a written safe conduct, sometimes referred to as *littere* or *breve de salvo conductu*[14]). Whatever the form, its giver assumed responsibility for the security of the traveller and his possessions.[15]

Although the Chancery at Westminster did occasionally issue safe conducts to English envoys going abroad or foreign envoys returning home,[16] there is no evidence of such documents being drawn up for Englishmen going to Avignon in the period under investigation. Resembling, as they did, letters patent of recommendation and credence, they were probably not considered sufficiently effective for this particular purpose. It seems that instead, if deemed necessary, letters of safe conduct were invariably procured from the French or the papal chancery, or from both; English envoys did not hesitate to state extra expenses for them in their accounts.[17] At the same time, we know that safe conducts were never issued indiscriminately and as a matter of course; rulers would decide from case to case whether they would grant them or not.[18] In view of these facts, we need to ask in which situations Edward III's envoys to Avignon tried to obtain them.

The English and Vatican sources show that during the pontificates of Clement VI and Innocent VI there were three main periods in which letters of safe conduct were requested by the English king and granted by the pope or the French king: 1343–4, 1348–50 and 1354. Following the truces or preliminary peaces of Malestroit (19 January 1343), Calais (28 September 1347) and Guines (6 April 1354), preparations were made for grand embassies to Avignon, the sending of which appeared too risky without prior written guarantees of their security.

Three different methods of giving written safety guarantees to

Edward's envoys were applied during these periods. The pope could have his own safe conduct issued by his chancery and have it taken to England by his couriers or by returning royal envoys. Such documents provided protection for the whole duration of a mission, from the day the diplomats left London to the day of their return.[19] Secondly, he could send a request for a 'one-way' safe conduct, sealed with the great seal of France, to the French king and/or his chancellor. If granted, it would be valid either for a journey from England to the curia or for a journey back north.[20] While these first two types of safe conduct contained a definite promise of security for as long as their recipients were staying in France and Avignon, safe conducts of the third type more resembled letters of recommendation (*littere recommendatorie*) in form and contents.[21] These were accompanying letters patent of safe conduct given to individuals shortly before they departed from the curia. In the course of their homeward journey such documents would have to be produced on demand, with the degree to which they took effect depending on the secular or ecclesiastical lord through whose territory their bearer was travelling.[22]

It is difficult to observe any clear patterns with regard to the issue of these documents. Safe conducts of the third type, those that Englishmen received from the papal chancery before starting their homeward journey, seem to have been readily available. Whether they were worth the additional expenses, or whether the money to be spent on scribes' fees could be better used for other purposes, will have been for the individual envoy to decide. Nicholas d'Amory and Thomas Fulnetby, for example, considered it prudent to invest some money in papal safe conducts in July 1357, as did William Burton in May 1360. What is striking is that safe conducts of the first and second categories occurred relatively seldom. We may assume that the time and administrative effort required to have them drawn up and sent to England was justified only in those cases where they were intended as a protection for larger and higher-ranking embassies, like the one headed by Henry, duke of Lancaster in 1354. Writing to the duke in May 1354 in response to his request for a letter of safe conduct, Cardinal Guy de Boulogne, then staying in Paris, promised to arrange for a draft to be sent to England for inspection, and, if necessary, correction, which was later to be followed by a final version stating the names of Edward III's envoys to Avignon and the size of their retinues.[23]

In the aftermath of the abduction of Edward III's envoy Niccolò

Fieschi from his lodgings in Avignon in the early hours of Good Friday 1340, two remarkable innovations in diplomatic practice were introduced that gave a unique status to English envoys to the Holy See, albeit in only a few, isolated cases.[24] These, however, are worth a more detailed discussion.

The truce of Malestroit had ended Edward III's short and unsuccessful Breton campaign.[25] Its terms were surprisingly favourable to the English, whose territorial gains in the duchy were to be left untouched. But the agreement stipulated that envoys from both sides arrive at the papal court by 8 September to negotiate for a final peace, and this was certainly not in the short-term interest of Edward, who intended to launch a follow-up campaign as soon as possible. What is more, he was probably hoping to be able to induce Clement VI to revise his policy regarding provisions in return for an English participation in the peace process.[26]

During the spring and summer of 1343 the king used every possible pretext to delay the dispatch of his envoys to Avignon. One strategy was to insist on legal technicalities: Philip VI's letters of safe conduct were repeatedly criticized as having been drawn up in the wrong form, or as generally ineffective.[27] In a letter taken to Avignon by Andrew Offord in July 1343 Edward made his first reference to Fieschi's abduction in more than three years. He refused to send his delegation unless Clement VI gave a written guarantee that effectively rendered it impossible to arrest its members and start legal proceedings of any kind against them during their stay in the curia:

Sanctitatem vestram [...] supplicamus, quatinus literas apostolicas speciales protectionis et defensionis vestrae et sedis apostolicae, ac salvi et securi conductus, tam pro dictis nunciis nostris, familiis, et rebus suis quam pro alligatis, amicis et fidelibus nostris, eorum nunciis, et rebus suis, ad sanctitatis vestrae curiam, occasione dicti tractatus, simul, vel separatim, venientibus, ibidem morantibus, et exinde redeuntibus; Et quod nec dicti nuncii, alligati, amici, et fideles nostri, nec aliquis eorum, vel familiarum suorum, in quacumque causa, beneficiali, civili, vel criminali, personali, reali, sive mixta, seu alia qualicumque, seu quovis colore, ex officio, seu ad partis instantiam, occasione cujuscumque obligationis, ex debiti causa qualicumque, seu cujuscumque contractus [...] aliave quacumque de causa, citentur, conveniantur, moneantur, arestentur, capiantur, excommunicentur, suspendantur, aut interdicantur, nec alio quocumque modo graventur, set ab omni vexatione et molestatione, in sic eundo, morando, et redeundo, tam in Romana curia quam alibi, liberi sint penitus et quieti.[28]

[We supplicate Your Holiness that special apostolic letters guaranteeing your protection and that of the Holy See, and of safe conduct, be written for our said envoys and their retinues and belongings as well as for our allies, friends and followers, their envoys and their belongings, coming to your court together or separately on the occasion of the said negotiations, and staying and returning from there. Furthermore, we supplicate Your Holiness that neither our said envoys, allies, friends and followers nor any one of them or their men be summoned, cautioned, arrested, seized, excommunicated, suspended, placed under interdict, or otherwise distressed, in any beneficial, civil, criminal, personal, real, mixed or any other case, be it under some pretext, *ex officio*, or at the instance of a third party, on the grounds of any obligation, because of any debt or in any other case, but that in going, staying and returning, both at the Roman court and elsewhere, they be entirely free from all persecution and molestation.]

Clement VI, eager as he was for the conference to begin as scheduled, responded by having a safe conduct in the desired form written on 1 August. Its first part was designed to ensure the physical safety of the English delegation on its way to the papal city and back. The kind of protection offered here was actually nothing new, and was based on Boniface VIII's bulls of 1302–3; anyone found guilty of laying hands on Edward's diplomats, or opening their correspondence, would face instant excommunication and condemnation:

Nos [...] omnes et singulos predictos nuncios, clericos et laicos, ex causa tractatus hujusmodi ad nostram presenciam destinandos, volentes cum omnibus familiis, rebus et bonis suis, que secum deferent, in veniendo ad Sedem predictam et eandem presenciam, ibidem morando et inde recedendo, plena securitate gaudere, ipsos sub nostra et ejusdem Sedis protectione suscipimus speciali, statuentes ac eciam decernentes quoscumque injuriatores, moles-tatores, offensores, captivatores aut spoliatores eorum, quamdiu in itinere veniendi et recedendi predicto, eciam pace predicta reformata vel non reformata, fuerint, aut moram in eadam curia propter hoc traxerint, excom-municationis et alias penas et sentencias, que adversus illos qui venientes ad Sedem prefatam, vel recedentes ab ea injuriis seu dampnis afficiunt, aut captivatores, spoliatores vel detentores eorum per nos et predecessores nostros, Romanos Pontifices, promulgate sunt generaliter incursos.[29]

[We take all of the said envoys and each of them individually, clerics and laymen, who are to be sent to us in connection with these negotiations, into our special protection and into that of the Holy See, desiring that they enjoy, with all the members of their retinues and all their belongings, full security in coming to the said See and into our presence and in staying and returning from there. What is more, we decide and decree that all those who harm, molest, offend, seize or rob them while they are on their way to the curia, returning from or staying there in connection with the peace negotiations (regardless of whether or not the peace has been renewed), have, in general, incurred excommunication and the other penalties and sentences that we ourselves and our predecessors have published against those who harm, injure, seize, rob or detain such persons coming to or returning from the said See.]

The real novelty lay in the second part of Clement's letter of safe conduct, which contained an almost verbatim copy of Edward's original request of 6 July. It amounted to nothing less than a written guarantee of full immunity: Edward III's envoys to Avignon became immune, in their persons and in their property, from actions in the law courts of Avignon and other cities, and from all other forms of interference. The only restriction was that this protection referred only to acts committed or debts contracted *before* their mission, not, as had originally been demanded by the king, during their actual stay in Avignon:

Et insuper eisdem nunciis [...] concedimus, quod, durante prosecutione negocii antedicti, ipsi vel familiares commensales eorum, clerici vel laici ex quacumque, sub quovis colore, ex officio seu ad partis instanciam occasione promissionum, obligationum contractuum [...] que ante iter eorum arreptum facta, habita vel commissa dicerentur, nullatenus citentur, conveniantur, moneantur, arrestentur, capiantur, excommunicentur, suspendantur, vel interdicantur, aut contra eos quomodolibet procedatur, sed ab omni molestatione ac vexatione in sic veniendo, morando et recedendo, tam in eadem Romana curia, quam alibi sint liberi penitus atque quitti.[30]

[And moreover we grant these envoys that they and their men be they laymen or clerics, are in no way to be summoned, cautioned, arrested, seized, excommunicated, placed under interdict or be taken legal action against, be it under some pretext, *ex officio* or at the instance of a third party, on the grounds of any promises or contractual agreements said to have been made before their journey. They are, for the duration of the aforementioned business, to be entirely free from all molestation and persecution in thus coming, staying and returning, both at the Roman court and elsewhere.]

Roman civil law offered a precedence for such a reformulation of the principle of diplomatic immunity. Eleven centuries earlier the legist Ulpian (d. 228) had come to the conclusion that while emissaries (*legati*) from the provinces and *municipia* of the Empire were justiciable at Rome for offences committed during their missions to the city, this was not the case with respect to offences committed prior to it. They should have the right to demand that any lawsuits concerning these be handled by the courts of their provinces and *municipia* alone.[31] Although this privilege, the *ius revocandi domum*, originally referred to the Roman *legati*, not to the emissaries of foreign rulers, it was in at least two instances transferred to the diplomatic world of medieval Europe. Around 1263 it found its way into *Siete Partidas* of Alfonso X 'the Wise' of Castile-León (1252–84), where it served to establish the inviolability of Moorish envoys.[32] Secondly, as has been shown by D. Queller, the exemption of envoys from the jurisdiction of the receiving court, as far as acts committed before their missions were concerned, was a principle adhered to by the Venetian authorities prior to 1343.[33] But not even Queller's exhaustive study mentions a written guarantee of the kind demanded in 1343 as a precondition for a continuation of contacts between Westminster and Avignon. Incidentally, Edward's demands of 6 July were not too far-fetched: had Avignon not, in Clement VI's own propaganda, become the 'New Rome'?[34]

Needless to say, Clement VI yielded to the king's demands only grudgingly. They could not but cause offence to him, implicitly casting doubt, as they did, on his capacity to offer protection to travellers moving within his sphere of influence—an essential component of what constituted 'power' in the Middle Ages, and a topos of the praise of rulers and their good governance since time immemorial.[35] In his letter of 1 August Clement pointed out that nobody had ever dared demand such guarantees from a Supreme Pontiff.[36] It had so far always been sufficient for himself and his predecessors to enforce the laws introduced by Boniface VIII.

Diplomatic immunity was certainly not 'invented' in the aftermath of the Fieschi affair; it was merely restated, with recourse to Roman law doctrines, as an exemption from the jurisdiction of the law courts of Avignon and of the territories to be crossed during the long and dangerous journey there and back. Subsequent English embassies could build up on this: new-style safe conducts were granted in August 1343 and in the autumn of 1344, as part of the preparations for the First Avignon Conference. According to two papal letters English diplomats in the curia had even dared to dictate these safe conducts to the scribes of the curial chancery![37]

In the winter of 1354–5 the duke of Lancaster and the earl of

Arundel requested the pope to grant the members of their retinues protection against any form of prosecution and hindrance. What they had in mind, however, was not letters of safe conduct granting partial immunity of the kind written in 1343–4. Their men were to be treated by the curial authorities as if they were not at all present at the papal court (*ab ipsa curia personaliter absens*). Innocent VI granted their petition on 29 January 1355.[38] This is nothing other than an early, if not the earliest, explicit formulation of the legal fiction of exterritoriality: during their stay in the curia the English envoys and their retinues would be treated, with respect to matters of jurisdiction, as if they were actually residing outside the papal city.

The development of the concept of exterritoriality has traditionally been seen as belonging into the context of the disintegration of the medieval *res publica Christiana*, the development of a distinctly territorial principle of jurisdiction and sovereignty, and of the rise of the permanent embassy as the ordinary channel of diplomatic intercourse; in short, as belonging to the context of the transition from the feudal to the early modern state and diplomatic system.[39] In 1576 the French judge and international law theorist Pierre Ayrault (1536–1601) advanced, for the first time, a theory of diplomatic immunity that came close in substance to the concept of immunity-as-exterritoriality: no matter what the ambassador does, he is to be treated as if he were absent from the place in which he is actually staying.[40] Half a century later, Hugo Grotius (1583–1645), in his *De jure belli ac pacis* (1625), restated diplomatic immunity in terms of an extra-territorial fiction by referring to envoys in a receiving state as being *quasi extra territorium*.[41]

It would appear that the unique characteristics of communication with the curia were catalytic in the innovations outlined above. Not only did mid-fourteenth-century English envoys have to spend three to four weeks passing through a potentially hostile territory on their way to Avignon; having arrived there, they would spend weeks, sometimes months, at a court at which they were more fully exposed to the jurisdictional power of their host than they could ever be anywhere else. As Christians staying at the court of the Vicar of Christ, they could not claim to be 'quasi-exterritorial' in the sense of being subject only to the laws of their peoples or home countries, laws that they were, so to speak, bearing with them. It was precisely this problematic legal status that the innovations of 1343 and 1354 were meant to address.

We now need to resume our discussion of the institution of *conductus*, which, as has been said above, could take two different forms: a letter patent of safe conduct or an escort literally 'conducting' a traveller on his way.

Protection was seldom the sole purpose of the latter. The further the English envoys deviated from their standard route to Avignon, the one through central France,[42] the more they depended on locals to guide them. Immediately after Richard Stafford's and William Burton's return to London on 5 July 1359, the king ordered the Exchequer to account with the two knights for their costs, specifically mentioning money spent 'pour messageries et conductz de gentz avoir sur le chemyn pour leur sauvete' (on messengers' errands and on men guiding them on the way for their safety).[43] The list of expenses on guidance that Stafford and Burton compiled shortly afterwards reads like an itinerary. Payments of between 12d. and 6 li. 10s., typically around 25s., had been made to subjects of rulers of the western regions of the Empire—for example, the duke of Guelders, the bishops of Speyer and Basle and the count of Savoy. A guide from Geneva had received 23s. 4d.[44] The 44 li. 6s. 8d. in cash and gifts that Nigel Loring and William Margaret spent on safe conducts four years later may have been intended to help alleviate their security concerns, but also to help them and their retinues find their way through Burgundy.[45] Unpleasant memories of his journey to the curia in the preceding summer must still have been fresh on John de Shepeye's memory in the first weeks of 1374, when he decided to hire guides, among them at least one knight, for parts of his return journey to England; he and his companions had been seized and imprisoned while passing through Dauphiné.[46]

Another motive for a ruler to provide a traveller passing through his territory with an escort was to do with the widespread view, in many cases well founded, that every foreign envoy was a potential spy. The escorts given in both England and France to the other side's messengers and envoys were intended to ensure their safety, but also to make certain that they did not make use of, and report back, information gleaned during their missions.[47] The earl of Arundel constantly had a royal French sergeant at arms by his side while travelling through France on his journeys to and from Avignon in 1354–5, leaving him with a bill of 86 li. 12d.[48] Guillaume de Grisac, a papal sergeant at arms, was reimbursed at the Apostolic Chamber in late April 1365 for his expenses 'pro associando et conducendo' (for accompanying and guiding) Nigel Loring, William Margaret and Thomas Fulnetby during their stay in Avignon.[49] A French sergeant by the name of Massy accompanied Bartholomew Burghersh, Richard Stafford, Thomas Bukton and John Carlton for a full three months during their mission in the summer and early autumn of the following year, leading them from Paris to Avignon and back again at a daily wage of 6s. 8d., which the Englishmen had to pay out of their own pockets. In the papal city itself, one *Massyot*, a papal sergeant at arms, stayed by the envoys' side, although he probably was no stranger to them and was there as much for their assistance as for their surveillance: this seems to have been none other than Massiolus de Monte Falco, who also bore the honorary title of Edward III's sergeant at arms from about 1343, and who had been at the English court as Clement VI's messenger in 1346.[50]

Having diplomats of elevated rank escorted was also a way of honouring them, an institution of chivalric as well as of legal culture. The agreement concluded by English and French representatives near Calais on 13 June 1350 stipulated that plenipotentiaries of both sides were to meet in the curia before 1 November. For its journey through France the English delegation would be given both letters of safe conduct and an escort, the members of which, it was explicitly stated, would be men of appropriate social status (*bons et honorables conducteurs*); in case the English delegation was headed by the earl of Lancaster the lords of Montgascon and Beaujeu and the marshal of Naele were to perform this task.[51] In late May 1354, while preparations for the Second Avignon Conference were being made in Paris and Westminster, Pierre de la Forêt, the chancellor of France, wrote to Henry of Grosmont and Richard Fitzalan, assuring them that, as soon as he received the names of the members of Edward III's delegation, they would be given royal letters of safe conduct, and would be escorted to Avignon by French notables.[52] The combined retinues of the duke and the earl indeed reached the size of a small army,[53] and there must have been some concern in France that their embassy would turn into a reconnaissance mission or, even worse, yet another *chevauchée*; on the other hand, the duke was the most powerful and respected English aristocrat of his day, and requirements of etiquette had to be met. We do not know who the French noblemen mentioned in the chancellor's letter were, but what is certain is that Henry eventually obtained a written safe conduct from the papal chancery, and that the English taxpayer had to bear the cost for his escort: he paid no less than 316 li. to the squires and sergeants at arms who accompanied him and his retinue on their outward and return journeys.[54]

4.1.3. *Plague and war: Diplomacy in times of crisis*

Between 1348 and 1362 southern France was hit by a unprecedented succession of crises, each lasting for several months and bringing with it grave risks for travellers to that region. What, if any, changes to diplomatic practice did the protagonists in London and Westminster make in response to these threats, and how did Edward III's diplomats cope with the problems encountered en route to the papal city?

From 1347 to 1350 Europe was devastated by the Black Death, the greatest demographic catastrophe in its recorded history. Provence and Languedoc were the worst affected regions of France.[55] The plague attacked Avignon in late January 1348 and does not seem to have died out much before the end of the year.[56] The best-known and most graphic eyewitness account of its effects on life in the papal city is that contained in the letter which Louis Heyligen (*Sanctus*) of Beringen wrote to a fellow canon of the chapter of Saint-Donatien, Bruges, on 27 April 1348.[57] Although the total number of victims stated in his report is doubtless too high,[58] his claim that half the population of the papal city had died over the preceding three months does not appear at all exaggerated in the face of what is known about the demographic consequences of the epidemic in Provence.[59]

The disruption in the curial administration must have been considerable, as can also be seen from the correspondence and account books of the envoys of the Hamburg city council.[60] The *Grandes chroniques* report that several cardinals left the city in haste.[61] According to the rumours that Louis Heyligen had heard, the curia was supposed to remain in Avignon, but Clement VI was preparing to retreat to his castle at Étoile-sur-Rhône. A general vacation until Michaelmas had been called while all those auditors, advocates and proctors who had not yet succumbed to the epidemic had left Avignon or were about to do so.[62] The German chronicler Matthias von Neuenburg gives rather different information regarding the whereabouts of the pope during the crisis: on the advice of his physician, Clement retreated to his chamber, saw nobody and spent all day and night sheltering between two enormous fires.[63] But some of the statements of the Flemish canon are corroborated by the observations that Reginald Bugwell, an English resident proctor, wrote down for one of his clients on 4 June 1348: three days earlier it had become necessary to call a general vacation until Michaelmas 'propter pestilencias et mortalitates que iam in curia mirabilior regnant' (because disease and death had taken up their ever stranger reign in the curia). The auditor who had originally been in charge of his client's lawsuit had been sent to Sicily, his substitute had died of the plague before proceedings could begin and the substitute's substitute had not yet had the time to familiarize himself with the details of the case.[64] In total, six cardinals and ninety-three officials (14 per cent of the curial personnel) are known to have met their end during the epidemic.[65]

The Black Death probably arrived in England in late June 1348, and in the course of the following year afflicted almost every town and village in the country. First cases occurred in London in November 1348, if not earlier, and at the beginning of 1349 the population began to feel the full force of the epidemic. Its main wave lasted for three or four months, but deaths were still common in the city until far into 1350.[66] However, as William Mark Ormrod has shown in an important study, it was not least thanks to the Crown's determination to sit out the period of disruption that the general crisis of confidence in England could be overcome within a relatively short time, and that the royal administration managed to emerge from the disaster with renewed strength. A very real panic had gripped Edward III's government in late 1348 and early 1349. The king himself had retired to the relative safety of his country estates, and the Privy Seal office had later joined him. But the Chancery remained in session throughout the plague, and the Exchequer, no less important for the conduct of the everyday business of diplomacy, continued to keep its terms. By Michaelmas, as it became clear that the Crown had succeeded in coping with the first and most catastrophic outbreak of the Black Death, the machinery of government was again running as usual.[67]

Ormrod's observations regarding the stability of Edward III's domestic government in 1348–50 are supported and complemented by what can be ascertained about diplomatic contacts with the Continent in that period. Between 1 March 1348 and 19 December 1350 no less than twenty-three English embassies crossed the Channel.[68] Throughout the crisis, English envoys continued to be sent to the papal court, which is all the more remarkable since it was known that their journeys would take them further into the plague-stricken Continent than most other missions. John Carlton, Hugh Neville and John Reppes were in Avignon at the time when the Black Death broke out there.[69] They seem to have experienced some problems in keeping up communication with England—on 14 February 1348 the king noted that he had expected to hear their report at the last meeting of Parliament, but that no news had arrived[70]—but Neville and Reppes returned safely to England on 16 March. There is no reference to the epidemic in the papal letter that they brought back with them,[71] or in their expense accounts, but they doubtless briefed the king and his councillors on what they had seen along the way. When Carlton arrived back in London on 14 May 1348, the pope had already asked for him to be sent back to the curia.[72] Carlton began his return journey in the company of Richard Saham shortly afterwards and presumably arrived in Avignon before 15 June, as he had announced he would.[73]

On their journeys through the French countryside all these envoys must have witnessed scenes testifying to the breakdown of social and economic bonds under the pressure of the plague. In July 1348 Jacques le Muisit, a councillor of the king of France, returned home from a sixteen-month mission to Aragon. He met his cousin, Gilles le Muisit, the chronicler, in the following winter and told him the news that he had gathered during stays in Paris and Avignon. Merchants, pilgrims and other travellers had brought disturbing reports from all over Christendom: they had spoken of cattle roaming the countryside unherded, of doors of barns and wine cellars standing wide open, of uncultivated fields and vineyards and of deserted houses, villages, castles and towns.[74]

And yet, even in the summer of 1349, at the height of the plague in their own country, Englishmen continued to be sent to Avignon both as royal and non-royal envoys: Michael Northburgh, John Carlton and Robert Askeby acted as representatives of Edward III, while Robert Stanton OFM, Richard Cleangre, Henry de Mons, Peter Gildesburgh, John Philippi of Thedelthorpe, Simon Beckingham, Guillaume de Savinhac, Thomas Dunclent and probably many others left England to promote the interests of individual prelates, aristocrats, religious houses, or secular or ecclesiastical corporations at the papal court.[75]

In the summer of 1361, the plague returned to ravage Avignon and its environs once more. The death toll among the curial personnel has been proved to have been even higher in those months than it had been thirteen years before, and we have reason to believe the chronicler Heinrich Taube of Selbach when he notes that the panic in the city was greater during this second outbreak than it had been during the first.[76] But, as before, the English royal administration did not suspend contacts with the curia. Thomas Fulnetby went on a mission in mid-May 1361, and Guy de Brian followed him five days later. The latter did not even abort his mission when the plague began to claim the lives of members of his household.[77] Another experienced knight-diplomat, Nigel Loring, even travelled twice between mid-June and mid-August. John Pigot, a messenger and a veteran of five journeys to the curia, also set out from London.[78] An extra allowance of 60s. was intended to help de Brian cope with the increased food prices in France and the papal city, but normally the envoys had to make do with their regular daily wages even in these most complicated of circumstances.[79]

In 1357 and 1360–2 the lower Rhône valley and Provence suffered heavily under the incursions of contingents (*routes*) of professional men-at-arms who, after the general demobilizations that had followed the truce of Bordeaux and the peace of Brétigny–Calais, assembled together to make war on their own account, or in the pay of whoever would hire them.[80] Independent units of freebooters began to conduct raids in the lands through which the standard route used by English envoys to Avignon led—the area between the rivers Seine and Loire and the Loire valley—in the late 1350s, and the problem persisted in the first half of the following decade. In about May 1357 a company of *routiers* under the leadership of Arnaud de Cervole, the infamous 'Archpriest', transferred its operations from western and northern France to the *Midi*. On 13 July they crossed the Rhône north of Valence, and until October of the following year carried out raids in the Comtat Venaissin, the county of Forcalquier, and Provence.[81] What is more, an alliance of several units, each in its turn made up of a number of *routes*, operated in the lower Rhône basin, the region around Avignon and Provence, between late 1360 and the spring of 1362, calling itself, and being called by others, the 'Great Companies'. The first of these descended on Pont-Saint-Ésprit above Avignon in late December 1360. They were joined by others in the spring of the new year.[82] The control of the fortress, town and bridge placed the *routiers* in a position to control the traffic up and down the corridor of the Rhône, to ransom merchants and travellers, including the lay and ecclesiastical dignitaries and others conducting business at the curia, and to intercept convoys of food and other merchandise: 'As the number of companies operating in the area was swollen to mega-proportions, Avignon was blockaded, and its supply lines to the north cut off.'[83] It was not until the end of April 1361, shortly before the return of the plague, that Pont-Saint-Ésprit and the lower Rhône valley were finally evacuated by the Great Companies.[84]

If Edward III and his councillors continued to send their diplomatic agents to Innocent VI's court throughout the crises of 1357–8 and 1360–1, this was certainly not because they had failed to gather sufficient intelligence about the *routiers*' movements. Nicholas d'Amory and Thomas Fulnetby were at the curia when news of Arnaud de Cervole's crossing of the Rhône and advance towards the papal city arrived (it was probably these pieces of news that prompted them to take precautions and request a papal letter of safe conduct[85]). Thomas Clipston left London after receiving 100s. for his expenses in late October 1357.[86] When Adam Hilton began his journey, in mid-November of the following year, de Cervole's company had only just begun to leave the *Midi*, and it is to be doubted whether clear, up-to-date information had arrived in Westminster by that time. Adam Hilton and William Burton were probably both still in Avignon when news about the fall of Pont-Saint-Ésprit arrived, but, as has been seen above, English envoys continued to be sent during the spring and summer of 1361, despite the double threat from the brigands and the plague.

Both the outbreaks of the plague and the raids of the *routes* in the Rhône valley and the area around Avignon might have been expected to have a disruptive effect on Anglo-curial communication, but, as has been shown, this was not the case. The *perception* of these crises, however—the fear that plague and war struck into men's hearts—seems to have exerted some influence on the protagonists of diplomacy, in that it accentuated the social stratification in the English 'diplomatic service'—that is, the circle of clerics and laymen selected for missions abroad. Already in June 1344 an informal meeting at Clement VI's court between Henry of Grosmont and several French peers under the leadership of the dukes of Normandy and Burgundy had come to a premature end because of the outbreak of an epidemic. After the duke of Normandy had been taken ill, neither Henry nor Duke Eudes IV of Burgundy was willing to take any chances and they left the city.[87] In May 1348 the earls of Lancaster and Arundel and the archbishop of Canterbury declared that, although they had been planning to come to the papal court before Michaelmas for a solemn prolongation of the Calais truce, they felt forced to remain at home, *timore concutiens* (shaking with fear), because of rumours about the horrors of the Black Death. Instead, it was decided to send John Carlton as a substitute with more limited powers.[88]

The general rule seems to have been that, the higher the rank of the envoys, the longer the expected duration of the stay in the curia, and the greater the perceived risks, the less likely it was that a particular embassy would actually leave England or remain in Avignon until its task was accomplished. Envoys of lesser status, however, even distinguished knights such as Thomas Fulnetby, Guy de Brian or Nigel Loring, who were not expected to engage in long-drawn-out negotiations, continued to be sent. Unfortunately, in the absence of personal statements on their part—for example, in the form of private letters or memoirs—it is impossible to say whether these men saw the diplomatic services that they rendered to their king in times of crisis as a potentially deadly risk, and went against their will, or whether they saw them as yet another opportunity for advancement.

How many ordinary travellers never reached the papal court, or perished there or on their way back, can only be guessed at. What little source material there is suggests that the risks of the road were considerable. We know that at least thirty-one Englishmen died in or near Avignon in 1348 and 1361, the years of the plague.[89] In the summer of 1344 Thomas Lunderthorpe, a cleric from the diocese of Lincoln, was seized near Vienne, robbed and subsequently held for ransom. In 1346 French officials arrested William Inge, the archdeacon of Surrey, at Nîmes, while others intercepted and opened the private letters addressed to the pope that a Franciscan friar was taking from England to Avignon. Two years later another cleric, Simon Brisley, was waylaid near Maastricht and released only after two citizens of Cologne had agreed to advance his ransom.[90] In 1352 or early 1353 Henry Ingelby, a king's clerk, tried to obtain permission to go to Avignon and defend himself against certain allegations made against him in the curial courts. There was, at that time, no truce or peace between England and France, and Edward III and his councillors denied Ingelby's request because of concerns about his safety. Edward's legal advisers had pointed out that he, a confidant (*secretarius*) of the king, would not be sufficiently protected by the general principles of immunity.[91] Lastly, John Derby, another king's clerk, who had been in the earl of Arundel's retinue during the Second Avignon Conference, was robbed and imprisoned at Saint-Omer in northern France, in spite of the fact that he had a letter of safe conduct from the marshal of France for his return journey. He was released only after he had sworn to pay a ransom of 1,423 florins à l'écu.[92]

The official envoy's life, by contrast, was a good deal safer than one might believe. To our knowledge only two missions to the Roman curia during the twenty-year period under investigation in this study were forcibly interrupted. In September 1342 Edmund von Birkelin, a Cologne knight and a veteran of Edward III's Scottish wars, and his men seized John Piers, took him to a castle near Cologne and held him for ransom for more than two weeks.[93] French officials arrested and imprisoned John Carlton somewhere between Avignon and Calais in the late summer of 1348.[94] But, if one considers the political instability of the time, the impressive overall number of diplomatic missions and the frequency with which private travellers were exposed to violence, these cases appear all but negligible. With remarkably few exceptions, Edward III's diplomatic agents, even the minor ones, did enjoy the privileges and immunities to which theory said they were entitled.

This is not to say that they relied on these privileges and immunities alone. On the contrary, they seem to have been quite aware of the precariousness of their situation abroad. The author of the *Anonimalle Chronicle* tells of an abortive attempt by the French to ambush the duke of Lancaster and the earl of Arundel on their return journey to England.[95] It was for a good reason that many English envoys chose to travel along the Rhine River and through the Low Countries rather than via Paris and France.[96] What is more, no privilege or immunity could protect them against disease and death. Edward's envoys in 1348 and 1361 may have evaded the plague, but in December 1366 Thomas Bukton died in Lyons, just days before reaching his destination.[97]

4.2. The Embassy: Structure and Self-image

If a royal embassy to Avignon comprised more than two envoys, and if a letter of procuration was drawn up for it, a *quorum* was usually specified in this document. Presumably this was intended as a precaution against the eventuality of one or more envoys being unable to leave England, and against the risks of the long journey: if, for whatever reason, a delegation arrived at the curia one or more men below strength, its procuration would not automatically become invalid.[98] Thus on 28 August 1354, as part of the preparations for the Second Avignon Conference, six diplomats—William Bateman, Michael Northburgh, Henry of Grosmont, Richard Fitzalan, Bartholomew Burghersh and Guy de Brian—were given plenary powers to negotiate for a final peace, to renounce Edward III's claims in France and to submit his dominions in France to the pope's jurisdiction, but their letter of procuration explicitly stated that Edward would also consider binding any agreement that had been negotiated by only five, four, three or even two of them.[99]

The *quorum* could also be used to establish a hierarchy among envoys. That William Bateman and John Offord were the leaders of the English delegation at the first Anglo-French peace conference can be seen from their first procuration (4 August 1344): the king guaranteed that he would accept agreements concluded on his behalf by as few as two members of his embassy, provided that either Bateman or Offord was one of them. John Thoresby and Ralph Spigournel were substituted for Thomas Fastolf and Andrew Offord as members of the English delegation in November 1344, but the stipulations of the *quorum* in the new letter of procuration remained unchanged.[100]

As has been noted above, most English envoys were selected from the ranks of the king's councillors, and in some cases there is evidence of men taking a formal councillor's oath shortly before departing for the Continent on diplomatic missions. It defined their duties both as royal advisers at home and as diplomatic representatives abroad: these were essentially the duties of loyalty and secrecy, and of defending the rights of the Crown.[101]

An interesting passage in one of John Offord's reports from the First Avignon Conference indicates the practical importance of these formalities. Thomas Fastolf, the auditor, was appointed as one of Edward III's delegates on 4 August 1344, but, having lived abroad for more than ten years, he was apparently not connected with the king's council at that time. At his first meeting with his future colleagues, Fastolf took an oath by virtue of which he became an affiliated member of the council. This enabled him to act as a full representative of the king; Offord could thus refer to him as 'Meistre Thomas Fastolfs [...] lequele j'ay feat jurer à vostre conseil, et nous purra après ces heures lieu tenir' (Master Thomas Fastolf, whom I had take the oath of your councillors, and henceforth he will be able to represent us).[102] It seems, then, that, in order to be able to function as a diplomat in the full sense, a person needed to swear the councillor's oath of allegiance, either before setting out on his mission or, less frequently, abroad when he joined a royal embassy at a later stage.

In fact, larger embassies charged with making decisions on the king's behalf or performing ceremonial functions constituted and perceived of themselves as branches of the king's council sitting abroad. Their very composition indicates as much: article seven of the preliminary peace signed at Guines on 6 April 1354 stipulated that Edward III's and John II's 'solemn embassies', which would meet before Innocent VI in the autumn of that year, should comprise both prelates and temporal lords.[103] The embassy's internal structure was thus made to mirror that of the ordinary king's council, with its balance between the clerical and lay elements.

That decision-making (as opposed to decision-conveying) envoys regarded themselves as king's councillors, and their embassy as 'the king's council in miniature', is also reflected in the terminology used in their correspondence. In his first intermediate report to Edward III, written on 14 September 1344, John Offord referred to himself and his colleagues as 'nous [...] de vostre conseil en court de Rome' (we, the members of your council at the Roman court).[104] Writing to the archbishop of Canterbury in late November or early December, he complained that Thomas Fastolf was keeping his distance from the rest of the English delegation—the *consilium regium* (royal council).[105] Four weeks earlier he had informed the king that he had requested an audience at which his 'council' and *le counseil de la partie adverse* (the council of the other side) could exchange their views.[106]

4.3. Diplomats on the Road

From a strictly logistic point of view, the 'working conditions' for English diplomatic agents sent to the Holy See were more favourable after 1316, when the newly elected John XXII chose Avignon as his permanent place of residence, than they had been during the previous three centuries. Never between the time of the Investiture Contest and John's election had the Supreme Pontiffs been truly sedentary; in fact, they had become used to spending more time on their estates in central Italy than in Rome, and some of them never went to the papal city at all.[107] This itinerant character of the curia must have created some difficulties for anyone who had business to transact at it: while

Robert of Béthune, son of the count of Flanders, was preparing a journey to the curia in the spring of 1298, he received an apologetic letter from two Flemish envoys who were already in Italy. The two had not yet booked accommodation for him and his retinue or made any other preparations since it had been impossible to ascertain where Boniface VIII and his court would be spending the summer.[108] After 1316, envoys and other travellers could expect to find the pope in Avignon or not too far from there, in his summer residences at Villeneuve-lès-Avignon, Châteauneuf-du-Pape or Sorgues. This may have saved them some time and money, yet they still had to cope with the travails of travel, which will be discussed in this section.

4.3.1. Travel routes

Following Yves Renouard's terminology, we may distinguish between two kinds of route descriptions. *Itinéraires théoriques* (for example, guide books or manuals for pilgrims) were intended to instruct intending travellers, whereas *itinéraires réels*, reconstructable on the basis of incidental topographical information provided in other kinds of sources (especially expense reports), describe the stages of actual journeys made by the authors of these texts.[109]

The route to Avignon, or at least the larger part of it, was probably well known to English travellers by the time the papacy moved to southern France; the existence of a thirteenth-century pilgrims' itinerary in the University Library, Cambridge, describing the stages of a journey from the Channel coast to Lyons, suggests as much.[110] A second 'theoretical' itinerary is preserved in the British Library. Written probably between 1309 and 1346, it provides remarkably detailed information on two different routes through central France: the outward journey leads through Artois, Picardy, the Île de France, the Orléanais, the Nivernais, the Bourbonnais, Auvergne, the Velay, the Vivarais and Bas-Languedoc, while for the return journey the route up the Rhône valley, through the Lyonnais, the Bourbonnais, the Nivernais, the Orléanais, the Île de France, Picardy and Artois is suggested.[111] Unfortunately, only two full *itinéraires réels* by English royal diplomatic agents survive: those contained in the expense accounts of Richard Plympstok and John Faukes, sent to the Roman court in 1315–16 and 1343, respectively. To these may be added the itinerary in the *compotus* of John Middleton, fellow and subwarden of Merton College, Oxford (1331).[112]

Map 1

*The standard route to Avignon
and the alternative route through the Empire*

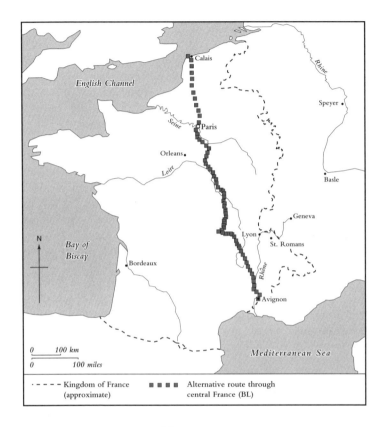

Map 2

An alternative route through central France (BL Royal MS A XVIII)

A comparison between these four texts shows that the royal diplomats and the Oxford cleric used exactly the same route through central France that the Cambridge itinerary describes. What is more, this route is largely identical with the one suggested for the return journey to England by the author of the London itinerary. All this indicates that soon after the transfer of the papacy to Avignon the institutions of the royal government were aware of there being a standard route available to their diplomatic agents. It was probably because this path was so well trodden that, unless the route that they took deviated much from the norm, the diplomats were not expected to give topographical details in their expense accounts.

Before its destruction by marauding English forces in early September 1346, Wissant was the place from which royal envoys to Avignon, like other travellers to the Continent, usually set out on their journey across central France. Calais took over this function after its capture (4 August 1347).[113] Turning due south, the envoys would traverse Artois, Picardy and the Île de France, calling at Boulogne-sur-Mer, Montreuil, Airaines, Poix, Beauvais and Beaumont-sur-Oise, before entering Paris from the north.

For the second major stage of their journey (from Paris to Lyons through the Orléanais, the Nivernais, the Bourbonnais and the Lyonnais), they would use the highway along the middle course of the Loire (*iter lugdunense, iter franciscum, magna via francisca, magna strata francheschi*).[114] A major trade route from the thirteenth century, it was also frequently used by northern French pilgrims to Rome. It acquired a more 'diplomatic', 'administrative' and 'political' character in the following century when the popes resided at Avignon. Later the road through the Bourbonnais and the Nivernais became—by comparison—economically more important, but in 1436 locals aged between 60 and 80 still remembered the Loire road being called 'the great road to Avignon' in their youth.[115] From Paris the envoys would travel south along the Seine up to what today is Corbeil-Essonnes, then continue in the same direction to Nemours on the Loing. Having followed that river upstream to Châtillon-Coligny they would reach the Loire valley at Bonny.[116] The *iter lugdunense* then took them in a south-easterly direction along the river bank via Cosne, Nevers and Decize to Marcigny in southern Burgundy, and out of the valley towards Charlieu and Thizy. Having crossed the southern range of the Beaujolais mountains, they would approach Lyons from the north-west.

An alternative route, detailed in the London itinerary, led from Nevers due south through the central Bourbonnais, Auvergne, the Velay, the Vivarais and Bas-Languedoc. It was not shorter but certainly more difficult than the one via Lyons and the Rhône valley, leading, as it did, through the heart of the Massif Central. It may have been due to this disadvantage that it never became the standard route for English travellers; we know of only one embassy that followed it— that of John Stratford in 1322.[117]

For the final stretch of their journey, the 210 kilometres from Lyons to Avignon, travellers could choose between two options. They could take the land route, following either of the old highways along the eastern or western bank of the Rhône, or go by boat. The expense accounts do not state what influenced the decision in each individual case, but envoys in more peaceful times like Plympstok, and less prosperous non-diplomats like Middleton usually seem to have taken the land route, while men like John Faukes and Robin of Arden in July 1343, John Offord and Hugh Neville in September 1344, Richard Stafford and William Burton in April 1359, Nigel Loring in November 1361 and John Cobham in November 1366 preferred to buy or hire boats in Lyons and ports further downstream such as Valence, Bourg-Saint-Andéol and Pont-Saint-Ésprit.[118] The purchase of a boat in Lyons cost Faukes and Arden as much as they had had to spend on hiring horses since disembarking at Wissant (18s.). In some instances saving time will have been the motive. A flat barge usually needed two to three days to go down the Rhône from Lyons to the Mediterranean coast[119], and Faukes and his companion even managed to make the river journey in a single day. Often the decision to buy or hire boats and the duration of the subsequent journey will have depended on the river conditions of the day, and on the advice of locals. The strength of the Rhône's current is subject to considerable seasonal variations and usually increases sharply in the spring (March to May) and autumn (October to December), especially on its middle and lower courses.[120] On their arrival in Lyons some travellers will have found the river unnavigable, while others will have reckoned that a journey by boat would enable them to achieve more than was possible by relying on the stamina of their horses. Safety concerns must sometimes also have played a major part, especially during the late 1350s and early 1360s, when the threat of attacks by *routiers* was at its greatest. Travellers by boat were less likely to be disturbed by marauders.[121]

In the summer of 1347 Giacomo Malabaila, the Asti merchant residing in Avignon, received what must have been long-expected letters from Flanders through a messenger who had just made his way through eastern France. Having kissed the letters (!), Malabaila rebuked the man for not having taken the safer route through Germany:

Trouant garson! Pourquoy as tu esté si hardis que tu es passés par le royaume de France à tout ces lettres, car qui te eust trouvé on te eust copé la teste. Et vraiment tu devoies venir par Almagne; et pour ce que tu n'i es venuz, et aussi car tu as failli de venir à terme, je ne te paie point.[122]

[Miserable fellow! Why were you so foolhardy to pass through the kingdom of France with all these letters? If they had found you they would have cut off your head. And truly you ought to have come via Germany, and because you did not do so, and because you failed to arrive on time, I won't pay you.]

After seven years of hostilities, which badly kept truces interrupted only for short periods, it had become customary for English envoys to travel through the western regions of the Empire, up or down the Rhine valley and through northern Savoy and the Dauphiné whenever the political or military situation in central France appeared too volatile for them to follow the normal route.

In August 1326, when Anglo-French tensions over the presence of Queen Isabella, Roger Mortimer and the young Prince Edward in France were mounting, Edward II imposed restrictions on the movements of Frenchmen travelling in and out of England. By way of retaliation, the arrest of all Englishmen in France and the confiscation of half their property were ordered.[123] Rumours of these reprisals prompted William Weston, Edward's envoy to the court of John XXII, to travel home through Germany (Saxonia) and embark at Antwerp.[124] In mid-April 1340 Laurence Fastolf decided to return to England after almost four years in Avignon, and deemed it prudent to make a long detour through the Empire.[125] When Richard Winkleigh and David Servington landed on the continental coast in early May of the same year, it was near Petten in West Friesland (a remote and unusual place, as Winkleigh remarked in his expense report), and their way south led them through Alemania.[126] Returning from Avignon in September 1342, John Piers, 'for fear of the king's adversaries of France', followed the Rhine valley down to Cologne and then turned west towards Brabant and Flanders, using the important trade route that linked Cologne with Mechelen, Ghent and Bruges, but before he could reach the Channel coast he was attacked by a Cologne knight and his men on the road from Hasselt to Herk-de-Stad in the county of Loon.[127] In early 1348 Simon Brisley was probably following the same route but got even less far: he was waylaid while crossing the Meuse at Maastricht in the duchy of Limburg.[128]

The most complete itinerary of a detour through the Empire is that given by Richard Stafford for his and William Burton's mission from 17 March to 5 July 1359. Since he was travelling in times of truce (a week after his departure English and French plenipotentiaries concluded the First Treaty of London), his decision not to take the standard route is likely to have come after he had learnt that bands of mercenaries were active in those areas that he would normally have had to pass through: in the spring of that year an army of mainly English and Breton *routiers* gathered around Châteauneuf-sur-Loire and began to march south towards the Rhône valley under the leadership of Robert Knolles, an English captain.[129] Like Winkleigh in 1340, Stafford and Burton probably disembarked somewhere along the coast of Holland and continued their way south across the duchy of Guelders. They then followed the whole length of the Rhine upstream to Basle, travelled through northern Savoy, Geneva, Chambéry and down the Isère valley before gaining the Rhône north of Valence. The information about their return journey is sketchy, but we know that they used the same route through Brabant and Flanders as Piers and Brisley had done, passing through Hasselt, Dendermonde, Ghent, Bruges and Gravelines.[130] John Gilbert, John de Shepey and Uthred of Boldon, the Benedictine theologian, decided to follow what seems to have been the same route when travelling to the curia in the summer of 1373, at the time when an English army commanded by John of Gaunt was sweeping from Calais through the central provinces of France to Bordeaux.[131] Several weeks earlier a German nobleman bound for Avignon had been mistaken for English and arrested in Lyons.[132]

If the way along the Rhine offered a real alternative to the standard route via Lyons and Paris, Edward III's diplomats appear to have been reluctant to cross France further to the west. As can be gathered from Cardinal Guy de Boulogne's reply to a letter from the duke of Lancaster (27 May 1354), the leading members of the English delegation to the Second Avignon Conference initially intended to travel to Guienne and from there to the papal court, but in the event, it seems, the dukes of Lancaster and Arundel took the standard route through central France.[133] Only in one case is there evidence of royal diplomats actually deviating from this route towards the west. For fear of French troops blockading the direct and shortest way back to England, Richard Stafford, accompanied by Bartholomew Burghersh the younger, John Carlton and Thomas Bukton, decided to make a detour via Poitiers on his return journey from the Avignon. They embarked at Saint-Malo in Brittany in September 1366.[134] Unfortunately, here again further details of the itinerary are absent from the envoys' accounts.

Like their compatriots who made the pilgrimage to Rome, English royal envoys to the papal court in the pre-Avignon period had been able to choose from a whole bundle of possible routes from the Channel coast to Italy, all of which had steered between the Paris–Lyons line on the west and the Rhine valley on the east.[135] Diplomatic traffic between the two protagonists, to use Marc Bloch's metaphor, had not yet been canalized in 'a few great arteries' but spread through 'a multitude of little blood-vessels'.[136] Once the popes had settled in the south of France, traffic along the standard route (Wissant/Calais–Paris–Loire valley–Lyons) was virtually monopolized by diplomats, prelates and private petitioners from England, whereas English pilgrims to Rome or the Holy Land, having reached Paris, would cross France further to the east on their way to the Alpine passes.[137] Two different kinds of mobility thus became disentagled from each other: the organized politico-administrative mobility of the royal diplomats and the individual and spontaneous religious mobility of the private travellers.[138]

4.3.2. Speed of travel, speed of communication

Throughout the Middle Ages and well into early modern times the individual remained the basic information-bearing unit—news could spread only as fast as man, travelling on foot, on horseback or by ship, managed to cross the spaces that lay between his place of departure and his destination. There was thus a direct connection between the speed of travel and the speed of communication.

Along most of the route from the Channel coast to Avignon, the lie of the land was conducive to easy and fast travelling. Being able to follow, as they were, the banks of rivers flowing from south to north or from north to south for most of the way, the diplomats did not confront elevations of more than approximately 750 metres (in the mountains to the south-west of Lyons). This also meant that the time of year was less of a determinant than it had been for journeys to Rome; unlike their predecessors in earlier times, English diplomats travelling to the curia during the autumn and winter months did not have to scale the icy heights of the Alps.[139] In the period under examination, the speed of travel was not subject to noticeable seasonal variations. It is to be assumed that even at times of war the important roads from the Channel coast to Paris, from Paris to Lyons and from Lyons to Avignon were in a comparatively good state. Where this was not the case, the traveller would often be able to choose one of several alternative routes; the density of the medieval French road system has been compared to the country's modern road network.[140]

The single most important factors influencing the speed of travel were the function of the individual diplomatic agent—that is, the nature of his journey—and his social rank. Both of these factors in turn had an influence on the size and composition of the accompanying party. Envoys travelling at great speed were almost invariably transmitters of pieces of information deemed to be of the highest importance. We have seen above that the news of Benedict XII's death reached Westminster in less than a week.[141] The flow of information in the opposite direction was potentially just as fast: John XXII had learnt about Edward III's seizure of power from Mortimer and Isabella (19 October 1330) by 26 October 1330.[142] The 'pressure to produce results'[143] also had a powerful effect on a diplomat's travel speed. Before their departure on 26 July 1343, John Faukes and Robin of Arden were told that they had to return to the royal court within eighteen days 'on pain of life and limb'; they thus had a tangible motive for exertion.[144] It took them a mere seven days to reach the papal city, an achievement that would not have been possible had they not been able to hire mounts in towns along the way: they changed horses in Wissant, Paris, Ouzouer-sur-Trézée, Cosne-sur-Loire and Nevers. They travelled fastest in northern France (Artois, Picardie, Île-de-France), slowed down as they went up the Loire, and picked up speed again towards the end of their way.[145] On his return journey (thirteen days) Faukes travelled by night on two occasions: between Avignon and Vienne and Châteauneuf-sur-Loire and Paris, the latter journey being made 'noet et iour sur diverses chivaux' (by night and day on several horses).[146] This enabled him to cover very considerable distances: 182 and 138 kilometres, respectively.

By contrast, it took Richard Plympstok and his companions almost five times as long to get to the papal court (thirty-three days, excluding those they spent negotiating at the royal court in Paris, waiting for Louis X's written reply in Essonnes, and deliberating among themselves in Valence), and twenty-seven days to return. This was mainly due to the fact that this was a mixed company of five horsemen and three pedestrians. They travelled at a more relaxed and constant rhythm than Faukes and Arden, usually doing between 32 and 42 kilometres a day, and very seldom more. On average, they covered approximately 34 kilometres a day, less than half of what Faukes and Arden, the two professional travellers, achieved (78 kilometres). Faukes alone did an even more impressive 85 kilometres a day on his way back to England. Like Faukes and Arden, John Middleton and his servant, both of them mounted, travelled fastest on their way from the Channel coast to Paris: 52 kilometres daily was the average speed on this part of their journey. Between Paris and Avignon they slowed down to an average of 48 kilometres daily.

Two passages in royal letters to Clement VI suggest that twenty days was regarded the minimal duration of a common clerk's outward journey.[147] Unfortunately, only in a few cases (apart from Faukes's and Plympstok's) do the expense accounts state both the day of departure from England and the day of arrival in Avignon, or vice versa, thus making it possible for us to establish how long the journey actually took. William Weston needed thirty-one days in 1325 and twenty-six days in 1328.[148] John Offord and Hugh Neville, two of the English delegates at the First Avignon Conference, were on the road for twenty-eight days before they reached the papal court, and their co-envoys John Thoresby and Ralph Spigournel for twenty-six days.[149] Henry Whitfield, provost of The Queen's College, Oxford, needed a full seven weeks, but, as he remarked in his account, this was 'propter intemperiem et periculum in via' (due to bad weather and danger on the way).[150] John Middleton, following the *iter lugdunense* on his return journey, arrived back in Oxford after twenty-five days. Obviously, the detour through the Empire took considerably longer—fifty-eight days in the case of William Weston (1326) and forty-two days in that of Laurence Fastolf (1340).[151]

Receptions of royal envoys are often mentioned in the opening lines of papal letters, even with exact dates, but, since we can only guess for how long after their arrival these men were kept waiting for an audience, it is not possible to establish with any precision the duration of their journeys. However, a comparison between the

Exchequer and papal chancery documents shows that the envoys' arrival was usually confirmed within three to four weeks of their departure from London[152]—a result that confirms what the direct references to travel speed tell us.

If, then, an envoy who was neither a *cursor* nor an aristocrat or prelate would normally complete his journey from London to Avignon within three or four weeks, and if he used the regular route through central France, he would do an average of about 37 kilometres a day.

The higher the rank of the travellers, the more slowly they moved. This was due to these persons' greater insistence on comfort in travel, to the rank-specific notion that slow travel was a more appropriate form of progress (Bernard du Rosier, writing in the 1430s, recommended that an embassy move in a style reflecting the dignity of its principal figure and at an adequate speed[153]), and to their custom of taking to the road in large parties. Having to prearrange every stage of their journey, these companies would inevitably face organizational difficulties much greater than those of individual travellers or small groups: retainers had to be sent ahead to arrange accommodation and provisions, and the length of the baggage train tended to hamper the progress.[154] All this must have applied to the travel group of Henry of Grosmont, duke of Lancaster, who participated in the Second Avignon Conference. His *compotus* does not contain any details of its progress through France, but we know that Lancaster and his men were on the road for fifty-eight days.[155] This would mean that they travelled at the rather modest rate of a little less than 18 kilometres daily.

The speed of travel of English envoys en route to the Avignonese curia did not differ from what was normal in late medieval Europe. Between 30 and 40 kilometres a day was common for travellers on land, although pedestrians would sometimes do up to 50 kilometres. A horseman could travel 60 or 70 kilometres in a day and substantially more in flat terrain.[156] Analysing textual evidence concerning the speed of travel in fourteenth-century France, Marjory Boyer came to the conclusion that, while most journeys were probably made at a rate of 32–48 kilometres a day, and while it was possible for royal messengers to achieve a speed of around 90 kilometres a day, 48–53 kilometres was considered a full day's journey. However, she points out that long journeys were usually made at a slower rate and frequently included stopovers.[157] As Appendix III shows, many, if not most, of the travel groups with which this study is concerned were made up of both horsemen and pedestrians. According to Boyer's findings, even such mixed companies could, if necessary, maintain a speed of at least 48 kilometres a day over a period of several days.[158] It would appear, thus, that the presence of pedestrians in their company did not hamper most journeys of English diplomats.

4.3.3. Accommodation and food

Information about where English envoys lodged on their way to Avignon and in the city itself is scarce, and an unclear terminology further complicates the interpretation of what few references there are. While we know that William Bateman, having left London on 4 October 1354, spent the nights before and after crossing the Channel in *hospitia* in Dover and Calais, the exact meaning of the word is as elusive here as it is in many other cases.[159]

Diplomats recruited from the ranks of England's secular and ecclesiastic elite will often have found accommodation at a friendly castle or monastic house, where hospitality was a tradition, but here again our sources remain silent. The extant itineraries show that the travellers of medium and lower rank usually spent the nights in the towns and villages that lay along the road. Exceptions were rare: John Middelton stayed at *la mala taverne*, apparently a rural inn of poor standard and/or dubious reputation, on 10 February 1331 and at the roadside establishment of one Jean Cortois (*Chescorteys*), situated between Decize and Beaulon, four days later.[160] John Faukes and Robin of Arden took up quarters at the same place in late July 1343. Public inns or hostels (*hospitia*), providing lodging and food on a commercial basis to travellers of all ranks, had by the middle of the fourteenth century become a typical feature of central European cities, towns, villages and roadsides. A traveller could expect to find up to ten such houses in villages and smaller cities near main roads, at least twenty in medium-sized towns (10,000 or less inhabitants), and far more in centres of international trade such as Paris or Lyons.[161]

In Avignon an unusually large number of inns and hostels was available to travellers brought to the curia by judicial, diplomatic or other business. The *Liber divisionis cortesanorum et civium Romanae curie et civitatis Avinionis*, written at the beginning of the pontificate of Gregory XI, lists sixty-one keepers of such establishments.[162] About one-third of these were situated in the parish of Saint-Étienne, in the immediate vicinity of the papal palace, and an especially large number were to be found in *Fustaria nova* (today rue Grande Fusterie),

through which visitors came immediately after leaving Pont-Saint-Bénézet. It is probable, however, that during the pontificate of Clement VI the city's eastern part, the area between the Imbert and Matheron gates, had the greatest density of *hospitia*.[163]
There are hints in the expense accounts of John Middleton (1331) and Henry Whitfield (1363) that these two non-diplomatic travellers found accommodation at an English college or hostel, frequented by their countrymen. For their first eight days Middleton and his servant remained at a common inn (*herbigerya*), but subsequently took up residence at what he called 'our house'. On the termination of his business at the curia he gave a feast for its inmates (*socii*). Whitfield apparently did the same shortly after moving in, which led to some expenditure on wine and other things.[164]
As a general rule, English proctors lived either as tenants in citizens' houses, or, probably less often, as permanent guests in *hospitia*. In either case they usually rented one or more rooms, often with cooking facilities and stables. Some opted for shared accommodation with a countryman.[165] Englishmen in senior positions in the curial administration doubtless had their own, permanent residences. At least this was the case with the auditors Thomas Fastolf and Simon Sudbury, who would sometimes transact part of their business there. *Dominus Richardus de Anglia* (Richard Wimundewold?), the advocate, owned a house in *Carreria Furni de Nabressa* in the south-east of the city (parish of Saint-Geniès, today rue du Four de la Terre) in the late 1350s. After the death of Richard Drax, the auditor, in 1361, the ownership of his *hospitium* was transferred to the parish church of Saint-Pierre, where he was buried.[166]
References to lodgings of English lower- and middle-rank diplomats are too scarce for any clear pattern to emerge, but it is likely that their decision as to where to take up quarters was largely influenced by the expected duration of their stay. The representatives of the council of the city of Hamburg rented a spacious house in the city centre, formerly owned by a cardinal, for a whole year in the spring of 1354, but they probably made this long-term investment only because they knew that their business would keep them in town for some more time.[167] Whereas William Weston rented the entire inn or hostel of one Guillaume Lamas for at least the last weeks of his stay in 1326, most of his colleagues seem to have sought short-term accommodation at inns and hostels, although it is quite possible that compatriots such as Fastolf, Sudbury, or Drax would have been

prepared to put them up at least temporarily.[168] In 1318 three commissioners (*taxatores* or *assignatores domorum*) allocated to a papal penitentiary 'hanc partem hospicii domine Bertrande Radulphe [...] quam tenent Anglici' (the part of the *hospitium* of mistress Bertrande Radulphe occupied by the English),[169] but it is not clear who these 'English' were or how long they had been living there. The quarters from which Niccolò Fieschi was abducted on the night of 13 April 1340 was a *hospitium*, according to an anonymous vita of Benedict XII, but is mentioned simply as a *domus* in the papal correspondence referring to the incident.[170] Whatever the status of the house may have been, we may infer that it was not top-of-the-range accommodation: it was situated in *Carreria Curaterie* or *mercati coriorum*, the street of the leather-traders (today rue Bonneterie),[171] and the smell created in the processing of that material will have caused the residents some inconvenience.

Finding affordable accommodation in the notoriously overcrowded city was a difficult task for any visitor. Richard Paveley, prior of the Knights Hospitallers in England, learnt in 1320 that he would have to start looking for new lodgings as soon as Richard Jean, a squire of the papal household, returned and took over his house in *Carreria Furni Fresicorum* (today rue Bertrand), conveniently situated very near the north-eastern corner of John XXII's palace.[172] To be able to accommodate a delegation expected in March 1331, the pope had to request the master of the Hospitallers to put certain city houses owned by the order at his disposal.[173]

For peers and prelates and their retinues, finding adequate lodgings posed a major problem. It seems that the religious houses of Avignon and the surrounding region frequently offered them accommodation. When Clemence, widow of Louis X of France and queen of Navarre, came to the curia in 1318, the pope's officers requisitioned the Franciscan convent, twelve hostels, three houses, two stables and several rooms in citizens' houses.[174] In the summer of the following year Adam Orleton, bishop of Hereford, visited Avignon; he moved into the former Austin priory of Saint-Ruf, situated a kilometre south of the city.[175] Finding sufficient space for men and horses was not the only imperative; for high-ranking visitors, finding adequate lodgings was also, and not least, a question of security and status. In October 1316 two Aragonese envoys, Pontius de Gualba, bishop of Barcelona, and Vidal de Villanova, a knight, complained to their king that they had been forced to stay 'like common folk' (*viliter*) at an ordinary and rather squalid *commune hospitium* (inn or hostel) since their arrival in the overcrowded city, and informed him that they intended to move into the Benedictine abbey of Saint-André in Villeneuve, where they expected to find cleaner and safer lodgings appropriate for the dignity of the Crown that they represented.[176]

Aristocratic visitors who enjoyed friendly relations with a member of the college of cardinals were sometimes given the opportunity to stay at that person's *livrée*. On his first visit to the curia in late 1339, Charles, margrave of Bohemia, was entertained as a guest in the lodgings of Pierre Roger, then cardinal priest of SS Nereus and Achilles, with whom he had been well acquainted since his time at the Parisian court.[177] The south wing of Benedict XII's new palace, built in 1337–9, contained separate guest rooms, among them a large room for guests of special importance (*camera regis* or—from 1365, when Emperor Charles IV stayed there—*camera imperatoris*), but there is no conclusive evidence of it being used before the visit of Peter IV of Aragon in December 1355.[178] Eudes IV of Burgundy was a resident guest in the palace in the early summer of 1344, but we do not know whether he used the *camera*.[179] Behind this diversity of strategies for housing visitors lay a deliberate 'hierarchy of accommodation': a glance at the quality of the lodgings assigned to him could help a guest gauge the importance attributed to him and his visit. As a general rule, the closer to the pope his lodgings were located, the more honoured could he consider himself.[180]

Advisers of the pope living in the palace were sometimes requested to vacate their rooms when high-ranking aristocratic envoys were expected. The lodgings of Audouin Aubert, nephew of Innocent VI and cardinal priest of SS John and Paul, were prepared at considerable cost for the arrival of the dukes of Lancaster and Burgundy in early December 1354. At the same time, a room usually occupied by Arnaud Aubert, bishop of Carcassonne, was prepared for Charles II of Navarre.[181] However, there is no evidence in the cameral sources that Lancaster actually made use of the rooms prepared for him.[182] What is more, the nature of the items purchased (cloth, benchcovers) suggests that this was a room for receptions and negotiations rather than residential purposes. It is quite possible that, by having a room inside the papal palace prepared for them, Innocent VI, following the protocol to be observed on such occasions, intended to signify to the dukes of Lancaster and Burgundy what importance he attached to their meeting, and that this gesture, while being recognized, had little or no practical consequences. Apparently Lancaster managed to find much larger quarters outside the palace walls, not only for his enormous retinue but also for himself. According to Henry Knighton, the cellar of his *hospitium* was stocked with a hundred barrels of wine before his arrival.[183] If, therefore, the rooms inside Innocent's palace were used at all, Henry must have changed lodgings frequently.

Two of the ledgers of the *Introitus et Exitus* series[184] record deliveries of basic foodstuffs such as grain, vegetables and wine, as well as of hay, straw and firewood, to visitors between 1342 and 1361. The Apostolic Camera distributed these goods only to persons lodging outside the papal palace, most of whom would be accompanied by one or more cooks who would then prepare the meals.[185] These documents thus give valuable information not only about how the curia entertained its guests but also as to whether these were accommodated inside the palace or not. Furthermore, it is instructive to see that only those among the English diplomats whose missions were responses to papal initiatives could expect to be looked after in this fashion, while all others were left to fend for themselves. When Robert Hereward came to Avignon with John Grey in September 1343 to make preparations for the first Anglo-French peace conference, he received copious quantities of food (grain, vegetables, wine and pigs) and firewood;[186] apparently, the cameral staff believed him to be the vanguard of a much larger English delegation. When this delegation eventually came, eleven months later and much reduced in size, a new delivery was made to its leading members.[187] In 1354 the picture was much the same: the households of William Bateman, Guy de Brian, Henry of Grosmont and Richard Fitzalan were supplied with foodstuffs and other essentials.[188] We may conclude that these envoys and their retinues did not stay in the papal palace during the conference, or at least not primarily.

4.4. The Diplomat and his *Familia*

While frequently mentioning the number of horses loaded onto ships at Dover, the expense accounts of Edward III's envoys to the curia only rarely provide precise information on the overall number of men in the retinue (*familia*) of a given envoy. All that can be said with certainty is that most royal embassies to Avignon, like those going to other continental destinations, comprised both horsemen and pedestrians, and that the latter usually outnumbered the former.[189]

Where exact numbers are given, these indicate that the size of Edward's embassies to the papal court did not differ from that of those sent to other continental destinations. The main determinant was the social status of the leading members of a mission, which, in turn, depended on the task assigned to it. The majority of the English diplomats sent to the curia were charged with presenting royal petitions, extending truces, preparing or conducting peace negotiations, or making propaganda for Edward III's policy while attempting to gain a clearer perception of the pope's goals.[190] A modestly sized embassy, between four[191] and forty strong, would normally suffice for such purposes.

More solemn and ceremonious occasions, on the other hand, required the presence of exceptionally high-ranking envoys, each of whom would invariably bring with him an accompanying party of adequate size. The English delegation sent to Avignon in 1354 to be present at the publication of the terms of the permanent peace and to make the solemn and public renunciations of rights and territories for which the treaty provided was probably the largest English diplomatic mission of the mid-fourteenth century. It comprised the retinues of one duke (Henry of Grosmont), one earl (Richard Fitzalan), two bishops (William Bateman and Michael Northburgh), one peer (Guy de Brian), the king's confessor (John Woderove) and a senior Privy Seal clerk (John Welwick). Its total strength was considerably more than 630 men, travelling with 602 horses. The English thus even outnumbered the combined domestic and administrative staff of the curia (between 460 and 650 men at any given point in time during the Avignon period)![192]

The larger his *familia*, the more logistic problems a diplomat could expect when preparing for the passage from Dover to Calais, but the majority of Edward's embassies seem to have been small enough to pass through this 'eye of a needle' without major difficulties. So far as can be seen from their expense accounts, the leading members of missions to the curia normally did not have to hire more than one ship, and even John Stratford, William Weston and William Dean, attended by forty-one men using twenty horses, did not need more vessels than that when they arrived at Dover in late July 1322.[193]

By contrast, William Bateman, bishop of Norwich, had to find three ships for his eighty-five men and sixty horses, and Henry of Grosmont, who took with him no less than 317 men-at-arms, plus an unknown number of household staff, will have needed at least ten. In fact, the

chronic shortage of suitable ships at Dover, together with the
problem of finding accommodation for an oversized travel group en
route and in the papal city, was probably the reason why combined
missions with two or more leaders would travel in successive 'waves'.[194]

From a purely organizational point of view, then, small travel
groups doubtless had a number of advantages over larger ones. It is,
therefore, necessary to ask why senior diplomats, as a general rule, still
deemed it indispensable to take with them up to several dozen clerics,
men-at-arms and domestic servants on their missions. First, the sheer
size of the *familia* was intended to produce an outward effect. A
diplomat's retinue, especially if dressed in the robes of the livery of its
head, could serve to emphasize the importance of the mission, the
power, status and wealth of both its sender and its leader, and the
esteem in which they held its receiver.

The diplomat's *familia* seems to have consisted of members of his
normal household who more or less permanently lived under his roof
(his actual 'travelling' or 'riding household' and the nucleus of his *familia*)
and also of persons who joined him for the duration of the mission.
Like the noble household in England, it was organized according to
the functions that it was expected to fulfil. The basic needs common
to the senior clerical and aristocratic envoys were twofold: the
demands of the social and economic tasks of any noble household in
the Middle Ages (the provision of food and clothing, the need for
personal service and entertainment, the fulfilment of religious duties,
perhaps even hospitality)[195] but also support for their diplomatic work.

There is evidence that a senior envoy's *familia* usually included a
small group of university-trained aides whose names did not appear in
his procurations and credentials. Before setting out for the curia in
early August 1344, John Offord applied to the Chancery for letters of
protection for himself, his secretary, Robert Morton, Richard Saham
DCL, later to be entrusted with a number of important missions to
the Iberian Peninsula, and two other clerks.[196] Even a man as experienced as William Bateman had his 'assistant envoys': on his last
mission he was accompanied by a doctor of both laws (Robert de
Stratton, the then master of Trinity Hall, Cambridge), a master of arts
(Thomas de Lexham), two bachelors of civil law (Roger de Freton
and Laurence de Littleton), a licentiate of civil law (Roger de Sutton)
and a notary public (Robert de Walton).[197]

Bateman's last expense account (E 101/313/21), drawn up
posthumously in the spring of 1355, is a unique source in that it offers

us some insight into the social composition of the travelling house-hold of a high-ranking English diplomat, as well as into the hierarchy, departmentalization and specialization within it. Only one of the senior clerics in his company, Thomas de Lexham, is identifiable as a chief household official. As Bateman's chamberlain, he supervised the staff of the inner, private enclave of the household, the *camera*, although the title 'master of the household'[198] suggests that he had additional, more general responsibilities within the *familia* as a whole.[199] Robert de Wissingsete and Stephen Nally (*Stephanus de Cressyngham*), Bateman's chaplains, belonged to the second layer of household officials. They were in charge of ordering the religious life of his retinue during the mission, officiating at the daily mass and hearing his and his men's confessions.[200] The seven *officiarii* whose names are listed in the account, probably minor officials or 'subheads', were also members of the 'middle management' of the *familia*. Their duties are not specified, but among them there will have been the bishop's marshal, his butler and his kitchen clerk.[201]

The largest group within Bateman's household was formed by the twenty-four grooms (*garciones*). They occupied the lowest position known in any noble household (with the possible exception of certain child servants) and performed a variety of duties: purchasing and preparing food and drink, serving at table, caring for and feeding the horses, cleaning, washing, and so on.[202] Four grooms mentioned in Bateman's account can be linked to the departments in which they were primarily employed: *Petrus de capella*, *Robertus* and *Galfridus de camera*, and *Andreas de coquina*. But it is not entirely clear whether these designations can actually be taken as proof of the existence of several departments within the bishop's travelling *familia*, or whether they refer to the grooms' positions in his regular household in England.

The fourth group comprised the squires of the bishop's household (*scutiferi de familia*), no doubt recruited from the ranks of the diocesan gentry; they functioned as an armed escort. John le Strange, a royal sergeant at arms specifically deputed for Bateman's service on this journey, commanded them.

Many details of the structure of this *familia* remain unclear, but Bateman's expense account furnishes some vital information from which it seems possible to generalize. As the *familia* of a clerical or aristocratic diplomat was a self-supporting unit, its duty was to insulate its head as much as possible from the rigours and difficulties of travel and to recreate the mode of life to which he was accustomed.

4.5. The Duration of Missions

As can be seen from Appendix II, the actual duration of English embassies varied considerably. Many envoys returned home after four or five months spent on the road and in the papal city, but any mission of between one and six months would have been considered of normal duration. However, embassies taking more than half a year were not at all uncommon, and we even know of cases where an envoy spent more than ten months abroad.

At first glance, these results may appear somewhat unsatisfactory, allowing merely, as they do, the conclusion that there were considerable fluctuations in the duration of diplomatic missions. But the absence of any standard draws our attention to the fact that it was virtually impossible for the royal administration to plan the duration of diplomatic missions to the curia with any accuracy: the equation simply contained too many variables. Most important among these were certainly the duration of an envoy's outward and return journeys and the amount and complexity of the actual business to be transacted. What is more, we may assume that most English embassies had to vie with the representatives of other rulers, or indeed with the rulers themselves, for the pope's attention. In January 1326 Guilhem Richer, envoy of James II of Aragon, wrote to his king to inform him that he had not yet had an opportunity to present his letters; John XXII was constantly busy receiving French and Italian diplomats.[203] Two examples from Anglo-papal diplomacy in the mid-fourteenth century may suffice. In May 1345, while John Reppes OC and William Ludeford were staying in Avignon, Clement VI was also engaged in negotiations with diplomats from Aragon, Hungary, Venice and the Order of the Knights of St John.[204] During the visit of John, king of Bohemia, to the curia in the winter of 1343–4, Robert Hereward will have had to accept some delays in the transaction of his own business.[205]

Secondly, any envoy to the Holy See had to take into consideration that the rhythm of daily life at the curia was to a large degree determined by the liturgical calendar.[206] The Supreme Pontiff himself would usually officiate at religious ceremonies on fifty or so occasions per year. On these and very many other days[207] the cardinals were not summoned for consistory, unless special events, such as the arrival of a king or an exceptionally important embassy, necessitated this. The administrative operations of the curia as a whole ceased during the long summer vacations (29 June–15 September) and during Holy Week.

Thirdly, whether or not the pope would receive an envoy on a given day would also depend on the state of his health. Both Clement VI and Innocent VI are known to have suffered from severe chronic illnesses that at times made it impossible for them to perform their administrative and liturgical functions. Clement was in particularly poor health in 1343, 1345 and 1349, when he suffered prolonged fever attacks, and in 1351–2, when tumours formed in the lumbar region and, finally, in his brain. On several occasions he had to undergo major surgery. Innocent VI was an old and infirm man at the time of his election, and his ability to participate in day-to-day governmental business was repeatedly curtailed by bouts of gout.[208] Though it is difficult to assess to what extent Clement's and Innocent's illnesses actually influenced their policies, 'it is certain that a constantly ill pope would have to slow his level of activity and rely more on the zeal of his subordinates and the suggestions of his entourage',[209] and that speculations about their state of health had some influence on the policy of the English Crown.

4.6. Payment

The *particule compoti*, which were submitted to the Wardrobe until the last years of Edward II's reign and afterwards to the Exchequer, stood at the centre of the administrative process preceding the reimbursement of envoys for their expenses. A detailed description of this procedure can be found elsewhere[210] and does not appear necessary in the context of the present study.

It should be added, however, that payment at the Wardrobe or Exchequer was not the only way by which royal envoys to Avignon could expect to receive remuneration. A journey to the papal court, the place where the distribution of benefices was organized, offered unique opportunities for profit, and the Registers of Supplications contain an abundance of information on petitions made by English diplomats for themselves or on behalf of relatives, friends and members of their households. Clerical envoys petitioned the pope for church posts, while laymen tried to obtain dispensations, indults and confirmations of rights and indulgences. The activities of Andrew Offord in the summer of 1343 are a case in point. During his nine-week stay[211] he managed to secure for himself no less than five provisions: a prebend of Salisbury on 6 August, a canonry and prebend of York a fortnight later, the canonry and prebend of Ramsbury in the diocese of Salisbury and the canonry and prebend of St Lawrence in the church of Romsey, with the adjacent chapel of Innere, on 4 September, and finally, shortly before his return to England, a canonry of London with expectation of a prebend.[212] Ironically enough, these provisions were made at the very time when the parliamentary protests in England reached their climax.

The prospect of being able to save time and money by taking personal action for the benefit of one's career while staying at the papal court at the Crown's expense will often have served as an incentive to undertake to go on such a long and arduous journey in the first place, especially when one takes into consideration the fact that the pay of the English medieval 'public servant' was scanty and irregular.[213] From the king's perspective, a practice that ensured the remuneration of his diplomatic agents without expense to the Crown must have been something to be tolerated, perhaps even actively encouraged. By tolerating this practice, Edward III and his councillors connived at the blurring of the dividing line between an envoy's official functions and his private interests.

Notes to Chapter 4

1. Geoffrey R. Berridge, 'Amarna diplomacy: A fully-fledged diplomatic system?', in Raymond Cohen and Raymond Westbrook (eds.), *Amarna Diplomacy: The Beginnings of International Relations* (Baltimore and London, 2000), 212–24 (213).

2. C. 17 q. 4 c. 29; *CIC* i. 822.

3. Étienne Magnin, 'Immunités ecclesiastiques', in *Dictionnaire de théologie catholique*, ed. Alfred Vacant and Eugène Mangenot (Paris, 1903–50), vii. 1218–62 (1220–4).

4. See e.g. Dig. 48.6.7 and Dig. 50.7.18. On the inviolability of the envoy in canon law, see e.g. D. 1 c. 9, D. 21 c. 2, D. 94 c. 2, and Guillaume Durand, *Speculum legatorum*, in *De legatis et legationibus tractatus varii*, ed. Vladimir E. Hrabar (Dorpat, 1905), 31–41 (32). Cf. Bernard du Rosier, *Ambaxiator brevilogus*, in *De legatis et legationibus tractatus varii*, ed. Vladimir E. Hrabar (Dorpat, 1905), chs. xxiii, xxvi and xxvii. On the theory and practice of diplomatic immunity in the Middle Ages, see in detail de Maulde La Clavière, *Diplomatie*, ii. 31–4, Ernest Nys, *Les Origines du droit international* (Brussels and Paris, 1894), 338–40, Mattingly, *Renaissance Diplomacy*, 39–44, Queller, *Office of Ambassador*, 175–84, and Nahlik, 46–8, 53–7.

5. *Registres et letters des papes du XIIIᵉ siècle: Les Registres de Boniface VIII: Recueil des bulles de ce pape, publiées ou analysées d'après les manuscrits originaux des Archives du Vatican*, ed. Georges Digard et al. (Paris, 1884–1939), 5345 (cf. 5016 and 5039–5040).

6. D 715, col. 441.

7. D 594, 596.

8. Montell Ogdon, *Juridical Bases of Diplomatic Immunity: A Study in the Origin,*

Growth and Purpose of the Law (Washington, 1936), 9–10, 29–30, 37–41, 166–94; Clifton E. Wilson, *Diplomatic Privileges and Immunities* (Tucson, AZ, 1967), 17–25; Grant V. McClanahan, *Diplomatic Immunity: Principles, Practices, Problems* (London, 1989), 32–4.

9. Geoffrey R. Berridge and Alan James, *A Dictionary of Diplomacy* (Basingstoke, 2001), 70.

10. Froissart, *Œuvres*, xviii. 228.

11. DGM 1574.

12. Hill, *King's Messengers: Contribution*, 32. A drawing on the inside cover of a Wardrobe book for 1360 shows a mounted king's messenger with his letter pouch at his belt, clearly marked with the royal arms (E 101/309/11). See also Chaplais, *English Diplomatic Practice*, 135–6 and n. 385.

13. For a detailed discussion of the origins and uses of *conductus* as a legal principle, see Georg Robert Wiederkehr, *Das freie Geleit und seine Erscheinungsformen in der Eidgenossenschaft des Spätmittelalters: Ein Beitrag zur Theorie und Geschichte eines Rechtsbegriffs* (Zurich, 1977), esp. 3–7, 22–7, 22–3, 33–9, 46–7, and, more recently, Martin Kintzinger, 'Cum salvo conductu: Geleit im westeuropäischen Spätmittelalter', in Schwinges and Wriedt, 313–63 (esp. 328–30).

14. Letters of safe conduct are discussed here and not in Section 5.1., since they were not, in a technical sense, diplomatic letters.

15. Wiederkehr, 53; Meinrad Schaab, 'Geleit', in *LexMA* iv. 1204–5; Kintzinger, 320.

16. Cuttino, *English Diplomatic Administration*, 158–9. See *EMDP*, docs. 165, 167, 173.

17. See e.g. E 403/377, m. 8 (John Woderove, 1354); E 372/202, m. 35ʳ (Nicholas d'Amory and Thomas Fulnetby, 1357).

18. Wiederkehr, 33–9, 46–7.

19. DGM 315, 581, 848, 899, 1039, 1332, 4169, 4682; GL 1019.

20. e.g. ASV RV 146, fo. 70ʳ; DGM 327–8, 451, 593–4, 860–1, 4710, 4819, 4828.

21. Cf. Cuttino, *English Diplomatic Administration*, 158–9.

22. DGM 452, 610, 657, 780, 848, 899, 3811, 4699, 5446–7, 5450, 5457; ASV Instr. Misc. 6306, ASV RV 240, ii. fos. 39ʳ⁻ᵛ; RV 241, fo. 55ᵛ.

23. Perroy, 'Quatre lettres', 163–4.

24. For what follows, see in detail Plöger, 'Entführung des Fieschi', 97–103.

25. See Section 2.3.1.

26. Eckert, 183–4.

27. DGM 327, 329, 743.

28. R II. ii. 1228. The first part of this petition ('Sanctitatem [...] redeuntibus'), as copied into C 70/19, m. 3 and printed in Rymer, does not contain a predicate.

29. DGM 315, col. 117, l. 26–col. 118, l. 7.

30. Ibid., col. 118, ll. 7–21.

31. Dig. 5.1.2.3–4. Cf. du Rosier, 26. On the *ius revocandi domum*, see Hans Ritter von Frisch, *Der völkerrechtliche Begriff der Exterritorialität* (Vienna, 1917), 9–10, and Mattingly, *Renaissance Diplomacy*, 39–41.

32. Part 7, title 25, law 9 (*Las siete partidas del Rey Don Alfonso el Sabio* (Madrid, 1807), iii. 680–1).

33. Donald E. Queller, 'Early Venetian legislation concerning foreign ambassadors', *Studies in the Renaissance* 12 (1965), 7–17 (16), and *Office of Ambassador*, 179–80.

34. Wood, 45–7.
35. Timothy Reuter, 'Die Unsicherheit auf den Straßen im europäischen Früh- und Hochmittelalter: Täter, Opfer und ihre mittelalterlichen und modernen Betrachter', in Johannes Fried (ed.), *Träger und Instrumentarien des Friedens im hohen und späten Mittelalter* (Sigmaringen, 1996), 169–201 (173–4); Kintzinger, 313–14.
36. DGM 315, col. 117, ll. 18–26.
37. R III. i. 18, cf. DGM 581, 1039, 1332. Dictated letters: DGM 743, col. 289, and 1844, 25.
38. ASV, *Registra Supplicationum* 28, fo. 8ᵛ, cf. *CPP* 269.
39. Edward R. Adair, *The Exterritoriality of Ambassadors in the 16th and 17th Centuries* (London and New York, 1929), 5–12; Ogdon, 63.
40. Pierre Ayrault, *De l'ordre et instruction judiciaire dont les Anciens Grecs et Romains ont usé en accusations publiques, conféré à l'usage de nostre France* (Paris, 1576), 55. The idea is expressed more clearly in the fourth edn. (Paris, 1610), 1.15, 76–7: 'L'ambassadeur [...] sera tenu pour absent, et pour present en son pays.' Cf. Nys, *Les Origines du droit international*, 340–1, Adair, 16–17, and Ogdon, 68–9.
41. Hugo Grotius, *De jure belli ac pacis libri tres* (Paris, 1625), 2.18.4.5, 371.
42. See Section 4.3.1.
43. E 159/135, m. 174ᵛ.
44. E 101/313/39, m. 2; cf. E 372/203, m. 40ᵛ.
45. E 101/314/27. Margaret's name was later crossed out.
46. *Anonimalle Chronicle*, 75, 179. Guides: E 101/316/28.
47. Hill, *King's Messengers: Contribution*, 95–8; J. R. Alban and Christopher T. Allmand, 'Spies and spying in the fourteenth century', in Christopher T. Allmand (ed.), *War, Literature, and Politics in the Late Middle Ages: Essays in Honour of G. W. Coopland* (Liverpool, 1976), 73–101 (77–8).
48. E 403/377, m. 11.
49. VQ vi. 97. On Loring's, Margaret's and Fulnetby's mission (Loring and Fulnetby: 1 Aug. 1364–21 Mar. 1365, Margaret: 24 Nov. 1364–21 Mar. 1365), see E 372/209, fo. 51ʳ⁻ᵛ.
50. E 101/315/16. Massiolus de Monte Falco: *CPR* 1343–5, E 403/336, m. 40. Cf. the note of payment to another papal sergeant at arms, 30 Apr. 1365: 'De mandato pape [...] Guillelmo de Grisaco bastardo [...] pro expensis pro associando et conducendo quosdam ambaxatores regis Anglie etc. in Romana Curia, 33 flor. cam.' (VQ vi. 97). The envoys referred to are Nigel Loring, William Margaret and Thomas Fulnetby, who had all returned to London on 21 Mar. (E 372/209, fo. 51ᵛ).
51. R III. i. 197.
52. Edinburgh University Library MS 183, fo. 53ᵛ, see Fowler, *King's Lieutenant*, 132.
53. See App. III.
54. Letter: GL 1019. Escort: E 101/313/25.
55. Édouard Baratier, *La Démographie provençale du XIIIᵉ au XVIᵉ siècle* (Paris, 1961), 82, 127–9.
56. Francis Aidan Gasquet, *The Black Death of 1348 and 1349*, 2nd edn. (London, 1908), 43–52; Sylvain Gagnière (ed.), *Histoire d'Avignon* (Aix-en-Provence, 1979), 260–2; Philip Ziegler, *The Black Death* (Stroud, 1997, repr. 2000), 47–8.
57. Andries Welkenhuysen, 'La peste en Avignon (1348) décrit par un témoin

oculaire, Louis Sanctus de Beringen (édition critique, traduction, éléments de commentaire)', in *Pascua Medievalia: Studies voor Prof. Dr J. M. de Smet* (Louvain, 1983), 452–90.

58. Heyligen notes that the epidemic claimed 62,000 lives in the city between 25 Jan. and 27 Apr. (Welkenhuysen, 467, l. 61; cf. 468, ll. 100–2). This seems quite impossible—its population never exceeded 45,000 in the years between 1345 and 1347 (Guillemain, *Cour pontificale*, 62, 556–8).

59. Baratier, 82, 127–9. Cf. Gagnière, 262, and Ziegler, 47.

60. *Rechnungsbücher*, intro. 96–101.

61. GC ix. 314.

62. Welkenhuysen, 469, ll. 137–42.

63. Matthias von Neuenburg, *Cronica*, in *Heinricus de Diessenhofen und andere Geschichtsquellen Deutschlands im Späteren Mittelalter*, ed. Alfons Huber (Stuttgart, 1868), 149–276 (261). The dating clauses of Clement VI's letters in fact do suggest that he remained in Avignon throughout the year. According to the account books of the Apostolic Chamber, he held only one banquet between 15 Mar. 1348 and 20 June 1349 (Stefan Weiß, *Die Versorgung des päpstlichen Hofes in Avignon mit Lebensmitteln (1316–1378): Studien zur Sozial- und Wirtschaftsgeschichte eines mittelalterlichen Hofes* (Berlin, 2002), 504).

64. E 30/1519. Unfortunately, the document is much stained and in large parts illegible.

65. Guillemain, *Cour pontificale*, 214, 447–8. This would suggest a somewhat lower mortality rate than among the townsmen (Ziegler, 47).

66. Gasquet, chs. V–VI; Ziegler, 92–3, 106–49.

67. William Mark Ormrod, 'The English government and the Black Death of 1348–9', in id. (ed.), *England in the Fourteenth Century* (Woodbridge, 1986), 175–88 (175–8).

68. I here give the dates of their departures from London: 1 Mar. 1348: Andrew Offord, Castile (E 101/312/32; MD no. CXXVI), 6/16 May 1348: John Carlton, Avignon (E 372/194, m. 45^v), 12 May 1348: Yvo Clinton and Hugh Neville, Brabant and Cologne (E 101/312/30–1; MD nos. CXXVII–CXXVIII), 10 Aug. 1348: William Stury, Flanders (E 372/194, m. 45^r), 8 Sept. 1348: John Mayn, Guienne (E 372/193, m. 34^v), 21–26 Sept. 1348: Robert Ufford, William Bateman, Henry Grosmont, John Carlton, Calais (E 101/312/33; E 372/193, m. 34$^{r–v}$, 45^v; MD no. CXXIX), 7 Nov. 1348: Richard of Carlisle, Castile (E 101/312/34), 7 Jan. 1349: John Carlton, Calais, Flanders, Brabant (E 372/194, m. 45^v), 28 Jan. 1349: Stephen Cusington, Flanders (E 372/196, m. 41v), 9 Feb. 1349: Richard Talbot, Flanders (E 372/193, m. 34v), 11 Mar. 1349: John Carlton, Flanders (E 101/319/40; MD no. CXXXI), 14–19 Mar. 1349: William Bateman, John de Shepey, Reginald Cobham, William Clinton, Calais (E 101/312/33, 37–9; MD nos. CXXXII–CXXXV), c.22 May 1349: Michael Northburgh, Avignon (E 403/347, mm. 9, 25; E 403/353, mm. 18, 20–1; E 403/355, m. 40), 19 June 1349: John Carlton, Avignon (E 101/312/40; MD no. CXXXVI), c. 30 Aug. 1349: Robert Askeby, Avignon (E 403/347, m. 26), 26. Sept. 1349: Walter Manny, Flanders (E 372/194, m. 45r), 17–27 Oct. 1349: William Burton and Yvo Clinton, Calais (E 101/312/35–6; MD nos. CXXXVII–CXXXVIII), 19 Apr. 1350: Yvo Clinton and Walter Stury, Zealand (E 372/194, m. 45^v; E 372/196, m. 44^r), 19–22 May 1350: Robert Ufford and William Bateman, Calais

(E 101/313/1; MD no. CXL; E 372/194, m. 45^v), 18 July 1350: Richard Totesham, Flanders (E 101/313/2; MD no. CXLI), 21 Oct. 1350: Andrew Offord, Calais (E 101/313/4), 23–26 Oct. 1350: Yvo Clinton and William Stury, Hainault (E 101/313/3; MD no. CXLII), 19 Dec. 1350: Yvo Clinton, Zealand (E 101/313/3; MD no. CXLIII).

69. For the chronology of what follows, see App. I, nos. XXVII/1–XXXVII.

70. R III. i. 151.

71. DGM 3742 (17 Feb. 1348).

72. DGM 3797, 3812.

73. On the chronological problems regarding Carlton's missions in 1348 see the note in App. I. By 30 May Clement knew that he was on his way back to Avignon (DGM 3890).

74. Gilles le Muisit, *Chronique et Annales*, ed. Henri Lemaître (Paris, 1906), 197.

75. Stanton: envoy of Queen Philippa (*CPP* 160). Cleangre: envoy of the University of Oxford (*CPP* 146–50). De Mons: envoy of Wenlok priory (*CCR* 1349–54, 75). Gildesburgh: envoy of the prince of Wales (*CPP* 154, 164). Philippi: envoy of Edward III, David Bruce, Charles of Blois, Henry of Grosmont, Ralph Stafford, John Darcy (*CPP* 164). Beckingham: envoy of the abp. of York (*CPP* 168). De Savinhac: envoy of Henry of Grosmont (DGM 4338). Dunclent: envoy of the bp.-elect of Worcester (*CPP* 191).

76. Heinrich Taube von Selbach, *Chronica*, ed Harry Bresslau (Berlin, 1922), 88–9; Guillemain, *Cour pontificale*, 214, 448–9.

77. CPP 369, 374.

78. See App. I, nos. LXXVI–LXXVIII.

79. The 60s. were granted by letter under the privy seal on 10 May 1361, eight days before his departure: 'Vous mandons qe vous lui facez livrer et allouer par celle cause quarante soldes le iour pour ses gages et outre ce par encheson de la cherete des vitailles quele y ad es parties dedela vers la dite court plus qe ne soleit sessante soldes le iour' (E 404/6/41). Cf. the note of payment of the sum 'pro regardo causa caristatis victualium in partibus exteris' (E 403/409, m. 19).

80. See esp. the recent study by Kenneth A. Fowler: *Medieval Mercenaries*, i: *The Great Companies* (Oxford, 2001), chs. 1–3.

81. Sumption, *Trial by Fire*, 359–65.

82. Fowler, *Medieval Mercenaries*, 4–5, 28–37.

83. Ibid. 32.

84. Ibid. 37.

85. ASV Instr. Misc. 6306, dated 21 July 1357, eight days after de Cervole's crossing of the river.

86. E 403/390, m. 8.

87. Eudes, himself ill, withdrew to Beaucaire and travelled onwards to Marseilles when it became clear that the talks would not be resumed (Petit, vii. 330–3, 372–3, 399–402; Dubois, 72–3, 88–9).

88. DGM 3890.

89. 1348: John Merton (*CPL* 278), Richard Prayers (*CPP* 142). 1361: *Richardus de Anglia* (*CPP* 358, 318), William Bradley (*CPP* 319, 369), Thomas Bridekirke (*CPP* 373, 375), John Burton (*CPL* 384), Thomas Clipston (*CPP* 320, 373; *CPL* 381; see *BRUO* 443), John Colste (*CPP* 374), Thomas David (*CPP* 369, 370),

William de Doune (*CPP* 320, 370, 371; *CPL* 381; see *BRUO* 587), Richard Drax (*CPP* 318), William Driffield (*CPP* 373), Thomas Fastolf (*BRUO* 2175), Richard Hornington (*CPP* 374), Thomas de Lisle (VQ vii. 377, 410), Thomas Michel DCL (*CPP* 377, 382; see *BRUC* 405), Walter Moring (*CPL* 377; see *BRUO* 1323), William Napton (*CPP* 373), Thomas Neville (*CPP* 321, 373–5; see *BRUO* 1351), John Noion (*CPP* 377), John Olney (*CPP* 365, 371), Henry Rocha (VQ vii. 357), John Suldan (*CPP* 374), William Sunderlond (*CPP* 318), Hugh Tessedale (*CPP* 375), Richard Thormerton (*CPP* 370, 394), John Thursteyn (*CPP* 373, 375; see *BRUO* 1873), John Tomstayn (*CPP* 320), John Tresulian (*BRUO* 1897), Henry With (*CPP* 373), Henry la Zouche (*CPP* 374).

90. Lunderthorpe: ASV RA 79, fos. 46^v–47^r. Inge: *CPL* 29 (see also *BRUO* 1001). Franciscan: DGM 2353. Brisley: ASV RA 98, fos. 282^v–283^r, and *CPP* 142.

91. C 70/25, m. 3.

92. *CCR* 1354–60, 164–5.

93. *CPR* 1343–5, 411; *CCR* 1343–5, 412–13, 422–3. Edmund von Birkelin in Edward III's service: Trautz, 205–6, 215. Presumably he kidnapped Piers because he felt that the king still owed him money. Two years earlier he had kidnapped an English knight and his brother, a squire (*Deutsch–englisches Bündnis*, doc. 558).

94. E 372/194, m. 45^v.

95. *Anonimalle Chronicle*, 32; Knighton, 128.

96. See in detail Section 4.3.1.

97. E 101/315/12. On Bukton, see *BRUO* 300.

98. See Chaplais, *English Diplomatic Practice*, 181.

99. R III. i. 283. For other examples of letters of procuration including a *quorum*, see C 76/19, m. 2 (20 Oct. 1344); R II. ii. 1224 (20 May 1343), 1231–2 (29 Aug. 1343); R III. i. 19 (4 Aug. 1344), 289 (20 Oct. 1354).

100. R III. i. 19; cf. C 76/19, m. 2.

101. Baldwin, 345–52.

102. Froissart, *Œuvres*, xviii. 204.

103. Bock, 'Some new documents', 93.

104. Froissart, *Œuvres*, xviii. 204.

105. Ibid. 234.

106. Ibid. 221.

107. Guillemain, *Cour pontificale*, 110; Mollat, *Papes d'Avignon*, 9–11; Agostino Paravicini Bagliani, 'Residences, Papal', in *PE* iii. 1300–5 (1302).

108. Kervyn de Lettenhove, *Histoire de Flandre* (Brussels, 1847–50), ii, doc. V, II.

109. Yves Renouard, 'Routes, étapes et vitesses de marche de France à Rome au XIIIe et au XIVe siècles d'après les itinéraires d'Eudes Rigaud (1254) et de Barthélemy Bonis (1350)', in id. (ed.), *Études d'histoire médiévale* (Paris, 1968), ii. 677–97 (677). See also Jean-Marie Cauchies, 'Les sources des itinéraires routiers en Europe occidentale au moyen âge', in *Bronnen voor de historische geografie van België—Sources de la géographie historique en Belgique*, ed. J. Mertens (Brussels, 1980), 75–104 (80).

110. Cambridge University Library, MS Hh.6.11, fo. 2^r, ed. Léon Le Grand ('Itinéraire de Wissant à Lyon', *BEC* 47 (1886), 197–8 (197)). The route mentioned in this manuscript is not identical with that described in Matthew Paris's famous pictorial itineraries from London to Rome and Apulia in BL Royal MS C VII, fo. 2$^{r–v}$ (cf. Debra J. Birch, *Pilgrimage to Rome in the Middle*

Ages: Continuity and Change (Woodbridge, 1998), 43–5). It is therefore unlikely that, as Mary C. Hill believes, English travellers to Avignon would consult Paris's work ('Jack Faukes', 24).

111. BL Royal MS 13 A XVIII, fos. 157$^{r–v}$ (App. VI, 1).

112. See App. II. Mary C. Hill's article on Faukes's journey ('Jack Faukes', 25) contains many topographical errors. John Middleton's account is printed in James E. T. Rogers, *A History of Agriculture and Prices in England* (Oxford, 1866–1902), ii. 631–4.

113. Destruction: Jean le Bel, *Chronique*, ed. Jules Viard and Eugène Déprez (Paris, 1904–5), ii. 109–10; Sumption, *Trial by Battle*, 532. On the change from Wissant to Dover, see also Chaplais, *English Diplomatic Practice*, 220–1. Hugh Neville and William de Cusance disembarked at Calais in mid-Feb. 1344, but only because contrary winds prevented them from reaching Wissant (E 101/312/9; cf. E 372/188, m. 50^{v}).

114. Léon Blin, 'Le grand chemin de Paris à Lyon par la vallée de la Loire aus bas moyen âge (de Decize à Marcigny par la rive gauche)', *BPH* 1958 (1959), 237–65, deals with this route in some detail. The word *magnus* was used in the Middle Ages to denote the importance of a road, not its physical qualities (M. Gilles-Guibert, 'Noms des routes et des chemins dans le Midi de la France au moyen âge', *BPH* 1960 (1961), 1–39 (28–9)). A late-13th-c. *itinéraire théorique*, describing the stages of a journey from Lyons to Orléans along the Loire (Brussels, Bibliothèque Royale, MS 3213, fo. 137^{r}) has been edited by Ferdinand Lot ('Itinéraires du XIIIe siècle', *BPH* 1920 (1922), 217–22 (219–20)). See also the map in Renoaurd, 'Routes', 688–9.

115. Blin, 248–9, 263.

116. On the route from Paris to Nevers, see Robert-Henri Bautier, 'Récherches sur les routes de l'Europe médiévale. i: De Paris et des foires de Champagne à la Méditerranée par le Massif Central', *BPH* 1960 (1961), 99–143 (135–8).

117. See App. VI.4.

118. Faukes: E 101/312/4, m. 2; Offord and Neville: Froissart, *Œuvres*, xviii. 206; Stafford: E 101/313/39, m. 2^{v}; Loring: E 372/206, m. 50^{r}, cf. E 159/138; Cobham did not take the *iter lugdunense* but crossed Champagne and Burgundy and travelled down the Saône and Rhône in boats hired in Chalon, Tournus, Mâcon and Lyons (E 101/315/18).

119. G. Salmon, 'Bateaux et bateliers sur le Rhône et Saône: Un voyage lexical en domaine franco-provençal au moyen âge', in *Voyage, quête, pèlerinage dans la littérature et la civilisation médiévales* (Aix-en-Provence and Paris, 1976), 139–51 (147).

120. D. Faucher, *L'Homme et la Rhône* (Paris, 1968), 71–2, 75–80 (esp. 77, fig.6).

121. Marjory Nice Boyer, 'Roads and rivers: Their use and disuse in late medieval France', *Medievalia et Humanistica* 13 (1960), 68–80 (75, 80).

122. *Documents parisiens*, ii. 367.

123. *Chronique anonyme parisienne de 1316 à 1339*, ed. A. Héllot, *Memoirs de la Société Historique de Paris* 11 (1885), 1–207 (104–7); R II. i. 638.

124. E 372/175, m. 45^{r}. On his journeys to Avignon in 1325–6, 1328–9 and 1329, see Fredric L. Cheyette, 'Paris B.N. ms. latin 5954: The professional papers of an English ambassador on the eve of the Hundred Years' War', in *Économies et sociétés au moyen âge: Mélanges offerts à E. Perroy* (Paris, 1973), 400–13 (402–3).

125. E 101/311/27.

126. 'Eundo intravi mare apud Orewell' et applicui inter Friseam et Holand' iuxta villa de Petten in loco non consueto' (E 101/311/38). Journey through Germany: E 372/185, m. 42ʳ. Winkleigh and Servington returned via Tournai and Sluis.

127. On the routes from Cologne to Bruges via Maastricht, see Friedrich Bruns and Hugo Weczerka, *Hansische Handelsstraßen* (Cologne, 1962–8), i, map V, pp. 16, 24, and map II, pp. 476, 499–502, 505–7. Attack on Piers: *CPR* 1343–5, 411; *CCR* 1343–6, 412–13, 422–3.

128. ASV RA 98, fo. 282ᵛ; cf. *CPP* 142.

129. Sumption, *Trial by Fire*, 411–17.

130. See App. VI.9.

131. Gilbert: E 101/316/29; De Shepey: E 101/316/28. On their mission, see Richard G. Davies, 'The Anglo-papal concordat of Bruges, 1375: A reconsideration', *AHP* 19 (1981), 97–146 (102–19). On Gaunt's 1373 expedition, see Anthony Goodman, *John of Gaunt* (Harlow, 1992), 232–4.

132. *CPL* iv. 125.

133. Perroy, 'Quatre lettres', 163.

134. Stafford: E 101/315/10. Burghersh's account (E 101/315/16) mentions the detour via Poitiers where the envoys arrived on 1 Sept. 1366. Brittany may have appeared a safer place than ever to the travellers, since the victory of the English-backed Montfortists at the battle of Auray (29 Sept. 1364) had led to a formal settlement of the Breton succession after more than twenty years of intermittent warfare (Christopher T. Allmand, *The Hundred Years War: England and France at War c.1300–c.1450* (Cambridge, 1989), 20–1). On the medieval routes through southern central France see the map in Bautier, 126.

135. On the travel routes from England to Italy in the early and high Middle Ages, see the detailed study by George B. Parks, *The English Traveler to Italy*, i: *The Middle Ages (to 1525)* (Rome, 1954), pts. 1 and 2, *passim*, and esp. 45–57, 180–93 and table 5.

136. Marc Bloch, *Feudal Society*, 2nd edn., trans. L. A. Manyon (London and New York, 1965; repr. 1989), i. 64.

137. We have two *itinéraires réels* of pilgrims from the British Isles from the Avignon period. In 1323 Symon Semeonis and Hugh le Luminour, two Irish Franciscans, took ship at Chalon-sur-Saône and sailed down the Saône and Rhône on their way to Egypt and Palestine, but this was only because the war between Matteo Visconti and Robert of Naples prevented them from taking the direct route from Châtillon-sur-Seine to Lombardy via Dijon and Lausanne (*Itinerarium Symonis Semeonis Ab Hybernia Ad Terram Sanctam*, ed. Mario Esposito (Dublin, 1960), 30–2). On 13 Oct. 1344 an anonymous English pilgrim left Avignon to make the pilgrimage to the Holy Land via Rome, Naples and Brindisi, but unfortunately his report does not provide any information on the route that he chose for his journey to the papal city (MS Corpus Christi College, Cambridge, 370: *Itinerarium cuiusdam Anglici Terram Sanctam et alia loca sancta visitantis*, in Girolamo Golubovich (ed.), *Biblioteca bio-bibliografica della Terra Santa e dell'Oriente Francescano* (Florence, 1906–23), iv. 427–60).

138. For a useful typology of medieval mobility, see Geert Berings, 'Transport and communication in the Middle Ages', in *Kommunikation und Alltag in Spätmittelalter und früher Neuzeit* (Vienna, 1992), 47–73.

139. See e.g. the *particule* of Thomas Wale and Thomas Delisle for a journey to the papal court at Anagni (E 101/308/29, printed in Edward L. G. Stones, 'The mission of Thomas Wale and Thomas Delisle from Edward I to Pope Boniface VIII in 1301', *Nottingham Medieval Studies* 26 (1982), 8–28, doc. B).

140. Bautier, 101, 103.

141. See Section 2.1.

142. ASV RV 116, no. 203, printed in *Deutsch–englisches Bündnis*, doc. 583.

143. Marjory Nice Boyer, 'A day's journey in medieval France', *Speculum* 26 (1951), 597–608 (606).

144. E 101/312/4, m. 1.

145. Northern France: daily distances of between 42 km (Saint-Riquier to Poix) and 108 km (Poix to Paris). Loire valley: between 17 km (*Chescurteis* to Beaulon) and 54 km (Cosne to Nevers). Beaujolais and Rhône valley: 143 km (Beaulon to Lyons), 210 km (Lyons to Avignon).

146. E 101/312/4, m. 3.

147. 'Dictos nuncios [Hugh Neville and William de Cusance] ad sanctitatis vestre presentiam [...] providimus [...] destinandos [...] qui [...] infra viginti dies ab instanti festo Sancte Trinitatis [30 May 1344] continue munerandos presentes erunt et parati in sanctitatis vestre curia' (Edward III to Clement VI, 12 May 1344; C 70/20, m. 2). 'Certos nuncios ad sanctitatis vestrae praesentiam [...] ordinavimus destinandos, sperantes quod infra viginti dies [...] continue munerandos praesentes fuissent in sanctitatis vestrae curia' (the same to the same, 3 Aug. 1344; R III. i. 18).

148. E 372/175, m. 45^r; E 101/309/32.

149. Offord and Neville (App. I, nos. XVI/1–2): E 372/189, m. 44^r; Froissart, *Œuvres*, xviii. 202. Thoresby and Spigournel (App. I, no. XVI/5): E 372/189, m. 44^r; Froissart, *Œuvres*, xviii. 232.

150. Oxford, The Queen's College, Long Rolls, Transcripts, ii, fo. 113^r.

151. Weston: E 372/175, m. 45^r (excluding the time of his imprisonment in Antwerp 30 Aug.–5 Oct. 1326). Fastolf: E 101/311/27.

152. Some examples of durations of journeys thus established: Andrew Offord and Richard Chamberlain (App. I, no. VI): 22 days or less (E 101/312/7, m. 1; *CPP* 20); Robert Hereward (no. VIII/1): 29 days or less (E 372/188, m. 50^r; VQ iii. 232); Andrew Offord (no. X): 21 days or less (E 101/312/7; DGM 581); Hugh Neville and William de Cusance (no. XI): 29 days or less (E 101/312/9; DGM 722); Andrew Offord and William Bateman (nos. XII/1–2): 25 days or less (E 101/312/7; DGM 759); Michael Northburgh and Nigel Loring (no. XVII): 30 days or less (E 372/189, m. 44^r; DGM 1574); Nicholas d'Amory and Thomas Fulnetby (no. LXI): 27 days or less (E 372/202, m. 35^r; *CPL* 625); Nigel Loring (no. LXXVI): 28 days or less (E 101/314/7; R III, ii. 623). Richard Stafford and William Burton (no. LXVII) completed their journey through the west of the Empire to Avignon within 74 days (E 101/313/39; *CPP* 340–1).

153. Bernard du Rosier, *Ambaxiator brevilogus*, in *De legatis et legationibus tractatus varii*, ed. Vladimir E. Hrabar (Dorpat, 1905), 1–28 (10–11).

154. Boyer, 'Day's journey', 598–601, 604. Two articles by Grace Stretton provide some insight into the specific problems that faced travelling kings and nobles: 'Some aspects of medieval travel', *TRHS*, 4th ser., 7 (1924), 77–97, and 'The travelling household in the middle ages', *Journal of the British Archaeological*

Association NS 40 (1935), 75–103. On travelling aristocrats and their retinues, see also Margaret W. Labarge, *Medieval Travellers: The Rich and Restless* (London, 1982), 15–16 and chs. 3 and 4.

155. E 101/313/25 (departure: 28 Oct. 1354); cf. Knighton, 126–9 (arrival: 24 Dec. 1354).

156. By kind information of Dr Harm von Seggern.

157. Boyer, 'Day's journey', 604–6.

158. Cf. also Renouard, 'Information et transmission des nouvelles', 113.

159. E 101/313/21, m. 1. *Hospicium*: hospitality, entertainment of guests; (temporary) lodgings; inn, place of entertainment; monastic guest-house; hospice, hospital for the poor and infirm; academic hall of residence; dwelling, house; household (*Dictionary of Medieval Latin from British Sources*, ed. Ronald Edward Latham and David R. Howlett (London, 1975–), 1178). Cf. Hans Conrad Peyer (ed.), *Gastfreundschaft, Taverne und Gasthaus im Mittelalter* (Munich and Vienna, 1983), 261.

160. Cf. BL Royal MS 13 A XVIII, fo. 157ʳ, where *Chescurteys* is described as being situated four leagues (*c*.19.3 km) from Beaulon and two leagues (*c*.9.7 km) from Decize, which means that it must have been near or in what today is Lamenay-sur-Loire. See also Blin, 244–5.

161. Peyer, *Gastfreundschaft*, x–xi, 261, 264, and id., 'Gasthaus', in *LexMA* iv. 1132–4 (1133).

162. Michel Hayez and Anne-Marie Hayez, 'L'hôtellerie avignonnaise au XIVᵉ siècle, à propos de la succession de Siffrède Trelhon (1387)', *Provence historique* 25 (1975), 275–84 (275). The *Liber divisionis* (ASV RA 204, fos. 428–507) has been analysed in some detail by Guillemain (*Cour pontificale*, 654–95), who identifies 66 *hostelarii* or *alberguerii* (ibid. 666).

163. Hayez and Hayez, 276–7.

164. Middleton: Rogers, ii. 633. Whitfield: Oxford, The Queen's College, Long Rolls, Transcripts, ii. fo. 112ʳ; cf. Rogers, ii. 136–7.

165. *Hospitia*: William Ottringham (1318, 1319), ASV Coll. 52. fos. 27ʳ, 33ʳ; Ralph Hornchester (1327), fo. 150ʳ. *Domus*: William Ottringham (1318, 1320), fos. 28ʳ, 51ᵛ; Robert Schuburn (1320), fo. 51ᵛ; Richard Thormerton and Robert Gonwardby (1320), fo. 62ʳ; Andrea Sapiti (1326), fo. 132, Alan Setrington and William Hytrecon' (reading doubtful) (1329), fo. 177ʳ; William Weston (*clericus domini regis Francie* (!)) (1329), fo. 198ᵛ. Schrader (*Rechnungsbücher*, intro. 65–6, 69) notes that the permanent envoys who represented Hamburg's city council in 1338–48 and 1354–5 took up residence in inns and hostels when their visits were short ones, and in rented houses or flats for the duration of longer stays.

166. Fastolf: SC 7/64/15; *Prozeß-Schriftgut*, doc. 15f. Sudbury: *Korrespondenz*, doc. 215; CPP 329. *Richardus de Anglia*: Coll. 53, fo. 114ʳ. *Carreria Furni de Nabressa*: Pierre Pansier, *Dictionnaire des anciennes rues d'Avignon* (Avignon, 1930), 94–5; Cf. Joseph Girard, *Évocation du vieil Avignon* (Paris, 1958), 79, 257. Drax: Archives départmentales Vaucluse, 9 G 37, n. 871, cited after Anne-Marie Hayez, 576 n. 48.

167. Nicholas Fransoyzer and Hinricus de Monte to the councillors, 22 Mar. 1354: 'Conduximus unam bonam domum in Avinione pro L florenis pro uno anno, in qua morabatur quidam cardinalis, et est sita prope Sabatariam, dictam proprie platea Sutorum, et est in illa platea ubi casei venduntur' (*Korrespondenz*, doc. 198). The *Carreria Sabaterie* is today's rue des Fourbisseurs (Pansier, *Dictionnaire*, 219–20).

168. Weston: E 372/175, m. 45^r; ASV Coll. 52, fo. 122^v. The Hamburg envoys Hinricus de Monte and Johannes Wunstorp stayed with Eckhart of Lübeck, a proctor from northern Germany, in the winter of 1354–5 (*Korrespondenz*, doc. 239).
169. ASV Coll. 52, fo. 26^v. As has been said above, the exact meaning of *hospitium* is often unclear, but since ordinary houses are called *domus* in this document it is to be assumed that the word here denotes a place where commercial accommodation was offered. On the *taxatores et assignatores domorum*, see Paul Maria Baumgarten, *Aus Kanzlei und Kammer: Erörterungen zur kurialen Hof- und Verwaltungsgeschichte im XIII., XIV. und XV. Jahrhundert* (Freiburg, 1907), 51, 53–4.
170. *VPA* i. 213; Dau 715, 721.
171. Pansier, *Dictionnaire*, 79; cf. Girard, 78.
172. ASV Coll. 52, fo. 57^v; Pansier, *Dictionnaire*, 94.
173. *Registres et letters des papes du XIVe siècle: Jean XXII (1316–1334): Lettres secrètes et curiales relatives à la France, publiées ou analysées d'après les registres du Vatican*, ed. Auguste Coulon and Suzanne Clémencet (Paris, 1900–72), 4472.
174. ASV Coll. 52, fos. 24^v–25^r; cf. Bernard Guillemain, 'Les logements des curialistes et des courtisans dans Avignon sous Jean XXII', in *Crises et réformes dans l'église de la Réforme Grégorienne à la Préréforme* (Paris, 1991), 181–7 (184).
175. *Reg. Orleton*, 110, 112–13, 115–16, 118–20.
176. *AA* i. 225–6. As far as the hygienic aspect was concerned, their moving house came too late: de Villanova became ill which he attributed to the sanitary conditions at their *hospitium* (ibid. 227).
177. See Charles IV's autobiography: *Vita ab eo ipso conscripta, et Hystoria nova de Sancto Wenceslao Martyre: Autobiography of Emperor Charles IV and his Legend of St. Wenceslas*, ed. Balázs Nagy and Frank Schaer (Budapest, 2001), 28, 142–4.
178. For much of what follows, see Weiß, *Versorgung*, 245–50. This room was probably normally used as accommodation for the pope's closest advisers, the use by guests being an exception (ibid. 248).
179. Eudes's retinue stayed at the residence of Pierre Bertrand, cardinal priest of S Clement, an old friend of his. The duke himself seems to have spent a considerable amount of time there (Petit, vii. 321, 371–2; Dubois, 84).
180. Weiß, *Versorgung*, 245–50.
181. The material was supplied by a Florentine merchant who later submitted his bill at the Camera. Rooms of Audouin Aubert: ASV IE 272, fos. 138$^{r–v}$. Rooms of Arnaud Aubert: ibid., fos. 138^r, 138^v, 139^v, 154^v, and VQ iii. 549. Cf. Mollat, 'Innocent VI et les tentatives de paix', 739–40, and Weiß, *Versorgung*, 249.
182. Unlike Mollat and Weiß, I am not convinced that the two dukes would have consented to becoming 'flatmates' for the duration of the conference (Mollat, 'Innocent VI et les tentatives de paix', 740; Weiß, *Versorgung*, 249).
183. It is very unlikely indeed that his retinue found lodgings in the palace, as Mollat maintains ('Innocent VI et les tentatives de paix', 740). Wine: Knighton, 128.
184. ASV IE 207 and 199.
185. Cf. Weiß, *Versorgung*, 250. William Bateman was accompanied by at least two kitchen staff (*Galfridus* and *Andrea de coquina*) in 1354 (E 101/313/21, m. 2).
186. Hereward received no less than 200 horse-loads (*saumatae*) of wheat, 250 horse-loads of oats, 16 horse-loads of vegetables, 80 casks (*dolia seu botae*) of wine, 18 pigs and 600 horse-loads of firewood (ASV IE 207, fo. 31^v; VQ iii. 232).
187. John Offord and Hugh Neville: 200 horse-loads of wheat, 200 horse-loads of

oats, 6 horse-loads of vegetables, 500 horse-loads of firewood on 4 Sept. 1344, the day after their arrival (ASV IE 207, fo. 43^v; VQ iii. 232) and 60 casks (*botae*) of wine on 9 Sept. 1344 (IE 207, fo. 47^r). William Bateman: 1,000 *quintales* (=between 41 and 49 tons, according to regional unit) of firewood on 3 Sept. 1344 (ibid., fo. 45^r), 100 horse-loads of wheat, one horse-load of vegetables and 20 casks (*botae*) of wine on 29 Jan. 1345 (ibid., fo. 55^r).

188. Bateman: 200 horse-loads of oats, 60 horse-loads of wheat on 6 Sept. 1354 (ASV IE 199, fo. 36^r) and 1,000 *quintales* (=between 41 and 49 tons) of firewood and 40 casks (*botae*) of wine on 12 Sept. (ibid., fo. 37^r). De Brian: 40 horse-loads (*saumatae grossae*) of wheat, 100 horse-loads (*saumatae grossae*) of oats, 24 casks (*botae grossae*) of wine, 500 *quintales* (between 20.5 and 24.5 tons) of hay, 500 *quintales* of firewood on 12 Sept. 1354 (ibid., fo. 37^r). Grosmont: 200 horse-loads (*saumatae grossae*) of wheat, 4 horse-loads (*saumatae grossae*) of vegetables, 1,000 horse-loads (*saumatae grossae*) of oats, 6,000 *quintales* (=between 246 and 294 tons) of hay, 200 casks (*botae*) of wine, 8,000 *quintales* (=between 328 and 392 tons) of firewood, 1,000 baskets (*banastunes*) of coal on 1 Oct. 1354 (ibid., fo. 40^r). Fitzalan: 100 horse-loads of wheat, 300 horse-loads of oats, 3,000 *quintales* (=between 123 and 147 tons) of firewood, 60 casks (*botae*) of wine on 26 Sept. 1354 (ibid., fo. 40^v). The French were given preferential treatment: the duke of Bourbon not only received 1,500 horse-loads (*saumatae grossae*) of wheat, 2,000 horse-loads (*saumatae grossae*) of oat, 50 horse-loads (*saumatae grossae*) of various sorts of vegetables, 12,000 *quintales* (= between 492 and 588 tons) of firewood, 4,000 baskets (*banastones*) of coal and 200 casks (*botae grossae*) of wine, but also pears, apples, chestnuts and cheese (20 Oct. 1354, ibid., fo. 42^r).

189. See App. III. Cf. the collection of examples from 1329 to 1336 in Lucas, 'Machinery', 321–3.

190. See Section 6.1.

191. The smallest mission to Avignon of a diplomatic agent who was not a king's messenger was the 1340 embassy of Richard Winkleigh and his *socius* David Servington, accompanied by two grooms (E 101/311/38; *EMDP*, doc. 377).

192. See App. III. This estimate is based on the assumption that Welwick had between five and fifteen men with him and that the 317 men-at-arms that accompanied the duke of Lancaster were only a part of his *familia*. Curial staff: Bernard Guillemain, *Les Papes d'Avignon, 1309–1376* (Paris, 1998), 36.

193. E 101/309/27 (*EMDP*, doc. 370). Other diplomats requiring only one ship were Robert Hereward and John Grey in 1343 (E 372/188, m. 50^r; E 101/312/3), Hugh Neville and William de Cusance in 1344 (E 101/312/9; E 372/192, m. 46^r), John Woderove, Richard de la Bere and Guy de Brian in 1354 (E 101/313/23; E 101/620/9) and Richard Stafford in 1359 (E 101/313/39). Cf. App. III.

194. See e.g. App. I, nos. VIII/1–2 and XII/1–2, and esp. nos. XLIX/1–6.

195. Given-Wilson, *English Nobility*, 87; Kate Mertes, *The English Noble Household, 1250–1600* (Oxford, 1988), 51.

196. C 76/19, m. 5. Robert Morton: *CPP* 178. On Richard Saham and his journeys to Portugal, Castile and Majorca between 1345 and 1348, see *BRUC* 501, and E 101/312/20 (MD no. CXI), E 101/312/23 (MD no. CXXII), and E 101/312/27 (MD no. CXXIV). Saham served once more as an assistant envoy to the curia under John Carlton in 1348 (App. I, no. XXIX; *CPP* 137, 143).

197. E 101/313/21, m. 2. Robert de Stratton (*alias* Sutton) DUJ: *BRUC* 562. Thomas

de Lexham MA, later DUJ (d.1382), the bp.'s chamberlain and master of his household: ibid. 366. Roger de Freton BCL (d.1382): ibid. 244. Laurence de Littleton BCL: ibid. 371. Roger de Sutton Lic.CL (d.1378): ibid. 568. Robert de Walton, a notary public (d.1376): ibid. 615.

198. *CPP* 276.
199. On the office of chamberlain, see Given-Wilson, *English Nobility*, 91, and Mertes, 23.
200. Given-Wilson, *English Nobility*, 92; Mertes, 24–5, 46–7.
201. Given-Wilson, *English Nobility*, 91; Mertes, 25.
202. Given-Wilson, *English Nobility*, 93; Mertes, 29–30.
203. *AA* iii. 504–5.
204. Reppes and Ludeford: see App. I, no. XVIII. Other envoys: VQ iii. 284.
205. King of Bohemia: ASV IE 220, fo. 81^r (cf. Weiß, *Versorgung*, 499–500). Hereward: see App. I, no. VIII/1.
206. Guillemain, *Cour pontificale*, 50–2.
207. Ibid. 51–2.
208. Clement VI: Henri Waquet, 'Note sur les médecins de Clément VI.', *MAHEF* 32 (1912), 45–8; *VPA* ii. 423 n. 4; Guillaume Mollat, 'Clément VI.', in *DHGE* xii. 1129–62 (1161); Guillemain, *Cour pontificale*, 114–15; John E. Wrigley, 'A papal secret known to Petrarch', *Speculum* 39 (1964), 613–34 (621–4, 628–31). See also the notes of expenses for the pope's apothecaries and physicians in VQ iii. 248, 258, 306, 473, and Clement VI's own references to his state of health in SC 7/11/8 and DGM 500, 518, 532, 592, 1671–2, 1724. Innocent VI: *VPA* i. 329; Guillemain, *Cour pontificale*, 115.
209. Pierre-André Sigal, 'Sickness of the Pope, Middle Ages', in *PE* iii. 1415–17 (1417).
210. Payment of envoys: Larson, 'Payment', *passim*; Lucas, 'Machinery', 330–1; Cuttino, *English Diplomatic Administration*, 167–71; More recently: Reitemeier, 75–80, and Plöger, 'Englische Gesandtschaftsrechnungen', 248–9. Payment of *nuncii regis* and *cursores*: Hill, *King's Messengers: Contribution*, 110–11.
211. See App. I, no. VI.
212. *CPP* 76–8, 71, 75, 97, 20–1.
213. Tout, 'English civil service', 201–3.

CHAPTER 5

Means of Communication

5.1. Diplomacy and Textuality

While in the early Middle Ages an envoy might be sent without any documents, by the mid-fourteenth century diplomatic practice had come to be marked by a well-calculated use of texts. This may be regarded as an aspect of a wider cultural, social and political development: as the use of written discourse spread from the religious and artistic into the administrative, legal and economic spheres in the course of the twelfth and thirteenth centuries, the 'pragmatic literacy' of Latin Christendom became increasingly diverse. Towns and courts became the centres of a new, practice-oriented approach to the written word.[1]

5.1.1. Informing the envoy

For diplomacy to be conducted with continuity, envoys needed to have access to papers that might include instructions given to, and memoranda drawn up by, their predecessors. Despite the absence of a central archive, the increasing volume and complexity of England's relations with the Continent had prompted the government by the end of the thirteenth century to devise a method by which important documents could be brought under one control and made available to the diplomatic personnel. Philip Martel DCL had been appointed keeper of the documents (*custos processuum*) relating to Aquitaine in 1299. Until the disappearance of the office forty years later, his successors were responsible for accumulating, preserving and cataloguing documents dealing with the problems of Aquitaine and of England's relations with France in general, and for briefing royal envoys and providing them with the necessary documents before they set off.[2]

Even after the abolition of the office of *custos processuum*, English diplomats would continue to take copies of diplomatic records with them. By the second half of the fourteenth century the Privy Seal office had begun to take over from the Exchequer as the normal place for the custody and consultation of diplomatic correspondence. It kept orderly files of diplomatic correspondence, giving its keeper and clerks a special knowledge and status in diplomatic matters.[3]

Precise knowledge of the legal status and boundaries of the Crown's continental possessions was crucial when English negotiators came face to face with their French counterparts before the pope. By the summer of 1354 Andrew Offord was presumably too old or too ill to travel to Avignon himself, but he used his expertise to supervise the compilation of four cartularies concerning Guienne, which were delivered to Michael Northburgh on 26 August.[4] On the following day, two days before his departure for the curia, Northburgh was given a special allowance for a horse 'ad ducendum monumenta et diversos alios libros versus curiam Romanam, tangentes tractatum inter Regem et illos de Francia' (to transport records and several other books pertaining to the negotiations between the king and the French to the Roman court).[5]

If it turned out during negotiations in Avignon that supplementary information was required, it could be obtained from the curial archives, which Benedict XII had had transferred from Assisi to Avignon in 1339–40.[6] The reports of John Offord, William Bateman and Hugh Neville offer some insight into how written records kept at the curia were consulted during the First Avignon Conference. At his first meeting with Clement VI on 6 September 1344, John Offord insisted that any discussion of the latest violations of the truce take account of the disruptive activities of Charles of Blois in Brittany, and cited the Malestroit agreement to support his argument. It took Clement's officials only a short while to find the original document, or a transcript of it, and check the exact wording of the relevant passage.[7] A month later, during a heated discussion about provisions, an infuriated Clement pointed out that the English king was still a vassal of the Holy See and asked Offord whether he was familiar with the correspondence between King John and Innocent III in which the nature of their relationship was clearly spelt out. When the dean replied in the negative, he had a servant fetch the volume of the chancery registers (*liber regestralis*) that contained the letters in question.[8]

5.1.2. Defining the purpose and scope of embassies

Unlike a *nuncius* or *cursor*, who would simply hand over the royal letters to the addressee and thereafter depart his court, any representative of the English king whose task it was to deliver an oral message and/or participate in negotiations (that is, a 'diplomat', according to our definition) was expected to produce written material identifying him and explaining the purpose of his mission.

The first essential document an envoy or embassy had to receive prior to departure was that which gave him or them full power (*plena potestas*) to discuss, concede and draft, sometimes even to sign and ratify in the principal's name.[9] English letters of procuration (*littere procuratorie, littere de potestate, mandata*) invariably took the form of great seal letters patent, with the addition of five significant clauses: clause of address, clause of constitution, clause of limitation, clause of guarantee or *ratihabitio*, and clause of signification.[10] The actual subject matter of the mission—the most important part of the document—was specified either in the clause of constitution or in the clause of limitation.[11]

The rarity of letters of procuration for English envoys dispatched to Avignon in the mid-fourteenth century is a reflection of the nature of Anglo-papal relations in this particular period. The use of *plena potestas* had long since become a characteristic feature of negotiations both between equals and between rulers and their subjects in which the representatives of either side would try to reach some form of mutually binding agreement.[12] Bilateral talks between English envoys and the pope, however, did not normally involve the kind of give-and-take typical of such discussions. Unlike their compatriots sent abroad to negotiate with secular rulers, Edward III's diplomats travelling to the curia in those years did not go there with the aim of 'striking deals' and entering into contractual agreements (this also distinguished them from the plenipotentiaries of Louis of Bavaria, who came to Avignon between 1335 and 1344 to negotiate the terms of the emperor's absolution; their procurations were closely scrutinized in consistory and played a central role in the subsequent discussions[13]). Instead, as has been suggested above, they would usually try to influence papal decisions regarding such problems as provisions, peace and marriage dispensations by force of legal argument and persuasion.[14] By contrast, the Anglo-French talks at the papal court, above all the peace conferences of 1344 and 1355, were designed to lead up to mutually binding agreements. What few letters of procuration were issued to Englishmen going to Avignon in the mid-fourteenth century all belonged in this context of trilateral negotiations.[15]

In order to give envoys, especially those operating far from home, some freedom of movement, the royal Chancery would sometimes issue them with multiple procurations. These represented progressive concessions that they were authorized to make: by gradually revealing these powers in order of their strength, the envoys could often extract concessions from the other party with a minimum commitment on their own part.[16] These procurations could be stated in deliberately unclear terms to provoke time-consuming discussions with the addressee, thus helping to obstruct negotiations. On 29 August 1343 three of the English envoys due to go to the papal court to talk about a prolongation of the Malestroit truce received a rather vague full power, authorizing them to discuss all points of controversy with Philip VI's plenipotentiaries, and to conclude a peace agreement (what exactly these points were was, of course, the crucial question).[17] On the same day, a second, longer and more detailed letter of procuration empowered all members of that delegation not only to address these issues but also to discuss a prolongation of the Malestroit truce, the question of Edward's possessions and rights in France, his rights to the French throne and restitutions for all damages incurred during the conflict.[18]

An additional letter of procuration could also be drawn up to allow envoys to adopt an increasingly intransigent stance in the course of their negotiations. On 4 August 1344 William Bateman, John Offord, Thomas Fastolf, Hugh Neville, Niccolò Fieschi and Andrew Offord were given powers similar in scope to those issued to the projected embassy of the previous year.[19] A second letter of procuration, issued on the same day, gave three of them carte blanche to revoke the Malestroit agreement altogether and to defy the French king formally should a prolongation of the truce prove impossible.[20]

The exact inverse, of course, was also possible. One of the three letters of procuration that Bateman, Offord, Thoresby, Neville, Spigournel and Fieschi received on 20 October 1344 concerned what had by then become the usual matters: the prolongation of the truce, the English possessions and rights in France and possible reparations.[21] Like previous letters, this one was written in Latin, and its style was of the usual solemnity. It was complemented by two other, shorter procurations giving the same persons powers regarding two specific points only: the prolongation of the truce until mid-Lent 1345 if a final settlement was unattainable, and violations of the truce, to be discussed during that period.[22] The fact that these two documents were written in French suggests that they were for the envoys' eyes only, and not to be handed over to the pope or his cardinals.

The production of the envoy's powers and their examination for formal adequacy were routine steps that preceded the actual negotiations.[23] On the other hand, there were situations in which the representatives of one side deemed it more prudent to withhold written evidence defining the scope of their authority for as long as possible in order not to curtail their own freedom of action. French envoys to Avignon refused to hand over their letters of procuration on at least two occasions—in 1321 and 1335.[24] During their meeting with Clement VI on 24 October 1344, the English delegation demanded that the French side made its *potestas* public. The pope rejected this proposal, but suggested that the documents in question be submitted to his vice chancellor for examination.[25]

In contrast to the letter of procuration, which came into use only after the revival of Roman law, letters of credence possessed a tradition going back to the early Middle Ages.[26] They would be handed over by the envoy as evidence of his ambassadorial character but contained no authority to obligate the sender to any agreement. Whether a diplomat took with him both a letter of procuration and one of credence depended on his status and task, but in those frequent cases where a more or less straightforward message was to be conveyed credentials would be the only document required. On the other hand, if full powers were held, the diplomatic pouch did not always contain credentials.[27]

Before 1400 there was a fixed and rather solemn form according to which credentials were drawn up, with the heart of the document, the clause of supplication asking for full faith to be given to the bearer's oral message, commonly occupying no more than a few lines.[28] For the sake of simplicity, elements typical of these letters could also be 'implanted' in other kinds of texts. It is not at all unusual to find documents in which the phraseology typical of both credentials and procurations is mingled. In many instances a section commending the bearer of a message to the pope's confidence ends a regular letter.[29]

Credentials occur most often in connection with embassies whose business did not require lengthy series of negotiations.[30] The comparatively high number of such letters relating to English envoys to

Avignon preserved in the archives can thus be said to be as illustrative of the character of Anglo-curial diplomacy as the low number of procurations. This presents a striking contrast with, for instance, English diplomatic missions to Germany: only few letters of credence are extant today for envoys dispatched there, but the number of procurations seems to have been much higher.[31] Regarding the question of who was expected to present letters of credence on arrival at the papal court, the sources do not allow us to recognize a coherent pattern. So far as can be discovered, however, men who were known to the pope and his officials from previous missions or stays at the curia in other capacities were not usually issued with separate, formal credentials, but might instead be briefly mentioned at the end of the main letter. William Bateman, for instance, was commended to the pope's confidence in the final paragraph of a royal letter of 6 March 1344 but never received credentials.[32] Similarly, there are no separate credentials for John Offord, who had been a *procurator Regis* before becoming one of the leading Crown envoys. What is more, no credentials of any form survive for envoys recruited from the higher aristocracy such as Richard Stafford, Richard de la Bere, Nigel Loring and William Burton, and were possibly never written.

Unlike powers and credentials, instructions and credences were informal documents. Though not essential to the medieval diplomat, they became increasingly common.[33] The purpose of instructions was to inform the envoy as to what he should do and say during his stay at the foreign court. It is not always clear whether a particular instruction was of a confidential nature, and for the envoys' eyes only, or whether it had to be produced on demand. This is certainly not an irrelevant question, since an examination of an embassy's written guidelines could show instantly how great the bargaining space—'the range within which acceptable agreements might be reached'[34]—in the subsequent negotiations would be. The truth of the matter seems to be that either could be correct: while *some* instructions were intended for an embassy's internal use only, in most cases such documents could be, and were, handed over to the person to whose court the diplomats had been dispatched.[35] In fact, the showing or reading-out of instructions was considered a sign of friendly relations.[36]

The question of which of the above procedures should be followed must at times have been a controversial one, and some diplomats will have been reluctant to reveal their aims in full. In Anglo-papal diplomacy, this point became especially touchy when English and

French representatives met for trilateral discussions at the curia. In order to speed up the progress of the talks, Clement VI at one point asked Philip VI's diplomats at the First Avignon Conference to 'put their cards on the table' and let him know what their instructions were. On the following day he informed Edward's envoys that he had seen the documents, signed by Philip VI's notary.[37] The English Chancery took special precautions before the conference of 1355; Henry of Grosmont and Richard Fitzalan received not only a *credence secree* (a short, 'semi-secret' credence saying very little) for their negotiations with the French, but also a much more specific and 'really secret' set of instructions. Neither document was to be shown to the pope unless it proved necessary.[38] Eighty years later Bernard du Rosier proposed what appears to have been the usual solution in situations like this. If ambassadors were asked to produce their non-public instructions, they should, unless properly authorized to do so, not give away the actual documents but instead offer to read aloud certain sections.[39]

While the making public of written instructions depended on the circumstances of the individual case, it was common practice for the envoy to hand over his credence (*credentia, creaunce, charge, messagerie*), a written summary of his message in the form of an itemized list on a separate slip of parchment (*cedula*), and to explain it orally.[40] In fact, the distinction between credences and 'open', publicizable instructions will often have been meaningless, simply because the message conveyed *was* what the envoy had been instructed to say. Having arrived in Avignon in December 1340, William Bateman drew up two documents: first, a summary of the oral message (*credentia*[41]) that he, John Offord and John Thoresby had been given to convey, followed by a statement concerning the king's short-term political plans, and, secondly, a separate *cedula* listing Edward's main arguments regarding his claim to the French throne. To both documents the diplomats affixed their personal seals.[42] In fact, numerous examples show that the English Chancery did not always deem it necessary to draw a distinction between instructions and credences, or even regarded them as synonyms. In their physical appearance and in their method of authentication,[43] they were identical.[44] Since they were of a less formal nature than credentials or procurations, both kinds of documents were given in French to English envoys in this period.[45]

5.2. Literacy, Orality and Aurality

An examination of diplomatic documents, reports and journals suggests that those who produced and used such texts took an ambivalent attitude towards the employment of written discourse. Around 1300 William of Sarden, a civil lawyer and adviser to Edward I, pointed out the risks of relying solely on envoys—especially less experienced ones— and their oral messages when communicating with the Holy See: 'Videtur [...] periculum esse quod [...] per interrogaciones subtiles et astutas faciendas, a papa posset nuncius hujusmodi injuncta sibi excedere, et aliqua prejudiciali forte fateri. Item [...] posset forsan compelli respondere et alia dicere quam sibi erant injuncta, quorum nulla vel difficilis valde foret revocacio in futurum' (There seems to be a risk that this sort of envoy might, after subtle and clever questions put by the pope, go beyond his instructions, and perhaps say things which are prejudicial. He may perhaps be forced to answer, and to say things other than he was instructed to say, and it would be impossible, or very difficult, to disavow them in future).[46] Secondly, as has been seen, texts were indispensable aids in the discussion of such complex politico-legal matters as the status of Guienne and the French succession. Where no such written material existed, the negotiating parties would soon recognize the problems thus created. It was at the pope's explicit request that William Bateman put his oral message and the king's declaration of his intentions into writing in mid-December 1340.[47] Some documents can thus be said to have fulfilled an evidential function. The purpose of others was legitimization: procurations and credentials defined an envoy's powers and served as proof of authorization. Texts thus served to create the framework within which oral negotiations could be conducted; in other words: 'diplomatic orality' performed its functions within a system of graphic representation for language.[48]

If there was an awareness of the problems inherent in oral communication and if the use of documents was markedly extended during this period, hints towards an extended use of oral discourse also occur frequently in our sources, thus indicating the limitations of 'diplomatic literacy'. Instructions were frequently given orally by the king in person and his council; in fact, the giving of verbal instructions seems to have been the rule rather than the exception.[49] Accompanying royal letters as well as letters of credence normally stated the subject of negotiations in broad terms, but were not considered the appropriate place for giving details. These were left for the envoy's supplementary oral message, which, as it were, filled the gap between what he was *allowed* to say (as specified in his pro-curation) and what he was *supposed* to say (as specified in his instructions).[50] The majority of the letters produced by English diplomats on their arrival at the curia contained references to the orations that they were to deliver. Their credentials asked the pope to grant them *aditum et auditum*—to receive them and listen to what they would expound *viva voce*.[51] In some cases the clause of credence was an assurance that the oral message that he was about to hear could be trusted as fully as if it came directly from the king's mouth.[52]

If, then, diplomatic texts, while serving to set the stage for negotiations, also point out their own limitations and the importance of the spoken word, one needs to look for reasons why it was deemed necessary to balance elements of orality with those of literacy. Perhaps the most straightforward one is the need for security, which was especially pressing when an envoy had to pass through potentially hostile territories. Letters carried by travelling diplomats were easy targets for interception.[53] In November 1324 or 1325 Raymond Subirani, a papal auditor counted by Edward II as being among his friends in Avignon, informed the king that he had certain news for him but did not dare commit them to paper; rumour had it that the French king's keepers of passages had taken to seizing and opening letters to England.[54] The greater the need for secrecy, the more likely was a message to be conveyed in oral form.

Secrecy and security concerns were not always the reason for a principal to have an additional oral message conveyed through his representative. It has been observed that, if designed to express the pope's disapproval or to clarify his position on a point in dispute, the letters emanating from his chancery tended to be longer and more detailed than usual. The ratio of speech to writing could be altered so as to reflect changes in the climate between the protagonists and in the pope's attitude towards the recipient.[55]

Beside these more pragmatic reasons for retaining a large degree of orality in the conduct of diplomacy, there seems to have been a third one, which was to do with a fundamental scepticism towards the reli-ability of the epistolary medium. When a certain piece of information was sensitive and required careful handling, letters were sometimes regarded unsuitable for conveying it, because the meaning of the written word was liable to be twisted or at least misinterpreted by the recipient. Thus the same William of Sarden who so astutely commented on the risks of oral diplomacy conceded, in the same memorandum: 'Si mittantur informaciones per litteras regias sub regis sigillo [...] deliberetur de periculis que possent accidere [...]. Et cavendum est summopere ne aliquid obscurum, scrupulosum, dubium vel prejudiciale quod possit contra regem interpretari in dictis litteris inserabitur pro eo quod ipse littere si mittantur ad papam ad perpetuam rei memoriam remanebunt' (If a statement is sent by royal letter under the king's seal one must consider the dangers which might arise. Above all, one must beware that nothing obscure, ill-expressed, doubtful, or prejudicial is inserted in the letter, which might be interpreted against the king, because if that letter is sent to the pope it will remain on record forever).[56] During an audience in the late hours of 7 September 1344 John Offord asked Clement VI for a written statement regarding his stance on alien provisions in England. To confirm its factual correctness, the text was to be read out aloud: 'Post aliqua verba supplicavi Sanctitati Suae quatinus illa quae finaliter dicere vellet in hac materia habere possem in scriptis et ea coram Sanctitate Suae perlegere et signare antiquam dominum meum certificarem, quia alias posset faciliter, ut videbatur, michi circa verborum dubietatem periculum exoriri' (After a few words had been passed, I requested that I be given in writing what His Holiness would choose to pronounce as his final decision on this matter, and that it be read out aloud and signed in his presence before I inform my master, the reason being that otherwise, it seemed, dangers might easily arise for me from the uncertainty of (written) words). Clement, for his part, agreed with Offord about his scepticism towards the production of a text without recourse to an additional oral cross-examination. He cited Plato as an authority on the subject: 'Et ipse annuit quod sic stat de materia hujus articuli, non sine causa Plato jubet quiescere in praesenti' (And he agreed that this was the case with the contents of this article, and that it was not without reason that Plato tells us to remain silent at present).[57] In the *Phaedrus*, the *locus classicus* of the philosophical criticism of writing, Plato expresses his reservations about writing, and insists upon the superiority of speech as an instrument of teaching and learning. A written text is passive and unresponsive: while a person can explain his statement, the written word cannot defend itself as the spoken word can. Writing thus invites misunderstandings, and texts are no substitute for the give-and-take of dialogue.[58] In diplomacy, the envoy's supplementary oral message could help avoid the pitfalls of writing.

Indeed, one may ask just how useful a rigid distinction between 'oral' and 'written' as different modes of diplomatic discourse is. Where writing was used, it would frequently be converted into speech. Written instructions might supply the exact words that had to be used, and in their introductory orations diplomats will often have done little more than recite these texts.[59] Letters were not simply handed over to the pope for individual, silent perusal; in at least some cases they were, as Offord's and Bateman's reports of 1344 and Murimuth's chronicle confirm, read out in consistory.[60] This was certainly not done to cater for the needs of an illiterate audience. Firstly, it was an efficient way of passing on information to the pope's counsellors, the cardinals, and thus of achieving a maximum of publicity within a minimum amount of time. Secondly, this practice was in tune with the preferred mode of text usage: 'The medieval recipient prepared himself to listen to an utterance rather than to scrutinize a document visually as a modern literate would.'[61] In other words, reading was linked in the medieval mind with hearing rather than seeing. As law or theology students, the popes and cardinals will have been used to listening to their masters reading aloud. The phenomenon that we are dealing with here—voiced textuality— occupies a middle space between the two poles of pragmatic orality and pragmatic literacy and I propose to term this particular type 'pragmatic aurality'—the reading-aloud of a practice-oriented text to one or a group of listeners.[62]

Inversely, oral exchange could be recorded in its original form and thus converted into writing while its typical features were preserved. Verbatim transcripts of statements by the pope or cardinals, or of dialogues between them and the English plenipotentiaries, make up a substantial part of Neville's, Offord's and Bateman's journal and intermediate reports.[63] In late medieval diplomacy oral and written discourse were interdependent, and the boundary between these modes of communication was permeable in both directions.

5.3. Communication Problems

John XXII, a native of Quercy, was educated at Orléans and Paris but was nevertheless unable to understand a letter that the king of France had addressed to him in Northern French.[64] In the summer of 1326 Edward II negotiated with two papal legates in French, but for John to gain the full picture of what had been discussed a final report in

Latin had to be written.[65] Benedict XII, Clement VI and Innocent VI, by contrast, were fluent in French. When Guillaume d'Auxonne, chancellor of the count of Flanders, visited the curia with his master in April 1336, he apologized to Benedict for addressing him in this language, rather than Latin, explaining that otherwise the count would be unable to follow their discussion.[66] Like their two predecessors, Clement VI and Innocent VI had been born in the *Midi* and had Gascon Occitan as their mother tongue, but both must have been fluent in the language of the Parisian court, where they had served Philip VI as councillors and diplomats.[67]

One of the most powerful reasons for sending clergy on embassies was that they, almost alone, spoke and wrote Latin, Europe's *lingua franca* and the formal language of diplomatic intercourse until well into the early modern period.[68] Reference has been made above to the academic backgrounds of Edward III's clerical envoys to the curia in the mid-fourteenth century; most of them, having spent several years at Oxford or Cambridge and having during that period participated in a variety of forms of written and oral discourse in Latin, belonged to the better-educated sections of the English clergy. Discussing legal niceties and consulting documents written in this language thus cannot have constituted any problem for them. In addition, although they may not originally have come from francophone families, they probably acquired a sound knowledge of French while serving in aristocratic households and at the royal court.

The post-Conquest generations of the English nobility were bilingual. They learned English in infancy from nurses and servants, and later in their lives it remained the language of their converse with social inferiors. On the other hand, up to the period that we are here concerned with, French (more precisely, its Anglo-Norman dialect) was commonly their spoken language among equals and their literary language, systematically learned at school and in the noble household: 'It was [...] the distinguishing mark of the ruling elite and the linguistic link with western Christendom.'[69] An English aristocrat's pronunciation and usages would certainly, by the middle of the four-teenth century, have become anglicized to some degree, and so he would have spoken what his continental peers, more used to the fashionable dialect of the Parisian court, would have considered not only 'provincial' but also 'bad' French. In his *Livre de seyntz medicines* (1354) none other than Henry of Grosmont, one of the most prominent diplomats of his time, deemed it necessary to apologize for what he thought was a poor command of the language (while understating, no doubt, his actual familiarity with it): 'Si le franceis ne soit pas bon, jeo doie estre escusee, pur ceo qe jeo sui engleis et n'ai pas moelt hauntee le franceis' (May I be forgiven if my French is not good; I am English and have not used it much).[70] Nevertheless, it is safe to assume that in general Edward III's aristocratic diplomats did not have any manifest difficulties conversing with their French counterparts and with anyone at the papal court who was fluent in the Langue d'oïl.

How many of them would have qualified for the epithet *miles litteratus* because they were 'literate' in the sense that they possessed a minimal ability to read, understand, and express themselves in Latin[71] is more difficult to assess. Henry G. Richardson and George O. Sayles in 1963 came to the conclusion that as early as the twelfth century the baronage and gentry belonged to the section of those among the English laity who had 'a limited knowledge of Latin, a knowledge to be easily and rapidly acquired by any intelligent youth'.[72] In fourteenth-century England even those noble boys who were not intended to become clerics or study the common law were usually given formal instruction in Latin grammar and vocabulary and even in composing Latin prose for some years.[73] Furthermore, most of the noblemen sent to Avignon had at some stage in their careers held offices demanding the use of Latin documents such as charters, accounts, writs or letters. As has been seen, some were performing, or had at some point performed, key functions in the royal household as chamberlains or stewards. Others had been judges, sheriffs, escheators or tax collectors in their counties. We may thus presume that they had at least a working knowledge of Latin, which enabled them to master their administrative business at home. That said, it is doubtful whether they would have been sufficiently fluent in it to give elaborate, formal speeches or take an active part in the negotiations that formed the core of the diplomat's work. But they would certainly have been able to participate in more informal and confidential conversations—for example, when invited to dine with the pope or called into his chamber for a private audience.

Presumably, it was not until the diplomats left the papal palace that they experienced real communication problems. Only a small number of the inhabitants of fourteenth-century Avignon spoke French; it was used more widely in the city alongside the local Provençal dialect only from the early fifteenth century onwards, and to the population

of the surrounding countryside it was still a foreign language some
five decades later.[74] The king's envoys and other English visitors will
often have had to rely on the assistance of bi- or trilingual curialists and
townspeople speaking French and Provençal, or English, French
and Provençal, when conducting their business at the papal court and
procuring food and lodgings in the city.

Notes to Chapter 5

1. Hagen Keller, 'Pragmatische Schriftlichkeit im Mittelalter: Erscheinungsformen
   und Entwicklungsstufen. Einführung zum Kolloquium in Münster, 17.–19. Mai
   1989', in Hagen Keller, Klaus Grubmüller and Nikolaus Staubach (eds.),
   Pragmatische Schriftlichkeit im Mittelalter: Erscheinungsformen und Entwicklungsstufen
   (Munich, 1992), 1–7 (1–3). On the growth of literacy for practical purposes in
   medieval England, see Michael Clanchy's seminal *From Memory to Written Record:
   England 1066–1307*, 2nd edn. (Oxford, 1993).
2. See George P. Cuttino's articles on the professional papers of Elias Joneston,
   keeper of processes and memoranda from 1306 to 1336: 'A memorandum book
   of Elias Joneston', *Speculum* 17 (1942), 74–85, and 'Another memorandum book
   of Elias Joneston', *EHR* 63 (1948), 90–103.
3. Brown, *Governance*, 51. On the archival functions of the Exchequer, see Cuttino,
   English Diplomatic Administration, 166.
4. C 62/131, m. 4: 'Liberate [...] magistro Andrea de Offord', quem ad
   supervidendum scripturam quorundam librorum nostrorum statum ducatus
   nostri Aquitanie contingentium oneravimus, 20 li. pro stipendio clericorum
   dictos libros scribentium et pro ligatura eorundem' (12 July 1354). Cf. the note
   of payment to Offord in E 403/374, m. 16. Delivery to Northburgh: *CCR
   1354–60*, 83–4. On 30 Jan. 1355 the books were brought back to the Chancery
   and handed over to one of the chamberlains, to be kept in the treasury (ibid. and
   The Antient Kalendars and Inventories of the Treasury of His Majesty's Exchequer, ed.
   Francis Palgrave (London, 1836), i. 178–9). They were kept at Bordeaux
   between 1355 and 1361 and taken to Paris by French officials after 1468. One of
   the four cartularies, known as *Recognitiones feodorum in Aquitania*, is still extant:
   Wolfenbüttel, Herzog-August-Bibliothek, MS 31 Aug. 2° (see Jean Paul Trabut-
   Cussac, 'Les cartulaires gascons d'Édouard II, d'Édouard III, et de Charles VII',
   BEC 111 (1953), 65–106 (69–71, 78–85); *English Royal Documents, King
   John–Henry VI, 1199–1461*, ed. Pierre Chaplais (Oxford, 1971), plate 15, and
   EMDP 189 n. 445).
5. E 403/374, m. 19.
6. Franz Ehrle, 'Zur Geschichte des Schatzes, der Bibliothek und des Archivs der
   Päpste im vierzehnten Jahrhundert', *Archiv für Literatur– und Kirchengeschichte des
   Mittelalters* 1 (1885), 1–48, 228–364 (296–8); Heinrich Denifle, 'Die päpstlichen
   Registerbände des 13. Jahrhunderts und das Inventar derselben vom Jahr 1339',
   Archiv für Literatur– und Kirchengeschichte des Mittelalters 2 (1886), 1–105.
7. Froissart, *Œuvres*, xviii. 203.
8. Ibid. 217.

9. Queller, *Office of Ambassador*, 114–22; Cuttino, *English Diplomatic Administration*, 154–6.

10. Cuttino, *English Diplomatic Administration*, 155–6; Chaplais, 'English diplomatic documents', 42.

11. In clause of constitution: e.g. *EMDP*, docs. 93, 94, 95. Subject matter specified in clause of limitation: e.g. ibid., docs. 91, 92, 97, 99.

12. Gaines Post, '*Plena potestas* and consent in medieval assemblies: A study in Romano–canonical procedure and the rise of representation, 1150–1325', *Traditio* 1 (1943), 355–408 (369, 407–8).

13. Franz Josef Felten, 'Kommunikation zwischen Kaiser und Kurie unter Ludwig dem Bayern (1314–1347). Zur Problematik der Quellen im Spannungsfeld von Schriftlichkeit und Mündlichkeit', in Heinz–Dieter Heimann and Ivan Hlavácek (eds.), *Kommunikationspraxis und Korrespondenzwesen im Mittelalter und in der Renaissance* (Paderborn, 1998), 51–89 (67–76).

14. It should be noted, however, that this was a historically contingent phenomenon rather than a basic structural feature of Anglo-papal relations. Full powers could in fact become necessary if some form of compromise between king and pope was to be worked out. When King John sent envoys to Rome in 1215, they received a letter of procuration containing a general mandate with *libera administratio* for all royal suits and business in the curia (R I. i. 139).

15. C 76/18, m. 12; C 76/19, mm. 1, 2; R II. ii. 1231–2; R III. i. 19, 22, 161, 188, 201, 283, 289.

16. Queller, *Office of Ambassador*, 121; Cuttino, *English Diplomatic Administration*, 155.

17. C 76/18, m. 12.

18. R II. ii. 1231–2.

19. R III. i. 19.

20. C 76/19, m. 3.

21. Ibid., m. 2.

22. Ibid.

23. Mattingly, *Renaissance Diplomacy*, 37; Queller, *Office of Ambassador*, 121.

24. Heinrich Otto, 'Die Eide und Privilegien Heinrichs VII. und Karls IV. mit ungedruckten Aktenstücken', *QF* 9 (1906), 316–78 (326), and Dau 103; cf. Felten, 75 n. 146.

25. Froissart, *Œuvres*, xviii. 237–8.

26. Ganshof has found them used in late-6th and early 7th-c. Frankish diplomacy ('Merowingisches Gesandtschaftswesen', in *Aus Geschichte und Landeskunde. Forschungen und Darstellungen, Franz Steinbach zum 65. Geburtstag gewidmet von seinen Freunden und Schülern* (Bonn, 1960), 177). On English letters of credence, see esp. Chaplais, *English Diplomatic Practice*, 175–91.

27. Mattingly, *Renaissance Diplomacy*, 33; Queller, *Office of Ambassador*, 111; Cuttino, *English Diplomatic Administration*, 156.

28. Mattingly, *Renaissance Diplomacy*, 33–4; Queller, *Office of Ambassador*, 111–12; Cuttino, *English Diplomatic Administration*, 156–7; Chaplais, *English Diplomatic Practice*, 177.

29. Credentials and procurations: C 70/18, m. 2 (two letters for Richard Winkleigh, May 1342), and C 70/20, m. 2 (letter for John Thoresby, Ralph Spigournel, 26 Oct. 1344). Cf. Menzel, 16–17, and Queller, *Office of Ambassador*, 121. Lucas, 'Machinery', 309–10, fails to note the difference between procurations and

credentials altogether. Credentials inserted in regular letters to the pope or cardinals: C 70/20, m. 2 (two letters to Clement VI mentioning Andrew Offord and William Bateman, 6 Mar. 1344), C 70/21, m. 3, C 70/22, m. 2, C 70/25, m. 2; VM 2870, 2926; R II. ii. 118; R III. i. 30–1, 35, 66, 342.

30. Cuttino, *English Diplomatic Administration*, 156.
31. Reitemeier, 49.
32. C 70/20, m. 2.
33. Queller, *Office of Ambassador*, 122–3.
34. P. Terrence Hopmann, *The Negotiation Process and the Resolution of International Conflicts* (Columbia, SC, 1996), 48.
35. Marie Alphonse René de Maulde La Clavière, 'Les instructions diplomatiques au Moyen-Age', *RHD* 6 (1892), 602–32 (603). Examining the instructions for Louis of Bavaria's envoys to the curia between 1330 and 1346, Alois Schütz reached the conclusion that in the Middle Ages all such documents were intended to be handed over and scrutinized before negotiations could begin (*Die Prokuratorien und Instruktionen Ludwigs des Bayern für die Kurie (1331–1345): Ein Beitrag zu seinem Absolutionsprozeß* (Kallmünz, 1973), 110–33, esp. 128, 133, 310). This view has convincingly been disputed by Felten (74–5).
36. Queller, *Office of Ambassador*, 125.
37. Froissart, *Œuvres*, xviii. 250–1, 253 (20 and 21 Nov. 1344).
38. *EMDP*, docs. 124(b) and (a); Chaplais, *English Diplomatic Practice*, 212.
39. Du Rosier, ch. xvi ('De discreta instruccionum comunicacione'), 16.
40. See Chaplais, *English Diplomatic Practice*, 211–14, and the examples in C 70/20, m. 2, SC 7/64/79, Froissart, *Œuvres*, xviii. 203–4 (cf. 215), DGM 607, 1155, 1322, 1323, 1326, 1591, and *EMDP*, doc. 58. In most cases this summary, which was enclosed with an accompanying letter as a *cedula interclusa*, no longer exists, and all that remains is the letter making references to it and mentioning the object of the envoy's mission in broad terms, if at all. See e.g. DM 2445, DGM 607. See Guillaume Mollat, 'Correspondance de Clément VI par cédules', *Bolletino dell'Archivio paleografico italiano* (1956–7), 175–8, and Felten, 56–7 and n. 37.
41. *Credentia* was also a word for the envoy's oral message. In this sense, *credentia* was synonymous with *nuncium* or *nunciacio* (Chaplais, *English Diplomatic Practice*, 162).
42. First document: (1) 'Credentia nunciis regis Anglie commissa [...] super exponendis ex parte ipsius regis domino pape [...] Hec sunt in effectu que dicta sunt vobis, sanctissimo patri et domino, per nos Willelmum de Norwico [...], Johannem de Offorde [...], et Johannem de Thoresby [...] ex parte domini nostri regis Anglie [...] et sub credentia nostra' (VM 2981, cols. 121–4, and *EMDP*, doc. 239(b), i; *CPL* ii. 584–5). (2) 'Sequitur intentio domini regis' (VM 2981, cols. 124–5, and *EMDP*, doc. 239(b), ii; *CPL* ii. 585–6. Second document: 'Tenor unius cedule per regis Anglie nuncios sub sigillis eorum propriis domino pape date et exhibite continentis causas et rationes propter quas idem rex Anglie in et desuper regno Francie pretendit et vendicat jus habere' (VM 2982 and *EMDP*, doc. 239(b), iii; *CPL* ii. 586–8).
43. From the reign of Henry III to the end of that of Edward III, English credences were drawn up in the form of bipartite indentures, one half of which was kept by the king and the other half by the envoy. By *c*.1340 the sealing practice already in use for indentures of military service was probably extended to diplomatic instructions and credences: the envoy's exemplar was sealed with the king's privy

seal, and the king's exemplar with the envoy's seal (*EMDP*, docs. 43(c), 50(c), 55(a), 119, 121, 122(a), (b), 123, 186; Chaplais, *English Diplomatic Practice*, 197–9).

44. *EMDP*, doc. 57(a): *Linstruccioun et charge* (15 June 1396); doc. 65: document referred to both as *charge* and *instruccion* (25 Jan. 1417); doc. 126: *Linstruccion et charge* (4 Apr. 1399). Examples of texts that identify themselves as *credentiae* or *credences/messageries* but that might with equal justification be called instructions are *EMDP*, docs. 55, 67, 68(b), (c), (f), 123, and 124(a), (b). See Chaplais, 'English diplomatic documents', 35 and 43–4, and *English Diplomatic Practice*, 199.

45. Queller, *Office of Ambassador*, 124; cf. the examples in *EMDP*, docs. 121–8.

46. C 47/31/15, printed in *Anglo-Scottish Relations, 1174–1328: Some Selected Documents*, ed. and trans. Edward L. G. Stones (London, 1965; repr. Oxford, 1970), 93–4.

47. VM 2981.

48. Cf. Brian Stock, *The Implications of Literacy: Written Language and Models of Interpretation in the Eleventh and Twelfth Centuries* (Princeton, 1983), 42.

49. Lucas, 'Machinery', 309; Queller, *Office of Ambassador*, 122.

50. Felten, 76.

51. e.g. R II. ii. 1220; R III. i. 18, 25, 31, 32, 35, 66, 145, 342; VM 2926. Cf. the confirmations of the reception and hearing of English envoys in the opening passages of Dau 800; DGM 595, 743, 781, 1155, 1322, 1326; GL 467, 468.

52. See e.g. Edward III's credential for Reginald Cobham of 18 Oct. 1340: 'Cui praebere velitis, si placet, aditum et auditum, et verbis ejus, tanquam ab ore nostro prolatis, credulam dare fidem' (R II. ii. 1139).

53. Cf. Chaplais, *English Diplomatic Practice*, 76–8.

54. SC 1/50/48, printed in Langlois, 'Notices et documents', 77.

55. Felten, 62–3.

56. C 47/31/15, see *Anglo-Scottish Relations*, 94–5.

57. Froissart, *Œuvres*, xviii. 210.

58. *Phaedrus*, 274b–278b, esp. 275d–276a.

59. Cf. Thomas Haye, 'Die lateinische Sprache als Medium mündlicher Diplomatie', in Schwinges and Wriedt, 15–32 (23), and see e.g. the intended credence drawn up between Edward II's council and two royal envoys to Clement V before 24 Feb. 1311: 'Cestes sont les paroles que mons' Henry Spigournel et mons' Johan de Benstede deivent dire au pape depar le roy Dengleterre' (*EMDP*, doc. 43(c)).

60. Froissart, *Œuvres*, xviii. 224, 225, 226, 227, 229, 230; *CC* 149, 230.

61. Clanchy, 266–7.

62. On aurality see esp. Joyce Coleman, *Public Reading and the Reading Public in Late Medieval England and France* (Cambridge, 1996), chs. 1–2.

63. See Froissart, *Œuvres*, xviii. 206–9, 216–18, 221–3, 228, 237–40, 242, 244, 245–8, 250–3.

64. Education: John E. Weakland, 'John XXII before his pontificate, 1244–1316: Jacques Duèse and his Family', *AHP* 10 (1972), 161–85 (163–4). Linguistic skills: Auguste Brun, *Recherches historiques sur l'introduction du français dans les provinces du Midi* (Paris, 1923), 31.

65. 'Nos [Edward II] [...] eisdem nunciis [i.e. the abp. of Vienne and the bp. of Orange] in verbis Gallicis, quae transferri fecimus in Latinum, pro pleniori intellectu sanctitatis vestrae, respondimus' (R II. i. 629).

66. 'Excusando me quod linga [sic] materna loquebar, quia pro domino sic fieri oportebat, qui non erat literatus' (Paul Thomas, 'Une source nouvelle pour l'histoire administrative de la Flandre: Le registre de Guillaume d'Auxonne, chancelier de Louis de Nevers, comte de Flandre', *Revue du Nord* 10 (1924), 5–38 (34)).

67. On Clement VI, see Guillemain, *Cour pontificale*, 151 and n. 292, and Wrigley, 'Clement VI before his pontificate', 450.

68. Haye, 19.

69. Nicholas Orme, *From Childhood to Chivalry: The Education of the English Kings and Aristocracy, 1066–1530* (London and New York, 1984), 122 and (in general) 121–5. See also Maurice H. Keen, *English Society in the Later Middle Ages, 1348–1500* (Harmondsworth, 1990), 223–4.

70. *Le Livre de Seyntz Medicines: The Unpublished Devotional Treatise of Henry of Lancaster*, ed. Émile Jules Arnould (Oxford, 1940), 239.

71. In 1318 an Aragonese knight told John XXII that he was unable to deliver his message in Latin: 'Eyo, san pare, no som clergue, ne som letrat, que sabes proposar en Lati.' He was encouraged to speak in his mother tongue instead (*AA* ii. 795). On the semantics and uses of the term *litteratus*, see in detail Herbert Grundmann, '*Litteratus—illiteratus*: Der Wandel einer Bildungsnorm vom Altertum zum Mittelalter', *Archiv für Kulturgeschichte* 40 (1958), 1–65 (3–15), and Clanchy, 226–30.

72. Henry G. Richardson and George O. Sayles, *The Governance of Medieval England from the Conquest to Magna Carta* (Edinburgh, 1963), 278 and, more generally, 269–83; cf. Clanchy, 234–6.

73. Orme, 145–7.

74. Brun, 45–7, 387–9, 398–9; Pierre Pansier, *Histoire de la langue provençale à Avignon du XIIeme au XIXme siècle* (Avignon, 1924–7), i. 35–9.

CHAPTER 6

❖

Protocol, Procedure and Ceremonial

6.1. Objectives of Missions to the Curia

It is possible to establish five basic analytical categories when looking for reasons for the dispatch of English diplomats to the papal court. Envoys charged with negotiating directly with the pope were expected to

1. present the king's letters and petitions and explain them orally, and
2. make propaganda for the king and his position while, at the same time, gather information that would allow him and his advisers to gain a clearer perception of the pope's views and policies, about other influential personalities in the curia and about the diplomatic activities of other rulers.

As we have seen above,[1] such bilateral negotiations were, from the diplomats' point of view, exercises in persuasive communication. On the other hand, Anglo-French negotiations presided over by the pope or committees of cardinals may be referred to as trilateral conferences (arguably, much of Anglo-curial diplomacy in the period under consideration was nothing other than indirect Anglo-French diplomacy). Envoys participating in these were charged with

3. prolonging a truce already in force where the original understanding had a time limit,
4. preparing or participating in negotiations for a final peace, or
5. confirming a preliminary peace.

These categories of course represent ideal types and in practice negotiations at the curia were often 'mixed' in character.

In what follows I will examine how the different purposes of royal embassies influenced the pope's decisions as to what rules of procedure were to be applied to regulate the external forms of diplomatic intercourse. It will be shown that the complexity of the interior structure of the Palace of the Popes at Avignon offered a range of possibilities for the stage managing of diplomatic ceremonies as well as for adapting the form of negotiations to their contents. The mediation techniques applied by Clement VI and Innocent VI are analysed in the fifth section of this chapter. The last two sections are devoted to aspects of 'diplomatic culture': I will discuss the significance of celebrations and gifts.

6.2. The Papal Palace as a Stage for Communication

Benedict XII's new palace (today known as the Palais-Vieux), whose construction began in early 1335 and was completed under Clement VI, was designed to perform a diversity of functions. It was, first of all, a fortress, equipped with a garrison of its own. It was a palace, providing all the facilities necessary for the display of wealth and power expected of the pontifical court. And it was, thirdly, the headquarters of an ever-expanding bureaucracy whose area of influence was co-extensive with Western Christendom.[2] The parts added later by Clement VI were designed primarily to house the departments of the papal administration, in particular the law courts. We have no evidence for diplomatic business being transacted here.

Some insight into the use of the rooms of the new papal palace—of 'public' and 'private' space—for diplomatic purposes during Benedict XII's and Clement VI's pontificates can be gained from the consistorial records kept by the papal chamber clerks Guillelmus de Petrilia, Guillelmus de Bos and Michael de Ricomanni.[3] The consistory, a large room on the ground floor of the east wing of the palace, finished in 1339, was the place where prelates, princes and their emissaries were usually received and where returning nuncios reported on their missions.[4] Work on Benedict XII's Grand Chapel (*capella magna*), which was to occupy the entire north wing of his new palace, began in early April 1335. It seems that not long after its consecration (23 June 1336) it came to be used as a venue for the transaction of diplomatic business of a more solemn character: it was here that the envoys of Peter IV of Aragon, the king himself and the envoys of the Knights Hospitallers swore their oaths of allegiance to Benedict XII and Clement VI.[5] On at least two occasions—in 1340 and 1346—the first-floor gallery (*porticus* or *deambulatorium*) surrounding the central courtyard (Cloister Court) was used for diplomatic ceremonies.[6]

The pope's private quarters and most of the rooms with a more ceremonial function were located on the first floor of Benedict's palace.[7] There is documentary evidence from the period *c.*1336 to 1346 that shows that almost all of these—the hall primarily used for official banquets (Grand Tinel), the pope's private dining room (Petit Tinel), his dressing room (*camera paramenti*) and not least his bedroom (*camera pape* or *camera privata*) and study (*studium*)—became the setting for diplomatic communication at one stage or other.[8] During the pope's stay in Villeneuve-lès-Avignon in the summer, envoys would be received at his residence there.[9]

Just as there was no one, fixed place for the transaction of diplomatic business (although the consistorial chamber clearly provided a focal point for this), so there was considerable flexibility regarding the time of day at which envoys could be received. Edward III's delegates at the First Avignon Conference meticulously recorded at what time they were admitted to the pope's presence: meetings could take place *hora matutina* (at the time of Mattins)—that is, before 7 a.m.—*de mane* (in the morning)—that is, between 7 and 9 a.m.—*hora vesperarum* (at the time of Vespers)—that is, between 2.30 and 4 p.m.—*post hora vesperarum, hore derreyn passé à heure de vespres* (after the evening service) and even *après heure de dormir* (past bedtime).[10] The bells of Notre-Dame-des-Doms, situated to the north of the palace, may have helped the envoys to find out what the exact time was.[11] We may assume that to some extent the pope's liturgical duties determined his availability for a meeting on a given day, and the exact time chosen for it.

The pope's choice of venue for a meeting depended on what mode of diplomatic discourse and degree of publicity he deemed appropriate. In this regard, Benedict XII's new palace offered more options to choose from than the papal palaces in Italy during the high Middle Ages.[12] Publicity in this context, it needs to be emphasized, was always publicity of a restricted, elitist nature. 'Public' diplomatic receptions were attended by members of the Sacred College, specifically invited prelates and nobles who themselves were visitors to the curia, and members of the papal 'family'. The townspeople and visiting petitioners of lower rank may have witnessed the arrival of grand embassies and marvelled at the display of wealth and status on such occasions, but only insiders with access to the palace were in a position to find out about the intricacies of the protocol observed in the subsequent receptions and negotiations.[13]

Formal receptions of diplomatic agents usually took place in public or extraordinary consistories—that is, before the pope, the assembly of the cardinals and a select number of ecclesiastical and lay dignitaries. These meetings followed a precise ceremonial pattern (the inclusion of chapters on such 'profane' matters as the reception of rulers or their envoys is a new feature of ceremonials compiled during the Avignon period—earlier compilations of this kind had focused on the pope and his liturgical role[14]). A passage in a treatise on the ceremonial to be observed at the papal court, written probably by a cardinal around 1320, describes the pivotal role of the *consistorium publicum* in diplomatic affairs: 'Attendendum etiam quod cum magna negotia publica tamen proponenda sunt, sive per ambassiatores imperatorum vel regum, provinciarum vel communitatum solemnium [...] dominus papa audire consuevit in consistorio publico [...] Et etiam quando summus pontifex multum vult honorare ambassiatores, vel solemnes nuntios venientes, etiam si tunc nichil magni proponant, in publico consistorio recipere consuevit.' (Also note that when important matters that concern all are to be expounded by the envoys of emperors or kings, provinces or important corporations, our lord the pope usually listens to these matters in public consistory. Also, when the Supreme Pontiff intends to bestow a great honour on high-ranking envoys to his court, even if they then put forward nothing of great importance, he usually receives them in public consistory.)[15] Clement VI attached more value to the 'stage managing' of significant diplomatic events than any of his predecessors. After 1342 public consistories increasingly provided the setting for the solemn publication of the results of negotiations rather than for these negotiations themselves.[16] It was in public consistories, in the presence of great numbers of witnesses, that Clement VI declared that he intended to take measures against Louis of Bavaria after his non-appearance at the curia (11 July 1343), and that he accepted the emperor's submission five months later.[17] Clement's solemn approbation of the election of the new king of the Romans, Charles IV (6 November 1346), is perhaps the most striking example of the propagandistic use of the public consistory. In order to achieve maximum publicity, and quite possibly because the consistorial chamber was simply too small, the scene of this convention was shifted to the gallery (*deambulatorium*) outside the Grand Tinel, and it is to be assumed that the whole of the Cloister Court was filled with spectators.[18]

'Diplomatic' consistories of a less public nature were attended—apart from the envoys themselves—only by the pope, some cardinals and an even smaller number of curial officials. These 'secret' or 'private'[19] consistories were sometimes held outside the consistorial chamber. The papal chamber in the Great Tower (today called the Tower of the Angels) was the place where the talks between the envoys of Joanna I of Naples and Clement VI, assisted by a committee of ten cardinals, began on 21 October 1343.[20] At such non-public consistorial meetings the main emphasis was on diplomatic debate and decision making rather than the publication of results.[21]

This was even more clearly the case with those meetings *in camera pape*, which did not have consistorial status. References to such assemblies occur frequently in the ledgers of the chamber clerks. Whereas early in Clement VI's pontificate so many prelates and nobles were invited that they are almost indistinguishable from regular consistories, the number of witnesses was deliberately reduced over the following years. It seems that such meetings were convened for discussions that did not necessarily have to be conducted in consistory, for which a smaller circle of participants seemed more suitable, and—most importantly—for discussions whose outcome was not to be made public too early, since the issue under negotiation was particularly sensitive.[22] Although John Offord does not explicitly mention the *camera pape* in his reports sent to the English court in October 1344, there is reason to assume that it was the location of his and Hugh Neville's preliminary talks with Clement VI earlier that month.[23]

There is, however, a certain risk of overlooking the 'human factor', and thus the role of historical contingency, in these considerations. Whether or not the pope would receive envoys in his private quarters—and, indeed, whether or not he would receive them at all—also depended on his health at a given point in time. We know, for example, that Benedict XII was bedridden in early May 1340, and that the business that required his attention had to be transacted 'in camera turris nove, ubi tunc iacebat' (in the chamber of the Great Tower, where he was lying at the time)[24]—that is, in his bedchamber. As has been mentioned above, his two successors also repeatedly went through patches of serious illness,[25] and it is to be assumed that they were at times simply unable to sit through long public consistories.

6.3. The Structure of Bilateral Negotiations

Our examination of the uses of 'private' and 'public' space has left us with the impression that receptions of diplomats in the papal palace were carefully orchestrated events. We must now turn our attention towards the sequencing of individual visits of embassies to the papal court. It is possible to distinguish between four main stages.

1. *The escort into the city.* The ceremonials from the period under examination state explicitly that only cardinals, emperors and empresses and kings and queens and their sons ought to be honoured by being met outside the papal city and accompanied in the final stage of their journey by members of the Sacred College.[26] Thus in early May 1322 a French embassy under the leadership of the count of Clermont was greeted at Pont-Saint-Ésprit (more than 40 kilometres north of Avignon!) by the *familiares* of some cardinals, and at Sorgues by the brother, nephews and some other relatives of the pope, but not by any cardinals or John XXII in person.[27] However, it seems that exceptions from this rule were occasionally made, and that guests were deliberately received with a higher degree of solemnity than their social status warranted; such a conspicuous, 'positive' violation of protocol was a means of showing a particular guest in what high esteem he and his principal were held at the papal court.[28] In this respect, the disagreement between Geoffrey le Baker and Henry Knighton over whether or not there were any cardinals present at the solemn entry of the duke of Lancaster and the earl of Arundel into Avignon on 24 December 1354[29] is not a disagreement over a minor detail: if there were, this could be interpreted as a gesture of goodwill from an otherwise anglophobe, or at least anglosceptic, college of cardinals.

2. *The first audience.*[30] The envoy's demonstration of his and his master's *reverentia* was the first part of the welcoming ritual. Since the early Middle Ages all clerics and laymen coming into the pope's presence were expected to kneel before him and kiss his right foot as a sign of reverence, obedience and submission.[31] This was usually followed by the *receptio ad osculum oris*, the granting of the licence to give the pope the kiss of peace on the cheek.[32] After offering their master's greetings, the envoys recommended him and his family to the pope, who usually responded by asking about the well-being of the king and his immediate family and by declaring his affection for and good intentions towards him.[33] After these courteous exchanges the head of the mission handed over the king's letters and, if he had been issued with such a document, his letter of credence.[34] At some point during this first meeting the envoys probably also presented their gifts. With its short speeches, in which set phrases dominated, and its gestural elements, this pre-negotiation phase was the most ritualized part of any mission.

3. *The second audience.*[35] After the presentation of the king's letters, the envoys were sometimes invited to deliver their oral message straight away. More frequently, they were given a later date for this, or told that they would in due course be summoned to appear before the pope.[36] Before this second audience the envoys would have had to decide which of them would speak. Presumably, this task would fall to the highest ranking cleric, if the embassy was a mixed one, and to the highest ranking noble in those rare cases where it was made up by laymen only. Some envoys mention in their reports that at some point during their receptions they knelt down to address the pope, but we also have references to stools or benches being provided.[37] After the speech the envoys were usually told that they would be given a detailed answer later on the same day or at a date to be notified to them later.

4. At their *third and final audience*[38] the envoys received the promised reply. Their mission was now completed, and it only remained for them to take their formal leave of the pope. Requesting licence to depart (*licentia recedendi*) was an indispensable part of the protocol, and it was considered shameful for envoys to leave furtively.[39] Hence in late 1344 and early 1345, after the breakdown of the Anglo-French negotiations, William Bateman, Hugh Neville and John Offord did not dare to leave Avignon without papal permission, which was repeatedly refused.[40] An official recall by their king would have added weight to their request, and was asked for several times, but it never came.[41] Envoys who had been given licence to depart were expected to repeat the *reverentia* and kiss the pope's foot as they had done at their first audience. However, it seems that in certain circumstances— especially if the preceding negotiations had gone well—the pope would exempt them from this and thus honour them. Having granted Louis of Nevers permission to depart at the end of his 1336 visit, Benedict XII received the kiss of peace from him. When Louis's chancellor knelt down to kiss his foot, Benedict did not allow this but insisted on exchanging the *osculum oris* with him, too.[42]

6.4. The Structure of Trilateral Negotiations

Our knowledge of what format Clement VI and his advisers chose for the peace conference of 1344 derives from the letters of John Offord and his colleagues, and from the minutes kept by them;

ceremonials remain silent on the question of how multilateral negotiations were to be structured. It is therefore difficult to say whether
the same protocol was observed when the Supreme Pontiff attempted
to arbitrate or mediate at other times, and between other protagonists.

The arrival of the French delegation on 18 October 1344 marked
the end of the bilateral consultations that had been going on between
Offord and his colleagues and Clement VI since early September, and
the beginning of the trilateral peace conference, presided over by the
pope and six cardinals (Pierre Després, Gaucelme de Jean Duèsne,
Jean de Comminges, Annibaldo Caetani da Ceccano, Pedro Gomez
da Barroso and Bertrand de Déaulx) and, between 28 October and 20
November, by two cardinals (Després and da Ceccano) alone.[43] From
the very start the conference took the form of a series of informal and
mostly relatively short bilateral discussions between the pope or the
cardinals' committee and the English delegation and between the
pope or the committee and the French delegation: On 24 October
1344, for example, Clement VI negotiated with the French from
between 3 and 4 (*hora vesperarum*) until around 6 p.m. (*ad noctis
tenebras*).[44] What little communication there was between the two
royal embassies was indirect—that is, conducted through the pope and
the cardinals, whose aim it was to determine whether or not any
bargaining space existed.[45] Only on two occasions did all three parties
come together for a plenary session.[46] This separation of the two
delegations, it seems, was maintained in order to promote flexibility
and productivity: Clement VI may have been concerned that plenary
meetings would all too soon turn into polemical exchanges of legal
arguments, and that the conference would reach a deadlock within
days. Bilateral exploratory talks with each delegation would give him
the opportunity to investigate the views of each government on the
thorny points under discussion. As for the diplomats, such confidential discussions with the pope or the cardinals alone allowed them
to adopt more constructive positions without the risk of losing face.[47]

In the absence of equally strong documentation, much less can be
ascertained about the format chosen for the Second Avignon Conference ten years later. Geoffrey le Baker tells us of a consistory in which
both parties were given the opportunity to make speeches before
Innocent VI and the cardinals.[48] There is evidence of the English and
French kings setting up committees or working parties of experts to
deal with any potentially problematic territorial issues before the
conference. On 30 October 1354 the Chancery issued a special

procuration to the three English delegates then at the curia (William Bateman, Michael Northburgh and Guy de Brian), together with four senior members of Edward's council in Guienne (over whose boundaries difficulties were likely to arise): Bernard Ezi, lord of Albret, Guillaume-Sanche, lord of Pommiers, Bertrand, lord of Montferrand and the lawyer Gérard du Puy. The document empowered these seven men to conduct, in cooperation with their French counterparts, an inquiry about the definition of the boundaries of the territories to be ceded to Edward, and to communicate their findings to the pope and the other envoys.[49] The heads of the English and French delegations, the duke of Lancaster and the earl of Arundel, and the duke of Bourbon and John II's chancellor, Pierre de la Forêt, respectively, were then, in a final step, to make the formal renunciations referred to above. The contrast between the dreary work of the specialist and the solemn functions of the aristocratic envoy, between the realms of 'legal' and 'ceremonial diplomacy', could hardly have been made clearer. Unfortunately, we do not know for sure whether the French appointed a similar committee of legal experts, and if so, whether they actually held consultations with their English counterparts.

6.5. Trilateral Negotiations: The Role of the Pope

If Clement VI and Innocent VI repeatedly intervened in the Anglo-French conflict without being explicitly invited to do so, it was first because they considered this their spiritual duty as popes, and, secondly, because they saw their own interests—namely, the renewal of the crusading movement—undermined by the war. Clement VI's intervention in 1344 took the form of mediation, and not, as has often been maintained, arbitration, the key difference being that the latter is a procedure in which a third party is asked to render a judgement about the conflict in question, whereas in the former the third party is requested to assist the disputants to reach agreement between themselves while the ultimate decision-making authority remains in their hands.[50]

There are different kinds of roles, ranging from relatively passive to very active and involved ones, that a mediator can play in assisting parties to resolve conflicts.[51] The first role is the mediator as process facilitator. This kind of mediator generally exerts little direct influence on the parties or on the substance of the agreement; his role rather is restricted to creating conditions that are conducive to reaching agreement. Providing a venue for the English and French delegates to meet and offering the logistical support for their negotiations were perhaps the most obvious aspects of the work of Clement VI and Innocent VI as facilitators. Moreover, their procedural functions comprised the opening, closing or adjourning of meetings, 'giving the floor' to delegates and the ruling on any points of order made.

The second role is the facilitator of communication and compromise. As we have seen, Clement VI and the committee of cardinals kept the two delegations separate most of the time during the First Avignon Conference and served as the main channel of communication between them. This was done in an attempt to help them to communicate basic information that was regarded essential for the peace talks to be successful. Moreover, part of their role as mediators was to facilitate mutual and simultaneous flexibility. In order to avoid appearing weak, each party involved in a mediation process may try to appear firm and unbending, often making excessively rigid commitments to their respective positions. For Philip VI's delegates to the 1344 conference, any discussion of the English claims to the French throne was out of the question. This, however, was the very cornerstone of the negotiating position of Edward III's diplomats.[52] The delegates of both kings were repeatedly criticized by Clement VI and the cardinals for their intransigence.[53] It was in vain that Clement VI tried to persuade William Bateman, John Offord and their colleagues to make their position more flexible by waiving, at least for a certain period, their maximum claim—that is, Edward's claim to the French throne—and negotiate about a solution to the problem of Guienne and possible marriage alliances instead.[54]

A third mediating role is that of formulator, someone who helps the parties to invent new solutions to their problems by helping to redefine the issues in conflict, or finding a formula for its resolution. The mediator thus becomes more than an intermediary; he is no longer a more or less passive third party but takes on the substantive function of a maker of proposals or suggestions. The English delegation clearly expected Clement VI to take on such an active role in the 1344 negotiations. On 26 October, for instance, they told him in no uncertain terms that it was his, not their, task to find a lasting solution: 'we answered him that it was not up to us to show any way towards peace, but only to stand on our stated demands for the kingdom and to listen to the ways he himself as mediator could show us.'[55] Clement and the cardinals rose to the challenge. At a meeting on 28 October he encouraged the English delegates to think about new ways towards a lasting peace, and said that he himself would do the same.[56] As head of the ecclesiastical hierarchy, he possessed sufficient resources to offer Edward III compensation if he agreed to renounce his claim to the French throne. During their consultations with his delegates on 4 November 1344, Cardinals Després and da Ceccano suggested as possible compensations the lands of the Hospitallers as well as of all other foreign ecclesiastics and laymen in his realm, the rule over all Scotland, a large sum of money and beneficial marriage alliances, but all of these offers were declined.[57]

I have so far referred to the functions performed by Clement VI during the First Avignon Conference as 'roles'. For him, as well as for his predecessors and successors, participation in diplomatic business entailed role playing in yet another, more literal sense. Attached to their status as Vicars of Christ was a bundle of normative expectations made upon their behaviour by the members of the curial public: cardinals, officials, domestics and visitors. According to these shared expectations, the pope, when interacting with foreign envoys, had to act as a severe but fair judge and as a champion of the liberties of the Church. In a letter of 8 March 1284 the English envoys Ellis de Hauville and Walter of Bath reported to their king that Martin IV had not allowed them to recite their message on their knees but had made them sit down. They pointed out, however, that this was unusual and only done after the pope's *familia* had been sent out; the audience had thus assumed a more private character.[58] Adam Murimuth includes in his chronicle what may well be a first-hand account by John Shoreditch of his reception at the papal court in October 1343.[59] Immediately after his arrival Shoreditch was led into the pope's chamber, where he presented his letters concerning provisions in England. He was then told to return to the dressing room (*camera paramenti*) and wait there while the pope summoned the cardinals present in the curia. The first, private audience was then publicly 're-enacted': Shoreditch was called back into the chamber and after the *reverentia* handed over the letters for a second time to Clement, now sitting on a throne, surrounded by his cardinals. He was then sent out again while the letters were read aloud. After he had been called back in, the pope gave his response, venting his anger at what he had just been given to hear. The same dichotomy between confrontation in public and cooperation in private can be observed in Clement's negotiation technique during the First Avignon Conference. He protested vigorously against Edward III's policy concerning provisions during his meeting with the royal delegation on 6 September 1344, when the six cardinals were present, but had a far more peaceful and constructive discussion with Offord, Fastolf, Bateman and Neville on the following day, when the five of them were alone in his chamber.[60]

6.6. Entertainment at Court

The account books kept by the head of the Apostolic Chamber contain a large number of marginal notes stating whom the Avignon popes invited to their table for particularly lavish and costly meals, the aim being to explain why the expenses incurred by the kitchen (*coquina*) as well as by the household departments responsible for the supply of wine, bread and wood (*buticularia* and *panataria*) were exceptionally high during a given period of time. It is possible, on the basis of these notes, to compile a kind of posthumous guest list—a list of persons deemed worthy of such an invitation.[61]

Grand banquets were held in the Grand Tinel (*tinellum magnum* or *aula*) on the first floor of the Consistory Wing. It is noteworthy that the cameral ledgers from the period 1342 to 1362, while containing dozens of references to Italian, Spanish and especially French guests, mention only one Englishman as being honoured by an invitation to a formal lunch or dinner: Henry of Grosmont, duke of Lancaster, guest at Innocent VI's table on Christmas Day 1354.[62]

If invitations to banquets were a means of honouring an envoy (and, indirectly, his principal), the same could be said of invitations to lunches or dinners in a smaller circle. The pope would sometimes entertain select diplomats and other visitors to his court in his private dining room, the Petit Tinel (*tinellum parvum*).[63] This was more than a gesture of goodwill; informal meetings of this kind could form an integral part of the diplomatic dialogue in that they could help to reduce uncertainty prior to the beginning of the negotiations proper. This was certainly the case with the lunch or dinner to which Clement VI treated John Offord and Hugh Neville on 5 September 1344, two days after their arrival in Avignon; this meal was followed by a preliminary discussion about the problems to be addressed during the following days and weeks.[64] Such conversations during and after meals could help both sides to reach an understanding about each other's interests and objectives and about what they might expect to achieve through negotiation. They thus offered an opportunity to lay the groundwork for the subsequent formal negotiations as well as to improve its atmospherics. While the absence of evidence that Englishmen other than the duke of Lancaster were entertained in the Grand Tinel would suggest that Edward III's diplomats were treated as second-class guests at the Avignonese curia, one should not be too hasty in drawing conclusions on this point. Not enough intermediate reports from English envoys survive for us to ascertain whether invitations to private lunches or dinners in the Petit Tinel, which are not documented in the cameral ledgers, were customary or an exception.

Some areas of medieval diplomatic culture overlapped with contemporary aristocratic culture (I here take 'diplomatic culture' to mean the ideals and operating norms of a diplomatic system; these comprise not only the recognized institutions and procedures that give structure and order to the diplomatic dialogue, but also the subjective attitudes, 'the common stock of ideas and values',[65] of those who participate in it). Both the English and the French aristocrats who performed diplomatic functions and the popes and cardinals who received them at the curia belonged to the same socio-economic class and shared a self-image of being part of an international community whose social and cultural values transcended local boundaries. These intra-aristocratic ties could be reinforced on such festive occasions as tournaments—which served as 'points of diffusion for chivalrous culture and for chivalrous standards'[66]—and banquets. We have some evidence suggesting that this is exactly what happened during the informal meeting between Henry, earl of Derby and the high-ranking French delegation in Avignon in June 1344. According to one source John, duke of Normandy, not only invited Henry to dinner at the palace of the cardinal of Boulogne (the uncle of his wife Jeanne) at Monteau but also organized a two-day Anglo-French tournament at Villeneuve at which Clement VI and the cardinals were present (the ecclesiastical ban on tournaments, in place since 1130, had been lifted by John XXII at the very beginning of his pontificate).[67]

6.7. Diplomatic Gifts: Functions, Structures, Symbolism

Throughout the Middle Ages the triad of the interlinking obligations of giving, accepting and returning gifts played a central role in the production and reproduction of the interpersonal ties that, in turn, formed the basis of social and political relations at large.[68]

Four lists of royal gifts to the pope and other recipients at the curia survive from the Avignonese period: three from the pontificate of John XXII and one from that of his immediate successor, Benedict XII.[69] In what follows I will discuss what the rationale behind the distribution of money or precious objects (*jocalia*) by English envoys was, and what precisely was expected in return from each of the individuals or groups who profited from the king's generosity (popes, their relatives, cardinals, members of the curial administration and of the papal household).

The presentation of the gift marked the point where the spheres of diplomatic communication and of court culture intersected. We may assume that, in order for their gifts to the higher-ranking individuals at the curia (popes, cardinals and their relatives) to appear genuine, Edward's envoys had to construct a 'polite fiction' of voluntariness and disinterestedness[70]—at least, that was what the courtly ideal of gift giving demanded.[71] The novelty of the medieval *ars donandi* was that it consciously stepped outside the context of any legal or moral obligation, depicting itself as purely honorific and motivated by the donor's free will as opposed to guided by the expectation of a return gift or an obligation of gratitude. In other words, in medieval court culture the 'ideal' gift, given gladly, freely and spontaneously, 'breaks the continuum of giving and taking, debt and payment of debt, and posits itself as a *unique* act determined only by the dialectic of honour'.[72]

The diplomats' expense accounts, however, speak a rather different language. Where they mention expenses for precious objects or gifts in cash, we often also find succinct explanations for the specific purpose behind these, as will be discussed below. On the other hand, they also tell us that certain gifts were made simply because it was customary to do so. By the mid-fourteenth century the courtly 'art of giving' had become the distinct practice of a noble rank in society and proof of an aristocratic mentality. At the same time, gift exchange functioned as 'the crucial medium of expression in the internal group structure of the nobility, as the relationship sign *par excellence*'.[73] Besides putting the success of their own mission at stake, any refusal on the part of Edward's representatives to follow this practice would have resulted in a loss of prestige for their king.

The payments that John Stratford, archdeacon of Lincoln, had made to four of the pope's doorkeepers on Christmas Eve 1322 had been made in keeping with a practice introduced by previous generations of English diplomats ('sicut moris est nunciorum domini regis'), the auditors at the Exchequer were given to hear after Stratford's return. Earlier, on 3 November, he had been obliged to give money to other members of Pope John's household because curial custom required this ('sicut moris est in curia Romana').[74] A fragmentary Wardrobe account of 1333–4[75] may simply state that Richard de Bury and John Shoreditch had distributed precious objects and money while in Avignon earlier in that year to expedite the processing of the king's requests, and generally to promote his interests at the Apostolic See ('pro celeriori expedicione et promocione negociorum suorum in curia' (for his affairs at the papal court to be handled and promoted more speedily)), but Edward's privy seal letter ordering the Exchequer staff to account with the two diplomats explicitly states that their gifts had been motivated by both practical necessity and etiquette: 'Et pour mielz exploiter les dites busoignes et pour nostre honour sauver [ils] eient aussint done coupes et deniers au dit Seint Piere, ses neveus et clercs de sa chambre, as cardinals, usshers et plusurs autres officiers de la dite court' (And to be better able to conduct the said business and to safeguard our honour they also gave cups and money to the Holy Father, his nephews and his chamber clerks, the cardinals and several others of the said court).[76]

Giving creates obligations. He who accepts a gift thereby also accepts the duty to reciprocate; he places himself in the moral debt of the donor until he has given something in return. Whether their gifts were occasioned by particular circumstances or given in accordance with an established custom, Edward III's envoys expected reciprocation. What form this was expected to take differed widely from one recipient to another.

As the head of the ecclesiastical hierarchy and the central figure around which curial life revolved, the Supreme Pontiff was the single most important recipient of gifts. There seems to have been fairly precise ideas in circulation among visitors as to what kind of presents were fit for him. While Baldwin, archbishop of Trier, was making preparations for a journey to Vienne and Avignon in the spring of 1310 or 1311, he received a letter from a friend who was already staying in the papal city. He advised Baldwin to bring along precious gifts for the cardinals and especially for the pope, touching upon the crucial question of the donor's honour: 'Credo, quod congruit honori vestro, immo necessarium est, quod visitetis papam et omnes cardinales [...] cum donis [...] vel in pecunia vel in bonis pannis de lana. Papam autem cum vasis pulcherrimis de auro et de aliis iocalibus pulcris visitetis' (I would believe it to be consistent with your honour, and indeed necessary, for you to bring gifts of money or good pieces of wool cloth when you visit the pope and all of the cardinals. When you visit the pope, moreover, you ought to bring the most beautiful dishes made of gold and other precious materials).[77]

The choir-cope that John XXII received in 1317 was the only ecclesiastical garment that we know to have been presented to him or his successors by English royal envoys. For the most part, their gifts were objects that could be used either at table or in liturgical ceremonies: cups, ewers, basins, plates, dishes, all made of gold or gilded silver.[78] The exchange of such 'bifunctional' artefacts was a characteristic of contacts at the highest social level.[79]

Of the dozens of extant diplomatic expense reports from the years 1309 to 1378 only three mention the distribution of precious objects to the pope and other recipients. According to these documents, they had either been entrusted to the royal diplomats before they departed from London, or purchased in Paris or Avignon; obviously, in the latter two cases the unusual additional expenses had to be accounted for. However, to deduce from this that all other English embassies turned up empty-handed at the curia would certainly be wrong. Especially a man like Clement VI, whose taste for luxury and pomp was commonly known (and, indeed, resented by more than one contemporary observer),[80] would have considered this an affront.

More probably, the English envoys received the objects they would later use as gifts directly from the keeper of the Wardrobe before leaving London. This would explain why the objects seldom appear in their *particule compoti* before 1337, and never after that date. The inventories of the papal treasury made in 1314–16, 1342–3 and 1353 show that a considerable number of items kept in that repository, mainly dishes made of gold or gilded silver, bore heraldic signs linking them to the English Crown: the arms of England, often combined with or next to those of France.[81] We also know that around that time many items of the same kind, adorned with the same devices, were stored in Edward III's Wardrobe, and that occasionally—for instance, during his continental expedition of 1338–40—the king would give some of these away as diplomatic gifts.[82]

Unilateral giving can be a way of indicating the social inferiority of the recipient and the generosity of the donor; at the very least, until it is reciprocated, a gift establishes an inequality of status between the two.[83] Indeed, there is much to be said for the thesis that a failure on the pope's part to show some sign of gratitude would have run counter to the expectations normally attached to his position. If stable relations between Westminster and Avignon were to be maintained, both sides would have had to adhere to some variation of the reciprocity principle.

How, then, are the facts that papal presents were rarely of considerable financial value,[84] and that there are only two documented instances of English diplomats receiving such presents,[85] to be accounted for? This apparent contradiction can be resolved if we accept the postulate that neither a gift itself nor its reciprocation must necessarily take material form.[86] The pope's counter-gift was his allocation of honour as social capital, the renewed esteem in which he held the king after the latter had had 'largesse by proxy' practised through his envoys. It has been noted that, by reacting in this way, 'the pope responded to material gifts of high value with immaterial gifts that were priceless'[87]. This seems to confirm the general observation that in the court context the gift was the most significant form in which relations of recognition were established and expressed.[88]

The diplomatic gift, then, could be used as a tool in the aspiration for, and protection of, prestige, which in turn could be transformed into power and political gain. The first to feel the consequences of failure or success in this would obviously be the king's diplomats themselves. The least they could expect was a favourable reception (benigna auditio). The maximum, of course, of what they could hope to achieve was to exert a direct influence on the pope's decisions, but it is not surprising to find that any evidence for this is lacking.

As has been shown above, one way for the Crown to ensure the gratitude and favour of certain cardinals deemed influential at court was to pay them annual pensions out of the Exchequer revenues. These payments would at times be complemented by spontaneous gifts; hence the presentation of cups and ewers of gilded silver to Cardinals Talleyrand de Périgord and Pierre Després, the vice-chancellor, in 1333.[89] Like the precious objects presented to John XXII or Benedict XII, these were designed to enhance the king's prestige in the eyes of members of the same stratum of society—after all, as aristocrats, the pope, the king, the cardinals and their relatives shared the same group-specific concept of honour. At the same time, however, more practical motives came into play here. Those cardinals to whom the handling of ecclesiastical or political matters had been delegated became 'targets' for the generosity of those who would be affected by their decisions, as can be seen from the account books of the envoys of Hamburg's city council.[90] Bérenger Frédol the younger, cardinal bishop of Porto, and Bertrand de Montfavès, cardinal deacon of S Maria in Aquiro, each received a Christmas gift of 20 florins from John Stratford in 1322. According to Stratford's *compotus*, this was money well invested: Frédol and Montfavès had been charged by John XXII with finding a solution to the Anglo-Scottish conflict, which had once more erupted into war over the summer.[91]

Besides the compliance with custom, two motives for English envoys to present gifts at the papal court have so far emerged: the preservation of the king's honour, and the hope of being able to influence curial decision-making procedures. Neither of this was really possible unless the diplomats managed to gain direct access to the pope himself, which, in turn, seems to have been no mean feat—Guilhem Richer, envoy of King James II of Aragon, complained in 1326 that even the road to Paradise was easier than the way into the pope's audience hall.[92]

Under John XXII, success was more likely if one managed to secure the goodwill of three of his nephews, Arnaud Duèze, Arnaud de Trian and Pierre de Via, all of whom wielded considerable influence at court.[93] The letters of the Aragonese diplomats tell of their repeated efforts to persuade these men to admit them to John's audience hall or lodgings.[94] In 1324–5 James II deemed it best to issue his envoys not only with letters of recommendation to several cardinals but also to these three *nepotes pape*.[95] In the early 1330s de Via, Duèze, de Trian and Bernardus Jordani de Insula, a distant relative of the pope,[96] were even invited to attend receptions of foreign princes or their envoys in consistory.[97] If these four men received gold florins from John Stratford in 1322, and gilded silver cups and ewers from Richard de Bury and John Shoreditch eleven years later, it was because the diplomats knew that they had the pope's ear, that it was in their power to grant or deny access to him, and that they possessed insider knowledge about consistorial negotiations.

Waiting for the much-coveted papal bulls to be drafted must have cost the English diplomats, as indeed any private petitioner, some time and money. Richard de Bury and John Shoreditch were apparently trying to speed up this process in 1333 by presenting Arnaldus Neapolinis with a gilded silver cup, and Robertus de Adria with 18 florins.[98] The difference in value between these gifts reflects the difference in status between the two recipients: Neapolinis was a prothonotary, one of the more distinguished notaries who were serving in John XXII's chancery. The *protonotarii pape*, as they were unofficially called, were responsible for keeping the minutes in consistory and putting them into their final written form, but also for drawing up all letters relating to judicial matters (*littere de iustitia*, as opposed to *littere de gratia*).[99] As an abbreviator (*abbreviator litterarum apostolicarum*), working under the direct supervision of the vice-chancellor, Robertus de Adria was one of the staff who changed petitions from the form of requests to rescripts.[100] But he was, at the same time, also a scribe (*scriptor litterarum apostolicarum*) in the engrosser's office, which suggests that he not only drew up the concepts or minutes of bulls but also set them up in definite form.[101] Two squires of the vice-chancellor were rewarded with 6 florins each for taking this 'end product' to de Bury and Shoreditch.

Among the members of the papal household, two groups stood out as recipients of gifts: those who were responsible for the pope's security, and those who carried out duties in his immediate surroundings. On their way into the old papal palace—the palace that Jacques Duèze had occupied as bishop of Avignon, and that he had moved back into as pope on 2 October 1316[102]—visitors usually had to come through the main gate (*prima porta*), which led into the south-eastern corner of the central courtyard. The guards (*janitores*) of this gate were given cash gifts by John Stratford at Christmas 1322 and Easter 1323, and by Richard de Bury and John Shoreditch in 1333, perhaps also at Easter.[103] The *secunda porta* mentioned in Stratford's account is more difficult to identify; in all probability it was the door of the audience hall (*aula magna*) on the first floor of the south wing of the palace.[104] The men standing guard there received payments on the same dates, and from the same envoys, as their colleagues of the 'first gate'. The rest of the inside of the apostolic palace was guarded by sergeants at arms (*servientes armorum*);[105] they too received money in 1333. A relatively modest present was made to the squires (*scutiferi* or *domicelli pape*), who escorted the pope every time he rode out,[106] by Stratford in 1322.

If doorkeepers, guards, sergeants at arms and squires[107] could be either a hindrance or a help in establishing personal contact with the pope, the same was true of the staff of the papal chamber, which was situated in a tower at the southern end of the west wing of John XXII's palace.[108] To each of its two master-doorkeepers (*magistri hostiarii*) and four doorkeepers (*hostiarii*) de Bury and Shoreditch gave silver cups in 1333. More than thirty years later Bartholomew Burghersh found the doorkeepers of Urban V's chamber a valuable source of first-hand information as to what was going on in the curia's 'inner sanctum': one of them informed him of Urban's decision to make Simon Langham the next archbishop of Canterbury and promptly received a generous payment of 16 li. 13s. 4d.[109] The range of the functions performed by the chamberlains (*cubicularii, camerarii,* or *cambrerii*) expanded markedly in the period under consideration. Besides vesting the pope when he went to consistory, solemn ceremonies or receptions of distinguished visitors, uncovering the papal slipper that visitors were to kiss at audiences and standing in rows on either side of their master on these occasions, the chamberlains came to be assigned a variety of other tasks both in the household and outside it.[110] Some of these personal attendants acted as the pope's private secretaries, receiving requests and presenting them, and sending them off once they had been signed.[111] Perhaps Jean Rigaud, who was given 30 florins and two pieces of clothing from de Bury and Shoreditch in 1333, was one of them. While a cup and a ewer went to Bertrand Demerii, a 'knight of the pope's chamber', the 'familiars of the pope's chamber' had to content themselves with their share in the 157 florins that were given to the domestic staff as a whole.

What has been noted so far may suggest that the sole purpose of diplomatic gift giving was to produce immediately tangible results not unlike the type characteristic of economic transactions. But to accept this view would mean to ignore the symbolic dimension of the gift; goods are not only economic commodities but also 'vehicles and instruments for realities of another order: influence, power, sympathy, status, emotion; and the skilful game of exchange consists of a complex totality of manoeuvres, conscious or unconscious'.[112] When churchmen like the archbishop of Canterbury, the bishop of Lichfield or the archdeacon of Nottingham sent altar cloths, choir copes and religious books to Avignon,[113] they did so not only because these objects befitted their rank but also because they gave visible expression to what they perceived as their own function in earthly society.

Among the gold dishes that the Bardi merchants delivered to Edward II's envoys at Avignon for presentation to John XXII in 1317 there were several items bearing the arms of both the king and the pope. This points towards a second aspect of symbolism: the diplomatic gift could be used to convey a visualized normative statement expressing the donor's ideas about his relations with other rulers and about his position within the wider political structure (one needs only to think of the tennis balls that Shakespeare has the Dauphin's ambassadors present to King Harry in *Henry V*, I. ii).[114] In this sense, Edward II's message in 1317 was that he was taking an interest in close cooperation with the new pope—which was all the more necessary for him since in the aftermath of the Battle of Bannockburn (23 June 1314) England and Scotland remained in a constant state of hostility, with Edward and Robert Bruce rapidly gaining influence in Ireland, and the inner-English conflict between the court party and Thomas of Lancaster was drifting towards the verge of civil war.[115]

By contrast, in the case of the artefacts bearing the English and French coats of arms—if these objects had actually been brought to Avignon by English diplomats, and if the *arma Francie et Anglie* mentioned in the inventories were the new arms as assumed by Edward III in 1340—the message was a highly political one. Whether these objects were used in liturgical ceremonies or at the papal table, they would silently remind those present of Edward's claim to the French throne, thus continuing his envoys' work by other means (it should be noted, however, that an acceptance of such gifts could have been interpreted as a tacit approval of these claims, which, in turn, would have been unlikely, given Benedict XII's adverse reaction when first receiving a letter with Edward's new seal in early March 1340[116]).

Besides establishing a specific relation between individuals or groups, then, a gift also has the potential to reveal something about its donor's ambitions, about how he wants to be seen by others: it is a mirror of identity. Whether this identity is consonant with social or political reality (Edward III as *rex Anglie*) or whether it is merely aspired to (Edward III as *rex Francie et Anglie*) is not crucial. Either way, every giving of a gift implies a self-definition of the donor; it makes a statement about his character, taste and economic and cultural resources. At the same time, the gift also imposes an identity on the recipient in that the donor's perceptions of the other's taste and status, but also of his needs and desires, are exposed in it.[117] In his letter of 20 April 1317 John XXII thanked Edward II for his coronation gifts, some of which he found 'suitable for divine worship, and others for the pope's use'.[118] If these gifts had been intended to please Jacques Duèze both as an aristocrat and as Vicar of Christ, this aim had been achieved.

Unfortunately, the expense accounts of 1316–17, 1322–3, 1333 and 1337 do not say much about the actual circumstances of the distribution of money or objects. The medieval court, and the papal curia in particular, were the stage for a continuous struggle for opportunities of gaining prestige and influence. In this respect, it would be of particular relevance to our analysis of diplomatic contacts as an aspect of courtly interaction to know whether the English and French delegations to the peace conferences of 1344 and 1355 entered into some kind of 'gift competition'. What seems clear is that, in making monetary gifts, Edward's diplomats were not obliged to follow a rigid set of instructions but had the authority to act at their own discretion, which allowed them to adapt quickly to changing situations. It was on the basis of a communal agreement (*per consilium nunciorum*) that John Stratford and his co-envoys in 1322–3 began handing out gold florins to Cardinals Frédol and Montfavès, their auditors, a clerk of Andrea Sapiti, the pope's nephews and his doorkeepers and guards. If it is possible to generalize from what is stated in Stratford's account, some cash gifts (*dona*) were handed to the recipient directly, while others (*exhennia*) were sent through a go-between. The former method was applied when money was given to persons of inferior or middle rank (messengers, doorkeepers, squires), the latter, more unobtrusive and discreet, when it was given to notaries, the pope's nephews and cardinals.

The example of Edward III's gifts to the Avignon popes may serve as a reminder of the fact that in all cultures and ages diplomacy, as a system of communication, is bound up with the articulation and mediation of identity. The partners in this dialogue use codes and symbols alongside verbal means.[119] If the constitution *Excommunicamus* (dated 1295) of Boniface VIII, which pronounced excommunication upon anyone who gave or received anything to obtain any kind of favour at the Roman court,[120] was not very effective at this time it was because the elaborate system of exchanging material gifts (money and *jocalia*) and immaterial counter-services (the allocation of prestige, the granting of access, deciding in the donor's favour and speeding up the processing of his requests) had come to be appreciated by all parties involved, including the popes themselves.

Notes to Chapter 6

1. Section 1.1.
2. Philippe Contamine, 'Les aménagements de l'espace privé, XIVe–XVe siècle', in Philippe Ariès and Georges Duby (gen. eds.), *Histoire de la vie privée*, ii: Georges Duby (ed.), *De l'Europe féodale à la Renaissance* (Paris, 1985), 421–501 (471).

Bernhard Schimmelpfennig has analysed the ceremonial functions of the various rooms of the papal palace at Avignon in three important publications: 'Die Funktion des Papstpalastes und der kurialen Gesellschaft im päpstlichen Zeremoniell vor und während des Großen Schismas', in Michel Hayez (ed.), *Genèse et débuts du Grand Schisme d'Occident (1362–1394)* (Paris, 1980), 317–28, '*Ad maiorem pape gloriam*: La fonction des pièces dans le palais des Papes d'Avignon', in Jean Guillaume (ed.), *Architecture et vie sociale: L'Organisation intérieure des grandes demeures à la fin du moyen âge et à la Renaissance* (Paris, 1994), 25–46, and 'Der Palast als Stadtersatz. Funktionelle und zeremonielle Bedeutung der Papstpaläste in Avignon und im Vatikan', in Werner Paravicini (ed.), *Zeremoniell und Raum* (Sigmaringen, 1997), 239–56. See also R. Lentsch, 'Le palais de Benoît XII et son aménagement intérieur', in Marie-Humbert Vicaire (ed.), *La Papauté d'Avignon et le Languedoc (1316–1342)* (Toulouse, 1991), 345–66 (349).
3. Schröder, 206–47.
4. Léon-Honoré Labande, *Le Palais des Papes et les monuments d'Avignon au XIVe siècle* (Marseilles, 1925), i. 60, 109; Gabriel Colombe, *Le Palais des Papes d'Avignon*, 2nd edn. (Paris, 1931), 22–4; Dominique Vingtain and Claude Sauvageot, *Avignon: Le Palais des Papes* (Saint-Léger-Vauban, 1998), 160–3. Diplomatic receptions in the new consistory: Schröder, nos. 49, 53, 59, 61, 70–1, 74, 76, 79, 85, 96, 101–4, 106, 108–9; Froissart, *Œuvres*, xviii. 240 (*domus consistorialis*), 245 (*locus consistorialis*).
5. Labande, *Palais des papes*, i. 52–4, 126–8; Vingtain and Sauvageot, 98–101. Oaths of allegiance: Schröder, nos. 40, 55, 111.
6. Gallery: Labande, *Palais des papes*, i. 119, and Vingtain and Sauvageot, 164. Negotiations: Schröder, nos. 60, 109.
7. See the maps in Schimmelpfennig, 'Funktion des Papstpalastes', between pp. 318 and 319, and id., 'Palast als Stadtersatz', 255.
8. Grand Tinel (*tinellum magnum* or *aula*): ASV IE 272, fos. 154^r–155^r; IE 277, fo. 118^v. Petit Tinel (*tinellum parvum*): Froissart, *Œuvres*, xviii. 203. Dressing room: CC 229–30. Papal chamber: Schröder, nos. 36–7, 40a, 41, 50, 56–8, 62, 64–5, 67–9, 73, 78, 80, 82, 84, 90, 95, 105, 107, 110; CC 229–30; Émile G. Léonard, *La Jeunesse de Jeanne Ire, reine de Naples, comtesse de Provence* (Monaco and Paris, 1932), ii. 400–1, 405. Study(?): Froissart, *Œuvres*, xviii. 216. See Labande, *Palais des papes*, i. 60, 109–10, Colombe, 38–40, and Vingtain and Sauvageot, 163–4 (on the Grand Tinel), Labande, *Palais des papes*, i. 55, 105, Colombe, 12, and Vingtain and Sauvageot, 139–40 (on the Petit Tinel), Labande, *Palais des papes*, i. 55, 103, Colombe, 12, and Vingtain and Sauvageot, 129–31 (on the *camera paramenti*), Labande, *Palais des papes*, i. 102, Colombe, 12–14, and Vingtain and Sauvageot, 107–21 (on the papal chamber).
9. Schröder, no. 72. The papal residence in Villeneuve was probably the venue for John Offord's and Hugh Neville's first four meetings with Clement VI in early Sept. 1344, before the start of the First Avignon Conference (Froissart, *Œuvres*, xviii. 202–4, 206–10, 215). After the death of Cardinal Napoleone Orsini (23 Mar. 1342) Clement VI used his *livrée*, situated in the south of Villeneuve, as his summer residence (Fernand Benoît, *Villeneuve-lez-Avignon* (Paris, 1930), 41). See Schröder, nos. 92–4, 98–100, 108.
10. I am here taking into consideration that the conference took place in the autumn (Sept.–Nov.). *Hora matutina*: Froissart, *Œuvres*, xviii. 241, 245, 250, 251. *Mane*:

ibid. 216, 222, 238. *Hora vesperarum*: ibid. 221, 237, 240, 245, 248, 254, 255, 256. *Post hora vesperarum*: ibid. 204, 220, 235. *Après heure de dormir*: ibid. 203, 204, 206, 208, 215. See also *CC* 229, on John Shoreditch's reception 'after lunch' (*post prandium*) in Oct. 1343. See Hermann Grotefend, *Zeitrechnung des deutschen Mittelalters und der Neuzeit* (Hanover, 1891–8), i. 117, 120–1, 184, 198–9.

11. See e.g. *Korrespondenz*, doc. 85.

12. Schimmelpfennig, 'Palast als Stadtersatz', 245.

13. *Die Zeremonienbücher der römischen Kirche im Mittelalter*, ed. Bernhard Schimmelpfennig (Tübingen, 1973), 38–9; id., 'Funktion des Papstpalastes', 321–2. Cf. Werner Paravicini, 'Zeremoniell und Raum', in id. (ed.), *Zeremoniell und Raum*, 11–27 (15).

14. Léon-Honoré Labande, 'Les manuscrits de la Bibliothèque d'Avignon provenants de la librairie des papes du XIVe siècle', *Bulletin historique et philologique du Comité des Travaux Historiques et Scientifiques* 1894 (1895), 145–60; Cf. Gottfried Kerscher, 'Das mallorquinische Zeremoniell am papstlichen Hof: *Comederunt cum papa rex maioricarum ...*', in Jörg Jochen Berns and Thomas Rahn (eds.), *Zeremoniell als höfische Ästhetik in Spätmittelalter und früher Neuzeit* (Tübingen, 1995), 125–49 (130, 137–8).

15. *Le Cérémoniel papal de la fin du moyen âge à la Renaissance*, ed. Marc Dykmans (Brussels and Rome, 1977–85), ii. 425.

16. Schröder, nos. 179–81.

17. Ibid., nos. 76, 85.

18. Ibid., no. 109.

19. See e.g. *AA* i. 167 (Vidal de Villanova to James II of Aragon, 27 June 1304): 'E soplegarem a gran instancia [...] al papa e als cardenals [...] en consistori secret en presencia del papa per los vostres fets.', and ii. 769 (Poncius de Lerida and Bernat des Fonollar to the same, 22 Mar. 1309): 'Aquel diluns en consistori privat, on eren tots les cardenals [Clement V] feu nos entrar.'

20. Léonard, ii. 402–5; Schröder, no. 80; cf. ibid.; no. 69.

21. Cf. Schröder, 176, 182.

22. Ibid. 183–4 and nos. 67–8, 73, 78, 80, 82, 84, 90–3, 95, 99–100, 103. On this point I disagree with Bernhard Schimmelpfennig, who maintains that the closer to the centre of the pope's private quarters a reception took place, and the smaller the circle of witnesses invited, the more could an envoy consider himself and his principal honoured ('Funktion des Papstpalastes', 322–3; cf. id., 'Ad maiorem pape gloriam', 37, and 'Palast als Stadtersatz', 245–6). The elaborateness of the interior arrangement of Benedict XII's palace certainly made possible a hierarchization of both curialists and visitors (cf. Kerscher, 139), but I hope to have shown that it was mainly practical requirements that influenced the choice of venue.

23. Froissart, *Œuvres*, xviii. 216, 220, 221, 222, 223 (references to meetings *devaunt lui* (Clement VI)).

24. Schröder, no. 57.

25. See Section 4.5.

26. *Zeremonienbücher*, no. XXVIII, 206. Cf. *Cérémonial papal*, iii. 324, 333–4.

27. François Guessard, 'Étienne de Mornay, chancelier de France sous Louis Hutin', *BEC* 5 (1843–4), 373–96 (393).

28. Cf. Weiß, *Versorgung*, 233–6.

29. While according to le Baker (124) the two nobles were met by 'many bishops and cardinals', Knighton (126) maintains that they were greeted by 'bishops, noblemen, citizens, and commons to the number of 2,000 horse'.
30. Cf. in general Chaplais, *English Diplomatic Practice*, 231–6.
31. See e.g. Paul Thomas, 'Source nouvelle', 33; *AA* ii. 531, iii. 346; Froissart, *Œuvres*, xviii. 255; Achim Thomas Hack, *Das Empfangszeremoniell bei mittelalterlichen Papst-Kaiser-Treffen* (Cologne, 1999), 146–9.
32. See e.g. *Acta Imperii, Angliae et Franciae ab anno 1267 ad annum 1313*, ed. Fritz Kern (Tübingen, 1911), nos. 38 and 48; Hack, 145–7.
33. Recommendation: see e.g. *EMDP*, doc. 124(a). Inquiry: see e.g. *AA* i. 218, ii. 531, iii. 346; Froissart, *Œuvres*, xviii. 202–3. Declarations of affection: see e.g. the report on the first meeting between Boniface VIII and an English delegation headed by the bp. of Winchester on 21 Aug. 1300: 'Et puis dit [Boniface]: "Nous amoms mult le Roi Dangleterre qar nous lavoms esprovee et lavoms trovee loial. Et certes il trouvera nous son peer et son amy, et ja no li faudroms a cele heure, nous faille diex qe nous lui faudroms" ' (C 47/29/4/15, printed in J. G. Black, 'Edward I and Gascony', *EHR* 17 (1902), 518–27 (522)).
34. Presentation of royal letters: see e.g. Froissart, *Œuvres*, xviii. 255.
35. See in general Chaplais, *English Diplomatic Practice*, 236–41.
36. See e.g. *AA* ii. 531, iii. 346, 484; Froissart, *Œuvres*, xviii. 203, 206, 255; Paul Thomas, 'Source nouvelle', 34.
37. Kneeling: e.g. *AA* ii. 531; Froissart, *Œuvres*, xviii. 208. Stools or benches: Paul Thomas, 'Source nouvelle', 35, 37; Froissart, *Œuvres*, xviii. 208.
38. On the third audience (*responsio*) in general, see Chaplais, *English Diplomatic Practice*, 241–4.
39. See du Rosier, 21; Queller, *Office of Ambassador*, 202. Berridge ('Amarna diplomacy', 214) rightly points out that this norm is inconsistent with modern notions of diplomatic immunity.
40. Froissart, *Œuvres*, xviii. 231–2, 253; DGM 1574.
41. Froissart, *Œuvres*, xviii. 228, 233, 234–5.
42. 'Et postea, cum vellem osculari pedem ejus, elevavit caput meum, et me similiter fuit osculatus' (Paul Thomas, 'Source nouvelle', 38).
43. Arrival: Froissart, *Œuvres*, xviii. 212, 220, 225, 226. Cardinals: ibid. 223, 240–1, 250.
44. Froissart, *Œuvres*, xviii. 237–8. Meetings between Clement VI or the cardinals and the English delegation: ibid. 225, 226, 238, 241, 245, 248, 251.
45. Ibid. 220, 231, 235, 237, 240, 241, 251–2, 252–3.
46. Ibid. 250 (20 Nov.), 254 (24 Nov.).
47. Cf. Johan Kaufmann, *Conference Diplomacy: An Introductory Analysis*, 3rd edn. (Basingstoke, 1996), 86–7.
48. Le Baker, 124.
49. R III. i. 289. This is not, as has been suggested by Bock ('Some new documents', 73, 76), a new commission replacing that of 28 Aug. (R III. i. 283). Cf. Fowler, *King's Lieutenant*, 134–5.
50. See e.g. Christer Jönsson, 'Diplomacy, bargaining and negotiation', in Walter Carlsnaes, Thomas Risse and Beth A. Simmons (eds.), *Handbook of International Relations* (London, 2000), 212–34 (221).
51. For what follows, see Hopmann, 231–43.

52. Froissart, Œuvres, xviii. 221, 223, 238, 240, 245.
53. Ibid. 222, 236, 237, 238–9, 242.
54. Ibid. 221, 237.
55. Ibid. 222; cf. 238. The translation is taken from Autrand, 269–70.
56. Froissart, Œuvres, xviii. 221.
57. Ibid. 243–4; cf. C. Taylor, 163.
58. Acta Imperii, no. 48; cf. EMDP 296 n. 203.
59. CC 229–30; cf. p. 149.
60. Froissart, Œuvres, xviii. 206–10.
61. See Weiß, Versorgung, 226, 449–515.
62. VQ iii. 558.
63. Schimmelpfennig, 'Ad maiorem pape gloriam', 34; Weiß, Versorgung, 241–2.
64. Froissart, Œuvres, xviii. 203.
65. Hedley Bull, The Anarchical Society: A Study of Order in World Politics, 3rd edn. (Basingstoke, 2002), 176, 304–5.
66. Maurice H. Keen, Chivalry (New Haven and London, 1984), 100.
67. Banquet: Petit, vii. 325, 371–2; Dubois, 84, 87, 90. Tournament: Petit, vii. 324–5 (Dubois, looking at the same sources, has not found any evidence of a tournament). Ban lifted: Extrav. comm. 9 (CIC ii. 1215); Keen, Chivalry, 94, 96–100.
68. See e.g. the chapter entitled 'Prendre, donner, consacrer' in Georges Duby, Guerriers et paysans, VIIᵉ–XIIᵉ siècle (Paris, 1973), 60–9; trans. Howard B. Clarke as The Early Growth of the European Economy: Warriors and Peasants from the Seventh to the Twelfth Century (London, 1974), 48–57.
69. London, Society of Antiquaries, MS 120, fos. 53ᵛ–54ʳ; E 101/309/27, m. 3 (EMDP, doc. 370); E 101/386/11, m. 1; E 101/311/25.
70. Marcel Mauss, The Gift: The Form and Reason for Exchange in Archaic Societies, trans. W. D. Halls (London, 1990), 3.
71. Helmuth Berking, Sociology of Giving, trans. Patrick Camiller (London, 1999), 113–16.
72. Ibid. 115–16: 'In the imaginary of the court space, a form of knowledge developed whereby the gift became what it was capable of being in the ideal case: a voluntary sign of recognition motivated by the pure intent of giving, situated beyond debt and any duty to reciprocate, and directed only towards the other's person.'
73. Ibid. 112.
74. See App. VII.2.
75. E 101/386/311; cf. John Welwick's payments in 1354–5 'pro celeri expedicione negociorum regis' (E 372/202, m. 37ʳ).
76. E 404/3/17 (27 Feb. 1334).
77. Nova Alamanniae, doc. 83.
78. See App. VII.1.
79. Ivan Hlaváček, 'Überlegungen zum Geschenkwesen im Mittelalter', Mitteilungen der Residenzen-Kommission der Akademie der Wissenschaften zu Göttingen 2/2 (1992), 12–15 (14).
80. Wood, 52–73.
81. Die Inventare des päpstlichen Schatzes in Avignon, 1314–1376, ed. Hermann Hoberg (Vatican City, 1944), 2–7, 91–111, 230–78, 339. Unfortunately, we do not learn

how many of these items were bearing the new coat of arms assumed by Edward III in Feb. 1340: the lions of England quartered with the lilies of France.

82. e.g. BL Cotton MS Nero C VIII, fos. 312^r–313^r; E 101/390/4 (cf. E 36/203, fos. 156^r–163^v); E 101/391/13; E 101/391/19. Diplomatic gifts: E 101/390/4 (cf. E 36/203, fos. 158^r–159^r).

83. Maurice Godelier, *The Enigma of the Gift*, trans. Nora Scott (Cambridge, 1999), 12.

84. Weiß, *Versorgung*, 260.

85. In the third week of July 1333 John XXII had Richard de Bury and John Shoreditch presented with a sturgeon (VQ ii. 119). Like dolphins, sturgeons were an expensive delicacy and, as a 'royal fish', a particularly prestigious gift to receive (Weiß, *Versorgung*, 228–9, 262). Henry of Grosmont was present at Innocent VI's Christmas banquet of 1354 and presumably received ginger, pepper and cloves, as did the other guests (ASV IE 272, fo. 100; VQ iii. 544, 558).

86. Cf. Mauss (5) on gift exchange in 'the economic and legal systems that have preceded our own': 'What they [clans, tribes and families] exchange is not solely property and wealth, moveable and immovable goods, and things economically useful. In particular, such exchanges are acts of politeness: banquets, rituals, military services, women, children, dances, festivals, and fairs, in which economic transaction is only one element, and in which the passing on of wealth is only one feature of a much more general and enduring contract.'

87. Weiß, *Versorgung*, 260.

88. Berking, 112.

89. See App. VII.4(b).

90. *Rechnungsbücher*, intro. 88, and text 93, 105–6, 107: gifts of game and fowl to Cardinals de la Mothe and de la Jugie at Easter and Christmas 1354 and Easter 1355. Occasionally the envoys would advise their superiors at home to send their petitions, accompanied by money or other gifts, directly to certain cardinals (*Korrespondenz*, docs. 26, 23, and pp. 241, 237).

91. See App. VII.2. The truce which had been arranged with Robert Bruce in 1319 had expired in the summer of 1322, and Scottish troops were crossing the border again to raid as far as Preston and into Yorkshire (Maurice H. Keen, *England in the Later Middle Ages* (London and New York, 1973, repr. 1986), 73).

92. 'Quodammodo strictior et difficilior est via qua intratur ad eum, quam que ducit ad paradisum' (*AA* iii. 505).

93. Cf. Weiß, *Versorgung*, 290–2. Arnaud Duèze (*de Osa* or *de Ozia*) was the son of John XXII's younger brother Pierre Duèze and a *scutifer* or *domicellus* (later *miles*) *pape* (*VPA* ii. 297; VQ ii. 87 n. 4, 197 n. 3, 198, 298 n. 2, 415 n. 2, 439, 551, 889; Weiß, *Versorgung*, 289 n. 10). Arnaud de Trian was the eldest son of John XXII's younger sister Huguette, a *miles pape*, and, as John's marshal (*marescallus curie* or *iustitie*), the highest-ranking layman at the curia (VQ ii. 82 n. 3, 198 n. 4; Weiß, *Versorgung*, 290). Pierre de Via, a *miles pape*, nephew and chamberlain of John XXII, was a son of John XXII's younger sister Marie (VQ ii. 54 n. 2; Weiß, *Versorgung*, 291–2). See the genealogical table in Guillemain, *Cour pontificale* (n. 333 between pp. 156 and 157).

94. In Mar. 1318 Johannes Burgundi was told not to return to the papal palace before he had drawn up a written version of his *credentia* (*AA* iii. doc. 163). On 7 Apr. 1325 Bernat de Boxados received word from Arnaud Duèze that he would be

granted an audience later that day (ibid. ii, doc. 503, 806). Arnaud Duèze was 'the man to get past' for Boxados on his way into the palace (ibid. iii. 468). See also ibid. i. 380 on Pierre de Via's and Arnaud Duèze's control over access to the pope: 'Post hec procuravi oportune et importune [...] cum dominis [...] P. de Via et Arnaldo de Osia domini pape nepotibus habere ingressum ad huismodi litteras presentandas eidem domino pape; cui per ministerium dicti domini Arnaldi, qui michi ingressum prebuit, huiusmodi litteras presentavi' (29 Sept. 1326). Two of John XXII's nephews had rooms on the mezzanine between the storeroom on the ground floor and the *magna aula* on the first floor of his palace, which allowed them to control access to the latter (Labande, *Palais des Papes*, i. 41).

95. *AA* ii. 805.

96. Bernardus Jordani de Insula was an uncle of Margarita de Insula, who had married Arnaud Duèze, the pope's nephew, in 1317 (VQ ii. 87 n. 4, p. 576; Weiß, *Versorgung*, 288).

97. Pierre de Via: Schröder, nos. 10, 13, 15. Arnaud Duèze: ibid., nos. 13, 15, 26, 32. Bernardus Jordani: ibid., no. 10. Arnaud de Trian: ibid.

98. App. VII.4(b).

99. Harry Bresslau, *Handbuch der Urkundenlehre für Deutschland und Italien*, 2nd edn. (Berlin and Leipzig, 1912–31), i. 195, 294–5; Guillemain, *Cour pontificale*, 308; Frenz, §90; Walter Koch, 'Protonotar', in *LexMA* vii. 273–4 (273).

100. Bresslau, i. 296–301; Thomas Frenz, 'Abbreviator', in *LexMA* i. 16–17.

101. Bresslau, i. 303–8; Olivier Guyotjeannin, 'Skriptor', in *PE* iii. 1398. Scribes ranked higher than abbreviators, bore the title of *magister*, and became members of the papal 'family' after 1347 (Thomas Frenz, 'Skriptor', in *LexMA* vii. 1991–2).

102. On the old episcopal palace, see esp. Labande, *Palais des Papes*, i. 18–19, 35–48, and Vingtain and Sauvageot, 67–86.

103. App. VII.2 and 4. On the *hostiarii* and *janitores*, see Guillemain, *Cour pontificale*, 418–34, and Mollat, *Papes d'Avignon*, 467.

104. Labande, *Palais des Papes*, i. 37–8. Vingtain and Sauvageot, 79–80. In May 1318 the construction of a second, smaller audience hall (*aula parva*) next to John XXII's study was completed. It was used for informal receptions and meals (Labande, *Palais des Papes*, i. 41).

105. Guillemain, *Cour pontificale*, 419–21; Mollat, *Papes d'Avignon*, 467.

106. Guillemain, *Cour pontificale*, 421–2.

107. There was a great amount of flexibility in the structure of the household in that one and the same person could perform the duties of a doorkeeper, a master-doorkeeper, a sergeant at arms and a pope's squire, depending to what the current situation demanded (ibid. 422–5).

108. The west wing housed both the *camera vetus* or *inferior* and the *camera nova* (Labande, *Palais des Papes*, i. 42). See also Schimmelpfennig, '*Ad maiorem pape gloriam*', 28–9, and Vingtain and Sauvageot, 72–4.

109. E 101/315/16.

110. Guillemain, *Cour pontificale*, 373–6.

111. Ibid. 375; id., 'Curia, 14th and 15th Centuries', in *PE* i. 455–61 (457).

112. Claude Lévi-Strauss, 'The principle of reciprocity', abridged and trans. Rose L. Coser and G. Frazer, in Lewis A. Coser and Bernard Rosenberg (eds.), *Sociological Theory: A Book of Readings* (New York, 1957), (86).

113. *CPL* ii. 417; *CPL* iii. 15.
114. Cf. *The Brut or the Chronicles of England*, ed. Friedrich W. Brie (London, 1906–8), ii. 374–5.
115. Keen, *England in the Later Middle Ages*, 61–2.
116. R II. ii. 1117.
117. Barry Schwartz, 'The social psychology of the gift', *American Journal of Sociology* 73 (1967), 1–11 (1–3).
118. *CPL* ii. 417.
119. Der Derian, 'Diplomacy', 244.
120. Extrav. comm. 5.10.1 (*CIC* ii. 1309–10). Cf. Wright, 124.

CONCLUSION

In a recent publication, a leading scholar of diplomatic theory and practice has asked what makes a 'sophisticated' diplomatic system. He suggested the following features: diplomatic immunity; continuous contact; well-qualified, if not necessarily professional, personnel; bureaucratic direction; provision for mediation; methods for under-pinning agreements; and flexibility of form and procedure.[1] To what extent did these features exist in the particular context under examination in this study?

For the French there would have been good reasons to take measures against English diplomats on their way to the curia in order to impair their functioning. After all, these were envoys of the 'intrinsically threatening'[2] variety, likely to relay back to the English court any piece of information that might prove helpful in organizing a new invasion and carrying with them messages clarifying the short- and mid-term political plans of their king. Immunity for them was a much needed privilege, not a luxury. Conventional forms of protection were observed, by and large (diplomats fared much better than private travellers!), and, as the innovations introduced in 1343-4 and further developed in 1355 show, the protagonists of diplomacy were quite capable of 're-thinking diplomatic immunity'. Secondly, there is ample evidence of exceptionally well-qualified diplomatic agents at work in Edward III's contacts with the curia; the qualifi-cations recommending laymen and clerics for missions to this parti-cular destination have been dealt with extensively in Section 3.1. Most of the king's envoys participated, at the same time, in the work of the governmental institutions that gave coordinated advice on foreign policy (the king's council) and helped to regulate its conduct by ensuring that diplomats had access to archives of correspondence and treaties, and that they were provided with the necessary documents before setting out on their missions (the Privy Seal office, the Chancery). Fourthly, there were clearly 'well-understood methods for reinforcing agreements':[3] one needs only to think of the diplomatic use of *plena potestas* from the thirteenth century onwards, of the much older notion that consanguinity with the monarch conferred on an individual the power to enter into binding agreements, or of the solemn publication and public renunciation of rights and territories that were supposed to convert the preliminary peace of Guines into a lasting arrangement. As regards flexibility, we have seen that both sides employed various forms and procedures of diplomatic intercourse. Besides dispatching royal envoys and messengers, the English Crown made ample provision for unofficial communication. The size and composition of embassies were adapted to their purposes, contact with the English court was maintained through secondary diplomacy and a secure channel of communication was found in the king's confessor. In the negotiations at the curia, a balance was sought between elements of written and oral discourse. The complexity of the interior structure of Benedict XII's new palace offered a range of possibilities for stage managing diplomatic ceremonies as well as for adapting the form of bilateral and multilateral discussions to their contents. Flexibility and diversity also characterized the papal attempts to settle the Anglo-French dispute; the various mediation techniques applied by Clement VI and Innocent VI have been dealt with in Section 6.5.

The greatest obstacle to referring to the diplomatic system examined here as 'sophisticated' is the apparent lack of continuity—that is, the absence of a permanent English embassy to the Holy See. After the abolition of the office of *procurator regis Anglie*, Edward III no longer had a resident diplomatic agent in Avignon, and, although frequent, Anglo-curial contacts remained episodic rather than regular or even continuous throughout the period under consideration. However, I hope to have shown that medieval diplomacy was governed by the necessity principle: no ruler or ruling body practised continuity for continuity's sake. If the duties of the *procurator regis* were transferred to itinerant envoys and independent (English) proctors from *c.*1340 onwards, this was done out of practical considerations, not organizational inadequacy. Thereafter, whenever continuity of contact appeared necessary, it was achieved through a rapid succession of missions, which would be dispatched to the curia even in the most adverse of circumstances.

The diplomatic system that provided the wider framework for Anglo-curial diplomacy, then, was not only adequate (that is, adapted to its environment) and effective (that is, able to achieve results), but also exhibited most of the 'features of sophistication'. There is, of course, no objective procedure by which to measure the efficiency of diplomatic systems, but the overall picture is that of a technique of communication no less efficient than the early modern practice of representation through resident ambassadors—its strength lay in its dynamism and adaptability.

Our primary aim, however, was not a wholesale rehabilitation of medieval 'ad hoc' diplomacy. Moving away from what has rightly been criticized as 'the traditional Anglo-French paradigm'[4] in British scholarship on medieval diplomacy, I have applied the social and cultural history approach and some concepts of International Relations to the interaction between two powers whose relationship was influenced by very specific determinants. Simultaneously, this has been, to some extent, a departure from previous, more 'static' approaches that focused on the institutional and administrative context of diplomacy (such as Queller's and Lucas') or on the features and functions of diplomatic documents (like Chaplais's). The authors of these standard works have paid little or no attention to differences in status between the protagonists that they were dealing with.

The aim of this study has been to explore the techniques and modes of diplomatic activity in the late Middle Ages. The particular dialogue chosen for investigation has revealed itself to have been the product more of ongoing social and cultural interaction than of the incessant operation of a 'machinery of diplomatic intercourse' and of administrative routine. For the English king and his advisers, the key to maintaining clear and nuanced communication with the curia was to create a solid social substratum for it: interpersonal connections, to be renewed at periodic intervals, were established with English or at least anglophile elements in the curial administration and papal household. Material means such as pensions, cash payments, trading privileges and gifts served to achieve this. The latter, at the same time, played a key function in the mediation of political identity.

This was no doubt an ambitious and cost-intensive strategy, but it was feasible thanks to the resources generated by an efficient, centralized bureaucracy. It enabled the Crown to make the best of the cosmopolitan character of the papal court at Avignon and made it possible to offset, to a considerable degree, the many problems caused by the unfavourable circumstances during this particular period (mainly logistical problems and the dominance of potentially anglophobe elements in Avignon, combined with the relative weakness of the English position) and by the power asymmetry intrinsic to the relationship between the *regnum Anglie* and the *sancta Romana ecclesia*.

Notes to Conclusion

1. Berridge, 'Amarna diplomacy', 212–13.
2. Cf. ibid. 214.
3. Ibid. 220.
4. Joseph P. Huffman, *The Social Politics of Medieval Diplomacy: Anglo-German Relations (1066–1307)* (Ann Arbor, 2000), 9.

EPILOGUE

A 'New Medievalism'?

The classic works on the history of diplomatic practice (and even more so, of the works produced by the exponents of the 'traditionalist' school in International Relations) seem to espouse a teleological view of diplomacy: the idea that we have reached, after a long-drawn-out but continuous development, the best and final form of diplomacy. Suggesting that there was 'a distinct upward curve of progress'[1] in the development of diplomatic theory, Harold Nicolson in his main work aimed 'to concentrate upon the continuity of development rather than upon the sudden spurts and long retardations by which it has been marked'.[2] This kind of approach has, over the past decades, led to many of 'the dynamic and dispersed forces behind the formation of diplomacy which defined purposes often antithetical to the traditional teleology'[3] to be left unexplored.

However, in recent years a number of theorists have listed the resident professional diplomat, the very embodiment of modern diplomacy, as an endangered species, citing as evidence increased physical risks as well as political and technological changes. The increase in attacks on diplomatic personnel, the growing frequency of direct contacts between actual *members* rather than *representatives* of governments (that is, between ministers rather than ambassadors), the development of summitry and shuttle diplomacy and revolutionary changes in transport and communication technology have led more than one theorist to argue that the system of representation through permanent embassies may soon be obsolete altogether.[4] Are we entering an age, then, where the travelling envoy will be regarded as a more efficient and flexible tool of communication than his resident colleague? In other words: are we heading back to the future (or rather: ahead into the past), towards a 'new medievalism' in diplomatic practice?

Opinions are certainly divided over this, and some more conser-

232

vative theorists have rightly pointed out that the number of resident embassies worldwide is, in fact, increasing.[5] The writing of the obituary of the modern ambassador may be premature, and even if it were not, it would appear unlikely that he will be replaced by bishops travelling on horseback. But if we are to understand what diplomacy is, and what it may be able to do for us in the future, we are well advised to look back at its origins and historical transformations.

Notes to Epilogue

1. Nicolson, *Diplomacy*, 17.
2. Ibid. 16.
3. Der Derian, *On Diplomacy*, 3.
4. For an up-to-date survey of recent research on the state of our diplomatic system, see Jönsson, 216–17.
5. e.g. Robert Wolfe, *Still Lying Abroad? On the Institution of the Resident Ambassador* (Leicester, 1997), 1–2.

APPENDIX I

English Royal Embassies to the Papal Court, 1342–62
(Departure from and return to London)

References to missions for which there is no sufficient evidence are printed in italics; missions of envoys who departed England individually but were members of larger delegations are marked with Roman numerals, followed by Arabic numerals (e.g. XLVIII/1).

I. 1342, early June–late Sept.
Richard Winkleigh, John Piers
TNA: PRO: C 70/18, m. 2; C 81/1331/45; C 81/1332/9; E 36/204, fo. 77^r; E 403/325C, m. 1; E 404/5/29; E 404/5/31; *CCR* 1343–6, 412–13, 422–3; *CPR* 1343–5, 411.
ASV: R I. 988–9 (wrong date, cf. *Orig. Papal Letters*, no. 177); *CPP* 2–4.

II. *1343, ?late Feb.–?*
Richard Winkleigh
TNA: PRO: E 36/204, fo. 5^v; CPR 1343–5, 87, 92.

III. 1343, c. 3 Apr.–a. 30 May
John Faukes
TNA: PRO: E 403/327, m. 38; E 403/328, m. 13.
ASV: *CPP* 18.

IV. 1343, c. 28 May–?
William Bateman
TNA: PRO: R II. ii. 1224.
ASV: IE 207, fo. 22^v.

V. 1343, 1 – 20 June
Andrew Offord
TNA: PRO: E 101/312/7, m. 1 (MD no. XC); E 372/189, m. 44^v; E 403/328, mm. 13, 32; C 70/19, m. 4; C 76/18, m. 3; R II. ii. 1224; *CPR* 1343–5, 39.
ASV: R I. 988–9 (wrong date, cf. *Orig. Papal Letters*, no. 177); *CPP* 2–4.
Other: *CC* 136–8.

VI. 1343, 16 July–5 Nov.

Andrew Offord, Richard Chamberlain

TNA: PRO: E 101/312/7, m. 1 (MD no. XCI); E 372/189, m. 44^v; E
403/328, mm. 24, 32; R II. ii. 1239.
ASV: DGM 326, 328, 420, 439, 449–52; CPP 20, 21, 32, 71.
Other: CC 143, 147–8.

VII. 1343, 26 July–23 Aug.

John Faukes, Robin of Arden

TNA: PRO: E 101/312/4 (MD no. XCII); E 372/188, m. 50^v; E 159/120,
m. 19^r; E 403/328, mm. 13, 28; E 403/330, mm. 8, 21; E 403/335, m. 34;
E 403/336, m. 4; R II. ii. 1239.
ASV: DGM 326, 328, 420, 439, 449–52; CPP 20, 21, 32, 71.
Other: CC 143, 147–8.

VIII/1. 1343, 29 Aug.–1344, 11 Feb.

Robert Hereward (John Siglesthorn, Richard Chamberlain?)

TNA: PRO: E 372/188, m. 50^r; E 159/120, m. 89^r; E 403/328, m. 32: E
403/374, m. 4; C 76/18, m. 2; R II. ii. 1232; CPR 1343–5, 122.
ASV: VQ iii. 232; CPP 19, 24, 28–9.
Other: CC 148–9.

VIII/2. 1343, 1 Sept.–1344, 19 Jan.

John Grey (John Siglesthorn, Richard Chamberlain?)

TNA: PRO: E 101/312/3 (MD no. XCIII); E 372/188, m. 50^v; E 403/328,
m. 32; E 403/330, mm. 7, 18; C 76/18, m. 2; R II. ii. 1232; CPR 1343–5,
122.
ASV: Archivum Arcis, Arm. I–XVIII, no. 5014, fo. 110 (Schröder, no. 84);
CPP 21, 24, 26, 31–3.
Other: CC 148–9.

IX. 1343, 26 Sept.–?

John Shoreditch

TNA: PRO: E 403/331, m. 2; C 76/18, m. 1; R II. ii. 1236.
Other: CC 143–6, 149, 229–30.

X. 1343, 17 Dec.–1344, 2 Feb.

Andrew Offord

TNA: PRO: E 101/312/7, m. 1 (MD no. C, with wrong date); E 372/189,
m. 44^v; E 403/330, mm. 18, 39; E 403/331, m. 19.
ASV: DGM 581, 594.
Other: CC 152–3.

XI. 1344, 12 Feb.–21 Apr.

Hugh Neville, William de Cusance
TNA: PRO: E 101/312/9 (MD no. XCV); E 372/188, m. 50ᵛ; E 159/120,
m. 88ʳ; C 70/20, m. 2.
ASV: DGM 722, 743, 749; *CPP* 45–6.

XII/1. 1344, 13 Mar.–7 Aug.

Andrew Offord
TNA: PRO: E 101/312/7, m. 1 (MD no. CVI, with wrong date); E
372/189, m. 44ᵛ; E 403/330, m. 39; C 70/20, m. 2; R III. i. 18–19.
ASV: DGM 957, 1844.

XII/2. 1344, 13 Mar.–1345, 15 Apr.

William Bateman
TNA: PRO: E 101/312/7, m. 1 (MD no. CVI, with wrong date); C 70/20,
m. 2; C 76/19, m. 2; *CCR* 1343–6, 383, 445; *CPR* 1343–5, 219, 224, 367;
R III. i. 18–19, 27, 32.
ASV: IE 207, fos. 45ʳ, 55ʳ; DGM 749, 759, 957, 1039, 1108, 1332, 1618.
Other: *The Register of William Bateman,* xv, nos. 61, 97, 150; *CC* 157, 162–3;
Froissart, *Œuvres,* xviii. 202–56; *EMDP,* doc. 155.

XIII. 1344, late May–*c.* 7 July

Henry of Grosmont
TNA: PRO: C 76/19, m. 19; R III i. 54.
ASV: DGM 780–1, 848, 864, 899, 1156, 1844; *CPP* 218.
Other: *CC* 158–9; *GC* ix. 248–9; Petit, vii. 325, 371–2; Déprez, 'Conférence
d'Avignon', 305; Fowler, *King's Lieutenant,* 48–9, 261 n. 37.

XIV. 1344, May/June–?

Guglielmo Fieschi
TNA: PRO: *CCR* 1343–6, 378.

XV. 1344, *c.* 28 June–?

Ralph le Messager
TNA: PRO: E 403/332, m.12.

XVI/1. 1344, 6 Aug.–1345, 5 Apr.

John Offord
TNA: PRO: E 372/189, m. 44ʳ; E 403/332, mm. 19, 21, 22; E 403/335, m.
8; E 403/336, mm. 25–32, 35–6; E 404/5/31; C 76/19, mm. 1–3, 5; R
III. i. 18–19, 25, 27, 32; *CCR* 1343–6, 447.
ASV: DGM 1039, 1043, 1108, 1158, 1332, 1574; IE 297, fo. 47ʳ; VQ iii. 232.
Other: Froissart, *Œuvres,* xviii. 202–56; *GC* ix. 251–2; *CC* 159, 162–3;
EMDP, doc. 155.

XVI/2. 1344, 8 Aug.–1345, 1 Jan.

Hugh Neville
TNA: PRO: E 372/189, m. 44^v; E 403/332, m. 22; E 403/335, mm. 9, 28;
C 76/19, mm. 1–2; R III. i. 18–19.
ASV: DGM 1039, 1043, 1108, 1305, 1332; *CPP* 80–1; IE 207, fo. 47^r; VQ
iii. 232.
Other: Froissart, *Œuvres*, xviii. 202–56; *GC* ix. 251–2; *CC* 159–61; *EMDP*,
doc. 155.

XVI/3. 1344, *c.* 9 Sept.–?

Niccolò Fieschi
TNA: PRO: E 101/390/12, fo. 1^r; E 403/336, m. 48; C 76/19, mm. 1–2; R
III. i. 22; *CCR* 1343–6, 456.
Other: Froissart, *Œuvres*, xviii. 202–56.

XVI/4. 1344, Sept.–early Nov.

John Reppes
TNA: PRO: E 403/335, m. 14; E 404/5/31.
ASV: DGM 1155, 1158; *CPP* 77, 80, 168.
Other: Froissart, *Œuvres*, xviii. 211–15; *CC* 160.

XVI/5. 1344, 29 Oct.–1345, 11 Jan.

John Thoresby, Ralph Spigournel
TNA: PRO: E 372/189, m. 44^r; E 403/335, m. 7; E 403/336, m. 24; C 70/20,
m. 2; C 76/19, m. 2; R III. i. 25; *CCR* 1343–6, 474; *CPR* 1343–5, 367.
ASV: DGM 1305, 1322–4, 1326–8, 1844, 2726; *CPP* 82.
Other: Froissart, *Œuvres*, xviii. 229, 232, 254–6; *CC* 159–60, 184.

XVII. 1345, 16 Feb.–23 Apr.

Michael Northburgh, Nigel Loring
TNA: PRO: E 372/189, m. 44^r; E 403/335, m. 27; R III. i. 32.
ASV: DGM 1574, 1582, 1587, 1590–1, 1597.

XVIII. 1345, 16 Apr.–30 Sept.

John Reppes, William Ludeford
TNA: PRO: E 372/191, m. 49^v; E 403/338, mm. 11, 14; C 70/21, mm. 1–3;
R III. i. 35, 41–2.
ASV: DGM 1801, 1844, *CPP* 93, 98–100, 204.

XIX. 1345, *c.* 8 Aug.–Dec.

Jean de la Porte
TNA: PRO: C 70/21, mm. 1, 12.
ASV: *CPP* 89–91.

XX. 1345, Nov.–?1346, mid-Jan.

Laurence Fastolf
TNA: PRO: E 403/336, m. 26.

XXI. 1345, c.20 Dec.–?

N.N. (quidam nuncius)
TNA: PRO: E 403/336, m. 24.

XXII. 1346, c.8 Jan.–c.11 March

Richard Vaughan
TNA: PRO: E 403/336, m. 24; R III. i. 66.
ASV: DGM 2358; CPP 121.

XXIII. 1346, c.14 Feb.–?

Thomas Dirland
TNA: PRO: E 403/336, m. 29.

XXIV. 1346, c.1 Mar. –?

John Thursteyn
TNA: PRO: C 70/22, m. 2.

XXV. 1346, c.10 Apr.–?

N.N. (two nuncii)
TNA: PRO: E 403/336, m. 48.

XXVI. 1347, Sept. – Oct.

Nicholas Herle
ASV: DM 1494; R III. i. 136.

XXVII/1. 1347, 9 Dec.–1348, 16 Mar.

Hugh Neville, John Reppes
TNA: PRO: E 372/192, m. 46^r; E 403/340, m. 23; E 403/341, m. 19; R III.
    i. 145, 151–2.
ASV: DGM 3703, 3742, 3756, 3812; RA 98, fo. 400^r.
Other: RP ii. 200.

XXVII/2. 1347, 12 Dec.–1348, 14 May[1]

John Carlton
TNA: PRO: E 101/312/29 (MD no. CXXX, with wrong date); E 372/192
    m. 46^r; E 403/340, mm. 19, 23; E 403/341, mm. 16, 36, E 403/342, m.
    12; R III. 145, 151–2.
ASV: DGM 3703, 3742, 3756, 3797, 3812, 3890; RA 98, fos., 392^v–393^r.
Other: RP ii. 200.

XXVIII. 1348, ?–May

Guy de Brian
ASV: DGM 3811–12; *CPP* 369.

XXIX. 1348, 6 (16?) May–15 Sept.[2]

John Carlton
TNA: PRO: E 372/194, m. 45ᵛ; E 403/341, mm. 16, 29, 36; R III. i. 161, 166.
ASV: DGM 3890; *CPP* 131, 137, 134–5, 143, 163.

XXX. 1348, c.29 July–?

N.N. (*nuncius* A)
TNA: PRO: E 403/341, m. 29; R III. i. 165.

XXXI. 1348, c.13 Aug.–?

N.N. (*nuncius* B)
TNA: PRO: E 403/341, m. 36.

XXXII. 1348, c.13 Aug.–?

N.N. (*nuncius* C)
TNA: PRO: E 403/341, m. 36.

XXXIII. 1349, May–June

Geoffrey de la Mare
ASV: DM 2009.

XXXIV. 1349, May–?

Bartholomew Burghersh
ASV: DGM 4169.

XXXV. 1349, c.22 May–18 Aug.

Michael Northburgh
TNA: PRO: E 403/347, mm. 9, 25; E 403/353, mm. 18, 20–1; E 403/355, m. 40; R III. i. 188.
ASV: *CPP* 174, 186, 190; *CPL* 318, 395, 399.

XXXVI. 1349, 19 June–7 Sept.

John Carlton
TNA: PRO: E 101/312/40 (MD no. CXXXVI); E 372/200 m. 41ᵛ; E 403/347, m. 13; E 159/126, m. 62ᵛ.

XXXVII. 1349, c.30 Aug.–mid-Dec.

Robert Askeby
TNA: PRO: E 403/347, m. 26; R III. i. 188.
ASV: DGM 4313; *CPP* 186–8; *CPL* 383–4, 395, 399.

XXXVIII. 1350, *c.*19 July–?

John Paris
TNA: PRO: E 403/353, m. 23.

XXXIX. 1350, *c.*2–*c.* 31 Aug.

John Pigot
TNA: PRO: E 403/353, m. 25.
ASV: DGM 4682, 4684.

XL. 1351, *c.*11 Mar.–?

Aubertyn de Plesence
TNA: PRO: E 404/5/33.

XLI. 1351, *c.*26 Sept.–?

John Faukes
TNA: PRO: E 403/358, m.29.

XLII. 1352, *c.*12 May–?

John Faukes
TNA: PRO: E 403/362, m. 7.

XLIII. 1352, *c.*14 July–?

N.N. (*nuncius*)
TNA: PRO: E 403/362, m. 19.

XLIV. 1352, *c.*1 Sept.–late Nov.

Hugh Pelegrini, Daniele Provana, Pietro Provana
TNA: PRO: *CPR* 1350–4, 325.
ASV: DGM 5446–8, 5450, 5457.

XLV. 1353, June

John Woderove
ASV: GLG 466; Perroy, 'Quattre lettres', doc. IV, 163.
Other: *RP* ii. 251–2; *EMDP* 190, ll. 5–15.

XLVI. 1353, *c.*6 July–late Aug.

William Whittlesey
TNA: PRO: E 403/368, m. 16; *RP* ii. 252.
ASV: GLG 466–8.

XLVII. 1353, *c.*8 Nov.–?

Raymond Pelegrini
TNA: PRO: R III. i. 269.

XLVIII/1. 1354, 20 May–10 Aug.
Richard de la Bere
TNA: PRO: E 101/313/23 (MD no. CLXVI); E 372/197, m. 48^v; E 403/374, m. 7; E 403/375, m. 4; E 159/131; C 76/32, m. 5.
ASV: GLG 1019, 1026; Perroy, 'Quattre lettres', doc. IV, 163; CPP 260–1.

XLVIII/2. 1354, 25 May–1355, 29 Mar.
John Woderove
TNA: PRO: E 403/374, m. 14; E 403/375, mm. 18, 27; E 403/377, m. 8; E 404/5/34.
ASV: GLG 1019, 1026; Perroy, 'Quattre lettres', doc. IV, 163; CPP 265–7, 279, 284; CPL 523–4.

XLIX/1. 1354, 28 Aug.–1355, 21 July
John Welwick
TNA: PRO: E 101/313/22 (MD no. CLXVII); E 372/202, m. 37^r; E 403/374, m. 19; E 403/377, m. 10; E 403/379, m. 17; E 403/390, m. 21; E 159/134; C 76/32, m. 4; R III. i. 284–5.
ASV: VQ iii. 589; CPL 569.
Other: see no. XLIX/5.

XLIX/2. 1354, 29 Aug.–1355, 31 Mar.
Michael Northburgh
TNA: PRO: E 101/620/9; E 372/200, m. 37^r; E 101/171/3, fo. 33^r; E 403/374, m. 19; E 403/375, m. 18; E 159/131; C 62/131, m. 4; C 81/1334/7; CCR 1354–60, 83–4; R III. i. 283, 289.
ASV: VQ iii. 589; CPP 264, 267.
Other: EMDP, doc. 156; see no. XLIX/5.

XLIX/3. 1354, 6 Sept.–1355, 28 Mar.
Guy de Brian
TNA: PRO: E 101/620/9; E 101/171/3, fo. 33^r; E 403/374, m. 19; E 403/375, m. 18; E 403/377, m. 11; E 404/5/34; R III. i. 283, 289.
ASV: IE 199, fo. 37^r; VQ iii. 589; CPP 265, 268, 276, 279–80.
Other: see no. XLIX/5.

XLIX/4. 1354, 4 Oct.–1355, 6 Jan.
William Bateman
TNA: PRO: E 101/313/21 (MD no. CLXVIII); E 372/199 m. 41^v; E 403/375, m. 2; E 159/131; R III. i. 283, 289.
ASV: IE 199, fos. 36^r, 37^r; VQ iii. 589; CPP 265, 275–81.
Other: Reg. Bateman, nos. 1874, 1918; see also no. XLIX/5.

XLIX/5. 1354, 28 Oct.–1355, 28 Mar.

Henry of Grosmont
TNA: PRO: E 101/313/25 (Bock, 'Some new documents', 96–7; MD no. CLXXII, with wrong date); E 101/620/9; E 101/171/3, fos. 30^v, 33^r; E 401/429, m. 10; E 403/375, mm. 2, 9, 22, 28; E 403/377, mm. 12, 22; E 404/5/34; C 76/32, m. 4; R III. i. 283, 289, 293, 303.
ASV: IE 199, fo. 40^r; GLG 2152; VQ iii. 558, 589; CPP 269–76, 281–3, 286.
Other: John of Reading, 118; *Chronicon Anonymi Cantuariensis*, 195; *Anonimalle Chronicle*, 31–2 (with wrong date), 163; Le Baker, 123–5, 289–90; Avesbury, 421; Knighton, 126–9; Higden, viii. 347–8, 407; Walsingham, i. 278–9; *Chronicon Angliae*, 31; Capgrave, 215–16; Froissart, *Chroniques*, iv. 131–2; *Chronique des règnes de Jean II et Charles V*, i. 47–9; *VPA* i. 311, and ii. 381, 443; *EMDP*, docs. 124, 157; *Prozeß-Schriftgut*, nos. 223, 225; *Korrespondenz*, doc. 241B.

XLIX/6. 1354, c.6 Nov.–1355, 8 Mar.

Richard Fitzalan
TNA: PRO: E 403/375, m. 8; E 101/171/3, fo. 33^r; E 403/377, mm. 8, 11; C 76/32, m. 4; R III. i. 283, 289, 293, 303; CCR 1354–60, 92–4, 164–5.
ASV: IE 199, fo. 40^v; VQ iii. 589; CPP 269, 278–81.
Other: see no. XLIX/5.

L. 1354, Nov./Dec.

N.N. (quidam nuncius)
TNA: PRO: E 403/379, m. 17.

LI. 1354, c.15 Nov.–?

Alan de Barley
TNA: PRO: E 403/375, m. 12.

LII. 1354, c.5 Dec.–?

John of Kent
TNA: PRO: E 403/375, m. 17.

LIII. 1354, c.5 Dec.–?1355, c.22 Jan.

quidam valettus (John Eymonderby?)
TNA: PRO: E 403/375, mm. 17, 22.

LIV. 1355, c.21 Jan.–?

Thomas Whittrost
TNA: PRO: E 403/375, m. 21.

LV. 1355, c.20 Feb.–?

John de Branketre
TNA: PRO: E 403/375, m. 27 (EMDP, doc. 380); CPR 1354–8, 183.

LVI. 1355, c.26 Sept.–?

John Pigot
TNA: PRO: E 403/377, m. 38.

LVII. 1356, c.24 Feb.–?

John Pigot
TNA: PRO: E 403/379, m. 28.

LVIII. 1356, ?Nov.–?

N.N. (*quidam nuncius*)
TNA: PRO: E 403/385, m.15.

LIX. 1356, c.12 Nov.–a.1357, 13 Mar.

Philip Codeford
TNA: PRO: E 403/386, m. 18; C 62/135, m. 1; R III. i. 342.

LX. 1357, ?Feb./Mar.

Martin Alman
TNA: PRO: E 403/387, m. 10.

LXI. 1357, 4 May–24 Aug.

Nicholas d'Amory, Thomas Fulnetby
TNA: PRO: E 372/202, m. 35^r; E 403/387, mm. 9, 11, 26; E 159/134; R
    III. i. 356.
ASV: *CPL* 625, 628; *CPP* 299–300.

LXII. 1357, c.17 June–a.28 Oct.

Hugh Pelegrini
TNA: PRO: C 76/35, m. 11.
ASV: Coll. 352, fo. 23^r.

LXIII. 1357, c.23 Oct.–?

Thomas Clipston
TNA: PRO: E 403/390, m. 8.
ASV: *CPP* 373.

LXIV. 1358, c.16 Nov.–1359, ?Feb./Mar.

Adam Hilton
TNA: PRO: E 403/395, m. 16; E 403/407, m. 39.
ASV: *CPL* 628–9.

LXV. 1358, c.5 Dec.–?

John Pigot
TNA: PRO: E 403/395, m. 20.

LXVI. 1359, *a*.5 Mar.

Thomas Bradeston
TNA: PRO: E 403/395, m. 37; E 404/6/36.

LXVII. 1359, 17 Mar.–5 July

Richard Stafford, William Burton
TNA: PRO: E 101/313/39 (MD no. CXCIII); E 372/203 m. 40^v; E 159/135, m. 174^v; E 403/394, m. 32; E 403/395, m. 41; E 403/397, m. 21; E 404/6/36.
ASV: SC 7/64/79; *CPP* 340–3, 345.

LXVIII. 1360, *c*.3 Mar.–?

John Bandinellis
TNA: PRO: E 101/393/11, fo. 72^r.

LXIX. 1360, 14 Mar.–31 July

William Burton
TNA: PRO: E 101/393/11, fos. 64^r, 72^v; E 403/401, m. 23.
ASV: R III. i. 484; *CPP* 353–4; *CPL* 630, 633.

LXX. 1360, *c*.12 May–1361, *c*.12 Feb.

Adam Hilton
TNA: PRO: E 101/393/11, fo.64^r; E 404/6/36; E 404/6/40.
ASV: *CPP* 356–7, 360.

LXXI. 1360, *c*.18 June–?

John Pigot
TNA: PRO: E 403/401, m.12.

LXXII. 1360, 26 Nov.–*a*.1361, 24 Mar.

William Burton
TNA: PRO: E 101/314/11; E 101/314/16.
ASV: R III. i. 554; *CPP* 360, 362.

LXXIII. 1361, *c*.8 May–?

Adam Hilton
TNA: PRO: E 403/408, m. 17.

LXXIV. 1361, 13 May–15 Sept.

Thomas Fulnetby
TNA: PRO: E 372/204, m. 43^v; E 403/408, m. 17; E 403/409, m. 20; E 159/138.
ASV: *CPP* 371, 374.

LXXV. 1361, 18 May–14 Sept.

Guy de Brian
TNA: PRO: E 403/408, mm. 17, 19; E 403/409, m. 19; E 404/6/41; *CPR*
1361–4, 18.
ASV: *Thesaurus novus*, ii. 1059–62; *CPP* 369–70, 380.

LXXVI. 1361, 12 June–28 July

Nigel Loring
TNA: PRO: E 101/314/17 (MD no. CCXI); E 372/206, m. 42^r; E 403/408,
mm. 25, 37; E 159/138.
ASV: R III. ii. 623; *CPP* 373.

LXXVII. 1361, c.6 July–?

John Pigot
TNA: PRO: E 403/408, m. 35.

LXXVIII. 1361, 11 Aug.–28 Sept.

Nigel Loring
TNA: PRO: E 101/314/17 (MD no. CCXV, with a wrong departure date);
E 372/206, m. 42^r; E 403/409, mm. 18–19; E 159/138.

LXXIX. 1361, a.14 Oct.

Philip Codeford
TNA: PRO: E 403/409, m. 5; C 62/137, m. 1.

LXXX. 1361, 20 Oct.–1362, 10 Feb.

Nigel Loring
TNA: PRO: E 372/206, m. 50^r; E 159/138; E 401/465 m. 12; E 403/409,
mm. 8, 37, 39, 44; E 403/411, m. 10; E 404/6/41; E 404/6/42;
E 404/7/43; *Reg. Black Prince*, iv. 456, 476.
ASV: *Thesaurus novus*, ii. 1065–6; *CPP* 381.

Notes to Appendix 1

1. See no. XXIX and n. 2 below.
2. There is an overlap of nine days (6–14 May 1348) between Carlton's expense
accounts as transcribed in E 372/192, m. 46r, and E 372/194, m. 45v. He
probably set out on or around 15 May 1348.

APPENDIX II

Duration of Missions

Name	No. (App. I)	Days[1]
A. Offord	V	20
A. Offord, R. Chamberlain	VI	113
J. Faukes	VII	29
R. Hereward	VIII/1	146
J. Grey	VIII/2	141
A. Offord	X	58
H. Neville, W. de Cusance	XI	70
A. Offord	XII/1	148
J. Offord	XVI/1	243
H. Neville	XVI/2	146[2]
J. Thoresby, R. Spigournel	XVI/5	74[2]
M. Northburgh, N. Loring	XVII	67
J. Reppes, W. Ludeford	XVIII	168
H. Neville, J. Reppes	XXVII/1	80
J. Carlton	XXVII/2	154[2]
J. Carlton	XXIX	133
J. Carlton	XXXVI	81
R. de la Bere	XLVIII/1	82
J. Woderove	XLVIII/2	308
J. Welwick	XLIX/1	327
M. Northburgh	XLIX/2	215
G. de Brian	XLIX/3	204
N. d'Amory, Th. Fulnetby	LXI	113
R. Stafford, W. Burton	LXVII	111
W. Burton	LXIX	140
Th. Fulnetby	LXXIV	126
G. de Brian	LXXV	125
N. Loring	LXXVI	47
N. Loring	LXXVIII	49
N. Loring	LXXX	114

1. Usually counting both the days of departure and of arrival as full days
(*utroque die computato*).
2. Counting the day of departure as a full day (*primo die computato*).

APPENDIX III

Size of Travel Groups

(Outward journey at Calais)

Name(s)	No.[1]	Men	Horses	Reference
A. Offord	V	?	7	E 372/189, m. 44^v
A. Offord	VI	?	4	E 372/189, m. 44^v
J. Faukes, R. of Arden	VII	2	2	E 372/188, m. 50^v
R. Hereward	VIII/1	8	7	E 372/188, m. 50^r
J. Grey	VIII/2	?	20	E 372/188, m. 50^v
A. Offord	X	?	3	E 372/189, m. 44^v
H. Neville, W. de Cusance	XI	16	10	E 372/188, m. 50^v
A. Offord	XII/1	?	2	E 372/188, m. 44^v
J. Thoresby	XVI/5	17	8	E 372/189, m. 44^r
R. Spigournel	XVI/5	15	8	E 372/189, m. 44^r
J. Reppes	XVIII	?	4	E 372/191, m. 49^v
H. Neville	XXVII/1	?	5	E 372/192, m. 46^r
R. de la Bere	XLVIII/1	?	6	E 101/313/23
J. Welwick	XLIX/1	?	4	E 372/202, m. 37^r
M. Northburgh	XLIX/2	20	20	E 101/171/3, fo. 33^r
G. de Brian	XLIX/3	30	30	E 101/171/3, fo. 33^r
W. Bateman	XLIX/4	85	60	E 372/199, m. 41^v
H. of Grosmont	XLIX/5	317[2]	317	E 101/171/3, fo. 33^r
R. Fitzalan	XLIX/6	175	175	E 101/171/3, fo. 33^r
R. Stafford	LXVII	14	14	E 372/203, m. 40^v
W. Burton	LXVII	7	7	E 372/203, m. 40^v
N. Loring	LXXVI	?	5	E 101/314/17
N. Loring	LXXVIII	?	6	E 101/314/17

1. See Appendix I.
2. TNA: PRO E 101/171/3, fo. 33r, gives only the number of men-at-arms in his retinue.

APPENDIX IV

Academic Backgrounds

(Counting only clerics directly commissioned to travel to the curia, not those accompanying others as members of their retinue and curial proctors collaborating with Crown diplomats)

Civil law

DCL	William Bateman	BCL	Laurence Fastolf
	John Carlton		William Ludeford
	Thomas Clipston		John Offord
	Philip Codeford		John Piers
	Michael Northburgh		John Thoresby
	Andrew Offord		John Thursteyn
	John Offord		John Welwick
	John Piers		
	John Shoreditch	Lic.CL	Robert Hereward
	Richard Vaughan		

Utriusque juris

DUJ	William Whittlesey
BUJ	William Whittlesey

Theology

D.Th.	Richard Winkleigh OP
	John Woderove OP

Magister	Robert Askeby
	John de Branketre
	Adam Hilton

APPENDIX V

Importance of the Cardinals to Edward III

(as reflected in the Roman Rolls, C 70/18–25)

Name	Letters/ months	Monthly average
1. Raymond Gulhem des Farges (card. dcn. of S Maria Nova)	7/66	0.1
2. Annibaldo da Ceccano (card. bp. of Tusculum)	11/104	0.1
3. Pedro Gomez da Barroso (card. bp. of Sabina)	7/75	0.09
4. Gaucelme de Jean Duèsne (card. bp. of Albano)	5/75	0.07
5. Pierre Després (card. bp. of Praeneste)	7/176	0.04
6. Étienne Aubert (card. p. of SS John and Paul/ card. bp. of Ostia)	5/128	0.04
7. Talleyrand de Périgord (card. p. of S Petrus ad Vincula/card. bp. of Albano)	4/176	0.02
8. Ademar Robert (card. p. of S Anastasia)	2/123	0.02
9. Giovanni Colonna (card. dcn. of S Angelus in Foro Pisc.)	1/74	0.01
10. Jean de Comminges (card. bp. of Porto)	1/79	0.01
11. Gailhard de la Mothe (card. dcn. of S Lucia in Silice)	2/176	0.01
12. Bertrand de Déaulx (card. p. of S Marcus/ card. bp. of Sabina)	1/162	0.006
13. Guy de Boulogne (card. p. of S Caecilia/ card. bp. of Porto)	1/172	0.006

The method here followed is the one established by Wright (app. 4): first the total number of letters to each cardinal recorded in C 70 was computed, then the total number of months that each cardinal lived during Clement VI's and Innocent VI's pontificates. The cardinals are listed and numbered in order of the greatest monthly average numbers of letters sent to them. Cardinals who lived during the period under consideration but whose names do not appear on this list are deemed not to have received any letters.

It must be emphasized that these figures represent only a relative evaluation. The C 70 series breaks off with the year 1357. Some other royal correspondence with cardinals from the period under consideration remains in CPR and CCR. Many additional letters were undoubtedly sent under the privy seal, but most of these do not survive; they might well present a different picture (Cf. Pierre Chaplais, 'Privy seal drafts, rolls, and registers (Edward I–Edward II)', EHR 73 (1958), 270–3). Letters directed to the college of cardinals as a whole have not been taken into consideration.

APPENDIX VI

Itineraries

1. BL Royal MS 13 A XVIII, fo. 157^{r-v}

[*c*.1284 (1309?)-1346[1]] Nomina villarum ab Anglia usque ad Avinonem per viam Recordan'[2] et regressus per Aurelianum cum distancia earum. *'Theoretical' itinerary for a journey from London to Avignon and back.*

London–Avignon

London – Dartford – Singlewell – Rochester – Newington – Sittingbourne – Ospringe – Canterbury – Dover – Gravelines – St-Omer – Thérouanne – Anvin (?) – Frévent (?) – Doullens – Amiens – Paillart – St-Just-en-Chaussée – Clermont – Rantigny – Creil – *Sovins* – St-Denis – Paris – Villejuif – Juvisy-s.-Orge – Corbeil-Essonnes – Perthes – Forges – *Beu Veyr* – Nemours – Dordives – Montargis – Montcresson – Montbouy – *Male Taverne* – *Mewe* – Bonny-s.-Loire – Neuvy-s.-Loire – La-Celle-s.-Loire – Cosne-s.-Loire – Pouilly-s.-Loire – Mesves-s.-Loire – La-Charité-s.-Loire – La Marche – Pougues-les-Eaux – Nevers – Magny-Cours – St-Pierre-le-Moûtier – St-Imbert – *Vile Fraunche* – Villeneuve-s.-Allier – Moulins – Châtel-de-Neuvre – St-Pourçain-s.-Sioule – Escolles – Le-Mayet-d'École – Gannat – Montpensier – Aigueperse – Riom – Montferrand – Pérignat-lès-Sarliève – Orcet – Veyre-Monton – Coudes – Issoire – Le-Breuil-s.-Couze – *Cartone* – Brioude – La Chomete – Boisseuge – Fix-St-Geneys – Borne –

---

1. 1284: date of the foundation of Villeneuve-de-Berg, Dép. Ardèche, mentioned in the MS (see Jean Régné, 'La première étape de la pénétration capétienne en Vivarais: La fondation de Villeneuve-de-Berg et la mise en pariage de son territoire (novembre 1284)', BPH 1 (1913), 121–40). 1309: new bridge over the Rhône (Pont-St-Ésprit) near the Benedictine priory of St-Saturnin opened for traffic (built 1265–1307) (Eugène Germer-Durand, *Dictionnaire topographique du Département du Gard* (Paris, 1868), 169). 1346: date of the destruction of Wissant (see Section 4.3.1.).

2. The *Regordane*, an ancient trade route stretching from Nîmes or Montpellier to Alès and north across the Cévennes to Le Puy, Brioude, Issoire, Clermont and beyond to Paris or east into Champagne (see Clovis Brunel, 'Le nom de la voie Regordane', *Romania* 79 (1958), 289–313, and Bautier, 111–23).

Le Puy – Coubon – Le Monastier-s.-Gazeille – Le Béage – Usclades-et-Rieutord – Montpezat-sous-Bauzon – Aubenas – Villeneuve-de-Berg – Gras – St-Remèze – St-Marcel-d'Ardèche – Pont-St-Ésprit – Bagnols-s.-Cèze – St-Laurent-des-Arbres – Pujaut – Avignon

Avignon–London

Avignon – Châteauneuf-du-Pape – Orange – Mornas – Mondragon – Bollène – Pierrelatte – Donzère – Châteauneuf-du-Rhône – Montélimar – Loriol-s.-Drône – Livron-s.-Drône – Valence – La Roche-de-Glun – Tain-l'Hermitage – St-Vallier – St-Rambert-d'Albon – Roussillon – Auberives-s.-Varèze – Vienne – St-Symphorien-d'Ozon – Lyons – Crele – St-Clément-s.-Valsonne – Thizy – Charlieu – Iguerande – Marcigny – Bourg-le Comte – Luneau – Bois-des-Forges – Pierrefitte-s.-Loire – Diou – Beaulon – Chescurteys – Decize – Béard – Nevers – Pogues-les-Eaux – La Marche – La Charité-s.-Loire – Mesves-s.-Loire – Pouilly-s.-Loire – Cosne-s.-Loire – La Celle-s.-Loire – Neuvy-s.-Loire – Bonny-s.-Loire – Briare – Gien – Mewer supra Leyre – La Lorde – Châteauneuf-s.-Loire – Jargeau – Mardié – Point-aux-Moines (?) – Orléans – Cercottes – La Engenerye – Arthenay – Toury – Foliernaut – Angerville – Monnerville – Villesauvage – Étampes – Étréchy – Bruyères-le-Châtel – Montlhéry – Longjumeau – Bourg-la-Reine – Paris – St-Denis – Pierrefitte-s.-Seine – St-Brice-sous-Forêt – Pounceles – Moisselles – Presles (?) – Beaumont-s.-Oise – Puiseux-le-Hauberger – St-Geneviève – Tillard – Abbecourt – Beauvais – Oudeuil – Rothois – Cempuis – Dargies – La Haye-St-Romain – St-Romain – Poix-de-Picardie – Gouy-l'Hôpital – Camps-en-Amiénois – Airaines – Long – St-Riquier – Domvast – Crécy-en-Ponthieu – Maintenay – Montreuil-s.-Mer – Frencq – Neufchâtel-Hardelot – Le Choquel – Boulogne-s.-Mer – Wissant – Dover

2. John de Benstede and Henry Spigournel, 1311

(Bodleian Library, MS Tanner 197, fo. 41v)

London – Dover – Wissant – St-Just-en-Chausée – Avignon

3. Richard Plympstok, 1315–16

(E 101/309/20)

(day 1) 20 Dec.	(arrival at) Rochester
(2) 21 Dec.	Canterbury
(3–10) 22–9 Dec.	Dover
(11–12) 30–1 Dec.	Wissant
(13) 1 Jan.	Montreuil-s.-Mer

(14) 2 Jan.	St-Riquier
(15) 3 Jan.	Poix
(16) 4 Jan.	Beauvais
(17) 5 Jan.	Beaumont-s.-Oise
(18–34) 6–22 Jan.	Paris
(35–41) 23–9 Jan.	Essonnes
(42) 30 Jan.	Perthes
(43–4) 31 Jan.-1 Feb.	Nemours
(45) 2 Feb.	Montargis
(46) 3 Feb.	Châtillon-Coligny
(47) 4 Feb.	Bonny-s.-Loire
(48) 5 Feb.	Pouilly-s.-Loire
(49) 6 Feb.	Nevers
(50) 7 Feb.	Decize
(51) 8 Feb.	Beaulon
(52) 9 Feb.	Marcigny
(53) 10 Feb.	Thizy
(54) 11 Feb.	St-Clément-s.-Valsonne
(55) 12 Feb.	Lyons
(56) 13 Feb.	Vienne
(57) 14 Feb.	St-Vallier
(58–61) 15–18 Feb.	Valence
(62) 19 Feb.	Montélimar
(63–4) 20–1 Feb.	Bollène
(65) 22 Feb.	Sorgues
(66–73) 23 Feb.-2 Mar.	Avignon
(74–9) 3–8 Mar.	Carpentras
(80–96) 9–25 Mar.	Avignon
(97–106) 26 Mar.-5 Apr.	Carpentras
(107–23) 6–22 Apr.	Avignon
(124) 23 Apr.	Mornas
(125) 24 Apr.	Cruas
(126) 25 Apr.	Valence
(127) 26 Apr.	Roussillon
(128) 27 Apr.	Lyons
(129) 28 Apr.	St-Clément
(130) 29 Apr.	Charlieu
(131) 30 Apr.	Pierrefitte-s.-Loire
(132) 1 May	Decize
(133–4) 2–3 May	Nevers
(135) 4 May	Pouilly
(136) 5 May	Ouzouer-s.-Trézée
(137) 6 May	Montargis

(138) 7 May	*Rupem*
(139) 8 May	St-Geneviève-des-Bois
(140–1) 9–10 May	Paris
(142) 11 May	Beaumont
(143) 12 May	Beauvais
(144) 13 May	Poix
(145) 14 May	St-Riquier
(146) 15 May	Montreuil-s.-Mer
(147–52) 16–21 May	Wissant
(153) 22 May	Sandwich
(154) 23 May	Newington
(155) 24 May	London

4. John Stratford, 1322–3

(E 101/309/27, m. 3)

York – Dover – Wissant – Montpezat-sous-Bauzon (*Montpessat in Recordan'*) – Avignon

5. John Middleton, 1331

(Oxford, Merton College, Subwarden's Rolls, 3967)

(day 1) 21 Jan.	Thame	(28–9) 17–18 Feb.	Lyons
(2) 22 Jan.	Acton	(30) 19 Feb.	Vienne
(3) 23 Jan.	London	(31) 20 Feb.	Champagne
(6) 26 Jan.	Newington	(32) 21 Feb.	La-Voulte-
(7) 27 Jan.	Dover		s.Rhône
(8) 28 Jan.	Calais	(33) 22 Feb.	Bourg-St-
(9) 29 Jan.	Boulogne		Andéol
(10) 30 Jan.	Crécy-en	(34) 23 Feb.	Avignon
	Ponthieu	(31 July)	Avignon
(11) 31 Jan.	Poix	(?)	La Charité-
(12) 1 Feb.	Tillard		s.-Loire
(13–15) 2–4 Feb.	Paris	(?)	Cosne
(16–19) 5–8 Feb.	Essonnes	(?)	Dourdan
(20) 9 Feb.	Nemours	(?)	Paris
(21) 10 Feb.	*La mala taverne*	(?)	Amiens
(22) 11 Feb.	Cosne	(?)	Wissant
(23–4) 12–13 Feb.	Nevers	(?)	Dover
(25) 14 Feb.	*Chescorteys*	(?)	Gravesend
(26) 15 Feb.	Les Forges	(?)	London
(27) 16 Feb.	Thizy	(24 Aug.)	Oxford

6. Richard de Bury and John Shoreditch, 1333

(E 101/386/11)

London – Dover – St-Riquier – Cosne-s.-Loire – La Charité-s.-Loire – Avignon

7. Laurence Fastolf, 1336

(E 372/185, m. 42^r)

London – Dover – Wissant – Paris – Pierrefitte-s.-Loire – Avignon

8. John Faukes and Robin of Arden, 1343

(E 101/312/4)

(day 1) 26 July	Westminster	(17–18) 11–12 Aug.	Vienne
	London	(18) 12 Aug.	Lyons
	Rochester	(19) 13 Aug.	Marcigny
	Dover	(20) 14 Aug.	Nevers
	Canterbury	(21) 15 Aug.	Bonny
(2) 27 July	Wissant	(22–3) 16–17 Aug.	Châteauneuf-
(3) 28 July	St-Riquier		s.-Loire
	Poix	(24) 18 Aug.	Paris
	Paris	(25) 19 Aug.	Beauvais
(4) 29 July	Dordives		Airaines
	Montcresson	(26) 20 Aug.	Montreuil-
	Ouzouer-		s.-Mer
	s.-Trézée		Wissant
(5) 30 July	Cosne	(27) 21 Aug.	Dover
	Nevers		Canterbury
	Chescurteis		Rochester
(6) 31 July	Beaulon		Dartford
	Lyons		London
(7–16) 1–10 Aug.	Avignon	(28) 22 Aug.	Westminster

9. Richard Stafford, 1359

(E 101/313/39)

Guelders – Avignon

Guelders – Speyer – Basle – Geneva – Savoy – St-Romans – Valence – Pont-St-Ésprit – Avignon

Avignon – Dover

Avignon – Hasselt – Dendermonde – Ghent – Ursel – Bruges – Gravelines – Calais – Dover

APPENDIX VII

❖

Diplomatic Gifts

1. John Salmon, John Hotham, Aymer de Valence, Bartholomew Badlesmere, John Cromwell and Antonio Pessagno, 1316–17
(London, Society of Antiquaries, MS 120, fos. 53v-54r[1])

(a) Gifts from Edward II to John XXII after his election[2]

1	choir cope	embroidered, with pearls; value 220 mk.
1	choir cope	embroidered; value 100 mk.
1	ewer (olla)	gold, translucent enamel; weight 4 li. 2s. 6d.
1	goblet (ciphus)	gold, translucent enamel; weight 64s. 7d. Both items (ewer and goblet) bought from Roger le Frowyk, London goldsmith; value 147 li. 1s. 8d.
1	container (panerum)	leather, bound in iron, for transport of ewer and goblet. Bought from Walter de Bardeneye, London coffrarius; value 12s.

Objects (jocalia) obtained by the Bardi merchants in London and Paris and delivered in Avignon to the envoys for presentation (total value 1,177 li. 3s. 4d.):

1	buckle (morsus)	gold, with gems, for choir-cope; weight 2 mk. 6 s. 2 d., value 66 li. 16 s. 8 d.
4	basins (pelves)	gold, partially enamelled, with papal and royal crests; weight 26 mk. 9 s. 9 d. ob.
3	ewers (olle)	gold, partially enamelled, with papal and royal crests.
1	salt cellar (salar')	———
		Total weight of ewers and salt-cellar 21 mk. 5 s. 2 d.
12	dishes (disci)	gold; weight 27 mk. 2 s. 1 d.
12	sauce-boats (salsar')	gold; weight 12 mk. 17 d. ob.
12	spoons (coclear')	gold; weight 3 mk. 14 d.
1	cup (coupa)	gold, with lid. Lid partly enamelled, with papal and royal crests; weight 6 mk. 7 s. 1 d.

| 2 | cruets (*fiolette*) | gold, partially enamelled, with papal and royal crests; weight 2 mk. 4 s. 10 d. |
| 1 | chalice (*calix*) | gold, with paten. Paten partly enamelled, with papal and royal crests; weight 6 mk. 20 d. |

(b) Gifts from Queen Isabella to John XXII, 1317

Objects obtained by the Bardi merchants and delivered to John de Jargolio, the queen's almoner, for presentation (total value 300 li.)

1	incense boat (*navis*)	
1	ewer (*olla*)	
1	buckle (*morsus*)	All items made of gold, with pearls and gems.

2. John Stratford, 1322–3

(E 101/309/27, m. 3)

Recipient(s)	Sum	Notes / transaction mode (date of payment)
Squires (*armigeri*) of John XXII, and masters of the stable (*mariscalli*)	10s. (3 flor.)	*de curialitate nomine regis Anglie, sicut moris est in curia Romana* / *datum* (3 Nov. 1322).
Johannes Doun[3]	13s. 4d. (4 flor.)	*duxit dictos nuncios ad presenciam domini cardinalis* / *datum* (3 Nov. 1322).
Couriers (*cursores pape*)	10s. (3 flor.)	*deservientes in palacio ante festum Natalis Natalis Domini* / *datum.*
4 guards of the palace gates (*janitores in prima porta*)	16s. 8d. (5 flor.)	*sicut moris est nunciorum domini regis* / *donacio* (24 Dec. 1322).
Guards of the audience hall (?) (*janitores secunde porte*)	44s. 4d. (13 flor.)	*datum* (24 Dec. 1322).
Servants of *Soldannus*, squire	6s. 8d. (2 flor.)	[*Soldannus*] *habet execucionem judiciorum temporalium et eciam liberacionum hospiciorum, sicut moris est* / *datum* (before Christmas).
Card. Bérenger Frédol the younger[4], Card. Bertrand de Montfavès[5]	10 mk. (40 flor.)	*qui cardinales habebant negocia Scocie in manibus, juxta consilium nunciorum* / *exhennia missa* (24 Dec. 1322).

Walter, clerk of Andrea Sapiti[6]	20s. (6 flor.)	[*Gualterus*] *laboravit in negociis predictis et in eisdem multa scripsit, pro labore suo / datum.*
Magolotus, mag., and Petrus de Bonaco (*de Castro Bonici*)[7], *mag.*	6 mk. (24 flor.)	*notarii in negocio Scocie / exhennia missa* (*contra dictum festum* [*Natalis Domini*])
Auditors of Cards. Frédol and Montfavès	8 mk. (32 flor.)	[*cardinales*] *habebant negocia Scocie in manibus, per consilium nunciorum / exhennia missa.*
Pierre de Via[8]	46s. 8d. (14 flor.)	*per consilium nunciorum / exhennium missum.*
Arnaud, nephew of John XXII[9]	5 mk. (20 flor.)	*per consilium nunciorum / exhennium missum.*
Guards (*janitores*) and doorkeepers (*hostiarii*)	5 mk. di. (22 flor.)	*sicut moris est, per consilium nunciorum* (*ante festum Pasche / datum.* [*a.*11 Apr. 1323]).

3. Adam Orleton, 1327–8

(E 101/309/38)

'Item dat' 5 camerariis dom. pape, 7 militibus hostiariis ac 12 janitoribus 150 florenos de florencia'.

4. Richard de Bury and John Shoreditch, 1333[10]

(E 101/386/11, m. 1)

All items bought in Avignon

(a) Gifts to John XXII[11]

1	cup	gilded silver, with stand and cover worked in divers gems.
2	ewers (*ollae*)	
1	salt cellar	of crystal, worked in pearls and divers other gems, with foot and circumference of gilded silver and enamel. Total value: 66 li. 13s. d.

(b) Gifts to Cardinals and Curial Officials

Card. Élie Talleyrand de Périgord[12]	1 cup, 1 ewer	gilded silver, enamelled, with stand and cover. Total value: 20 li. 17 d. 1 s. (Entry crossed out in MS.)
Card. Pierre Després[13]	1 cup, 1 ewer 200 flor. (33 li. 6s. 8d.)	gilded silver, enamelled, with stand and cover. Total value of both items: 15 li
Arnaud Duèze (de Osa)	1 cup, 1 ewer	gilded silver, enamelled, with stand and cover. Total value: 10 li
Socius of A. Duèze, kt.	1 cup	silver, with stand and cover. Value: 40 s.
Pierre de Via	1 cup, 1 ewer	gilded silver, with stand and cover. Total value: 13 li. 6s. 8d.
Socius of P. de Via, kt.	1 [cup]	silver, with stand and cover. Value: 40s.
Arnaud de Trian	1 cup, 1 ewer	gilded silver, with stand and cover. Total value: 10 li.
Son of A. de Trian	1 cup, 1 ewer	gilded silver Total value: 6 li. 13s.
Bernardus Jordani de Insula[14]	1 cup	gilded silver, with stand and matching cover. Value: 12 li. 13s. 4d.
Arnaldus Neapolinis[15]	1 cup, 1 ewer	gilded silver, with stand and cover. Total value: 10 li. 13s. 4d.
Bertrand Demerii (de Mari)[16]	1 cup, 1 ewer	gilded silver, with stand and cover. Total value: 113s. 4d.
Robertus de Adria[17]	18 flor. (60s.)	*pro formacione et scriptura peticionum domini nostri regis.*
2 kts., master-doorkeepers of John XXII's chamber (*magistri hostiarii camere pape*)	2 cups	plain silver, with cover, without stand. Value: 48s.
4 doorkeepers of John XXII's chamber (*hostiarii camere pape*)	4 cups	plain silver, with stand and cover. Value: 64s.

Jean Rigaud[18]	30 flor.(6 li. 13 s. 4 d.)	
	1 surcoat (*alverus*)	surcoat made of silk.
	1 robe	Total value of clothes: 30s.
familiares camere pape, servientes armorum, ianitores, et alii ministri infra palacium pape	157 flor. (26 li. 3s. 4d.)	*ad participandum inter eosdem.*
2 squires of the vice-chancellor	12 flor. (40s.)	*deferentes domino* [Richard de Bury] *et domino Johanni de Sordich' literas supplicatorias per dominum papam concessas.*

5. Paolo Montefiore, 1336–7

(E 101/311/25)

All items made of gold and manufactured in Paris (total cost 2,686 li. 8s. 4d.)

12	esquelles (bowls?)	*de peur et de fin or.*
2	——	*grosses et graundes (cest assavoir chargeours pour ent porter les viaundes).*
12	sausers (sauceboats?)	
12	cups (*hanaps*)	*bels.*
3	——	*petitz, a la manere des bels godetz pour ent faire soupe en vernasche.*
1	cup (*coupe*)	*grant, od pie ovesques leuwer.*
2	pots (*basins, potels*)	*pour doner eawe.*
2	dageours (knives?)	*bels, pour especerie.*
1	salt cellar (*saler*)	*tresbien fait.*
24	spoons (*cuillers*)	
2	pots (*pootz*)	*grantz et larges, pour y mettre du vin*
2	forks (*fourchetz*)	*pour ent tenir la char.*

Notes

1. Cf. Wright, App. 2,1.
2. Cf. *CC* 25–6, and *CPL* ii, 417.
3. Nephew and squire of Pierre Després, card. bp. of Praeneste (vice-chancellor) (E 101/309/27).
4. Card. bp. of Porto.
5. Card. dcn. of S Maria in Aquiro.
6. On Walter see Zutshi, 'Proctors', 24 and n. 45.
7. A notary from Limoges diocese (VQ ii. 470, 833).
8. A pope's knight (*miles pape*), nephew and chamberlain of John XXII (VQ ii. 54 n. 2; Weiß, *Versorgung*, 291–2).

9. Arnaud Duèze (*de Osa, de Ozia*), or Arnaud de Trian (*de Trianno*).
10. Cf. TNA: PRO E 404/3/17.
11. All four entries crossed out in MS.
12. Card. p. of S Petrus ad Vincula.
13. Card. bp. of Praeneste and vice-chancellor.
14. *Scutifer* or *domicellus pape* (VQ ii. 87 n. 4, 576; Weiß, *Versorgung*, 288). The two terms had become synonyms during Clement V's pontificate and denoted a pope's squire (Guillemain, *Cour pontificale*, 421).
15. Prothonotary of John XXII (TNA: PRO E 101/386/11).
16. *Miles in camera pape* (TNA: PRO E 101/386/11). Bertrand was a squire and master-doorkeeper in 1316 and pope's knight from 1330 (VQ ii. 605, 592, 887, 889).
17. *Scriptor et abbreviator pape* in 1342 (VQ iii. 204).
18. One of the five chamberlains of John XXII in Oct. 1332 (VQ ii. 594, 597).

BIBLIOGRAPHY

Manuscript Sources

Archivio Segreto Vaticano (ASV), Città del Vaticano
Armarium (Arm.) XXXI, 2; XXXV, 140
Camera Apostolica
Collectoriae (Coll.) 38, 47, 50, 52–4, 350, 352, 382, 387, 388, 448–51, 456, 458,
    459, 475, 497–9
Introitus et Exitus (IE) 130, 185, 199, 207, 216, 220, 228, 232, 242, 262, 272,
    277, 282, 293
Instrumenta Miscellanea (Instr. Misc.) 1493, 2006, 5103, 6306
Registra Avenionensia (RA) 54–149
Registra Vaticana (RV) 137–244N

Biblioteca Apostolica Vaticana (BAV), Città del Vaticano
Cod. Barb. lat. 2126

British Library (BL), London
Cotton Manuscripts
Nero C VIII
Cleopatra E II
Harley Manuscripts 69, 136, 320, 739–41, 782, 861, 1757, 3120
Royal MS 13 A XVIII

Bodleian Library, Oxford
MS Tanner 197
MS Bodley 462

Merton College Archives, Oxford
Subwarden's Rolls, 3967

The Queen's College Archives, Oxford
2 P (Long Rolls), 12

The National Archives of the United Kingdom: Public Record Office
(TNA: PRO), Kew, Richmond, Surrey
Chancery
C 62 (Liberate Rolls) 113–38
C 70 (Roman Rolls) 14–25
C 76 (Treaty Rolls) 17–45
C 81 (Warrants for the Great Seal, Series I) 261–395, 908–10, 1330–5, 1394,
1538, 1673, 1709–12

Exchequer
E 30 (Treasury of the Receipt, Diplomatic Documents) 1367, 1519
E 36 (Treasury of the Receipt, Miscellaneous Books) 203–4
E 43 (Treasury of the Receipt, Ancient Deeds, Series WS)
E 101 (King's Remembrancer, Accounts Various)
France: 171/3
Nuncii: 309/20, 25, 27, 32, 37, 38; 310/ 32, 40; 311/8, 15, 25, 27, 38; 312/3,
4, 7, 9, 29, 40; 313/21–3, 39; 314/17, 27, 39; 315/10, 12, 16, 18; 316/22,
28; 620/9; 694/18
Wardrobe and Household: 313/11, 386/11, 390/12, 392/12
E 159 (King's Remembrancer, Memoranda Rolls and Enrolment Books)
116–39
E 361 (Pipe Office, Enrolled Wardrobe and Household Accounts) 2–3
E 364 (Pipe Office, Foreign Accounts Rolls) 2–12
E 372 (Pipe Office, Pipe Rolls) 154–212
E 401 (Exchequer of Receipt, Receipt Rolls and Registers) 393, 427, 429,
465
E 403 (Exchequer of Receipt, Issue Rolls and Registers) 288–413
E 404 (Exchequer of Receipt, Warrants for Issues) 3–7

Special Collections
SC 1 (Ancient Correspondence)
SC 7 (Papal Bulls)

Printed Record Sources

*Acta Aragonensia: Quellen zur deutschen, italienischen, französischen, spanischen,
zur Kirchen- und Kulturgeschichte aus der diplomatischen Korrespondenz
Jaymes II. (1291–1327)*, ed. Heinrich Finke, 3 vols. (Berlin and Leipzig:
Rothschild, 1908–22).
Acta Imperii, Angliae et Franciae ab anno 1267 ad annum 1313, ed. Fritz Kern
(Tübingen: Mohr, 1911).
Anglo-Scottish Relations, 1174–1328. Some Selected Documents, ed. and trans.
Edward L. G. Stones (Oxford Medieval Texts; London: Nelson, 1965; repr.
Oxford: Clarendon Press, 1970).

The Antient Kalendars and Inventories of the Treasury of His Majesty's Exchequer, ed. Francis Palgrave, 3 vols. (London: Eyre and Spottiswoode, 1836).

BOCK, FRIEDRICH, 'Some new documents illustrating the early years of the Hundred Years War (1353–1356)', *BJRL* 15 (1931), 60–99.

Bullarium Ordinis fratrum praedicatorum, ed. Thomas Ripoll and Antonius Bremond, 8 vols. (Rome, 1729–40).

Calendar of Chancery Warrants Preserved in the Public Record Office, i: *1244–1326*, ed. H. C. Maxwell Lyte et al. (London: HMSO, 1927; no further vols. published).

Calendar of the Close Rolls Preserved in the Public Record Office, 1272–1509, 61 vols. (London: HMSO, 1900–63).

Calendar of Entries in the Papal Registers Relating to Great Britain and Ireland: Calendar of Papal Letters, 1198–1419, ed. William H. Bliss et al., 15 vols. in 16 (London: HMSO, 1893–1960, Dublin, 1978).

Calendar of Entries in the Papal Registers Relating to Great Britain and Ireland: Calendar of Petitions to the Pope, 1342–1419, i: *1342–62*, ed. William H. Bliss (London, 1896; no further vols. published).

Calendar of Letters from the Mayor and Corporation of the City of London, c.AD 1350–1370, Enrolled and Preserved among the Archives of the Corporation at the Guildhall, ed. Reginald Robinson Sharpe (London, 1885).

Calendar of the Patent Rolls Preserved in the Public Record Office, 1232–1509, 54 vols. (London: HMSO, 1891–1916).

Calendar of the Register of Wolstan de Bransford, Bishop of Winchester, 1339–49, ed. Roy Martin Haines (Worcestershire Historical Society, NS 4; London: HMSO, 1966).

Cartulaire des comtes de Hainaut, de l'avènement de Guillaume II à la mort de Jacqueline de Bavière, ed. Léopold Devillers, 6 vols. in 7 (Brussels, 1881–96).

Le Cérémonial papal de la fin du moyen âge à la Renaissance, ed. Marc Dykmans, 4 vols. (Bibliothèque de l'Institut historique belge de Rome, 24–7; Brussels and Rome: R. de Ruysbroeck, Institut historique belge de Rome, 1977–85).

Chartulary of Winchester Cathedral, ed. Arthur W. Goodman (Winchester: Warren and Son, 1927).

Constitutiones Concilii quarti Lateranensis una cum Commentariis glossatorum, ed. Antonio García y García (Monumenta Iuris Canonici, Ser. A: Corpus Glossatorum, 2; Vatican City: Biblioteca Apostolica Vaticana, 1981).

Das deutsch–englische Bündnis von 1335–1342: I. Quellen, ed. Friedrich Bock (Quellen und Erörterungen zur Bayerischen Geschichte, NF 12; Munich: C. H. Beck, 1956).

Documents parisiens du règne de Philippe VI de Valois (1328–1350), extraits des registres de la Chancellerie de France, ed. Jules Viard, 2 vols. (Paris, 1899–1900).

English Medieval Diplomatic Practice, ed. Pierre Chaplais.
    Part I, Documents and Interpretation, 2 vols. (London: HMSO, 1982).
    Part II, Plates (London: HMSO, 1975).

English Royal Documents, King John–Henry VI, 1199–1461, ed. Pierre Chaplais (Oxford: Clarendon Press, 1971).

Foedera, Conventiones, Litterae et cuiuscunque generis Acta Publica inter Reges Angliae et alios quosvis Imperatores, Reges, Pontifices, Principes, vel Communitates, ed. Thomas Rymer, 5th edn. ['Record Commission edn.'], ed. Adam Clarke, Frederick Holbrooke and John Caley, 4 vols. in 7 (London, 1816–69).

Gascon Rolls Preserved in the Public Record Office, 1307–1317, ed. Yves Renouard (London: HMSO, 1962).

GOLUBOVICH, GIROLAMO (ed.), *Biblioteca bio-bibliografica della Terra Santa e dell'Oriente Francescano*, 5 vols. (Florence: Quaracchi, 1906–23).

Die Inventare des päpstlichen Schatzes in Avignon, 1314–1376, ed. Hermann Hoberg (Studi e Testi, 111; Vatican City: Biblioteca Apostolica Vaticana, 1944).

Literae Cantuarienses: The Letter Books of the Monastery of Christ Church, Canterbury, ed. Joseph B. Sheppard, 3 vols. (RS 85; London: printed for HMSO by Eyre and Spottiswoode, 1887–9).

Munimenta Academica, or Documents Illustrative of Academical Life and Studies at Oxford, ed. Henry Anstey, 2 vols. (RS 50; London: Longman, Green, Reader and Dyer, 1868).

Nova Alamanniae: Urkunden, Briefe und andere Quellen besonders zur deutschen Geschichte des 14. Jahrhunderts, ed. Edmund E. Stengel, 2 vols. (Berlin and Hanover: Weidmannsche Buchhandlung, 1921–76).

Original Papal Letters in England (1305–1415), ed. Patrick N. R. Zutshi (Index Actorum Romanorum Pontificum ab Innocentio III ad Martinum V electum, 5; Vatican City: Biblioteca Apostolica Vaticana, 1990).

Die päpstlichen Kanzlei-Ordnungen von 1200–1500, ed. Michael Tangl (Innsbruck: Wagner, 1894).

Rat und Domkapitel von Hamburg um die Mitte des 14. Jahrhunderts (Veröffentlichungen aus dem Staatsarchiv der Freien und Hansestadt Hamburg, 9):

   Die Korrespondenz zwischen dem Hamburger Rat und seinen Vertretern an der päpstlichen Kurie in Avignon 1337 bis 1359, ed. Richard Salomon (Hamburg: Christians, 1968) [vol. 1].

   Das Prozeß-Schriftgut aus den Streitigkeiten des Hamburger Rates und einzelner Bürger mit dem Domkapitel 1336 bis 1356, ed. Jürgen Reetz (Hamburg: Christians, 1975) [vol. 2].

   Ergänzungen sowie Namen- und Sachweiser zu dem in Teil 1 und 2 edierten Schriftgut der seit 1336 ausgetragenen Streitigkeiten, ed. Jürgen Reetz (Hamburg: Christians, 1980) [vol. 3].

Die Rechnungsbücher der hamburgischen Gesandten in Avignon 1338 bis 1355, ed. Th. Schrader (Hamburg and Leipzig: Leopold Voß, 1907).

The Red Book of the Exchequer, ed. Hubert Hall, 3 vols. (RS 99; London: HMSO, 1896).

Register of Edward the Black Prince, Preserved in the Public Record Office, 4 vols. (London: HMSO, 1930–3).

The Register of John de Grandisson, bishop of Exeter (AD 1327–1369), ed. Francis C. Hingeston-Randolph, 3 vols. (London: G. Bell, 1894–9).

The Register of John Kirkby, Bishop of Carlisle (1332–1352), and the Register of John Ross, Bishop of Carlisle (1325–1332), ed. Robin L. Storey, 2 vols. (CYS 79, 81; Woodbridge: Boydell Press, 1993–5).

The Register of William Bateman, Bishop of Norwich, 1344–1355, ed. Phyllis E. Pobst, 2 vols. (CYS 84, 90; Woodbridge: Boydell Press, 1996–2000).

Registres et lettres des papes du Xiii^e siècle (BEFAR, 2nd ser.):

Les Registres d'Innocent IV, publiées ou analysées d'après les manuscrits originaux des Archives du Vatican et de la Bibliothèque Nationale, ed. Élie Berger, 4 vols. (Paris: Thorin and Fontemoing, 1884–1911). [vol. 1]

Le Registre de Benoît XI: Recueil des bulles de ce pape, publiées ou analysées d'après le manuscrit original des archives du Vatican, ed. Charles Grandjean (Paris: Fontemoing, 1905). [vol. 2]

Les Registres de Boniface VIII: Recueil des bulles de ce pape, publiées ou analysées d'après les manuscrits originaux des Archives du Vatican, ed. Georges Digard et al., 4 vols. (Paris: Boccard; 1884–1939). [vol. 4]

Registres et lettres des papes du XIVe siècle (BEFAR, 3rd ser.):

Jean XXII (1316–1334): Lettres secrètes et curiales relatives à la France, publiées ou analysées d'après les registres du Vatican, ed. Auguste Coulon and Suzanne Clémencet, 3 vols. (Paris: Fontemoing and Boccard, 1900–72). [vol. 1]

—— *Lettres communes, analysées d'après les registres dits d'Avignon et du Vatican*, ed. Guillaume Mollat, 16 vols. (Paris: Fontemoing and Boccard, 1904–46). [vol. 1 bis]

Benoît XII (1334–1342): Lettres closes, patentes et curiales se rapportant à la France, publiées ou analysées d'après les registres du Vatican, ed. Georges Daumet, 2 vols. (Paris: Boccard, 1920). [vol. 2]

—— *Lettres communes, analysés d'après les registres dits d'Avignon et du Vatican*, ed. Jean-Marie Vidal, 3 vols. (Paris: Fontemoing, 1903–11). [vol. 2 bis]

—— *Lettres closes, patentes et curiales intéressant les pays autres que la France*, ed. Jean-Marie Vidal and Guillaume Mollat, 2 vols. (Paris: Fontemoing and Boccard, 1913–50). [vol. 2 bis]

Clément VI (1342–1352): Lettres closes, patentes et curiales interéssant les pays autres que la France, ed. Eugène Déprez and Guillaume Mollat (Paris: Boccard, 1960–1). [vol. 3]

—— *Lettres closes, patentes et curiales se rapportant à la France*, ed. Eugène Déprez, Jean Glénisson and Guillaume Mollat, 3 vols. (Paris: Fontemoing and Boccard, 1901–61). [vol. 3]

Innocent VI (1352–1362): Lettres closes, patentes et curiales se rapportant à la France, publiées ou analysées d'après les registres du Vatican, ed. Eugène Déprez (Paris: Fontemoing, 1909). [vol. 4]

—— *Lettres secrètes et curiales, publiées ou analysées d'après les registres des Archives Vaticanes*, ed. Pierre Gasnault, Marie-Hyacinthe Laurent and

Nicole Gotteri, 4 vols. (Paris and Rome: Boccard and École française de Rome, 1959–). [vol. 4]

Registrum Ade de Orleton, episcopi Herefordensis, AD MCCCXVII–MCCCXXVII, ed. Arthur T. Bannister (CYS 5; London: Canterbury and York Society, 1908).

Registrum Johannis de Trillek, episcopi Herefordensis, AD MCCCXLIV-MCCCLXI, ed. Joseph Henry Parry (CYS 8; London: Canterbury and York Society, 1912).

Registrum Palatinum Dunelmense: The Register of Richard de Kellawe, Lord Palatine and Bishop of Durham, 1311–1316, ed. Thomas D. Hardy, 4 vols. (RS 62; London: Longman, 1873–8).

Rotuli parliamentorum; ut et petitiones et placita in parliamento (1278–1503), ed. John Strachey, 6 vols. (London, 1767–77).

Las siete partidas del Rey Don Alfonso el Sabio, 3 vols. (Madrid: Imprenta real, 1807).

The Statutes of the Realm (from Magna Charta to the End of the Reign of Queen Anne), and a Chronological Index, 10 vols. (London: G. Eyre and A. Strahan, 1810–28).

Thesaurus novus anecdotorum, ii: Urbani Papae IV. epistolae LXIV, Clementis Papae IV. epistolae DCCXI, Joannis XXII. processus varii in Ludovicum Bavarum et ejus asseclas, Innocentii VI. registrum epistolarum anno MCCCLXI, aliaque plura de schismate pontificum Avenionensium monumenta, ed. Edmond Martène (Paris, 1717).

THOMAS, PAUL, 'Une source nouvelle pour l'histoire administrative de la Flandre: Le registre de Guillaume d'Auxonne, chancelier de Louis de Nevers, comte de Flandre', *Revue du Nord* 10 (1924), 5–38.

Treaty Rolls Preserved in the Public Record Office, ii: 1337–1339, ed. John Ferguson (London: HMSO, 1972).

Vatikanische Quellen zur Geschichte der päpstlichen Hof- und Finanzverwaltung, 1316–1378:

Die Einnahmen der Apostolischen Kammer unter Johann XXII., ed. Emil Göller (Paderborn: Schöningh, 1910). [vol. 1]

Die Ausgaben der Apostolischen Kammer unter Johann XXII., nebst den Jahres-bilanzen von 1316–1375, ed. Karl Heinrich Schäfer (Paderborn: Schöningh, 1911). [vol. 2]

Die Ausgaben der Apostolischen Kammer unter Benedikt XII., Klemens VI. und Innocenz VI., 1335–1362, ed. Karl Heinrich Schäfer (Paderborn: Schön-ingh, 1914). [vol. 3]

Die Einnahmen der Apostolischen Kammer unter Benedikt XII., ed. Emil Göller (Paderborn: Schöningh, 1920). [vol. 4]

Die Einnahmen der Apostolischen Kammer unter Klemens VI., ed. Ludwig Mohler (Paderborn: Schöningh, 1931). [vol. 5]

Die Ausgaben der Apostolischen Kammer unter den Päpsten Urban V. und Gregor

XI., 1362–1378, ed. Karl Heinrich Schäfer (Paderborn: Schöningh, 1937). [vol. 6]

Die Einnahmen der Apostolischen Kammer unter Innozenz VI., ed. Hermann Hoberg (Paderborn: Schöningh, 1955–7). [vols. 7, 8]

The Wardrobe Book of William de Norwell, 12 July 1338 to 27 May 1340, ed. Mary Lyon, Bryce Lyon and Henry Stephen Lucas (Académie royale de Belgique, Commission royale d'histoire/Koninklijke Academie van België, Koninklijke commissie voor Geschiedenis, 91; Brussels: Palais des Académies, 1983).

Die Zeremonienbücher der römischen Kirche im Mittelalter, ed. Bernhard Schimmelpfennig (Bibliothek des Deutschen Historischen Instituts Rom, 40; Tübingen: Max Niemeyer, 1973).

Printed Narrative and Literary Sources

ROBERT OF AVESBURY, *De gestis mirabilibus regis Edwardi Tertii*, ed. Edward M. Thompson (RS 93; London: HMSO, 1889).

Anonimalle Chronicle, 1333–1381, ed. Vivian H. Galbraith (PUM/HS 45; Manchester, London and New York: Manchester University Press, Longman, Green and Co., 1927).

GEOFFREY LE BAKER, *Chronicon*, ed. Edward M. Thompson (Oxford: Clarendon Press, 1889).

JEAN LE BEL, *Chronique*, ed. Jules Viard and Eugène Déprez, 2 vols. (SHF 317, 324; Paris: Renouard, 1904–5).

The Brut or the Chronicles of England, ed. Friedrich W. Brie, 2 vols. (Early English Text Society, Original Series, 131, 136; London: Kegan Paul, Trench, Trübner, 1906–8).

JOHN CAPGRAVE, *The Chronicle of England*, ed. Francis C. Hingeston-Randolph (London, 1858).

CHARLES IV, *Vita ab eo ipso conscripta, et Hystoria nova de Sancto Wenceslao Martyre: Autobiography of Emperor Charles IV and his Legend of St Wenceslas*, ed. Balázs Nagy and Frank Schaer (Central European Medieval Texts; Budapest: Budapest Central European University Press, 2001).

Chronicon Angliae, ab anno Domini 1328 usque ad annum 1388, auctore monacho quodam Sancti Albani, ed. Edward M. Thompson (RS 64; London: Longman, 1874).

Chronicon Anonymi Cantuariensis, in *Chronica Johannis de Reading et Anonymi Cantuarensis, 1346–67*, ed. James Tait (PUM/HS 20; Manchester: Manchester University Press, 1914), 187–227.

Chronicon de Lanercost, MCCI–MCCCXLVI, ed. Joseph Stevenson (Edinburgh: Publications of the Maitland Club Glasgow, 1839).

Chronique anonyme parisienne de 1316 à 1339, ed. A. Héllot, *Memoirs de la Société Historique de Paris* 11 (1885), 1–207.

Chronique des règnes de Jean II et Charles V, ed. Roland Delachenal, 4 vols. (SHF 348, 375, 391–2; Paris: Renouard and Société de l'histoire de France, 1910–20).

Desiderata Curiosa, new corr. edn., ed. Francis Peck, 2 vols. (London: Thomas Evans, 1779).

GUILLAUME DURAND, *Speculum legatorum*, in *De legatis et legationibus tractatus varii*, ed. Vladimir E. Hrabar (Dorpat, 1905), 31–41.

—— *Speculum juris*, ed. Alessandro Nievo (Frankfurt, 1594).

JEAN FROISSART, *Œuvres complètes: Chroniques*, ed. Joseph Marie Bruno Constantin Baron Kervyn de Lettenhove, 25 vols. (Brussels, 1867–77).

—— *Chroniques*, ed. Siméon Luce et al., 15 vols. (SHF; Paris: Renouard and Klincksieck, 1869–1975).

Les Grandes chroniques de France, ed. Jules Viard, 10 vols. (SHF 395, 401, 404, 415, 417, 423, 429, 435, 438, 457; Paris: Champion and Klincksieck, 1920–53).

WALTER HEMINGBURGH, *Chronicon*, ed. Hans C. Hamilton, 2 vols. (London, 1848–9).

RANULPH HIGDEN, *Polychronicon*, ed. Churchill Babington and J. R. Lumby, 9 vols. (RS 41; London: HMSO, 1865–86).

Itinerarium cuiusdam Anglici Terram Sanctam et alia loca sancta visitantis, in Girolamo Golubovich (ed.), *Biblioteca bio-bibliografica della Terra Santa e dell'Oriente Francescano*, 5 vols. (Florence: Quaracchi, 1906–23), iv. 427–60.

Itinerarium Symonis Semeonis Ab Hybernia Ad Terram Sanctam, ed. Mario Esposito (Scriptores Latini Hiberniae, 4; Dublin: Dublin Institute for Advanced Studies, 1960).

HENRY KNIGHTON, *Chronicle, 1337–1396*, ed. and trans. Geoffrey H. Martin (Oxford Medieval Texts; Oxford: Clarendon Press, 1995).

RICHARD LESCOT, *Chronique (1328–1344), suivie de la continuation de cette chronique (1344–1364)*, ed. Jean Lemoine (SHF 278; Paris, 1896).

Le Livre de Seyntz Medicines: The Unpublished Devotional Treatise of Henry of Lancaster, ed. Émile Jules Arnould (Anglo-Norman Texts, 2; Oxford: Blackwell, 1940).

GILLES LE MUISIT, *Chronique et Annales*, ed. Henri Lemaître (SHF 322; Paris: Renouard, 1906).

ADAM MURIMUTH, *Continuatio Chronicarum*, ed. Edward M. Thompson (RS 93; London: HMSO, 1889).

MATTHIAS VON NEUENBURG, *Cronica*, in *Heinricus de Diessenhofen und andere Geschichtsquellen Deutschlands im Späteren Mittelalter*, ed. Alfons Huber (Fontes Rerum Germanicarum, Geschichtsquellen Deutschlands, ed. Johann Friedrich Böhmer, 4; Stuttgart: J. G. Cotta, 1868), 149–276.

Memorials of St Edmund's Abbey, ed. Thomas Arnold, 3 vols. (RS 96; London, 1890–6).

PERROY, ÉDOUARD, 'Quattre lettres du cardinal Guy de Boulogne (1352–54)', *Revue du Nord* 36 (1954), 159–64.

JOHN OF READING, *Chronica*, in *Chronica Johannis de Reading et Anonymi Cantuarensis, 1346–67*, ed. James Tait (PUM/HS, 20; Manchester: Manchester University Press, 1914), 99–186.

BERNARD DU ROSIER, *Ambaxiator brevilogus*, in *De legatis et legationibus tractatus varii*, ed. Vladimir E. Hrabar (Dorpat, 1905), 1–28.

HEINRICH TAUBE VON SELBACH, *Chronica*, ed Harry Bresslau (Monumenta Germaniae Historica, Scriptores Rerum Germanicarum, NS 1; Berlin: Weidmannsche Buchhandlung, 1922).

MATTEO VILLANI, *Cronica, con la continuazione di Filippo Villani*, ed. Giuseppe Porta, 2 vols. (Parma: Fondazione Pietro Bembo: U. Guanda, 1995).

Vitae paparum Avenionensium: Hoc est historia pontificium qui in Gallia sederunt ab anno Christi MCCCV usque ad annum MCCCXCIV, ed. Étienne Baluze, new edn. by Guillaume Mollat, 4 vols. (Paris, 1914–27).

THOMAS WALSINGHAM, *Historia Anglicana*, ed. Henry T. Riley, 2 vols. (RS 28, pt. 1; London, 1863–4).

WELKENHUYSEN, ANDRIES, 'La peste en Avignon (1348) décrit par un témoin oculaire, Louis Sanctus de Beringen (édition critique, traduction, éléments de commentaire)', in *Pascua Medievalia: Studies voor Prof. Dr J. M. de Smet* (Mediaevalia Lovaniensia, ser. 1, studia, 10; Louvain: Universitaire Pers Leuven, 1983), 452–90.

Works of Reference

BERGER, ADOLF, *Encyclopedic Dictionary of Roman Law* (Transactions of the American Philosophical Society, NS 42/2; Philadelphia: American Philosophical Society, 1953).

BERRIDGE, GEOFFREY, and JAMES, ALAN, *A Dictionary of Diplomacy* (Basingstoke: Macmillan, 2001).

BOYLE, LEONARD E., *A Survey of the Vatican Archives and of its Medieval Holdings* (Pontifical Institute of Mediaeval Studies, Subsidia Mediaevalia, 1; Toronto: Pontifical Institute of Mediaeval Studies, 1972).

BRESSLAU, HARRY, *Handbuch der Urkundenlehre für Deutschland und Italien*, 2nd edn., 3 vols. (Berlin and Leipzig: Veit, de Gruyter, 1912–31).

BRUNS, FRIEDRICH, and WECZERKA, HUGO, *Hansische Handelsstraßen*, 3 vols. (Quellen und Darstellungen zur Hansischen Geschichte, NF 13; Cologne: Böhlau, 1962–8).

CERCHIARI, EMMANUELE, *Capellani papae et apostolice sedis auditores causarum palatii apostolici seu Sacra Rota, ab origine ad diem usque 20 Septembris 1870*, 4 vols. (Rome, 1919–21).

C[OKAYNE], G[EORGE] E[DWARD], *The Complete Peerage of England, Scotland, Ireland, Great Britain and the United Kingdom*, rev. and enl. edn., ed. Vicary Gibbs et al., 14 vols. (London, 1910–98).

Corpus Iuris Canonici, ed. Emil Friedberg, 2nd edn., 2 vols. (Leipzig: Tauchnitz, 1879–81).

Dictionary of Medieval Latin from British Sources, ed. Ronald Edward Latham and David R. Howlett (London: Oxford University Press, 1975–).

Dictionnaire de droit canonique, ed. Raoul Naz, 7 vols. (Paris: Letouzey et Ané, 1935–65).

Dictionnaire d'histoire et de géographie ecclésiastiques, ed. Alfred Baudrillart et al. (Encyclopédie des sciences ecclésiastiques, 4; Paris: Letouzey et Ané, 1912–).

Dictionnaire de théologie catholique, ed. Alfred Vacant and Eugène Mangenot, 15 vols. in 19 (Encyclopédie des sciences ecclésiastiques, 2; Paris: Letouzey et Ané, 1903–50).

EMDEN, ALFRED B., *A Biographical Register of the University of Oxford to AD 1500*, 3 vols. (Oxford: Clarendon Press, 1957–9).

—— *A Biographical Register of the University of Cambridge to A.D. 1500* (Cambridge: Cambridge University Press, 1963).

—— *A Survey of Dominicans in England Based on the Ordination Lists in Episcopal Registers (1268 to 1538)* (Institutum historicum fratrum praedicatorum Romae ad S Sabinae, dissertationes historicae, 18; Rome: Santa Sabina, 1967).

EUBEL, KONRAD, *Hierarchia catholica medii aevi sive summorum pontificum, S.R.E. cardinalium, ecclesiarum antistitum series, e documentis tabularii praesertim Vaticani collecta, digesta, edita*, 3 vols. (Münster: W. Regenberg, 1898–1910).

FRENZ, THOMAS, *Papsturkunden des Mittelalters und der Neuzeit* (Historische Grundwissenschaften in Einzeldarstellungen, 2; Stuttgart: F. Steiner, 1986).

GERMER-DURAND, EUGÈNE, *Dictionnaire topographique du Département du Gard* (Dictionnaire topographique de la France; Paris, 1868).

GIUSTI, MARTINO, *Inventario dei Registri Vaticani* (Collectanea Archivi Vaticani, 8; Vatican City: Archivio Vaticano, 1981).

GROTEFEND, HERMANN, *Zeitrechnung des deutschen Mittelalters und der Neuzeit*, 2 vols. (Hanover: Hahnsche Buchhandlung, 1891–8).

Handbook of British Chronology, 3rd edn., ed. Edmund B. Fryde et al. (Royal Historical Society Guides and Handbooks, 2; Cambridge: Cambridge University Press, repr. 1996).

HOLTZMANN, WALTHER, *Papsturkunden in England*, 3 vols. (Abhandlungen der Akademie der Wissenschaften zu Göttingen, phil.-hist. Klasse, 3. Folge; Göttingen: Weidmannsche Buchhandlung, 1930–52).

Lexikon des Mittelalters (Munich and Zurich: Artemis and Lexma, 1977–99).

Medieval France: An Encyclopedia, ed. William W. Kibler and Grover A. Zinn (Garland Encyclopedias of the Middle Ages, 2; New York and London: Garland, 1995).

PANSIER, PIERRE, *Dictionnaire des anciennes rues d'Avignon* (Avignon: Roumanille, 1930).

The Papacy: An Encyclopedia, ed. Philippe Levillain, Engl. edn., ed. John W. O'Malley, 3 vols. (New York and London: Routledge, 2002).

Secondary Works

ABERTH, JOHN, *Criminal Churchmen in the Age of Edward III: The Case of Bishop Thomas de Lisle* (University Park, PA: Pennsylvania State University Press, 1996).

ADAIR, EDWARD R., *The Exterritoriality of Ambassadors in the 16th and 17th Centuries* (London and New York: Longman, Green and Co., 1929).

ALBAN, J. R., and ALLMAND, CHRISTOPHER T., 'Spies and spying in the fourteenth century', in Christopher T. Allmand (ed.), *War, Literature, and Politics in the Late Middle Ages: Essays in Honour of G. W. Coopland* (Liverpool: Liverpool University Press, 1976), 73–101.

ALLMAND, CHRISTOPHER T., 'The civil lawyers', in Cecil Holdsworth Clough (ed.), *Profession, Vocation, and Culture in Later Medieval England. Essays Dedicated to the Memory of A. R. Myers* (Liverpool: Liverpool University Press, 1982), 155–80.

—— *The Hundred Years War: England and France at War c.1300–c.1450* (Cambridge Medieval Textbooks; Cambridge: Cambridge University Press, 1989).

ANDERSON, MATTHEW S., *The Rise of Modern Diplomacy, 1450–1919* (London: Longman, 1993).

ARIÈS, PHILIPPE, and DUBY, GEORGES (gen. eds.), *A History of Private Life*, ii: Georges Duby (ed.), *Revelations of the Medieval World*, trans. Arthur Goldhammer (Cambridge, MA, and London: Belknap Harvard, 1988).

AUTRAND, FRANÇOISE, 'The peacemakers and the state: Pontifical diplomacy and the Anglo-French conflict in the fourteenth century', in Philippe Contamine (ed.), *War and Competition between States* (The Origins of the Modern State in Europe, 13th to 18th Centuries, Theme A; Oxford: Clarendon Press, 2000), 249–77.

AYRAULT, PIERRE, *De l'ordre et instruction judiciaire dont les Anciens Grecs et Romains ont usé en accusations publiques, conféré à l'usage de nostre France* (Paris, 1576); 4th edn. (Paris, 1610).

AYTON, ANDREW, 'Edward III and the English aristocracy at the beginning of the Hundred Years War', in Matthew Strickland (ed.), *Armies, Chivalry and Warfare in Medieval Britain and France: Proceedings of the 1995 Harlaxton Symposium* (Harlaxton Medieval Studies, NS 7; Stamford: Paul Watkins, 1998), 173–206.

BAGLIANI, AGOSTINO PARAVICINI, 'Innocent IV.', in *PE* ii. 790–3.

—— 'Residences, Papal', in *PE* iii. 1300–5.

BAKER, JOHN H., 'Dr Thomas Fastolf and the history of law reporting', *Cambridge Law Journal* 45 (1986), 84–96.

BALDWIN, JAMES F., *The King's Council in England during the Middle Ages* (Oxford: Clarendon Press, 1913).

BARATIER, ÉDOUARD, *La Démographie provençale du XIIIe au XVIe siècle* (École pratique des hautes études, VIe section: Centre des recherches historiques. Démographie et sociétés, 5; Paris: SEVPEN, 1961).

BARBICHE, BERNARD, 'Les procureurs des rois de France à la cour pontificale d'Avignon', in *Aux origines de l'état moderne: Le Fonctionnement administratif de la papauté d'Avignon. Actes de la table ronde organisée par l'École française de Rome avec le concours du CNRS, du Conseil Général de Vaucluse et de l'Université d'Avignon (Avignon, 23–24 janvier 1988)* (Collection de l'École française de Rome, 138; Rome: École française de Rome, 1990), 81–112.

BARRACLOUGH, GEOFFREY, *Papal Provisions: Aspects of Church History, Constitutional, Legal and Administrative, in the Late Middle Ages* (Oxford: Blackwell, 1935).

—— *The Medieval Papacy* (London: Thames and Hudson, 1968: repr. 1992).

BARRELL, ANDREW D. M., 'The Ordinance of Provisors of 1343', *Historical Research* 64 (1991), 264–77.

BARSTON, RONALD PETER, *Modern Diplomacy*, 2nd edn. (London: Longman, 1997).

BARTON, JOHN L., *Roman Law in England* (Ius Romanum Medii Aevi, pars V, 13a; Milan: Giuffrè, 1971).

—— 'The study of civil law before 1380', in *The History of the University of Oxford*, i: Jeremy I. Catto (ed.) *The Early Oxford Schools* (Oxford: Clarendon Press, 1984), 520–30.

BAUMGARTEN, PAUL MARIA, *Untersuchungen und Urkunden über die Camera collegii cardinalium für die Zeit von 1295–1437* (Leipzig, 1898).

—— *Aus Kanzlei und Kammer: Erörterungen zur kurialen Hof- und Verwaltungsgeschichte im XIII., XIV. und XV. Jahrhundert* (Freiburg: Herder, 1907).

—— *Von der apostolischen Kanzlei: Untersuchungen über die päpstlichen Tabellionen und die Vicekanzler der Heiligen Römischen Kirche im XIII., XIV. und XV. Jahrhundert* (Görres-Gesellschaft zur Pflege der Wissenschaft im katholischen Deutschland, Sektion für Rechts- und Sozialwissenschaften, 4; Cologne: Bachem, 1908).

BAUTIER, ROBERT-HENRI, 'Confesseur du roi', in *LexMA* iii. 125–8.

—— 'Récherches sur les routes de l'Europe médiévale. i: De Paris et des foires de Champagne à la Méditerranée par le Massif Central', *BPH* 1960 (1961), 99–143.

BEHRENS, BETTY, 'The office of English resident ambassador', *TRHS*, 4th ser., 16 (1933), 161–92.

—— 'Origins of the office of English resident ambassador in Rome', *EHR* 49 (1934), 640–56.

BENOÎT, FERNAND, *Villeneuve-lez-Avignon* (Petites Monographies des Grandes Édifices de la France; Paris: H. Laurens, 1930).

BENTHAM, JAMES, *The History and Antiquities of the Conventual and Cathedral Church of Ely*, 2nd edn. (Norwich: Stevenson and Co., 1812).

BERG, DIETER, *England und der Kontinent: Studien zur auswärtigen Politik der anglonormannischen Könige im 11. und 12. Jahrhundert* (Bochum: Winkler, 1987).

—— *Deutschland und seine Nachbarn, 1200–1500* (Enzyklopädie deutscher Geschichte, 40; Munich: Oldenbourg, 1997).

—— Kintzinger, Martin, and Monnet, Pierre (eds.), *Auswärtige Politik und internationale Beziehungen im Mittelalter (13. bis 16. Jahrhundert)* (Europa in der Geschichte. Schriften zur Entwicklung des modernen Europa, 6; Bochum: Winkler, 2002).

BERINGS, GEERT, 'Transport and communication in the Middle Ages', in *Kommunikation und Alltag in Spätmittelalter und früher Neuzeit. Internationaler Kongress Krems an der Donau 9. bis 12. Oktober 1990* (Österreichische Akademie der Wissenschaften, phil.-hist. Klasse, Sitzungsberichte 596, Veröffentlichungen des Instituts für Realienkunde des Mittelalters und der frühen Neuzeit, 15; Vienna: Verlag der Österreichischen Akademie der Wissenschaften, 1992), 47–73.

BERKING, HELMUTH, *Sociology of Giving*, trans. Patrick Camiller (London: Sage, 1999).

BERRIDGE, GEOFFREY R., 'Amarna diplomacy: A fully-fledged diplomatic system?', in Raymond Cohen and Raymond Westbrook (eds.), *Amarna Diplomacy: The Beginnings of International Relations* (Baltimore and London: Johns Hopkins University Press, 2000), 212–24.

BEUTTEL, JAN-ERIK, *Der Generalprokurator des Deutschen Ordens an der Römischen Kuri: Amt, personelles Umfeld und Finanzierung* (Quellen und Studien zur Geschichte des Deutschen Ordens, 55; Marburg: Elwert, 1999).

BIRCH, DEBRA J., *Pilgrimage to Rome in the Middle Ages: Continuity and Change* (Woodbridge: Boydell and Brewer, 1998).

BLACK, ANTONY, *Political Thought in Europe, 1250–1450* (Cambridge Medieval Textbooks; Cambridge: Cambridge University Press, 1992).

BLACK, J. G., 'Edward I and Gascony in 1300', *EHR* 17 (1902), 518–27.

BLIN, LÉON, 'Le grand chemin de Paris à Lyon par la vallée de la Loire aus bas moyen âge (de Decize à Marcigny par la rive gauche)', *BPH* 1958 (1959), 237–65.

BLOCH, MARC, *Feudal Society*, 2nd edn., trans. L. A. Manyon, 2 vols. (London and New York: Routledge, 1965; repr. 1989).

BOCK, FRIEDRICH, 'Einführung in das Registerwesen des Avignonesischen Papsttums (I. Textteil, II. Tafelbeilagen)', *QF* 31 (1941), 1–107.

BORCHGRAVE, CHRISTIAN DE, *Diplomaten en diplomatie onder Hertog Jan Zonder Vrees. Impact op de vlaamse politieke situatie* (Anciens pays et assemblées d'etats—Standen en landen, 95; Courtrai: UGA, 1992).

BOYER, MARJORIE NICE, 'A day's journey in medieval France', *Speculum* 26 (1951), 597–608.

—— 'Roads and rivers: Their use and disuse in late medieval France', *Medievalia et Humanistica* 13 (1960), 68–80.

BROWE, PETER, 'Das Beichtgeheimnis in Altertum und Mittelalter', *Scholastik* 9 (1934), 1–57.

BROWN, ALFRED L., *The Early History of the Clerkship of the Council* (Glasgow University Publications, NS 131; Glasgow: University of Glasgow, 1969).

—— *The Governance of Late Medieval England, 1272–1461* (Governance of England, 3; London: Edward Arnold, 1989).

BRUCE, HERBERT, *Notes on the Chronicle Ascribed to Geoffrey le Baker of Swinbrook* (Cardiff: William Lewis, 1918).

BRUN, AUGUSTE, *Recherches historiques sur l'introduction du français dans les provinces du Midi* (Paris: Champion, 1923).

BRUNEL, CLOVIS, 'Le nom de la voie Regordane', *Romania* 79 (1958), 289–313.

BUCKLAND, WILLIAM W., *A Textbook of Roman Law from Augustus to Justinian*, 3rd, rev. edn., ed. Peter Stein (Cambridge: Cambridge University Press, 1963).

BULL, HEDLEY, *The Anarchical Society: A Study of Order in World Politics*, 3rd edn. (Basingstoke: Palgrave, 2002).

BURNS, CHARLES, 'Sources of British and Irish history in the *Instrumenta Miscellanea* of the Vatican Archives', *AHP* 9 (1971), 7–141.

—— 'Vatican sources and the honorary papal chaplains in the fourteenth century', in Erwin Gatz (ed.), *Römische Kurie. Kirchliche Finanzen. Vatikanisches Archiv. Studien zu Ehren von Hermann Hoberg*, 2 vols. (Miscellanea Historiae Pontificiae, 45–6; Rome: Università Gregoriana, 1979), i. 65–95.

CAUCHIES, JEAN-MARIE, 'Les sources des itinéraires routiers en Europe occidentale au moyen âge', in *Bronnen voor de historische geografie van België—Sources de la géographie historique en Belgique. Handelingen van het Colloquium te Brussel—Actes du Colloque de Bruxelles, 25.–27. IV. 1979*, ed. J. Mertens (Brussels: Archives générales, 1980), 75–104.

CAZELLES, RAYMOND, *La Société politique et la crise de la royauté sous Philippe de Valois* (Bibliothèque elzévirienne, nouvelle sér., études et documents; Paris: Librairie d'Argences, 1958).

CHAPLAIS, PIERRE, 'Règlement des conflits internationaux franco-anglais au xive siècle (1293–1337)', *Le Moyen âge* 57 (1951), 269–302.

—— 'Privy seal drafts, rolls, and registers (Edward I–Edward II)', *EHR* 73 (1958), 270–3.

—— 'English diplomatic documents to the end of Edward III's reign', in Donald A. Bullough and Robin L. Storey (eds.), *The Study of Medieval Records: Essays in Honour of Kathleen Major* (Oxford: Clarendon Press, 1971), 23–56.

—— *Essays in Medieval Diplomacy and Administration* (London: Hambledon Press, 1981).

—— *English Diplomatic Practice in the Middle Ages* (London and New York: Hambledon Press and London, 2003).

CHENEY, CHRISTOPHER R., *Notaries Public in England in the Thirteenth and Fourteenth Centuries* (Oxford: Clarendon Press, 1972).

CHEYETTE, FREDRIC L., 'Paris B.N. ms. latin 5954: The professional papers of an English ambassador on the eve of the Hundred Years War', in *Économies et sociétés au moyen âge: Mélanges offerts à E. Perroy* (Publications de la Sorbonne, Série 'Études', 5; Paris, 1973), 400–13.

CHIAUDANO, MARIO, 'Note sui mercanti astigniani: I Malabaila', *Bollettino storico-bibliografico subalpino* 41, NS 5 (1939), 213–28.

CHRIMES, STANLEY B., *An Introduction to the Administrative History of Medieval England* (Studies in Medieval History, 7; Oxford: Blackwell, 1952).

CLANCHY, MICHAEL T., *From Memory to Written Record: England 1066–1307*, 2nd edn. (Oxford: Blackwell, 1993).

CLARK, JOHN W., 'Bishop Bateman', *Proceedings of the Cambridge Antiquarian Society* 9, NS 3 (1894–8), 297–336.

COLEMAN, JOYCE, *Public Reading and the Reading Public in Late Medieval England and France* (Cambridge Studies in Medieval Literature, 26; Cambridge: Cambridge University Press, 1996).

COLOMBE, GABRIEL, *Le Palais des Papes d'Avignon*, 2nd edn. (Petites Monographies des Grands Édifices de la France; Paris: H. Laurens, 1931).

CONSTABLE, GILES, *Letters and Letter-Collections* (Typologie des sources du moyen âge occidental, 17; Turnhout: Brepols, 1976).

CONSTANTINOU, COSTAS M., *On the Way to Diplomacy* (Minneapolis: University of Minnesota Press, 1996).

CONTAMINE, PHILIPPE, 'Les aménagements de l'espace privé, XIVᵉ–XVᵉ siècle', in Philippe Ariès and Georges Duby (gen. eds.), *Histoire de la vie privée*, ii: Georges Duby (ed.), *De l'Europe féodale à la Renaissance* (Paris: Éditions du Seuil, 1985), 421–501.

CRAIG, GORDON A., 'Political and diplomatic history', in Felix Gilbert and Stephen R. Graubard (eds.), *Historical Studies Today* (New York: W. W. Norton, 1972), 356–71.

—— 'On the nature of diplomatic history: The relevance of some old books', in Paul G. Lauren (ed.), *Diplomacy: New Approaches in History, Theory, and Policy* (New York and London: Free Press, Collier Macmillan, 1979), 21–42.

CRUMP, CHARLES G., 'The arrest of Roger Mortimer and Queen Isabel', *EHR* 26 (1911), 331–2.

CUTTINO, GEORGE P., 'A memorandum book of Elias Joneston', *Speculum* 17 (1942), 74–85.

—— 'Another memorandum book of Elias Joneston', *EHR* 63 (1948), 90–103.

—— *English Diplomatic Administration, 1259–1339*, 2nd, rev. and enl. edn. (Oxford: Clarendon Press, 1971).

—— *English Medieval Diplomacy* (Bloomington, IN: Indiana University Press, 1985).

DAVIES, C., 'The Statute of Provisors of 1351', *History*, NS 38 (1953), 116–33.

DAVIES, RICHARD G., 'The Anglo-papal concordat of Bruges, 1375: A reconsideration', *AHP* 19 (1981), 97–146.

DEELEY, ANNE, 'Papal provisions and royal rights of patronage in the early fourteenth century', *EHR* 43 (1928), 497–527.

DELACHENAL, ROLAND, *Histoire de Charles V*, 5 vols. (Paris, 1909–31).

DENIFLE, HEINRICH, 'Die Constitutionen des Prediger-Ordens vom Jahre 1228', *Archiv für Literatur- und Kirchengeschichte des Mittelalters* 1 (1885), 165–227.

—— 'Die päpstlichen Registerbände des 13. Jahrhunderts und das Inventar derselben vom Jahr 1339', *Archiv für Literatur- und Kirchengeschichte des Mittelalters* 2 (1886), 1–105.

DÉPREZ, EUGÈNE, *Les Préliminaires de la guerre de cent ans: La papauté, la France et l'Angleterre (1328–1342)* (BEFAR 86; Paris, 1902).

—— 'La guerre de cent ans à la mort de Benoît XII: L'intervention des cardinaux avant le conclave et du Pape Clément VI avant son couronnement (25 avril–19 mai 1342)', *Revue historique* 83 (1903), 58–76.

—— 'La conférence d'Avignon (1344)', in Andrew G. Little and F. Maurice Powicke (ed.), *Essays in Medieval History Presented to T. F. Tout* (Manchester: Manchester University Press, 1925), 301–20.

DER DERIAN, JAMES, *On Diplomacy: A Genealogy of Western Estrangement* (Oxford: Blackwell, 1987).

—— 'Diplomacy', in *Oxford Companion to Politics of the World*, 2nd edn., ed. Joel Krieger et al. (New York: Oxford University Press, 2001), 217, 222–3.

DEVLIN, MARY AQUINAS, 'Bishop Thomas Brunton and his sermons', *Speculum* 14 (1939), 324–44.

DIBBEN, L. B., 'Secretaries in the thirteenth and fourteenth centuries', *EHR* 25 (1910), 430–44.

DOLEZALEK, GERO,'*Quaestiones motae in Rota*: Richterliche Beratungsnotizen aus dem vierzehnten Jahrhundert', in Stephan Kuttner and Kenneth Pennington (ed.), *Proceedings of the 5th International Congress of Medieval Canon Law* (Monumenta Iuris Canonici, Ser. C: Subsidia, 6; Vatican City: Biblioteca Apostolica Vaticana, 1980), 100–37.

DUBOIS, HENRI, 'Un voyage princier au XIVe siècle (1344)', in *Voyages et voyageurs au moyen âge: XXVIe congrès de la SHMES (Limoges-Aubazine, mai 1995)* (Histoire Ancienne et Médiévale, 39; Paris: Publications de la Sorbonne, 1996), 71–92.

DUBY, GEORGES, *The Early Growth of the European Economy: Warriors and Peasants from the Seventh to the Twelfth Century*, trans. Howard B. Clarke (London: Weidenfeld and Nicolson, 1974).

—— *France in the Middle Ages 987–1460: From Hugh Capet to Joan of Arc*, trans.

Juliet Vale (A History of France; Oxford and Cambridge, MA: Blackwell, 1991; repr. 1999).

DUNBABIN, JEAN, 'Careers and vocations', in *The History of the University of Oxford*, i: Jeremy I. Catto (ed.), *The Early Oxford Schools* (Oxford: Clarendon Press, 1984), 565–606.

DYKMANS, MARC, 'Le cardinal Annibal de Ceccano (vers 1282–1350): Étude biographique et testament du 17 juin 1348', *Bulletin de l'Institut historique belge de Rome* 43 (1973), 145–315.

EBAN, ABBA S., *Diplomacy for the Next Century* (New Haven and London: Yale University Press, 1998).

ECKERT, THOMAS, 'Nichthäretische Papstkritik in England vom Beginn des 14. bis zur zweiten Hälfte des 15. Jahrhunderts', *Annuarium Historiae Conciliorum* 23 (1991), 116–359.

EHM, PETRA, *Burgund und das Reich: Spätmittelalterliche Außenpolitik am Beispiel der Regierung Karls des Kühnen (1465–1477)* (Pariser Historische Studien, 6; Munich: Oldenbourg, 2002).

EHRLE, FRANZ, 'Zur Geschichte des Schatzes, der Bibliothek und des Archivs der Päpste im vierzehnten Jahrhundert', *Archiv für Literatur- und Kirchengeschichte des Mittelalters* 1 (1885), 1–48, 228–364.

ERNST, F., 'Über Gesandtschaftswesen und Diplomatie an der Wende vom Mittelalter zur Neuzeit', *Archiv für Kulturgeschichte* 33 (1950), 64–95.

FAUCHER, DANIEL, *L'Homme et la Rhône* (Paris: Gallimard, 1968).

FAVIER, JEAN, *Les Finances pontificales à l'époque du Grand Schisme d'Occident* (BEFAR 211; Paris: École française de Rome, 1966).

FELTEN, FRANZ JOSEF, 'Kommunikation zwischen Kaiser und Kurie unter Ludwig dem Bayern (1314–1347): Zur Problematik der Quellen im Spannungsfeld von Schriftlichkeit und Mündlichkeit', in Heinz-Dieter Heimann and Ivan Hlavácek (eds.), *Kommunikationspraxis und Korrespondenzwesen im Mittelalter und in der Renaissance* (Paderborn: Schöningh, 1998), 51–89.

FLINIAUX, ANDRÉ, 'Contribution à l'histoire des sources du droit canonique: Les anciennes collections de "Decisiones Rotae romanae"', *Revue historique de droit français et étranger*, 4ᵉ sér., 4ᵉᵐᵉ année (1925), 61–93, 382–410.

FOWLER, KENNETH A., *The King's Lieutenant: Henry of Grosmont, First Duke of Lancaster, 1310–1361* (London: Elek, 1969).

—— 'News from the front: Letters and despatches of the fourteenth century', in Philippe Contamine, Charles Giry-Deloison and Maurice H. Keen (eds.), *Guerre et société en France, en Angleterre et en Bourgogne, XIVᵉ–XVᵉ siècle* (Collection 'Histoire et littératures régionales', 8; Lille: Centre d'histoire de la région du Nord et de l'Europe du Nord-Ouest, Université Charles de Gaulle, 1991), 63–92.

—— *Medieval Mercenaries*, i: *The Great Companies* (Oxford: Blackwell, 2001).

FRENZ, THOMAS, 'Skriptor', in *LexMA* vii. 1991–2.

—— 'Abbreviator', in *LexMA* i. 16–17.

FRISCH, HANS RITTER VON, *Der völkerrechtliche Begriff der Exterritorialität* (Vienna: A. Hölder, 1917).

FRYDE, EDMUND B., 'The financial resources of Edward III in the Netherlands, 1337–40 (2nd part)', *Revue belge de philologie et d'histoire* 45 (1967), 1142–1216.

—— 'Italian merchants in medieval England, *c.*1270–*c.*1500', in *Aspetti della vita economica medievale: Atti del Convegno di Studi nel X Anniversario della morte di Federigo Melis, Firenze-Pisa-Prato, 10–14 Marzo 1984* (Florence: Istituto di storia economica, Università degli studi Firenze, 1985), 215–31.

FRYDE, NATALIE M., 'John Stratford, bishop of Winchester, and the Crown, 1323–30', *BIHR* 44 (1971), 153–61.

GAGNIÈRE, SYLVAIN (ed.), *Histoire d'Avignon* (Aix-en-Provence: Édisud, 1979).

—— and Granier, Jacques, *Avignon, de la préhistoire à la papauté* (Avignon: Rullière-Libeccio, 1970).

GALLAND, BRUNO, 'La publication des registres de lettres pontificales par l'École française de Rome', *BEC* 154 (1996), 625–34.

—— *Les Papes d'Avignon et la maison de Savoie (1309–1409)* (Collection de l'École française de Rome, 247; Rome: École française de Rome, 1998).

GANSHOF, FRANÇOIS LOUIS, *Le Moyen Âge* (Pierre Renouvin (ed.), *Histoire des relations internationales*, i; Paris: Hachette, 1953).

—— 'Merowingisches Gesandtschaftswesen', in *Aus Geschichte und Landeskunde. Forschungen und Darstellungen, Franz Steinbach zum 65. Geburtstag gewidmet von seinen Freunden und Schülern* (Bonn: L. Röhrscheid, 1960), 166–83.

GASQUET, FRANCIS AIDAN, *The Black Death of 1348 and 1349*, 2nd edn. (London: G. Bell, 1908).

GAUDEMET, JEAN, 'Le Rôle de la papauté dans le règlement des conflits entre états aux xiiie et xive siècles', *Recueils de la Société Jean Bodin pour l'histoire comparative des institutions* 15 (1961), 79–106.

GILLES-GUIBERT, M., 'Noms des routes et des chemins dans le Midi de la France au moyen âge', *BPH* 1960 (1961), 1–39.

GILLET, P., 'Avocat', in *DDC* i. 1524–35.

GIRARD, JOSEPH, *Évocation du vieil Avignon* (Paris: Éditions de Minuit, 1958).

GIVEN-WILSON, CHRIS, *The Royal Household and the King's Affinity: Service, Politics and Finance in England, 1360–1413* (New Haven and London: Yale University Press, 1986).

—— *The English Nobility in the Later Middle Ages: The Fourteenth-Century Political Commmunity* (London and New York: Routledge and Kegan Paul, 1987).

GODELIER, MAURICE, *The Enigma of the Gift*, trans. Nora Scott (Cambridge: Polity, 1999).

GOETZ, HANS-WERNER, *Moderne Mediävistik: Stand und Perspektiven der Mittelalterforschung* (Darmstadt: Wissenschaftliche Buchgesellschaft, 1999).

GÖLLER, EMIL, *Die päpstliche Pönitentiarie von ihrem Ursprung bis zu ihrer Umgestaltung unter Pius V.*, 2 vols. in 4 (Bibliothek des Königlich Preußischen Historischen Instituts in Rom, 3, 4, 7, 8; Rome: Loescher, 1907–11).

GOODMAN, ANTHONY, *John of Gaunt: The Exercise of Princely Power in Fourteenth-Century Europe* (Harlow: Longman, 1992).

GRANSDEN, ANTONIA, *Historical Writing in England*, ii: *c.1130 –c.1415* (London: Routledge and Kegan Paul, 1982).

GRAVES, EDGAR B., 'The legal significance of the Statute of Praemunire of 1353', in Charles H. Taylor and John L. La Monte (eds.), *Anniversary Essays in Medieval History Presented to Charles Homer Haskins* (Boston and New York: Houghton Mifflin, 1929), 68–80.

GREWE, WILHELM GEORG, *The Epochs of International Law*, trans. and rev. Michael Byers (Berlin and New York: Walter de Gruyter, 2000).

GROTIUS, HUGO, *De jure belli ac pacis libri tres* (Paris: Nicolas Buon, 1625).

GRUNDMANN, HERBERT, '*Litteratus—illiteratus*: Der Wandel einer Bildungsnorm vom Altertum zum Mittelalter', *Archiv für Kulturgeschichte* 40 (1958), 1–65.

GUENÉE, BERNARD, *States and Rulers in Later Medieval Europe*, trans. Juliet Vale (Oxford: Blackwell, 1985).

GUESSARD, FRANÇOIS, 'Étienne de Mornay, chancelier de France sous Louis Hutin', *BEC* 5 (1843–4), 373–96.

GUILLEMAIN, BERNARD, *La Politique bénéficiale du pape Benoît XII (1334–1342)* (Bibliothèque de l'École des hautes études. Sciences historiques et philologiques, 299; Paris: Champion, 1952).

—— 'Les chapelains d'honneur des papes d'Avignon', *MAHEF* 64 (1952), 217–38.

—— 'Les tentatives pontificales de médiation dans le litige franco-anglais de Guyenne au XIVe siècle', *BPH* 1957 (1958), 423–32.

—— *La Cour pontificale d'Avignon (1309–1376): Étude d'une société* (BEFAR 201; Paris: Boccard, 1962).

—— 'Les Français du Midi à la cour pontificale d'Avignon', *Annales du Midi* 74 (1962), 29–31.

—— 'Le Sacre Collège au temps du cardinal Albornoz (1350–1367)', in Evelio Verdera y Tuells (ed.), *El Cardenal Albornoz y el Colegio de España*, 3 vols. (Studia Albornotiana, 11–13; Bologna: Real Collegio d'España, 1972–3), i. 355–68.

—— 'Les Italiens à Avignon au XIVe siècle', in *Rapporti culturali ed economici fra Italia e Francia nei secoli dal XIV al XVI. Atti del colloquio italo-francese (Roma 18–20 febbraio 1978)* (Rome: Giunta centrale per gli studi storici, 1979), 57–72.

—— 'Les logements des curialistes et des courtisans dans Avignon sous Jean

XXII', in *Crises et réformes dans l'église de la Réforme Grégorienne à la Pré-réforme. Actes du 115e Congrès National des Sociétés Savantes (Avignon, 1990), Section d'histoire médiévale et de philologie* (Paris: Éditions du CTHS, 1991), 181–7.

—— 'Les tribuneaux de la cour pontificale d'Avignon', in *L'Église et le droit dans le Midi (XIIIe–XIVe s.)* (Cahiers de Fanjeaux, Collection d'histoire religieuse du Languedoc aux XIIIe et XIVe siècles, 29; Toulouse: Privat, 1994), 339–60.

—— *Les Papes d'Avignon, 1309–1376* (Paris: Éditions du Cerf, 1998).

—— 'Curia, 14th and 15th Centuries', in *PE* i. 455–61.

GUMBLEY, WALTER, *The Cambridge Dominicans* (Oxford: Blackfriars, 1938).

GUYOTJEANNIN, OLIVIER, 'Skriptor', in *PE* iii. 1398.

HACK, ACHIM THOMAS, *Das Empfangszeremoniell bei mittelalterlichen Papst-Kaiser-Treffen* (Forschungen zur Kaiser- und Papstgeschichte des Mittelalters, 18; Cologne: Böhlau, 1999).

HALLER, JOHANNES, *Papsttum und Kirchenreform: Vier Kapitel zur Geschichte des ausgehenden Mittelalters*, i (Berlin, 1903; no further vols. published).

HAMILTON, KEITH A., and LANGHORNE, RICHARD, *The Practice of Diplomacy: Its Evolution, Theory and Administration* (London and New York: Routledge, 1995).

HAYE, THOMAS, 'Die lateinische Sprache als Medium mündlicher Diplomatie', in Rainer Christoph Schwinges and Klaus Wriedt (eds.), *Gesandt-schafts- und Botenwesen im spätmittelalterlichen Europa* (Vorträge und Forschungen, 60; Sigmaringen: Jan Thorbecke, 2003), 15–32.

HAYEZ, ANNE-MARIE, 'Anglais présents à Avignon dans le pontificat d'Urbain V', in *La 'France anglaise' au moyen âge: Colloque des historiens médiévistes français et britanniques. Actes du 111e congrès national des sociétés savantes (Poitiers 1986), section d'histoire médiévale et de philologie* (Paris: Éditions du CTHS, 1988), 569–86.

HAYEZ, MICHEL, and HAYEZ, ANNE-MARIE, 'L'hôtellerie avignonnaise au XIVe siècle, à propos de la succession de Siffrède Trelhon (1387)', *Provence historique* 25 (1975), 275–84.

HECKEL, RUDOLF VON, 'Das Aufkommen der ständigen Prokuratoren an der päpstlichen Kurie im 13. Jahrhundert', in *Miscellanea Francesco Ehrle: Scritti di storia e paleografia pubblicati sotto gli auspici di S. S. Pio XI in occasione dell'ottantesimo natalizio dell' E.mo cardinale Francesco Ehrle* (Studi et Testi, 37–42; Rome: Biblioteca Apostolica Vaticana, 1924), ii. 290–321.

HERDE, PETER, *Beiträge zum päpstlichen Kanzlei- und Urkundenwesen im drei-zehnten Jahrhundert*, 2nd edn. (Münchener historische Studien, Abteilung geschichtliche Hilfswissenschaften, 1; Kallmünz: M. Lassleben, 1967).

—— *Audientia litterarum contradictarum. Untersuchungen über die päpstlichen Justizbriefe und die päpstliche Delegationsgerichtsbarkeit vom 13. bis zum Beginn des 16. Jahrhunderts* (Bibliothek des Deutschen Historischen Instituts Rom, 31–2; Tübingen: Max Niemeyer, 1969–70).

HIGHFIELD, J. ROGER L., 'Correspondence', *History*, NS 39 (1954), 331–2.

HILL, MARY C., 'A study, mainly from royal wardrobe accounts, of the nature and organisation of the king's messenger service from the reign of John to that of Edward III inclusive', *BIHR* 18 (1940), 33–5.

—— 'Jack Faukes, king's messenger, and his journey to Avignon in 1343', *EHR* 57 (1942), 19–30.

—— 'King's messengers and administrative developments in the 13th and 14th centuries', *EHR* 61 (1946), 315–28.

—— *The King's Messengers, 1199–1377: A Contribution to the History of the Royal Household* (London: Edward Arnold, 1961).

—— *The King's Messengers, 1199–1377: A List of All Known Messengers, Mounted and Unmounted, Who Served John, Henry III, and the First Three Edwards* (Stroud: Alan Sutton, 1994).

—— 'The King's messengers in England, 1199–1337', *Medieval Prosopography* 17/2 (1996), 63–96.

HINNEBUSCH, WILLIAM A., 'Diplomatic activities of the English Dominicans in the thirteenth century', *Catholic Historical Review* 28 (1942), 309–39.

—— *The Early English Friars Preachers* (Institutum historicum fratrum praedicatorum Romae ad S. Sabinae, dissertationes historicae, 14; Rome: Santa Sabina, 1951).

HLAVÁCEK, IVAN, 'Überlegungen zum Geschenkwesen im Mittelalter', *Mitteilungen der Residenzen-Kommission der Akademie der Wissenschaften zu Göttingen* 2/2 (1992), 12–15.

HOBERG, HERMANN, 'Die Rotarichter in den Eidregistern der Apostolischen Kammer von 1347–1494', *QF* 34 (1954), 159–72.

HOPMANN, P. TERRENCE, *The Negotiation Process and the Resolution of International Conflicts* (Columbia, SC: University of South Carolina Press, 1996).

HOUSLEY, NORMAN, *The Avignon Papacy and the Crusades, 1305–1378* (Oxford: Oxford University Press, 1986).

—— 'France, England, and the "national crusade", 1302–1386', in Gillian Jondorf and D. N. Dumville (eds.), *France and the British Isles in the Middle Ages and Renaissance: Essays in Memory of Ruth Morgan* (Woodbridge: Boydell Press, 1991), 183–98.

—— *The Later Crusades, 1274–1580: From Lyons to Alcazar* (Oxford: Oxford University Press, 1992).

HUFFMAN, JOSEPH P., *The Social Politics of Medieval Diplomacy: Anglo-German Relations (1066–1307)* (Studies in Medieval and Early Modern Civilization; Ann Arbor: University of Michigan Press, 2000).

HUNT, EDWIN S., 'A new look at the dealings of the Bardi and Peruzzi with Edward III', *Journal of Economic History* 50 (1990), 149–62.

IGGERS, GEORG G., *Historiography in the Twentieth Century: From Scientific Objectivity to the Postmodern Challenge* (Hanover, NH, and London: Wesleyan University Press, 1997).

JARRETT, BEDE, *The English Dominicans* (London: Burns, Oates and Wash-
burn, 1921).

JERVIS, ROBERT, 'Systems theory and diplomatic history', in Paul Gordon
Lauren (ed.), *Diplomacy: New Approaches in History, Theory, and Policy* (New
York and London: Free Press, Collier Macmillan, 1979), 212–44.

JOHNSON, J. H., 'The king's wardrobe and household', in James F. Willard
and William A. Morris (eds.), *The English Government at Work, 1327–1336*,
i: *Central and Prerogative Administration* (Mediaeval Academy of America,
Publication 37; Cambridge, MA: Mediaeval Academy of America, 1940),
206–49.

JONES, MICHAEL, 'Relations with France, 1337–1399', in Michael Jones and
Malcolm G. A. Vale (eds.), *England and her Neighbours, 1066–1453: Essays in
Honour of Pierre Chaplais* (London: Hambledon Press, 1989), 239–58.

JONES, MICHAEL, and VALE, MALCOLM G. A. (eds.), *England and her
Neighbours, 1066–1453: Essays in Honour of Pierre Chaplais* (London:
Hambledon Press, 1989).

JONES, W. R., 'Relations of the two jurisdictions: Conflict and cooperation
in England during the thirteenth and fourteenth centuries', in *Studies in
Medieval and Renaissance History* 7 (1970), 77–210.

JÖNSSON, CHRISTER, 'Diplomacy, bargaining and negotiation', in Walter
Carlsnaes, Thomas Risse and Beth A. Simmons (eds.), *Handbook of
International Relations* (London: Sage, 2002), 212–34.

JUGIE, PIERRE, 'Les cardinaux issus de l'administration royale française:
Typologie des carrières antérieures à l'accession au cardinalat (1305–1378)',
in *Crises et réformes dans l'église de la Réforme Grégorienne à la Préréforme. Actes
du 115e Congrès National des Sociétés Savantes (Avignon, 1990), Section
d'histoire médiévale et de philologie* (Paris: Éditions du CTHS, 1991), 157–80.

—— 'Innocent VI.', in *PE* ii. 794–7.

—— 'Consistory', in *PE* i. 413–15.

KAUFMANN, JOHAN, *Conference Diplomacy: An Introductory Analysis*, 3rd edn.
(Basingstoke: Macmillan, 1996).

KEEN, MAURICE H., *England in the Later Middle Ages: A Political History*
(London and New York: Routledge, 1973; repr. 1986).

—— *Chivalry* (New Haven and London: Yale University Press, 1984).

—— *English Society in the Later Middle Ages, 1348–1500* (Harmondsworth:
Penguin, 1990).

KELLER, HAGEN, 'Pragmatische Schriftlichkeit im Mittelalter: Erscheinungs-
formen und Entwicklungsstufen. Einführung zum Kolloquium in
Münster, 17.–19. Mai 1989', in Hagen Keller, Klaus Grubmüller and
Nikolaus Staubach (eds.), *Pragmatische Schriftlichkeit im Mittelalter:
Erscheinungsformen und Entwicklungsstufen (Akten des Internationalen
Kolloquiums, 17.–19. Mai 1989)* (Münstersche Mittelalter-Schriften, 65;
Munich: Fink, 1992), 1–7.

KERSCHER, GOTTFRIED, 'Das mallorquinische Zeremoniell am päpstlichen Hof: *Comederunt cum papa rex maioricarum ...*', in Jörg Jochen Berns and Thomas Rahn (eds.), *Zeremoniell als höfische Ästhetik in Spätmittelalter und früher Neuzeit* (Frühe Neuzeit. Studien und Dokumente zur deutschen Literatur und Kultur im europäischen Kontext, 25; Tübingen: Max Niemeyer, 1995), 125–49.

KERVYN DE LETTENHOVE, BARON JOSEPH MARIE BRUNO CONSTANTIN, BARON, *Histoire de Flandre*, 6 vols. (Brussels: A. Vandale, 1847–50).

KINTZINGER, MARTIN, '*Cum salvo conductu*: Geleit im westeuropäischen Spätmittelalter', in Rainer Christoph Schwinges and Klaus Wriedt (eds.), *Gesandtschafts- und Botenwesen im spätmittelalterlichen Europa* (Vorträge und Forschungen, 60; Sigmaringen: Jan Thorbecke, 2003), 313–63.

KIRSCH, JOHANN PETER, 'Andreas Sapiti, englischer Prokurator an der Kurie im 14. Jahrhundert', *HJb* 14 (1893), 582–603.

KNOWLES, DAVID, *The Religious Orders in England*, 3 vols. (Cambridge: Cambridge University Press, 1948–59).

KOCH, WALTER, 'Protonotar', in *LexMA* vii. 273–4.

LABANDE, LÉON-HONORÉ, 'Les manuscrits de la Bibliothèque d'Avignon provenants de la librairie des papes du XIVe siècle', *Bulletin historique et philologique du Comité des Travaux Historiques et Scientifiques* 1894 (1895), 145–60.

—— *Le Palais des papes et les monuments d'Avignon au XIVe siècle*, 2 vols. (Marseilles: F. Detaille, 1925).

LABARGE, MARGARET W., *Medieval Travellers: The Rich and Restless* (London: Hamish Hamilton, 1982).

LANGLOIS, CH.-V., 'Notices et documents relatifs à l'histoire du XIIIe et du XIVe siècle', *Revue historique* 87 (1905), 55–79.

—— 'Le fonds de l'*Ancient Correspondence* au *Public Record Office* de Londres', *Journal des Savants* (Aug. 1904), 446–53.

LARSON, ALFRED, 'The payment of fourteenth-century English envoys', *EHR* 54 (1939), 403–14.

—— 'The English embassies during the Hundred Years' War', *EHR* 55 (1940), 423–31.

LAUREN, PAUL G., 'Diplomacy: History, theory, and policy', in id. (ed.), *Diplomacy: New Approaches in History, Theory, and Policy* (New York and London: Free Press, Collier Macmillan, 1979), 3–18.

LEFEBVRE, CHARLES, 'Les origines et le rôle du cardinalat au moyen âge', *Apollinaris: Commentarius canonicus* 41 (1968), 59–70.

—— 'Rote Romaine (Tribunal de la Sainte)', in *DDC* vii. 742–71.

LE GOFF, JACQUES, 'Is politics still the backbone of history?', in Felix Gilbert and Stephen R. Graubard (eds.), *Historical Studies Today* (New York: W. W. Norton, 1972), 337–55.

LE GRAND, LÉON, 'Itinéraire de Wissant à Lyon', *BEC* 47 (1886), 197–8.

LENTSCH, ROBERTE, 'Le palais de Benoît XII et son aménagement intérieur', in Marie-Humbert Vicaire (ed.), *La Papauté d'Avignon et le Languedoc (1316–1342)* (Cahiers de Fanjeaux, Collection d'Histoire religieuse du Languedoc aux XIIIᵉ et XIVᵉ siècles, 26; Toulouse: Privat, 1991), 345–66.

LENZENWEGER, JOSEF, 'Das Vatikanische Archiv unter besonderer Berücksichtigung seiner spätmittelalterlichen Bestände', in Erwin Gatz (ed.), *Römische Kurie, kirchliche Finanzen, Vatikanisches Archiv: Studien zu Ehren von Hermann Hoberg*, 2 vols. (Miscellanea Historiae Pontificiae, 45–6; Rome: Università Gregoriana, 1979), i. 445–58.

—— 'Clemens VI.', in *LexMA* ii. 2143–4.

LÉONARD, ÉMILE G., *La Jeunesse de Jeanne Iʳᵉ, reine de Naples, comtesse de Provence*, 2 vols. (Monaco and Paris: Imprimerie de Monaco, 1932).

LE PATOUREL, JOHN, 'The Treaty of Brétigny, 1360', *TRHS*, 5th ser., 10 (1960), 19–39.

LÉVI-STRAUSS, CLAUDE, 'The principle of reciprocity', abridged and trans. Rose L. Coser and G. Frazer, in Lewis A. Coser and Bernard Rosenberg (eds.), *Sociological Theory: A Book of Readings* (New York: Macmillan, 1957).

LOT, FERDINAND, 'Itinéraires du XIIIᵉ siècle', *BPH* 1920 (1922), 217–22.

LUCAS, HENRY STEPHEN, *The Low Countries and the Hundred Years War, 1326–1347* (University of Michigan Publications, History and Political Science, 8; Ann Arbor: University of Michigan Press, 1929).

—— 'The machinery of diplomatic intercourse', in James F. Willard and William A. Morris (eds.), *The English Government at Work, 1327–1336*, i: *Central and Prerogative Administration* (Mediaeval Academy of America, Publication 37; Cambridge, MA: Mediaeval Academy of America, 1940), 300–31.

LUNT, WILLIAM E., *Studies in Anglo-Papal Relations during the Middle Ages*, i: *Financial Relations of the Papacy with England to 1327* (Mediaeval Academy of America, Publication 33; Cambridge, MA: Mediaeval Academy of America, 1939).

—— *Studies in Anglo-Papal Relations during the Middle Ages*, ii: *Financial Relations of the Papacy with England, 1327–1534* (Mediaeval Academy of America, Publication 74; Cambridge, MA: Mediaeval Academy of America, 1962).

—— *Papal Revenues in the Middle Ages*, 2 vols. (Columbia University Records of Civilization, Sources and Studies, 19; New York: Octagon Books, 1965).

MCCLANAHAN, GRANT V., *Diplomatic Immunity: Principles, Practices, Problems* (London: Hurst, 1989).

MACFARLANE, LESLIE J., 'The Vatican Archives: With special reference to sources for British medieval history', *Archives* 4 (1959), 29–44, 84–101.

MAGNIN, ÉTIENNE, 'Immunités ecclesiastiques', in *Dictionnaire de théologie catholique*, ed. Alfred Vacant and Eugène Mangenot, 15 vols. in 19 (Encyclopédie des sciences ecclésiastiques, 2; Paris: Letouzey et Ané, 1903–50), vii. 1218–62.

MAJIC, TIMOTHEUS, 'Die Apostolische Pönitentiarie im 14. Jahrhundert', *RQ* 50 (1955), 129–77.

MATTINGLY, GARRET, 'The first resident embassies: Medieval Italian origins of modern diplomacy', *Speculum* 12 (1937), 423–39.

—— *Renaissance Diplomacy* (New York: Dover, 1970).

MAULDE LA CLAVIÈRE, MARIE ALPHONSE RENÉ DE, 'Les instructions diplomatiques au Moyen-Age', *RHD* 6 (1892), 602–32.

—— *La Diplomatie au temps de Machiavel*, 3 vols. (Paris, 1892–3).

MAUSS, MARCEL, *The Gift: The Form and Reason for Exchange in Archaic Societies*, trans. W. D. Halls (London: Routledge, 1990).

MENACHE, SOPHIA, *Clement V* (Cambridge Studies in Medieval Life and Thought, 4th ser., 36; Cambridge: Cambridge University Press, 1998).

MENZEL, VIKTOR, *Deutsches Gesandtschaftswesen im Mittelalter* (Hanover: Hahnsche Buchhandlung, 1892).

MERTES, KATE, *The English Noble Household, 1250–1600: Good Governance and Politic Rule* (Family, Sexuality and Social Relations in Past Times; Oxford: Blackwell, 1988).

MIETHKE, JÜRGEN, 'Der Kampf Ludwigs des Bayern mit Papst und avignonesischer Kurie in seiner Bedeutung für die deutsche Geschichte', in Hermann Nehlsen and Hans-Georg Hermann (eds.), *Kaiser Ludwig der Bayer: Konflikte, Weichenstellungen und Wahrnehmung seiner Herrschaft* (Quellen und Forschungen aus dem Gebiet der Geschichte, NF 22; Paderborn, Munich, Vienna and Zurich: Schöningh, 2002), 39–74.

MINOIS, GEORGES, *Le Confesseur du roi: Les Directeurs de conscience sous la monarchie française* (Nouvelles études historiques; Paris: Fayard, 1988).

MIROT, LÉON, and DÉPREZ, EUGÈNE, 'Les ambassades anglaises pendant la Guerre de Cent Ans: Catalogue chronologique, 1327–1450', *BEC* 59 (1898), 550–77; 60 (1899), 177–214; 61 (1900), 20–58.

MOLLAT, GUILLAUME, 'Innocent VI et les tentatives de paix entre la France et l'Angleterre (1353–55)', *RHE* 10 (1909), 729–43.

—— 'La collation des bénéfices ecclésiastiques à l'époque des papes d'Avignon (1305–1378)', in id. (ed.), *Jean XXII (1316–1334): Lettres communes, analysées d'après les registres dits d'Avignon et du Vatican*, 16 vols. (BEFAR, 3rd ser., 1 *bis*; Paris: Fontemoing and Boccard, 1904–46), i. 9–152.

—— 'L'œuvre oratoire de Clément VI', *Archives d'histoire doctrinale et littéraire du moyen âge* 3 (1928), 239–74.

—— 'La diplomatie pontificale au XIVe siècle', in *Mélanges d'histoire du moyen âge dédiés à la mémoire de Louis Halphen* (Paris: Presses universitaires de France, 1951), 507–12.

—— 'Contribution à l'histoire du Sacre Collège de Clément V à Eugène IV', *Revue d'histoire ecclésiastique* 46 (1951), 22–112, 566–94.

—— 'Correspondance de Clément VI par cédules', *Bolletino dell'Archivio paleografico italiano* (1956–7), 175–8.

—— *The Popes at Avignon, 1305–1378*, trans. Janet Love (London: Thomas Nelson and Sons, 1963).

—— *Les Papes d'Avignon (1305–1378)*, 10th edn. (Paris: Letouzey et Ané, 1965).

MORAW, PETER, 'Über Rahmenbedingungen und Wandlungen auswärtiger Politik vorwiegend im deutschen Spätmittelalter', in Dieter Berg, Martin Kintzinger and Pierre Monnet (eds.), *Auswärtige Politik und internationale Beziehungen im Mittelalter (13. bis 16. Jahrhundert)* (Europa in der Geschichte. Schriften zur Entwicklung des modernen Europa, 6; Bochum: Winkler, 2002), 31–45.

NAHLIK, STANISLAW EDWARD, 'Völkerrechtliche Aspekte der frühen Diplomatie', in Gerhard Pferschy (ed.), *Siegmund von Herberstein—Kaiserlicher Gesandter und Begründer der Rußlandkunde und die europäische Diplomatie* (Veröffentlichungen des Steiermärkischen Landesarchives, 17; Graz, 1989), 43–62.

NICOLSON, HAROLD GEORGE, *Diplomacy*, 3rd edn. (Home University Library of Modern Knowledge, 192; London: Oxford University Press, 1963).

NYS, ERNEST, *Les Origines de la diplomatie et le droit d'ambassade jusqu'à Grotius* (Brussels, 1884).

—— *Les Origines du droit international* (Brussels and Paris: A. Castaigne, 1894).

OFFLER, H. S., 'Über die Prokuratorien Ludwigs des Bayern für die römische Kurie', *Deutsches Archiv* 8 (1951), 461–87.

OGDON, MONTELL, *Juridical Bases of Diplomatic Immunity: A Study in the Origin, Growth and Purpose of the Law* (Washington: J. Byrne and Co., 1936).

ORME, NICHOLAS, *From Childhood to Chivalry: The Education of the English Kings and Aristocracy, 1066–1530* (London and New York: Methuen, 1984).

ORMROD, WILLIAM MARK, 'The English government and the Black Death of 1348–9', in id. (ed.) *England in the Fourteenth Century: Proceedings of the 1985 Harlaxton Symposium* (Woodbridge: Boydell Press, 1986), 175–88.

—— *The Reign of Edward III: Crown and Political Society in England, 1327–1377* (New Haven and London: Yale University Press, 1990).

OTTO, HEINRICH, 'Die Eide und Privilegien Heinrichs VII. und Karls IV. mit ungedruckten Aktenstücken', *QF* 9 (1906), 316–78.

—— 'Das Avignoneser Inventar des päpstlichen Archivs vom Jahre 1366 und die Privilegiensammlungen des Fieschi und des Platina: Ein Beitrag zur Geschichte des Vatikanischen Archivs im 14. und 15. Jahrhundert', *QF* 12 (1909), 132–88.

PALMER, C. F. R., '*Fasti Ordinis Fratrum Praedicatorum*: The Provincials of the Friar-Preachers, or Black Friars, of England', *Archaeological Journal* 35 (1878), 134–65.

—— 'The king's confessors', *The Antiquary* 22 (1890), 114–20, 159–61, 262–6.

PALMER, JOHN J. N., 'The war aims of the protagonists and the negotiations for peace', in Kenneth A. Fowler (ed.), *The Hundred Years War* (London: Macmillan, 1971), 51–74.

PANSIER, PIERRE, *Histoire de la langue provençale à Avignon du XIIeme au XIXme siècle*, 4 vols. in 2 (Avignon: Librairie Aubanel Frères, 1924–7).

PANTIN, WILLIAM A., *The English Church in the Fourteenth Century* (Cambridge: Cambridge University Press, 1955).

—— 'The fourteenth century', in Clifford H. Lawrence (ed.), *The English Church and the Papacy in the Middle Ages*, rev. edn. (Stroud: Sutton, 1999), 157–94.

PARAVICINI, WERNER, 'Zeremoniell und Raum', in id. (ed.), *Zeremoniell und Raum. 4. Symposium der Residenzen-Kommission der Akademie der Wissenschaften in Göttingen, veranstaltet gemeinsam mit dem Deutschen Historischen Institut Paris und dem Historischen Institut der Universität Potsdam, Potsdam, 25. bis 27. September 1994* (Residenzenforschung, 6; Sigmaringen: Jan Thorbecke, 1997), 11–27.

PARKS, GEORGE B., *The English Traveler to Italy*, i: *The Middle Ages (to 1525)* (Rome: Edizioni de Storia e Letteratura, 1954).

PÉLISSIER, ANTOINE, *Clement VI le Magnifique, premier pape limousin (1342–1352)* (Brive: Imprimerie Catholique, 1951).

—— *Innocent VI le Réformateur, deuxième pape limousin (1352–1362)* (Collection 'Les papes limousins'; Tulle, 1961).

PERROY, ÉDOUARD, *L'Angleterre et le grand schisme de l'occident: Étude sur la politique religieuse de l'Angleterre sous Richard II (1378–1399)* (Paris: Librairie J. Monnier, 1933).

—— *The Hundred Years War* (London: Eyre and Spottiswoode, 1951).

PETIT, ERNEST, *Histoire des Ducs de Bourgogne de la race capétienne*, 9 vols. (Dijon: Imprimerie Darantière, 1885–1905).

PEYER, HANS CONRAD (ed.), *Gastfreundschaft, Taverne und Gasthaus im Mittelalter* (Schriften des Historischen Kollegs, Kolloquien, 3; Munich and Vienna: Oldenbourg, 1983).

—— 'Gasthaus', in *LexMA* iv. 1132–4.

PHILLIPS, JOHN R. S., *Aymer de Valence, Earl of Pembroke 1307: Baronial Politics in the Reign of Edward II* (Oxford: Clarendon Press, 1972).

PLÖGER, KARSTEN, 'Englische Gesandtschaftsrechnungen des Spätmittelalters', in Harm von Seggern and Gerhard Fouquet (eds.), *Adel und Zahl: Studien zum adligen Rechnen und Haushalten in Spätmittelalter und früher Neuzeit* (Pforzheimer Gespräche zur Sozial-, Wirtschafts- und Stadtgeschichte, 1; Verlag Regionalkultur: Ubstadt-Weiher, 2000), 247–54.

—— 'Die Entführung des Fieschi zu Avignon (1340): Zur Entwicklung der diplomatischen Immunität in der Frühphase des Hundertjährigen Krieges', *Francia* 30/1 (2003), 73–105.

POST, GAINES, '*Plena potestas* and consent in medieval assemblies: A study in Romano-canonical procedure and the rise of representation, 1150–1325', *Traditio* 1 (1943), 355–408.

PRESTWICH, MICHAEL, *Edward I* (Yale English Monarchs; New Haven and London: Yale University Press, 1997).

QUELLER, DONALD E., 'Thirteenth-century diplomatic envoys: *Nuncii* and *procuratores*', *Speculum* 35 (1960), 196–213.

—— 'Early Venetian legislation concerning foreign ambassadors', *Studies in the Renaissance* 12 (1965), 7–17.

—— *The Office of Ambassador in the Middle Ages* (Princeton: Princeton University Press, 1967).

—— 'Western European diplomacy', in Joseph R. Strayer (ed.), *Dictionary of the Middle Ages*, 12 vols. (New York: Scribner, 1982–9), iv. 201–14.

RÉGNÉ, JEAN, 'La première étape de la pénétration capétienne en Vivarais: La Fondation de Villeneuve-de-Berg et la mise en pariage de son territoire (novembre 1284)', *BPH* 1 (1913), 121–40.

REITEMEIER, ARND, *Außenpolitik im Spätmittelalter: Die diplomatischen Beziehungen zwischen dem Reich und England, 1377–1422* (Veröffentlichungen des Deutschen Historischen Instituts London, 45; Paderborn, Munich, Vienna and Zurich: Schöningh, 1999).

RENOUARD, YVES, 'Comment les papes d'Avignon expédaient leur courier', *Revue historique* 180 (1937), 1–22.

—— 'Compagnies mercantiles lucquoises au service des papes d'Avignon', *Bollettino storico lucchese* 11 (1939), 42–50.

—— *Les Relations des papes d'Avignon et les compagnies commerciales et bancaires de 1316 à 1378* (BEFAR 151; Paris: Boccard, 1941).

—— *Recherches sur les compagnies commerciales et bancaires utilisées par les papes d'Avignon avant le grand schisme* (Paris: Presses universitaires de France, 1942).

—— 'Interêt et importance des Archives Vaticanes pour l'histoire économique du moyen âge spécialement du XIVe siècle', in *Miscellanea archivistica A. Mercati* (Studi e Testi, 165; Vatican City: Biblioteca Apostolica Vaticana, 1952), 21–41.

—— *La Papauté à Avignon* (Que sais-je?, 630; Paris: Presses universitaires de France, 1954).

—— 'Information et transmission des nouvelles', in Charles Samaran (ed.), *L'Histoire et ses méthodes* (Encyclopédie de la Pléiade, 11; Paris: Gallimard, 1961), 95–142.

—— 'Routes, étapes et vitesses de marche de France à Rome au XIIIe et au XIVe siècles d'après les itinéraires d'Eudes Rigaud (1254) et de Barthélemy Bonis (1350)', in id. (ed.), *Études d'histoire médiévale*, 2 vols. (Bibliothèque générale de l'École pratique des hautes études, VIe section; Paris: SEVPEN, 1968), ii. 677–97.

—— *The Avignon Papacy, 1305–1403*, trans. Denis L. T. Bethell (London: Faber and Faber, 1970).

REUTER, TIMOTHY, 'Die Unsicherheit auf den Straßen im europäischen Früh- und Hochmittelalter: Täter, Opfer und ihre mittelalterlichen und modernen Betrachter', in Johannes Fried (ed.), *Träger und Instrumentarien des Friedens im hohen und späten Mittelalter* (Vorträge und Forschungen, 43; Sigmaringen: Jan Thorbecke, 1996), 169–201.

RICHARDSON, HENRY G., and SAYLES, GEORGE O., *The Governance of Medieval England from the Conquest to Magna Carta* (Edinburgh University Publications, History, Philosophy, and Economics, 16; Edinburgh: Edinburgh University Press, 1963).

RITZLER, R., 'Die Verschleppung der päpstlichen Archive nach Paris unter Napoleon I. und deren Rückführung nach Rom in den Jahren 1815–1817', *Römische Historische Mitteilungen* 6–7 (1962–3, 1963–4), 144–90.

ROGERS, JAMES E. T., *A History of Agriculture and Prices in England*, 7 vols. (Oxford: Clarendon Press, 1866–1902).

RUSSELL, E., 'The Societies of the Bardi and Peruzzi and their dealings with Edward III, 1327–45', in George Unwin (ed.), *Finance and Trade under Edward III* (London: Frank Cass, 1962), 93–135.

SÄGMÜLLER, JOHANN BAPTIST, *Die Thätigkeit und Stellung der Cardinäle bis Papst Bonifaz viii, historisch-canonistisch untersucht und dargestellt* (Freiburg, 1896).

SALMON, G., 'Bateaux et bateliers sur le Rhône et Saône: Un voyage lexical en domaine franco-provençal au moyen âge', in *Voyage, quête, pèlerinage dans la littérature et la civilisation médiévales* (Sénéfiance, 2; Aix-en-Provence: Édition CUERMA and Paris: Champion, 1976), 139–51.

SALT, MARY C. L., 'English embassies to France in the reign of Edward I: Their personnel, powers, equipment and objects', *BIHR* 6 (1929), 29–31.

—— 'List of English embassies to France', *EHR* 44 (1929), 263–78.

SAYERS, JANE E., 'Canterbury proctors at the court of *Audentia Litterarum Contradictarum*', *Traditio* 22 (1966), 311–45.

—— 'Proctors representing British interests at the papal court, 1198–1415', in Stephan Kuttner (ed.), *Proceedings of the Third International Congress of Medieval Canon Law, Strasbourg, 3–6 September 1968* (Monumenta Iuris Canonici, Ser. C: Subsidia, 4; Vatican City: Biblioteca Apostolica Vaticana, 1971), 143–63.

SCHAAB, MEINRAD, 'Geleit', in *LexMA* iv. 1204–5.

SCHÄFER, KARL HEINRICH, 'Päpstliche Ehrenkapläne aus deutschen Diözesen im 14. Jahrhundert', *RQ* 21 (1907), 97–113.

SCHIMMELPFENNIG, BERNHARD, 'Die Organisation der päpstlichen Kapelle in Avignon', *QF* 50 (1971), 80–111.

—— 'Zur Versorgung der Kurie in Avignon mit Lebensmitteln', in Erwin
Gatz (ed.), *Römische Kurie, kirchliche Finanzen, Vatikanisches Archiv. Studien
zu Ehren von Hermann Hoberg*, 2 vols. (Miscellanea Historiae Pontificiae,
45–6; Rome: Università Gregoriana, 1979), ii. 773–87.

—— 'Die Funktion des Papstpalastes und der kurialen Gesellschaft im
päpstlichen Zeremoniell vor und während des Großen Schismas', in
Michel Hayez (ed.), *Genèse et débuts du Grand Schisme d'Occident
(1362–1394): Colloques internationaux du Centre National de la Recherche
Scientifique no. 586 (Avignon 25–28 septembre, 1978)* (Éditions du Centre
National de la Recherche Scientifique; Paris: Centre National de la
Recherche Scientifique, 1980), 317–28.

—— *Das Papsttum: Von der Antike bis zur* Renaissance, 4th edn. (Darmstadt:
Wissenschaftliche Buchgesellschaft, 1996).

—— '*Ad maiorem pape gloriam*: La fonction des pièces dans le palais des Papes
d'Avignon', in Jean Guillaume (ed.), *Architecture et vie sociale: L'Organisation
intérieure des grandes demeures à la fin du moyen âge et à la Renaissance. Actes
du colloque tenu à Tours du 6 au 10 juin 1988* (De Architectura; Paris: Picard,
1994), 25–46.

—— 'Der Palast als Stadtersatz: Funktionelle und zeremonielle Bedeutung
der Papstpaläste in Avignon und im Vatikan', in Werner Paravicini (ed.),
*Zeremoniell und Raum. 4. Symposium der Residenzen-Kommission der
Akademie der Wissenschaften in Göttingen, veranstaltet gemeinsam mit dem
Deutschen Historischen Institut Paris und dem Historischen Institut der
Universität Potsdam, Potsdam, 25. bis 27. September 1994* (Residenzen-
forschung, 6; Sigmaringen: Jan Thorbecke, 1997), 239–56.

—— 'Beichtvater', in *LexMA* i. 1819.

SCHMITZ, PHILIBERT, 'Les Sermons et discours de Clément VI, OSB', *Revue
bénédictine* 41 (1929), 15–34.

SCHNEIDER, FRANZ EGON, *Die römische Rota: Nach geltendem Recht auf
geschichtlicher Grundlage* (Görres-Gesellschaft zur Pflege der Wissenschaft
im katholischen Deutschland, Veröffentlichungen der Sektion für Rechts-
und Sozialwissenschaft, 22; Paderborn, 1914).

SCHREINER, KLAUS, 'Fußkuß', in *LexMA* iv. 1063–6.

SCHRÖDER, HELMUT, 'Die Protokollbücher der päpstlichen Kammerkleriker
1329–1347', *Archiv für Kulturgeschichte* 27 (1937), 121–286.

SCHÜTZ, ALOIS, *Die Prokuratorien und Instruktionen Ludwigs des Bayern für die
Kurie (1331–1345): Ein Beitrag zu seinem Absolutionsprozeß* (Münchener
Historische Studien, Abt. Geschichtliche Hilfswissenschaften, 11;
Kallmünz: M. Lassleben, 1973).

SCHWARTZ, BARRY, 'The social psychology of the gift', *American Journal of
Sociology* 73 (1967), 1–11.

SCHWINGES, RAINER CHRISTOPH, and WRIEDT, KLAUS (eds.), *Gesandtschafts-
und Botenwesen im spätmittelalterlichen Europa* (Vorträge und Forschungen,
60; Sigmaringen: Jan Thorbecke, 2003).

SCHWÖBEL, HERMANN OTTO, *Der diplomatische Kampf zwischen Ludwig dem Bayern und der römischen Kurie im Rahmen des kanonischen Absolutionsprozesses, 1330–1346* (Quellen und Studien zur Verfassungsgeschichte des Deutschen Reiches in Mittelalter und Neuzeit, 10; Weimar: Böhlau, 1968).

SELLE, XAVIER DE LA, *Le Service des âmes à la cour: Confesseurs et aumôniers des rois de France du XIIIe au XVe siècle* (Mémoires et documents de l'École des chartes, 43; Paris: École des chartes, 1995).

SERRAO, FELICIANO, *Il procurator* (Pubblicazioni dell' Istituto di Diritto Romano, dei Diritti dell' Oriente Mediterraneo, e di Storia del Diritto, 26; Milan: Giuffrè, 1947).

SHARP, P., 'For diplomacy: Representation and the study of international relations', *International Studies Review* 1 (1999), 33–57.

SIGAL, PIERRE-ANDRÉ, 'Sickness of the Pope, Middle Ages', in *PE* iii. 1415–17.

SMITH, NATHANIEL B., 'Occitan Language', in *Medieval France: An Encyclopedia*, ed. William W. Kibler and Grover A. Zinn (Garland Encyclopedias of the Middle Ages, 2; New York and London: Garland, 1995), 677–80.

SOHN, ANDREAS, *Deutsche Prokuratoren an der römischen Kurie in der Frührenaissance (1431–1474)* (Norm und Struktur. Studien zum sozialen Wandel in Mittelalter und Früher Neuzeit, 8; Cologne, Weimar and Vienna: Böhlau, 1997).

STOCK, BRIAN, *The Implications of Literacy: Written Language and Models of Interpretation in the Eleventh and Twelfth Centuries* (Princeton: Princeton University Press, 1983).

STONE, LAWRENCE, 'Prosopography', in Felix Gilbert and Stephen R. Graubard (eds.), *Historical Studies Today* (New York: W. W. Norton, 1972), 107–40.

STONES, EDWARD L. G., 'The mission of Thomas Wale and Thomas Delisle from Edward I to Pope Boniface VIII in 1301', *Nottingham Medieval Studies* 26 (1982), 8–28.

STRETTON, GRACE, 'Some aspects of medieval travel', *TRHS*, 4th ser., 7 (1924), 77–97.

——— 'The travelling household in the middle ages', *Journal of the British Archaeological Association*, NS 40 (1935), 75–103.

SUMPTION, JONATHAN, *The Hundred Years War*, i: *Trial by Battle* (London and Boston: Faber and Faber, 1990).

——— *The Hundred Years War*, ii: *Trial by Fire* (London: Faber and Faber, 1999).

SWANSON, ROBERT N., *Church and Society in Late Medieval England* (Oxford: Blackwell, 1989).

TAMBURINI, FILIPPO, 'La Penitenzieria apostolica durante il papato avignonese', in *Aux origines de l'état moderne. Le fonctionnement administratif de la papauté d'Avignon. Actes de la table ronde organisée par l'École française de Rome avec le concours du CNRS, du Conseil Général de Vaucluse et de l'Université d'Avignon (Avignon, 23–24 janvier 1988)* (Collection de l'École française de Rome, 138; Rome: École française de Rome, 1990), 251–68.

TAYLOR, CRAIG, 'Edward III and the Plantagenet claim to the French throne', in James S. Bothwell (ed.), *The Age of Edward III* (Woodbridge: York Medieval Press, 2001), 155–69.

TAYLOR, JOHN, *English Historical Literature in the Fourteenth Century* (Oxford: Clarendon Press, 1987).

TELLENBACH, GERD, 'Beiträge zur kurialen Verwaltungsgeschichte im 14. Jahrhundert', *QF* 24 (1932–3), 150–87.

THOMAS, HEINZ, *Deutsche Geschichte des Spätmittelalters 1250–1500* (Stuttgart, Berlin, Cologne and Mainz: Kohlhammer, 1983).

THOMPSON, ALEXANDER H., 'William Bateman, Bishop of Norwich, 1344–1355', *Norfolk and Norwich Archaeological Society* 25 (1933–5), 102–37.

TOUT, THOMAS F., *Chapters in the Administrative History of Medieval England: The Wardrobe, the Chamber, and the Small Seals*, 6 vols. (PUM 126–7, PUM/HS 48–9, 57, 64; Manchester: Manchester University Press, 1920–33).

——— 'The English civil service in the fourteenth century', *BJRL* 3 (1916), 185–214.

TRABUT-CUSSAC, JEAN PAUL, 'Les cartulaires gascons d'Édouard II, d'Édouard III, et de Charles VII', *BEC* 111 (1953), 65–106.

TRAUTZ, FRITZ, *Die Könige von England und das Reich, 1277–1377: Mit einem Rückblick auf ihr Verhältnis zu den Staufern* (Heidelberg: Carl Winkler Universitätsverlag, 1961).

TUCK, ANTHONY, *Crown and Nobility: England 1272–1461*, 2nd edn. (Blackwell Classic Histories of England; London: Blackwell, 1999).

TURNER, BRYAN S., *Status* (Concepts in the Social Sciences; Milton Keynes: Open University Press, 1988).

ULLMANN, WALTER, *Principles of Government and Politics in the Middle Ages*, 4th edn. (London: Methuen, 1978).

URBAN, WILLIAM, 'The diplomacy of the Teutonic Knights at the curia', *Journal of Baltic Studies* 9 (1978), 116–28.

VALE, MALCOLM G. A., *War and Chivalry* (London: Duckworth, 1981).

——— *The Princely Court: Medieval Courts and Culture in North-West Europe, 1270–1380* (Oxford: Oxford University Press, 2001).

VINCKE, JOHANNES, 'Volkstum und Apostolische Pönitentiarie im 14. Jahrhundert', *Zeitschrift der Savigny-Stiftung für Rechtsgeschichte* 58, Kanonistische Abteilung 27 (1938), 414–44.

VINGTAIN, DOMINIQUE, and SAUVAGEOT, CLAUDE, *Avignon: Le Palais des Papes* (Le Ciel et le pierre, 2; Saint-Léger-Vauban: Zodiaque, 1998).

WALSH, KATHERINE, *A Fourteenth-Century Scholar and Primate: Richard FitzRalph in Oxford, Avignon and Armagh* (Oxford: Clarendon Press, 1981).

WAQUET, HENRI, 'Note sur les médecins de Clément VI', *MAHEF* 32 (1912), 45–8.

WAUGH, SCOTT L., *England in the Reign of Edward III* (Cambridge: Cambridge University Press, 1991).

WAUGH, W. T., 'The Great Statute of Praemunire, 1353', *EHR* 37 (1922), 173–205.

WEAKLAND, JOHN E., 'John XXII before his pontificate, 1244–1316: Jacques Duèse and his Family', *AHP* 10 (1972), 161–85.

WEIß, STEFAN, *Die Versorgung des päpstlichen Hofes in Avignon mit Lebensmitteln (1316–1378): Studien zur Sozial- und Wirtschaftsgeschichte eines mittelalterlichen Hofes* (Berlin: Akademie Verlag, 2002).

—— *Rechnungswesen und Buchhaltung des Avignoneser Papsttums (1316–1378): Eine Quellenkunde* (Monumenta Germaniae Historica, Hilfsmittel, 20; Hanover: Hahnsche Buchhandlung, 2003).

WIEDERKEHR, GEORG ROBERT, *Das freie Geleit und seine Erscheinungsformen in der Eidgenossenschaft des Spätmittelalters: Ein Beitrag zur Theorie und Geschichte eines Rechtsbegriffs* (Rechtshistorische Arbeiten namens der Forschungsstelle für Rechtssprache, Rechtsarchäologie und Rechtliche Volkskunde beim Rechtswissenschaftlichen Seminar der Universität Zürich, 16; Zurich: Juris, 1977).

WILKINSON, BERTIE, *The Chancery under Edward III* (PUM/HS 51; Manchester: Manchester University Press, 1929).

WILKS, MICHAEL J., *The Problem of Sovereignty in the Later Middle Ages: The Papal Monarchy with Augustinus Triumphus and the Publicists* (Cambridge Studies in Medieval Life and Thought, NS 9; Cambridge: Cambridge University Press, 1963).

WILLARD, JAMES F., 'The Memoranda Rolls and the remembrancers, 1282–1350', in Andrew G. Little and F. Maurice Powicke (eds.), *Essays in Medieval History Presented to T. F. Tout* (Manchester: Manchester University Press, 1925), 215–29.

WILLIAMS, GEORGE L., *Papal Genealogy: The Families and Descendants of the Popes* (Jefferson, NC, and London: McFarland, 1998).

WILSON, CLIFTON E., *Diplomatic Privileges and Immunities* (Tucson, AZ: University of Arizona Press, 1967).

WOOD, DIANA, *Clement VI: The Pontificate and Ideas of an Avignon Pope* (Cambridge Studies in Medieval Life and Thought, 4th ser., 13; Cambridge: Cambridge University Press, 1989).

WOLFE, ROBERT, *Still Lying Abroad? On the Institution of the Resident Ambassador* (Diplomatic Studies Programme, Discussion Papers 33; Leicester: University of Leicester, Centre for the Study of Diplomacy, 1997).

WRIGHT, J. ROBERT, *The Church and the English Crown, 1305–1334: A Study Based on the Register of Archbishop Walter Reynolds* (Pontifical Institute of Mediaeval Studies, Studies and Texts, 48; Toronto, 1980).

WRIGLEY, JOHN E., 'A papal secret known to Petrarch', *Speculum* 39 (1964), 613–34.

—— 'Clement VI before his pontificate: The early life of Pierre Roger (1290/91–1342)', *Catholic Historical Review* 56 (1970), 433–73.

—— 'The conclave and the electors of 1342', *AHP* 20 (1982), 51–82.

YOUNG, GEORGE M., *Victorian England: Portrait of an Age* (London: Oxford University Press, 1936).

ZACOUR, NORMAN P., *Talleyrand: The Cardinal of Périgord* (Transactions of the American Philosophical Society, NS 50, pt 7; Philadelphia: American Philosophical Society, 1960).

ZIEGLER, PHILIP, *The Black Death* (Stroud: Sutton, 1997; repr. 2000).

ZUTSHI, PATRICK N. R., 'Proctors acting for the English petitioners in the chancery of the Avignon popes (1305–1378)', *Journal of Ecclesiastical History* 35 (1984), 15–29.

—— 'The letters of the Avignon popes (1305–1378): A source for the study of Anglo-papal relations and of English ecclesiastical history', in Michael Jones and Malcolm G. A. Vale (eds.), *England and her Neighbours, 1066–1453: Essays in Honour of Pierre Chaplais* (London: Hambledon Press, 1989), 259–75.

—— 'Notaries public in England in the fourteenth and fifteenth centuries', *Historia, instituciones, documentos* 23 (1996), 412–33.

—— 'The Avignon papacy', in Michael Jones (ed.), *The New Cambridge Medieval History*, vi: *c.1300–c.1415* (Cambridge: Cambridge University Press, 2000), 653–73.

Unpublished Theses

CLARKE, R. D., 'Some secular activities of the English Dominicans during the reigns of Edward I, Edward II, and Edward III (1272–1377)', MA diss. (London, 1930).

HIGHFIELD, J. ROGER L., 'The relations between the church and the English crown 1349–1378—from the death of Archbishop Stratford to the outbreak of the Great Schism', D.Phil. thesis (Oxford, 1951).

ORMROD, WILLIAM MARK, 'Edward III's government of England, c.1346–1356', D.Phil. thesis (Oxford, 1984).

PHILLIPS, JOHN R. S., 'The career of Aymer de Valence, Earl of Pembroke, with special reference to the period from 1312 to 1324', Ph.D. thesis (London, 1968).

INDEX

to English benefices 5, 7, 23, 29, 42–53, 52–3, 64 n. 199, 82–3, 91, 97–8, 129, 165–6, 180–1, 188, 207–8
Provisors, Statute of (1351) 50–1, 64 nn. 200 & 210

qualifications of envoys 76, 80–3, 226
Queller, Donald E. 5, 87–8, 132, 193 n. 29, 228

receptions 11, 13, 154, 159, 199–203, 207, 213–14, 216, 220 n. 22, 224; *see also* audiences
recommendation, letters of *see* documents, diplomatic
Regordane 250 n. 2
Renouard, Yves 145
reports, envoys' 11–12, 80, 186, 189
Reppes, John 33, 36–7, 57 n. 76, 76–7, 89, 94–5, 110 n. 100, 115 n. 176, 138, 164, 236–7, 245–6
retinues (*familiae*), envoys' 130, 133–6, 158, 160–3, 246–7
Rhine, river 142, 150–2
Rhône, river 139–40, 145–7, 149, 151, 172 n. 118, 173 n. 137, 174 n. 145, 250 n. 1
Richardson, Henry G. 191
Richer, Guilhem 164, 214
Rigaud, Gil, card. 27–8
Rigaud, Jean 216, 259
Rimini, Gozo Battaglia di, card. 27
Ringstead, Thomas 89, 95
Robert, Ademar, card. 248
Roche, Androin de la, abbot of St Seine and Cluny, card. 27, 38, 41, 59 n. 124
Roger, Pierre 24–8, 43, 159
Rome 76, 124, 131–2, 144, 148, 152–3, 171 n. 110
Rosier, Bernard du, *Ambaxiator brevilogus* 155, 185
Ross, John 91
Rota (Court of Audience, *Audientia sacri palatii*) 43, 51, 84, 91–4, *see* also auditors
routiers 139–40, 149, 151, *see also* Great Companies

Rymer, Thomas, *Foedera* 7, 11
safe conduct 167 n. 13
written (letters of) 11, 126–36, 167 n. 14
'physical' (escort) 127, 134–6, 163
Saham, Richard 138, 162, 177 n. 196
Saint-Martial, Pierre de 100–1
Salmon, John 255
Salt, Mary C. 5
sanctity of envoys (*sanctitas legatorum*) 124–5
Sapiti, Andrea 84–5, 88, 257
Sarden, William of 186–8
Savoy 150–1, 254
counts of 5, *see also* Amadeus VI
Sayles, George O. 191
Scotland 8, 207, *see also* war
scribes, curial 10, 84, 87, 128, 132, 215, 224 n. 101
seals, royal English:
great seal 11, 181
privy seal 11, 68, 73, 194 n. 43, 249
Seine, river 139, 148
Selbach, Heinrich Taube of 139
sergeants at arms, papal 134–5, 168 n. 50, 215, 224 n. 107
Servington, David 150, 177 n. 191
Setrington, Alan 86, 175 n. 165
Shakespeare, William, *Henry V* 217
ships 152, 160–2, 177 n. 193 *see also* boats
Shoreditch, John 44, 56 n. 53, 105 n. 16, 207, 211, 214–16, 223 n. 85, 234, 247, 254, 257
Shepeye, John de 134, 151, 169 n. 68
Siglesthorn, John 31, 234
Sorgues 145, 202, 252
sovereignty 39–40, 42, 61 n. 144, 82, 133
national 14, 16, 30
papal 42, 46, *see also* supremacy, papal
Spigournel, Henry 195 n. 59, 251
Spigournel, Ralph 35, 47, 63 n. 185, 104, 105 n. 16, 143, 154, 182, 193 n. 29, 236, 245–6
squires:
cardinals' 215, 259 and n. 3
papal household 100–1, 158, 215, 218, 224 n. 107, 256, 260 nn. 14 & 16
royal English household 67–8, 106 n. 17
Stafford, Ralph 30, 35